Sport Development in the United States

The development of both elite, high performance sport and mass participation, grassroots-level sport is a central concern for governments and sports governing bodies. This important new study is the first to closely examine the challenges and opportunities for sports development in the United States, a global sporting giant with a unique, market-driven sporting landscape.

Presenting an innovative model of integrated sport development, the book explores the inter-relationship between elite and mass sport across history, drawing on comparative international examples from Australia to the former USSR and Eastern bloc countries. At the heart of the book is an in-depth empirical study of three (traditional and emerging) sports in the U.S. – tennis, soccer and rugby – that offer important lessons on the development of elite sport, methods for increasing participation, and the establishment of new sports in new markets.

No other book has attempted to model sport development in the United States in such depth before. This should therefore be essential reading for all students, researchers, administrators or policy-makers with an interest in sport development, sport management, sport policy, or comparative, international sport studies.

Peter Smolianov is an Associate Professor of Sport Management at Salem State University. Educated in Australia, Russia and the U.S., he has over 50 publications and conference presentations, including chapters in two 2013 books by Routledge – *Managing High Performance Sport*; and *Sport Governance: An International Case Study Perspective*.

Dwight H. Zakus is an Adjunct Professor at the University of Regina, Canada (being recently retired from Griffith University, Australia). He has over 65 publications, has co-authored a book on sport ethics, and has completed many industry consultancies and research projects worth over $480,000.

Joseph Gallo is a certified athletic trainer, physical therapist, and teaching tennis professional. He is Director and Associate Professor of the Athletic Training Program at Salem State University, and the Men's Tennis coach. His main area of research is in sport and rehabilitation sciences.

Routledge Research in Sport, Culture and Society

Sport Development in the United States

High performance and mass participation

Peter Smolianov, Dwight H. Zakus
and Joseph Gallo

Routledge
Taylor & Francis Group

LONDON AND NEW YORK

First edition published 2015
by Routledge
2 Park Square, Milton Park, Abingdon, Oxon, OX14 4RN

and by Routledge
711 Third Avenue, New York, NY 10017

Routledge is an imprint of the Taylor & Francis Group, an informa business

British Library Cataloguing in Publication Data
A catalogue record for this book is available from the British Library

Library of Congress Cataloging-in-Publication Data
Smolianov, Peter.
Sports development in the United States : mass participation and
high performance / Peter Smolianov, Dwight Zakus, Joseph Gallo.
– First edition.
       pages cm – (Routledge research in sport, culture and society)
    Includes bibliographical references and index.
    1. Sports – Psychological aspects. 2. Team sports. 3. Social groups.
    4. Social participation. I. Title.
    GV706.4.S56 2014
    796.01'9-dc23   2013044972

ISBN13: 978-0-415-81087-6 (hbk)
ISBN13: 978-0-203-06660-7 (ebk)

Typeset in Baskerville
by HWA Text and Data Management, London

With hope that this work makes sport more nurturing and enriching for all. To my wife, Natasha, our children, Vika, Max, and Matt, and their grandparents, especially Tata.

Peter Smolianov

For my family—Janelle, Natasha, Nicholas, Abby, and Amelia—and for the departed ones: Mercedes, Boy, and Gracie.

Dwight H. Zakus

To my father, Anthony M. Gallo, who taught me the value of sport.

Joseph Gallo

Contents

Illustrations

Preface

This book was written to provide a model of how a holistic sport system should look and operate; in particular, how the sport system of the United States of America (USA) might look now and into the future. The first purpose of the book is to present a holistic ideal-type model for a national sport system. Other published works we identify in the second chapter, present materials on various aspects of many national sport systems. We feel, however, they do not broadly or wholly combine all the necessary elements for a successful sport system. The second purpose is to present an analysis of the U.S. sport system. Christine Green, Laurence Chalip, and Matthew Bowers (2013), while focusing on the governance of sport, none the less argued that "distilled to its essential premises, sport in the United States lacks systematic national level governance," which in turn implies a lack of aligned structures and organizations for sport and coherence of purpose and funding of sport. Though there is clear evidence for the USA's domestic and global sport success, many other countries are catching up to the U.S. sporting outputs as well as in terms of other social and economic indicators. We argue that the U.S. sport system must continue to develop and expand as it would be perilous to rest on its past successes. This book provides a focused way in which we believe this might happen.

The USA has long been a leader in developing sport. It gave the world some of the most popular sport and fitness pursuits such as basketball and aerobics. Its indigenous, mainly territorial leagues and competitions, whether in terms of its professional teams or in terms of its schools, colleges, and universities, have been better organized than many other leagues and competitions in the world of sport: They have served as a benchmark for other countries. Other nations have recognized and emulated U.S. sport organizations, leagues, and management. Many U.S. scientists continue to lead the world in exercise- and health-related research. This then begs the following questions: Why do we observe a certain decline in participation rates and a rise in serious health problems in the USA? And how might the entire U.S. sport system be improved to address these issues and maintain its global leadership?

Our disparate group of authors came together to look into these questions and contradictions through the lens of a recently created theoretical model for the overall development of a national sport system. In particular, what are the gaps in the U.S. sport system based on the model and how might other sport systems contribute to closing these gaps? In our view, prospects for the U.S. sport development are consistent with the country's economic vision outlined in *The Post-American World* by Zakaria (2011). Zakaria argued that the fast growth of other countries, particularly China, presents opportunities for the USA to advance itself through better engagement with foreign nations. In particular, a deeper understanding of progressive international sport practices is important for the USA to be a leader in the world in elite and mass sport (Dittmore, Mahony, & Andrew, 2008; Sparvero, Chalip, & Green, 2008). Perhaps that is why this book was written by authors with knowledge of sport systems in the USA as well as in other successful sport nations. The first author grew up in the Union of Soviet Socialist Republics (USSR) and went through the Soviet system of athlete development during the 1970s to 1980s, starting in the Moscow Spartak club in swimming and then competing for the Moscow Dynamo in modern pentathlon and for Moscow University in fencing and swimming. While completing his MSc degree in the USA and PhD degree in Australia in the 1990s, Peter continued to compete in fencing and modern pentathlon, coached and managed athletes, including Australian pentathletes in preparation for world cups and championships and the 2000 Olympic Games. He also provided business research, analysis, and strategic planning as an internal and external consultant to corporations as well as governmental and sporting organizations. His output includes more than fifty sport management-related publications and conference presentations. Since 2004, Peter has been teaching sport management at Salem State University near Boston and publishing research that established him as a leading scholar in sport development systems from a holistic perspective.

The second author is a Canadian who is also now an Australian. He earned his bachelor's and master's degrees at the University of British Columbia and his doctorate at the University of Alberta. Dwight's sport background was in ice hockey and then rugby union football, first as an athlete and then as coach, manager, board member, club founder, professional sport manager, and now as arm-chair dilettante. Other than living for one year in Santa Barbara, California, at the start of John Kennedy's fitness program, his knowledge of U.S. sport is from studying published works and attending scholarly conferences on that topic. Dwight has more than sixty-five publications including books, book chapters, refereed journal articles, refereed conference articles, and industry reports. Dwight also delivered over 300 coaching courses through the National Coaching Certification Program (NCCP) in Canada. Canada, of course, has well-developed state sport structures and policies.

The third author is actually from the USA. Joseph Gallo, DSc, teaches sports medicine and rehabilitation at Salem State University and tennis-related seminars throughout the USA and serves as the Salem State head men's tennis coach. He is the founder and director of Tennis Operations for Summer's Edge Tennis School. He is a USPTA tennis teaching professional, certified athletic trainer, and physical therapist. He serves as associate professor and director of Athletic Training

Education at Salem State. He was a member of the West Virginia University tennis team and worked as an intern athletic trainer and tennis coach at IMG Academies in Florida. His research has been published in various rehabilitation and physical education journals. Recently he co-authored a text on drugs in rehabilitation.

While the third author has broad life involvement with sport in the USA, the first and second authors have more of a "consultant" approach driven by deep scholarly interest given the rich history of U.S. domination in international sport, particularly Olympic sport before World War II. More important, the USA produces sport leagues and wealth matched only by soccer in England, Europe, and possibly parts of the South American continent. In terms of the business of sport the USA is an exemplar. It also is strongly liberal in its outlook, in how government regulates life in the country, and in how it holds capitalism as the model of economic development, including in its sport system.

Despite this leadership, globalization has presented challenges and contradictions for the U.S. sport system. During the post-WWII "Cold War" period, sport competitions between the USA and the former USSR could be regarded as a surrogate for real wars. Countries that followed the Soviet Union in sport development challenged the U.S. sport system to advance in order to maintain its prominence in world sport.

This book identifies particular areas for further improvement of the U.S. sport machine based on surveys of U.S. coaches and on international practices. Concepts considered include those published in such journals as the *International Journal of Sport Management* in the USA, *Managing Leisure* in the United Kingdom, *Sport Science Bulletin* in Russia, and in papers presented at various international sport and sport management conferences in Europe, North America, Australia, and New Zealand.

By no means do we claim to offer an exhaustive plan for the integrated development of mass and elite sport. Rather, we suggest a holistic approach to the systematic development of sport and propose ideas for improvement of a sport system at all levels. The commercial and political powers of elite sport could help increase mass participation and reverse the trend of increasingly inactive, unhealthy, negative lifestyle options detrimental not only to the USA but to the rest of the world. We not only feel obligated to describe and predict but seek to positively influence sport development. We therefore focus on showing the value of various international approaches, which might help debate and move U.S. and global sport in a more optimal direction. Continuing our dialogue through our conference presentations and journal articles, this book's authors challenge readers with a question: Could the practices discussed here be useful in your local conditions, and if so, how could they be implemented? If you wish to contribute to this discussion, please e-mail Peter Smolianov at peter_smolianov@yahoo.com.

Acknowledgments

This work would not be possible without critique provided by reviewers and the Routledge editorial team as well as our close ones and colleagues, particularly Janelle Mullaly Johnstone, Gonzalo Bravo, John Passarini, Shelley Jordan, and Christopher Proulx. Peter Smolianov's students contributed to the book: Mark Carney studied U.S. rugby, and John Murphy researched U.S. soccer. Particular thanks go to peers and administrators of our universities for their support and inspiration.

Abbreviations

ACE	Athlete Career and Education program in Australia
ADM	American Development Model (based on LTAD)
ATP	Association of Tennis Professionals
CISM	Conseil International du Sports Militaire
CODP	Community Olympic Development Program
FIFA	Federal International Football Association
GDR	the former East Germany, the German Democratic Republic
GTO	Ready for Labor and Defense (Gotov k Trudu i Oborone), lifelong Russian fitness program involving gender-specific tests for all to progress through age-appropriate levels
HP(S)	high performance (sport)
HPM	high performance management
IMG	International Management Group
INSEP	Institut National du Sport et de l'Éducation Physique in France
IOC	International Olympic Committee
IRB	International Rugby Board
ISF	International Sport Federation
ITF	International Tennis Federation
LTAD	Long-term athlete development
MASF	Massachusetts Amateur Sports Foundation
MLB	Major League Baseball
MLS	Major League Soccer
NASPE	National Association for Sport and Physical Education
NBA	National Basketball Association
NCSG	National Congress of State Games
NFL	National Football League (American gridiron football)
NGBs	national governing bodies for particular sports
NGOs	non-governmental organizations
NHL	National Hockey League (the North American professional ice hockey league)
NOC	National Olympic Committee
NSCAA	National Soccer Coaches Association of America
ODA	Olympic Development Academies by USA Rugby

OJOP	Olympic Job Opportunities Program by USOC
OTP	Own the Podium program funded by Sport Canada
PAL	Police Athletic Leagues
PCFSN	President's Council on Fitness, Sports, and Nutrition
PE	physical education
POP	Préparation Olympique et Paralympique (France's agency for Olympic success funded through the national sports ministry)
RFU	Rugby Football Union
TAP	Talented Athlete Program in United Kingdom
TIA	Tennis Industry Association
TID	talent identification and development
UK	United Kingdom
UNESCO	United Nations Educational, Scientific and Cultural Organization
UN	United Nations
U.S. Soccer	United States Soccer
USADA	United States Anti-Doping Agency
USAID	United States Agency for International Development
U.S.	an accepted acronym for the USA (United States of America)
USASA	United States of America Adult Soccer Association
USL	United Soccer League
USOC	United States Olympic Committee
USPTA	United States Professional Tennis Association
PTR	Professional Tennis Registry
USSA	United States Ski and Snowboard Association
USSF	United States Soccer Federation
USSR	the Union of Soviet Socialist Republics, the former Soviet Union
USTA	United States Tennis Association
USYS	U.S. Youth Soccer
WADA	World Anti-Doping Agency
WCAP	World Class Athlete Program at U.S. Army
WCP	World Class Program in UK
WCA	Young Men's/Women's Christian Association

1 Introduction

Phenomenon of elite and mass sport

Sport is known to serve a great variety of social, cultural, political, and economic purposes for countries of the world. It also serves nationalistic purposes, as witnessed in most of the mega events in the past fifty years. National governments around the world increasingly invest resources into the systematic development of sport and athletes. Often this is part of a governing political party platform: for example, the use of sport as a policy tool to reduce health care costs, improve education and social inclusion, or prepare the nation's population to enhance competitiveness and reputation, whether militarily or chauvinistically.[1] Simply, a well-coordinated, successful sport system can achieve a range of goals. The reality of such a sport system is, however, complex.

It is this complexity of sport development systems that overwhelms most sport managers, sport specialists, coaches, policy makers, government workers, and students. In the next chapter we present a model of a sport development system to illustrate and deal with this complexity. Any sport development system for a particular nation that is holistic and comprehensive will be complex. And it must be remembered that each nation is unique in its origin and in its flux. While the current fad is to identify and implement what is seen as "best practice" in another nation's sport development system this can be a fraught process, like fitting square pegs into round holes. There can only be approximations of "best practice" across nations. That many people, even those studying or operating in one, are not aware of or do not understand the complexity of sport development systems is not derogatory, it is a fact.

As with any systemic aspect of society, a sport system evolves out of the historical circumstances of that civilization and out of the founding ideology and the policy devices through which the society seeks to better its members' lives. Overall, the way a country or society has sought to defend itself ideologically and militarily over history gives an indication of its sport philosophy and system.

The onerous conditions imposed by Britain on its American colonies that became the United States of America (USA) led these colonies to revolt. The religious and military nature of many of the founding settlers of the USA resulted in a strongly liberal constitution which emphasized protection of individual freedoms for this new nation, along with a strong military establishment. This history combined with strong political and economic market conservatism point to the founding U.S. ideology: a constitutional republic[2] and capitalist society backed by a large and strong military. The U.S. sport system differs greatly from nations with a "socialist" or a welfare State position.[3] It is market-driven, directing resources to activities that are financially self-sustaining. The pluses and minuses of this approach will be the analytical center piece of this book. We do not presume to say what the USA should do with its sport system, merely indicate where it might better maximize its sporting potential.

Sport in the USA embodies the particular historical development of capitalism and constitutionalism in the country. Under a strong neo-liberalist ideology and austerity-focused economic policy that began in the Reagan presidency, the marketability of sport at high school, college, university, and the professional/Olympic (elite) continues to evolve along market and business principles generating large revenues and social focus. Following the global financial crisis of 2007/2008, mass sport (i.e., sport for the broader population and all levels of sport development below the elite level) has suffered as the middle class was hollowed out and had less discretionary funds to spend on sport. Despite this, questions remain of what the future might hold for all U.S. citizens.

The level and degree of government regulation in the USA is markedly different from many other nations in the world. The U.S. Constitution supports individual freedom, reduced government intervention in peoples' lives, and a number of cherished freedoms. Though a particular type of liberalism exists in the USA, the reality is that government involvement in everyday U.S. life is rather considerable. Elected politicians cannot abide by this constitutionalism, as they become more involved with every piece of legislation they produce and pass. There is always some type of State intervention and therefore regulation at all levels of the nation and its governments. That is a reality of life in any country, big or small. If you have a political system and government bureaucracies, they make, pass, and implement legislation and policies, but little of this activity has direct involvement in U.S. sport.

To best understand how the U.S. sport system evolved, it is important to look at the key reasons for sport itself. In earlier times, sport was not always based on a contradiction between elite and mass sport. Many pre-capitalist civilizations, from ancient China and Greece, and State socialist societies such as the Soviet Union, saw "sport" as an activity for all citizens: as a form of controlling the population with healthy, productive activity not otherwise obtainable in society. The centrality of sport to lives and cultures through various historical periods is evident from scholarly work. Civilizations in different historical periods provided modern nations with many of the values, ideals, and goals that frame the relationship and purpose of sport for a society. The following overview sets the scene through which we can analyze modern sport systems, because what we currently have is a product of the past in more ways than are often understood.

History and purpose of elite and mass sport development

Since ancient Chinese, Egyptian, Indian, Greek, Mayan, and other civilizations, national leaders stimulated the masses and their elite leaders to practice "sport" and physical exercise for many purposes. These included military preparedness, health maintenance, excellence, and religious and cultural participation. Each of these purposes has importance at all times, although at certain historical points, some take on more immediate salience. In more immediate past centuries, the most common reason for physical training was readiness for war.

Sport for military preparedness

Throughout history, the preparation of warriors was critically important to a society's survival. Human history revolved around the need to either defend populations and resources or to attack other societies for their human and material assets. In either case, this meant that physical preparedness, of males in particular, was a central activity. What is now identified as sport was often training for military personnel (and society's elites). The rise and fall of various empires in history was associated with a rise in fitness when winning wars; and as Paul Kennedy (1988) noticed analyzing Persian, Roman, and other empires, fitness deteriorated after lands were conquered.

Sport and war also connect on physical and ideological levels. Both demand courage, endurance, exertion, and patriotism from participants. Many mass sporting activities developed out of army exercises (fitness programs) and games played by the military and other elites, especially in exclusive schools for these upper class males (who then became leaders of colonization in all of its forms). From colonial times, militia and military preparation for war drove physical training in what became the USA.

After the American Civil War, public school systems began to adopt physical education programs, and many states passed laws mandating the teaching of physical education programs. Concurrently and for the first time, specialized training was developed for physical education instructors. While physical education appeared universal, such authors as Dalleck and Kravitz (2012) and Krause (2012) noted that the necessity for improvement of soldiers' fitness drove the advancement of physical training methods throughout U.S. history.

During World War I, one of every three American draftees was deemed physically unfit for military service. Many of those drafted were highly unfit prior to the beginning of their military training (Barrow & Brown, 1988; Wuest & Bucher, 1995). This led to many efforts between wars to extend physical education to all levels of schooling. During World War II, the physical fitness of draftees again fell short. The armed forces had to reject nearly half of all draftees or give them noncombat positions (Rice, Hutchinson, & Lee, 1958). Again, U.S. schools instituted rigorous post-war physical education requirements, and there was greater interest in the teaching of physical education, including the preparation of physical education teachers, and an increasing recognition of the scientific foundations of physical education.

In the second part of the twentieth century, the "Cold War" between the USA and the Union of Soviet Socialist Republics (USSR) led to the expansion of both mass and high-performance sport to prepare for a possible war and to show ideological supremacy in global competitions. Fitness of the U.S. military in the Korean War again fell short of expectations, which moved the federal government to set up the President's Council on Fitness, Sport and Nutrition in 1956 to raise fitness standards in schools across the country. The striving for military advantage continued to unite and mobilize U.S. and Soviet societies and drive excellence in such areas as sport, medicine, education, and science. New methods of fitness and adaptation to extreme conditions, innovative medical care, and technology developed for military purposes first served the army elite, then passed to other troops and, finally, to the masses. Today, the military continues to drive fitness and sport in both the USA and Russia.

The above-said indicates that the military around the world and in the USA in particular contributed to high performance and to the fitness and health of the masses. However, today one question arises whether the armed forces benefit from society and sporting organizations through youth being fit for military service. For example, every ten days in Ancient Sparta, the youth passed in public review before assessment officials. If the youth were solid and vigorous as the result of exercise, they were praised; if they were fat or flaccid and lacked vigor, they were punished. This extreme approach allowed Sparta to prepare some of the best soldiers in history. We are unfortunately moving to the other extreme: this convenient, physically easy, entertaining, consumerist life makes most of the population weak and unhealthy.

As people tend not to give an hour a day to exercise, the pool of potential military personnel and athletes is depleted. If our armies are becoming more professional and relying less on mass conscription, they involve a smaller number of recruits and have a weaker connection to their society. The days of standing armies will increase with many nations becoming vulnerable in terms of the ability to draw on enlisted armed forces. This may also limit the transferability of knowledge and practices to the masses, particularly that pertaining to the science of fitness.

Sport for education and health maintenance

The basic tenets of the modern ideology for Western sport, Olympism, according to IOC dogma involves

> a state of mind, not a system, exalting and combining in a balanced whole the qualities of body, mind and will *(Mens sano e corpore sano)*, or a doctrine of the fraternity between the body and the soul *(Mens fervida e corpore lacertoso)*, where this state of mind has emerged from a double cult: that of effort and that of Eurhythmy (a taste of excess and a taste of measure combined) (Zakus, 2005).

This is at least the guiding philosophy. The key idea is that it is not just the body that needs improvement and challenge through sport development and competition. The mind and the soul (i.e., mental and moral) elements of the individual also required such improvement.

De Coubertin's proselytizing points to a wider excellence through sport in education or as noted in "la pedagogic sportive." De Coubertin's monograph *L'Education anglaise en France*, set out his beliefs of how English sport education provided the necessary ingredients for a vibrant French nation and strong males for military availability.[4] Here we again see the relationship between sport and "general values associated with physical education–health, patriotism, military preparedness, character development, and the socialization of a democratic elite" (MacAloon, 2008, p. 116). His political activities in the 1870–1880 period were focused on physical education and mass sport. In this context, de Coubertin argued for a British model of formal sport rather than on German or Swedish models of gymnastics, but these were not the only versions of elite and mass sport.

In Eastern traditions, the martial arts originally developed for warriors were actually ancient forms of fitness training and as such also served as a form of preventative medicine for the broader population. For example, yoga was once closely connected to ancient Indian fighting. Individualistic, highly spiritual and elitist, yoga has transformed into a mass physical regime movement. For example, in 2011, yoga had an estimated 20 million U.S. participants compared with about 4 million in 2001 (Broad, 2012). Interestingly, yoga still finds a place in modern military training. For example, U.S. specialist military forces, such as the Navy Seal unit, are trained in yoga because they see its application to situations where stealth and calm could make the difference between life and death. Some of these military specialists even set up their own yoga schools, blending yoga training with martial arts and their special combat techniques (Lawrence, 2011), completing the circle of its Ancient purpose.

Despite spending more on health care than other developed countries, the USA lags behind European nations such as France and the United Kingdom in both human longevity and health outcomes. Many examples provided by Luzi (2012) showed the numerous ways in which, although spending more, the overall health outcomes in the USA are lower. Luzi argued that preventive health interventions such as physical exercise can reduce health costs for society and may be a solution for indebted governments in an era of shrinkage of national health resources. Luzi suggested that one possible way to deliver the expertise and the practice of physical exercise is through a national health system.

Such a system could possibly introduce reimbursement to professionals who deliver physical training programs. This approach has the drawback of adding some costs to public administration in the short term, although the final balance in the medium/long term would be favorable (Luzi, 2012). Luzi also suggested elevating the vast number of existing fitness centers (mainly private, but also public) to the status of medical fitness centers. These centers, with a mission of providing training programs aimed at maintaining health and treating specific diseases, could enhance health in the USA. Their success would, however, depend largely on having highly qualified exercise specialists operating these facilities and that these services were affordable for the broader U.S. population. A similar practice has emerged in Canada, where health insurance fully covers services of certified physiotherapists who supervise exercise programs, for example, at Wynn Fitness centers aimed at maximizing both performance and the well-being of mass participants.

Similarly, well-educated PE teachers and daily PE classes can prevent obesity-related illnesses, particularly if integrated with after-school sport programs. According to an analysis by Baker (2012), childhood fitness has been a public concern for more than a half-century in the USA. Since President Dwight D. Eisenhower formed the Council on Fitness in 1956, obesity has become an epidemic, but many U.S. students are still being provided little or no PE instruction. PE classes have recently been cut for prevailing economic reasons. Nearly half of U.S. high school students had no PE classes in an average week in 2012. In New York City, that number was 20.5 percent, compared with 14.4 percent a decade earlier. Just 20 percent of elementary schools in San Francisco met the state's requirements of twenty minutes per day (Baker 2012). Obesity was among the key factors why in 2010 the USA fell to thirty-sixth place in the global ranking of life expectancy, down from twenty-second in 1990 (Tavernise, 2012). Knox (2013) was alarmed that people in the USA have not only shorter lives but also more illness and injury than citizens of sixteen other wealthy nations, and the gap is widening.

Mass and elite sport programs are also used to improve psychological and moral health. According to Parker-Pope (2013), the suicide rate among people in the USA aged thirty-five to sixty-four rose by nearly 30 percent from 1999 to 2010, to 17.6 deaths per 100,000 people, up from 13.7. Suicides may be under-reported, and the reasons for suicide are complex.[5] Though the rise in suicides may stem from the economic downturn, the risk for suicide is unlikely to abate for future generations who are also going to be facing many of the current conditions. Sports activities may reduce suicide risk (Müller, Georgi, Schnabel, & Schneider, 2009). For both male and female high school youths, sport participation protected against hopelessness and reduced suicide risk; frequent, vigorous activity is particularly required to help male adolescents. (Taliaferro, Rienzo, Miller, Pigg, & Dodd, 2008).

For sport to better divert us from daily concerns and improve our emotions, we all could be assisted by physical activity plans for holistic well-being at a young age; ideally as part of school PE and through sporting programs focused on fun and events that involve all participants. Analyzing the role of competent coaches in the promotion of mental health through competitive sports, Bell (1997) stressed that qualified sport staff have the potential to influence school and community cultures and provide guidance for developing skills to enhance physical health, intellectual growth, character development, spirituality, and maturation. Able coaches can instill confidence, inner peace, courage, ethics, initiative, discipline, concentration; and toward an enhanced and sound respect for nutrition, training, a drug-free body, and a balanced lifestyle in their athletes. As Bell (1997) argued, proficient trainers should promote efforts toward self-fulfillment and self-actualization.

Another social issue where physical activity is argued as a policy tool relates to reducing crime. Though there is a wide argument that sport can help with this issue, the research and outcomes of programs are not widely valid. Certainly the Victorian rational recreation movement viewed sport as a means to alleviate poor moral and living conditions of the masses (Bailey, 1978). Some of the programs of this movement, including those that transferred to the USA (e.g., the YM/WCA movement), continue, but this still does not allow such claims, as with the "sport for development" movement, to be generalized. The poor and hard living conditions that most people must return to after their sporting exposure limit such claims and leave us with the "bread and circuses" and "cakes and ale" diversions that sport provides. The veneer of social capital likewise attempts to hide the harsh reality in which most people are living in these current economic times (and with less State support for sport). More research is required to make solid claims that sport reduces crime, let alone other social ills (Coalter, 2007a, 2007b).

Sport for excellence: for all citizens

When Baron Pierre de Coubertin revived the Olympic Games in 1894, he widely borrowed from Ancient Greek culture. The Ancients practiced sport together with philosophy, music, literature, painting, and sculpture; again with the idea of a harmonized balance of mind and body, of body symmetry, and bodily beauty in repose and in action. We, like the Ancient Greeks, have commercialized and professionalized our sport systems (see Young, 1984 for a well-documented analysis of the myth of Ancient Greek amateur sport). Likewise, the modern Olympics have changed from amateur competitions into another money-making professional circus (see below). Two key questions arise: Are we going to do a better job retaining the value of sport for the development and well-being of everyone? And will we be able to avoid the fate of sport in the Greek and Roman civilizations by revitalizing the true goal of sport: physical, mental, and broad cultural excellence?

The twenty-one disciplines of the Ancient Olympics were part of a circuit of major events (e.g., Pythian, Isthmian, Nemean Games) scheduled to ensure that one major contest was held every year. There were also numerous other athletic festivals in nearly every city and town in Greece. Over several centuries, however, the original purpose and spirit of the Ancient Olympics, as a religious ceremony for Greek citizens, gave way to a narrow focus on highly competitive and trained athletes who sought fortune and fame. Citizenship was no longer a requirement, and an athlete would often hire out for the city that provided him with the most money and attendant luxuries. During the Roman Republic and Empire, sport became more a spectacle than a method for developing an all-around individual, similar to the influence of commercial professionalism in U.S. sport today.

The modern Olympics started as festivals of "amateur athletes." The concept of "amateurism" became one of the longest debates and battles in the IOC and global sport. It was IOC President Juan Samaranch who ended the hypocrisy by opening the Olympics up to the best athletes regardless of how they made a living. By the end of the twentieth century, the Olympics became one of the world's most powerful economic and political tools of governments and corporations with the world's largest "league" of paid professional athletes.

Fortunately, in contrast with other professional leagues, the principles of Olympism still make the Games a powerful vehicle of social development and nationalistic identity. The IOC and many national Olympic organizations invest in both mass sport programs and the systematic preparation of athletes for competitions. The best expression for the holistic integration of mass and elite sport with education, health, fitness, identity, and broader cultural aspects (music, dance, the arts, etc.) is physical culture. This term was widely used in the Eastern bloc and other state socialist countries as it was inclusive and did not put sport ahead of other cultural elements. As Pettavino and Pye (2014) noted in their analysis of Cuba: "To the Cubans, both goals [mass and elite sport outcome] mutually support each other in a continual cycle of interdependence. The road from mass participation leads to international competition. Success abroad then inspires more Cubans at home to participate." With the seemingly advanced athlete services of today, opportunities for healthier sport participation are still great.

In this respect, modern managers of both mass and elite sport programs have much to learn from managers of the Ancient Olympics and Greek sport. Today we know more than ever that the elite, Olympic-athlete preparations of this period included much of what we currently find in sport (Palaelogos, 1976; Platonov, 2005; Platonov & Guskov, 1994; Poole, 1965; Winniczuk, 1983). From these studies, we find that the Ancients selected talented athletes for major Games that included a multi-year preparation for the Olympic Games. This included a mandatory rational/systematic athlete preparation ten months prior to major competitions; a specialized, targeted thirty-day preparation before an athlete would compete in an Ancient Olympic Games occurring at the competition location (often disregarded today); a rationalized system of resistance loading in macro (e.g., several years) and micro (e.g., four days) training cycles; a specialized techno-tactical preparation; the use of traditional and advanced training equipment; the use of methods and substances for psychological preparation, to enhance performance, and for recovery from training, competition, and injury (many of which are overlooked today); and athlete support teams that included coaches, doctors, physiotherapists, and massage therapists as a rudimentary development of training process based on knowledge in anatomy, physiology, and psychology. Added to this were features which are standard today such as ongoing development of competition rules, objective refereeing, technical devices (starting blocks for running), and competitive equipment (javelin, discus, boxing gloves); and formal, systematic, and major organizational activities for annual local and major Games.

Modern high-performance systems started to develop slowly in the second part of the nineteenth century as sport around the world was becoming more popular, intense, and varied. Athletes trained every day for two to five hours in many European and American countries (e.g., in soccer, baseball, athletics) but not effectively, as there were no professionally trained and employed coaches and only limited interest from the biological, medical, psychological, and pedagogical sciences (except where such study overlapped with increased human productive capacities). Only in a few sports (fencing, baseball, horse riding) did former elite athletes work as coaches. By the end of the nineteenth century, a number of scientific works on training methods started to appear in the USA and Europe (Platonov 2005).

Intensive development of sport education and science started after the resurrection of the Olympics in 1896. During the 1920s and 1930s, the USA developed its high school and university sport, where athletic departments employed many professional physical educators and coaches. By the 1960s, the sport systems of high schools and universities were developed and served as a foundation for mass participation or as a sport development structure for professional leagues in terms of athlete progression (i.e., acting as key athletic sites for generating elite athletes for the expanded professional sport leagues). Physical education classes introduced students to sports, often as a mandatory requirement, while athletic programs and departments prepared students for competitions among schools and universities, integrating mass and elite participation often through the public purse.

The philosophy embraced by professional sports and their competitive teams (franchises) and leagues surrounds moneymaking and consumer entertainment. In college and university sport, where elite athletes received no direct performance payments but rather varying levels of scholarship and other direct support,[6] there was a similar philosophy. Through the ongoing professionalization of college and university sport, mass participation in many unprofitable competitive sports and many mass participation or recreation sports were subsidized by profitable sports and through government grants provided to public educational institutions. This systematic process also provided an "amateur" and a no-cost development pathway for the elite athletes.

Again, the USA led the world in its development of successful athletes from the earliest days of sport. Their sport development system was structured and operated very much along U.S. ideological and capitalist lines. With the size of the USA's population and its large middle class (until 2008), the number of potential elite athletes grew immensely. What the global financial crisis will mean to this in terms of the future development of the overall sport system remains to be seen. In later chapters we suggest how the USA can adapt its sport development to evolving challenges and become more efficient in achieving excellence of mass and elite participants.

In the second part of the twentieth century, the Olympic Games and various sport-specific world cups and championships (e.g., rugby, soccer, tennis) were transformed into profitable professional competitions, further demanding support systems for the development of highly organized and sophisticated athlete preparation and management processes. During the twentieth century, many national governments invested and became involved in sport development, significantly increasing sport funding around the world. Many of these national sport systems started in the social democratic nations of Scandinavia or central Europe (e.g., Sweden, Norway, Germany) or later were "welfare-State" responses to State socialist developments and successes (e.g., United Kingdom, Canada, Australia).

To increase the participation base from which talent can be developed and through which to achieve national social policy goals (such as improved health and education, reduced health care costs, and reduced crime statistics), sport has become a policy tool, mostly through a neo-liberal theory of social capital (Brooks, 2005). The ancient Greek ideas of arête[7] and agon[8] continue to inform modern sport. It was a striving by all for personal excellence, in this case through sport, that would contribute to the lifelong development of each individual and lead to "excellence" in all realms of life and peace and harmony in one's society. For these purposes, governments and different national governing bodies (NGBs) consider participants as the center of sport development effort ("athlete-centered," "participant-based"), trying to connect excellence with physical education and recreation and with high-performance (HP) and professional participation. In the USA, this was primarily implemented at schools and universities.

Mass sport provides for a continuous supply of elite athletes and can also contribute to their income. According to Van Bottenburg's (2002) analysis of statistical data from multiple studies, people who practice or have practiced a sport watch more sport on television, attend more sporting events, and read more about sport. Sport participants understand better the challenges faced by top athletes and the effort required from them and have more sport-specific reasons for following sporting events. By increasing mass participation, therefore, sporting organizations increase media audiences and sponsorship budgets that feed elite sport. From the NGBs' point of view, this is an important economic reason for developing integrated mass and elite sport despite superficially different goals and policy directions. Van Bottenburg (2002) noted that, though elite athletes are increasingly regulated according to the interests of the media, the business community, and consumers (spectators, viewers, readers), mass sport policies (e.g., for physical education and recreation programs) concentrate on developing a wide range of organizations primarily for the well-being of the participants themselves.

As corporate sponsors are more interested in increasing viewing audiences, they invest in elite athletes and events rather than in mass participation (Sleight, 1989; Thoma & Chalip, 1996). Most governments acknowledge the importance of mass participation but direct more funding to elite sport, which allows politicians to show a quick return on investment compared to mass sport where benefits are realized by future generations. However, governments responsible for the health of their nations (especially through the provision of universal health care) are more interested in increasing mass participation to prevent illness and reduce medical costs. If the current U.S. health care reform continues to move in the direction of universal medical coverage, mass sport/physical activity illness prevention programs might become a more important task of the U.S. government.

Thoma and Chalip (1996) pointed out that mass participation is sacrificed to prepare athletes for elite competitions. In a country with a market-based ideology, this does not appear unusual. The quest for excellence and for consumers does not align well with mass participation initiatives, especially in a federalist and non-interventionist-credo government structure. Though sport organizations promise the public to develop both elite and mass participation programs, as noted in the charters of the IOC, International Sport Federations, and NGBs, they are not able to do so, as attention and funding driven by short-term profit continue to focus on elite sport. The benefits of increased participation need, therefore, to be better documented and accounted for if mass sport is to receive a fairer share of all resources. The profitability of events for both mass and elite participants (such as marathons) should be relatively comparable to elite events (aside from international sport festival events such as the Olympics, and world cups organized by FIFA/IRB/IAAF). Economic justifications based on improvements to the quality of life of citizens and that lead to increased investments and industry, or which attract sport tourists are also required (De Knop, 1992; Kotler, Haider, & Rein, 1993; Thoma & Chalip, 1996).

An HP sport system integrated with mass participation seeking health and harmonious social development, as envisioned by Fetisov (2005), Isaev (2002), Matveev (2008), and Tumanian (2006), strives to create optimal living conditions for all members of society. Such an integrated system, which also teaches skills, knowledge, and abilities, empowers each individual to reach the highest possible level of physical, intellectual, and spiritual development within a culture that promotes maximum sport and life performance and harmony. This requires a systematic, holistic approach to understanding and improving all aspects of fitness and health, such as the personalized preventative medicine that David Agus (2011) called for in his book, *The End of Illness.*

Much of what Agus calls for in a new U.S. system of health care is historically well known. Elements of Agus's proposals are consistent with Asian mass exercise traditions and part of East European practices of mass and HP athlete monitoring and illness prevention. All of these elements are contained in the model presented below. Further global recognition of the need for joint efforts through both mass and elite sport is reflected in the Declaration of the IX World Sport for All Congress held in 2002. The 450 participants from 95 countries called for the provision of lifetime sport and physical activities to all citizens and for ensuring professional support for all sport programs. The declaration pointed out that people's personal movement behavior is increasingly independent of the services of organized sports and that the sporting idols may have only a marginal impact.

Participation in sports continues to show striking variations according to age, disability, ethnicity, and social class in particular, indicating an ongoing imbalance between the demand and supply of sports opportunities and services. Social challenges such as public health, equity, tolerance, and environmental sustainability call for a sensible response from both sport for all and elite sport, as declared at the World Sport for All Congress (2002). In line with this declaration, the U.S. National Physical Activity Plan (NPAP, 2010) recognized the need for better prevention of diseases through sport and recreation. The plan's authors called for Olympic and professional corporations and NGBs, and event venue operators, to help increase active physical participation in the community by shifting the current culture from watching sport to doing it, supported by sustained federal funding of $100 million annually.

Overview of the book

The above reasons provide the broad societal parameters for the importance and use of sport. To deal with the current situation of sport in the USA, the book is organized into five chapters. This chapter and the next one (Chapter 2) focus on the background and methods used to develop a sport development system model that is subsequently applied to two analyzes of the U.S. sport system. Chapter 3 completes an historical analysis of the U.S. sport development system against the ideal-type model outline in Chapter 2. Chapter 4 relates the findings and arguments from three recent empirical case studies in the sports of U.S. soccer, tennis, and rugby. Chapter 5 provides a summary of how the U.S. sport system can move forward.

The first two chapters set the scene for the analyses and recommendations made in further parts. In the next chapter (Chapter 2), we provide an ideal-type model for comparing current sport systems. This model developed by Smolianov and Zakus outlines a holistic sport development system, but it is an abstraction of the practices and structures of many successful sporting nations. The Model does not exist in any one country; rather, it is indicative of the elements of a sport development system that, if approximated, would lead to the successful practice of both mass and elite sport. We also outlined how the Model was developed and how it should be used.

Chapter 3 is an overview of the interactions and developments between the Western and the socialist blocs of countries, which occurred during the Cold War period. This period became identified as one of "war without weapons" that saw international sport and internal national sport development expand rapidly. Athletes came to be the warriors with their country's national pride, lifestyle, and ideology at stake. There was much "borrowing" of sport science and management techniques during this period in both directions: capitalist from socialist, and vice versa. By analyzing the Cold War roots of the current U.S. mass and elite sport developments, Chapter 3 provides a basis for understanding the emerging trends.

Chapter 4 presents a summary of studies on how three highly advanced global sports are developing in the USA. The methods used to compare current U.S. sport practices and structures in the sports of tennis, rugby, and soccer through the Model are detailed in other published works. The data were obtained from the people directly involved in the management of these sports. This allows the reader to observe where these sports are reaching some form of global "best practice" and where they could improve their practices and structures. All nations, including the USA, can improve, and this Model shows where positive changes could be made or at least the direction in which change might take place.

Chapter 5 contains suggestions and conclusions based on the elements of the sport development system model identified in Chapter 2, and on the historical and empirical research results discussed in Chapters 3 and 4. At best we can suggest a possible direction based on the identified current and predicted future realities of the USA sport system. Key to this are a better resource input and focus on the balance between mass and elite sport. Such forecasting is, of course, debatable, but we are confident in the Model and that its empirical value makes such proposals viable.

Notes

1 We initially also included content about the possibility of sport as a panacea for the large crime and incarceration rates in the U.S. but decided against this because the evidence that exists is insubstantial at best.

2 The preamble to the *U.S. Constitution* starts with "We the people." In President Abraham Lincoln's Gettysburg Address (1863) he made a speech that lasted for just over two minutes, and ended with his hope "that this nation, under God, shall have a new birth of freedom–and that *government of the people, by the people, for the people, shall not perish from the earth.*" Those words have been quoted ever since as the supreme vindication of representative government. Indeed, they are often quoted as proof of American exceptionalism. But the words were not Lincoln's" (Hannan, 2013; italics added). Both of these expressions of fundamental membership in the republic have come under considerable question in recent times. More of this questioning is discussed in Chapter 5.

3 Although there have been programs that are much like welfare State ones, these are limited and not the norm. For example, programs and projects developed and delivered through the New Deal period in U.S. history were very similar.

4 This was especially so after the French defeat at the hands of the Germans in the 1870–1871 Franco-Prussian War that led to great enmity of anything German (such as their system of gymnastics) (see MacAloon, 2008).

5 See David Stuckler and Sanjay Basu (2013, *The Body Economic: Why Austerity Kills*. New York: Basic Books) for how these issues are overcome in research. The notion of increased suicides during this period is noted in many countries that followed this economic policy.

6 This mellowed former IOC President Avery Brundage's position on the Soviet bloc using military and university elite sport performers. Despite his many idiosyncrasies, Brundage knew the USA sport development system at the college and university level was close to a fully professionalized one (Guttmann, 1984).

7 This is translated as "virtue," but also refers to excellence of any kind, courage, strength, intelligence in any part of one's life. More fully, it is "a striving for excellence or quality, coupled with the concept of man (in the generic sense of mankind) as a total being not divided into mind, body, and spirit. Beauty, strength, and wisdom are necessary ingredients of the balanced individual one is striving to become. Arête is possible only while one is striving; those who think they have attained arête have lost it, and have passed into hubris" (Olsen, 1983, frontispiece). Readers should also see Alasdair MacIntyre's discussion of this value in his book *After Virtue: A Study of Moral Theory* (1984; Notre Dame, IN: University of Notre Dame Press).

8 This refers to an individual contest or system of contests where individuals in contests struggle for self-assertion, success, and fame through the use of their physical capacities and endurance. Victory alone, however, was not sufficient; rather it was the quality of the victory that counted, victory as judged by one's peers.

2 Ideal-type model for an integrated elite and mass sport system

The field of comparative sport studies existed for many decades before it became an area of specialized research. That is, the exchange of ideas, structures, and systems for the development of athletic talent evolved from athletes, coaches, and all other sport specialists interacting and observing what other means for talent development were being used. It went to the limits of "espionage" in elite sport, although this was more common in terms of the military, economic, and political areas.

Though the field of comparative sport studies now has a long history, much of its focus has been on building taxonomies.[1] These sport taxonomies can be identified as "vernacular folk taxonomies" rather than scientific taxonomies such as those found in biology. It is through the socially developed knowledge of sport researchers that empirical, conceptually based categories are identified. It is in such categories that existing sporting practices are located. The result is a list of taxonomies such as "sport and – whatever categories (see the chapter outlines of the Bennett, Howell, & Simri [1975, 1983] books) – that makes the analysis and understanding of sport development systems more synthetic and less helpful.

Smolianov and Zakus (2008), compared with many other sport development researchers, whose primary focus has been in the policy and politics fields (see these references below), built an ideal-type model that is based on constructs. These mental constructs are the key elements necessary for a holistic sport development system to exist. The resultant elements then become the basis of analysis and comparison of different empirical possibilities. This model is presented in Figure 2.1, and its development and use are discussed in the next sections.

Basis of building an ideal-type model

The field of comparative sport evolved from the older and wider field of comparative education and then from comparative physical education. As physical education is, however, such an important starting point for people in most nations and in their sport development system (i.e., mass sport), this provided a positive basis for most comparative analyses. For some time now, in some form, comparative research and its purpose have been part of sport studies. The founding documents of comparative sport studies include seminal pieces by Gilbert (1980), Riordan (1978, 1980), Shneidman (1978), and books by Bennett, Howell, and Simri (1975, 1983).

These works and most subsequent articles, chapters, and books are highly descriptive. Though theory is mentioned, it is often at a low level of comparing structures and systems without an overall guiding theory. It is more like biology and the development of taxonomies of species in that it looks at elements to determine where a species might fit within an existing classification or whether it is, indeed, a new, different species. In sport studies, this generally leads to a bifurcation of sport systems being identified as fundamentally either more socialist or more capitalist. To avoid these issues, Smolianov and Zakus (2008) developed an ideal-type model, or construct, that one cannot find in its totality or in reality in any global sport development system. There are sport development systems that are more or less aligned with the elements of their model but not wholly so.

The Smolianov and Zakus model follows German social scientist Max Weber's methodology. Weber's ideal-type formation is discussed below.[2] It must be noted that the first ideal-type model of sport in the USA was constructed by Alan Ingham (1978) in his doctoral dissertation. We use both Ingham's and Weber's words to define such a model.

We begin with Weber's definition (1949, p.90; emphasis in original) of such a model from his book on this methodology:

> An ideal-type is formed by the one-sided *accentuation* of one or more points of view and by the synthesis of a great many diffuse, discrete, more or less present and occasionally absent *concrete individual* phenomena, which are arranged according to those one-sidedly emphasized viewpoints into a unified *analytical* construct (*Gedankenbild*). In its conceptual purity, this mental construct (*Gedankenbild*) cannot be found empirically anywhere in reality. It is a *utopia*.

As Ingham (1978) notes, the notion of an ideal-type as utopian does not mean it is biased or subjective. Rather, it is a logical accentuation of the real, "not a normative ideal" (p. 43), of "those essential features of meaningful, sociocultural reality which [could be] subjected to systematic historical and comparative analysis" (p. 41). The key value is that it

> provides an exaggerated vision of a social phenomenon ... which is heuristically[3] useful, as a measuring rod, in helping us to ascertain the similarities and deviations of concrete reality [e.g., the U.S. sport system] with our hypothesized and accentuated formulation [e.g., the Smolianov & Zakus Model]. As such, it provides a basic method for historically interpretative and contemporary analytic comparative study (p. 43).

Many different national, historical, and empirical elements of sport development systems were observed to begin to construct a model. To propose hypotheses for change to a particular national sport development system involves more than the straight borrowing of elements. In fact, the existing elements of past and present sport development systems merely provide ideas that are accentuated into the model developed in this work.

The model developed by Smolianov and Zakus, discussed below, is one which designates "abstract elements of the historical reality" (p. 45) to construct a comprehensive high-performance (HP) sport system, which "refers to an institution of which one finds many examples at different moments in history and in different political regimes" (p. 46). Finally, it also, as Ingham notes, "facilitates the construction of causal hypotheses" (p. 47), such as identifying where a particular sport system might be improved. Such a model provides a vision that is heuristically useful in that it can be utilized as a benchmark for ascertaining the achievements and shortcomings of real sport development systems. Further chapters demonstrate that this model helps to advance not only the developing U.S. sport of rugby but also tennis in which U.S. players have been highly successful and supported by expansive mass participation and sophisticated training systems.

Development of the Smolianov and Zakus model

The Smolianov and Zakus model (hereafter, the Model) was first published in the peer-reviewed *International Journal of Sport Management* in 2008. Since then, it has been used in teaching by the authors and tested against current models (see Chapter 4). It reflects the hierarchy of HP system development. We offer this Model and supporting research data as a heuristic typology against which current and future systems, structures, and practices at the macro-, meso-, and micro-levels of delivery can be measured and compared. Our heuristic differs in that we incorporate what is now identified as "best practice" at each level of current and past sport development systems and against which current sport systems can be benchmarked. It is very much a commingling of Eastern (China, the former USSR, the former East Germany) and Western (U.S., British, Commonwealth, European) systems.

Being a heuristic, however, this Model contains elements identified in existing models: models that are empirically evident but that are not directly based on identifiable theoretical constructs.[4] Many models specific to individual national entities have been so identified, such as Baumann (2002) on Australia and Green and Oakley (2001) on the UK. Other such studies focused more specifically on macro-level sport organizations (e.g., Digel, 2002) or on athlete service meso-level infrastructures (e.g., Houlihan & Green, 2008). While many previous models focused on elite sport (e.g., De Bosscher, De Knop, Van Bottenburg, & Shibli, 2006), our Model was developed in reference to integrated mass and elite sport practices of the current and former socialist nations.

For many, the Soviet model was held as an exemplar for a holistic sport development model (Isaev, 2002; Matveev, 2008; Riordan, 1980). Smolianov, being Russian, was able to explore, much like Jim Riordan, literature in Russian. He also carried out many interviews with Russian sport managers. As he currently publishes in Russian, Smolianov adds much to the Model's content and validity. Finally, as he was a product of the USSR sport system, he knows that system intimately. He was, therefore, well placed to develop the Model and to interact with colleagues around the world on its veracity.

The Model has, however, been shown to be a framework for program analysis that is not culturally limited. The Model incorporates concepts of authors not previously cited or mentioned. Many practices developed in Eastern Europe spread around the world. These practices were adapted by "Western" countries from Australia and Canada to the USA, as detailed further in this book.

The Smolianov and Zakus Model is based on an important premise. This is that "the foundation of an HP sport system lies in the macro-level societal support of mass sport participation" (Smolianov and Zakus 2008, p. 6). Also argued was that "balanced development of mass and elite sport depends on the national traditions of participating in sport and developing significant resources for sport programs" (p. 7) and that the "conditions for all to gradually progress from grass roots to excellence should be provided by integrating the key tools of systematic . . . development in key areas (e.g., educational systems, clubs, workplaces, communities)" (p. 7). Again, this Model is holistic. To maximize the overall development of a nation's population demands that they have easy access to shelter, food, education, and health care. With this in place, sport can truly deliver on its values and higher goals (e.g., public health, people's longevity, increased fitness, and positive social interaction).

In the Model, the relevant HP systemic elements and practices merged into seven levels of sport development, which taken together provide a methodical progression from mass to elite sport, as a real-world system might seek to emulate. By considering the HP elements as a system for developing participants from recreation and physical education to competitive and HP levels, we retain the key idea of the "macro-, meso-, and micro"-level concept used in different modifications by Green and Houlihan (2005), who analyzed elite sport policies, and others who summarized successful sport policy factors (De Bosscher et al., 2006; De Bosscher, Shibli, Van Bottenburg, De Knop, & Truyens, 2010).

In the Model, the macro-level (see Figure 2.1) embraces elements of socioeconomic, cultural, legislative, and organizational support for a national sport system by the whole of civil society and by the State. The meso-level includes infrastructure, personnel, and services enabling sport programs. The micro-level consists of operations, processes, and methodologies for development of individual athletes. Even though the HP elements overlap at different levels (cf. De Bosscher et al., 2006), we numbered the elements to express their relative magnitude and importance in a sport system. As the Model is holistic, all elements are interdependent and interrelated.

Smolianov and Zakus's wide and integrated analyses of Australasian, European, and North American sport systems aligned with the examination of Latin American countries by Bravo et al. (2012) in that in both developed and developing countries, governments intervene in sport by creating structures, enacting policies, and allocating resources to support sporting activities at all levels of participation. The current global challenge is to develop sport systems that nurture participants on their pathways from grass roots to the national teams. In all parts of the world, HP and mass participation sport are identified as distinct, often bipolar, areas that are more often now developed in integration under one organization such as a federal/national sport agency/ministry.

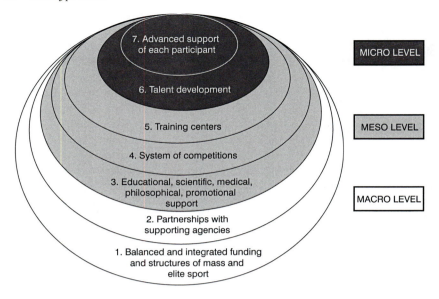

Figure 2.1 The Smolianov and Zakus Model (Smolianov & Zakus, 2008)

The balance and focus on both mass and elite sport continue to be a key dilemma for sport managers and developers and for government policy makers, as they are challenged by insufficient conceptual and practical frameworks, resulting in disintegrated sport systems that are disadvantageous for participants, particularly in the USA (Green, 2005). How to balance both sides of a sport development system is an issue that is endemic in sport across the globe. Added to this dilemma are wider issues of economic and political ideology (especially under lingering neo-liberalism).

In the next chapter (Chapter 3), we present historical and comparative examples following this Model. The evidence from the past is separated and analyzed through the seven elements of the Model. This material indicates that the USA has not, nor could it have ever, evolved in isolation. Throughout history, athletes, coaches, and other sport specialists have interacted continuously. Global interaction through, for example, competitions and research conferences put many aspects of different systems forward to be tested and integrated into national sport delivery systems. The globalization of sport is not new.

A final note for readers on this method. The Model provides a measuring stick; it is a heuristic. All one can do is to see where a current sport development system aligns or varies from the ideal-type model presented here. The Model presented here is a way to see where the U.S. sport development system is operating efficiently and effectively but also where it might be improved to meet such criteria. The Model is abstract. The currently evolving U.S. sport system is real. It is to improve that reality that this method, the Model, and book seek.

Notes

1 Taxonomies are a way in which scientists categorize and link together what exists in the world. It is based on gathering as much (empirical) information as possible to structure the categories and to fit or compare new findings into an existing category or establish a new category. In the natural sciences, taxonomizing is the basis of determining what living things belong to which category of species. In the social sciences, this is a more difficult process. Not all nations and their sport systems are easily categorized.

2 Students and scholars in sport studies are familiar with his model of bureaucracy that is also widely used in sociology and business studies and in research of large, complex organizations (Weber, 1978). Also widely known is his ideal-type model of the Protestant ethic that serves as a basis for modern sport (see Weber's *The Protestant Ethic and the Spirit of Capitalism*, 1958, New York: Charles Scribner's Sons).

3 There are many definitions and types of heuristics. A philosophy definition states that "heuristic" (or the designation "heuristic device") is used when an entity X exists to enable understanding of, or knowledge concerning, some other entity Y. A good example is a model, which, as it is never identical with what it models, is a heuristic device to enable understanding of what it models (Askdefine, 2013). It is this notion that is used in this work. More ideas can be gathered from the quotes of Ingham and Weber in the main body of the text.

4 We refer readers to the original article for more detail on the development of the Model and the very extensive literature review that was fundamental to the construction of that model.

3 From one Cold War to another

Recent U.S. sport development

Any sport development system is in a constant state of change. To properly study them is, therefore, difficult. As noted in Chapters 1 and 2 there are many theories, approaches, and foci to analyzing these systems, each with its own strengths and weaknesses. To deal with both of these issues this chapter uses evidence from U.S. history (yesterday is part of history) against the Model and then makes suggestions on what might be considered to further develop the U.S. sport development system. Readers will see that there are many points of alignment with the Model in past activities of the U.S. sport system.

As noted, we analyze developments in the U.S. sport system through the seven levels of the Smolianov and Zakus Model. We will look at the macro-societal aspects, then at the meso-level structural elements, and finally proceed to discuss those of the individual athletes at the micro-level of the U.S. sport machine. The purpose of this chapter is to examine the internal changes to the country's sport development system in relation to external challenges.

The U.S. sport system followed a unique development compared to other countries, as outlined by sport historians and more recently by Green, Chalip, and Bowers (2013). As was mentioned in Chapter 1, particular aspects are historically common, such as military preparedness, health maintenance, and mass and elite sport excellence. In the United States, educational and, to a certain degree, military institutions have been central to the development of the sport system. Tied to a strongly capitalist orientation, the United States, through its professional and increasingly professionalized sport structure and its highly education-based sport system, has achieved much in terms of global outcomes (e.g., in the Olympic and Winter Olympic Games (WOGs) – see Tables 3.1a,b).

An Olympic medal is the key achievement for many athletes. For athletes from long-time professionalized sports, this might not be as major a goal, but for the many sports more recently enjoying professional status, an Olympic medal brings not only fame but the fortune that sponsorship revenues can bring. Likewise Olympic success serves nationalistic and ideological purposes for many countries.

Throughout the history of the twenty-seven modern Olympic Games from 1896 to 2012, the United States won more medals overall (2,400) and more gold (974) medals than any other country in the twenty-six Games they entered.[1] During the pre—World War I period, with the exception of the home 1904 St.

Louis Olympic Games, the United States finished second to various European countries. Through the inter-war period (1920–1936), the United States was the top nation in both gold and overall medals, except for the 1936 Berlin Olympic Games. In the Cold War[2] era, except for the boycotted Games of 1980 and 1984, U.S. athletes were top in gold medals in the 1952 Helsinki, 1964 Tokyo, and 1968 Mexico City Olympic Games. They also won the most medals in the 1952 and 1968 Olympic Games.

During its existence from 1922 to 1991, the former USSR participated in nine of the possible ten Olympic Games (1952 to 1988) and as the Unified Team in the 1992 Barcelona Games. During this time, the country was second in both overall (1,122) and gold (440) medals won. Though competing in only 38 percent of the overall Games during its history, the USSR/Unified Team was more successful, comparatively speaking, in both overall and gold medals than any other country during this time.

For the six Olympiads from the 1956 Melbourne to the 1976 Montreal Olympic Games, the USSR was first in overall medals, except for 1968.[3] After the disintegration of the USSR in 1991, a "Unified Team" competed in the 1992 Barcelona Games, finishing with both the highest gold and overall medal tallies. Since 1992, the United States has ruled the summer Games, except for the 2008 Beijing Games when host China won more gold but fewer overall medals. China, with its sport system based on the Soviet pattern, has progressively moved up the medal rankings since its return to the Olympic Games in 1984 in Los Angeles[4] and appears to be the next superpower to battle the United States in the sport arena. Overall, the USA's share of total medals per Games declined over the 1952–2012 period (see Table 3.2).

This is consistent with the analysis made by Sparvero et al. (2008), who pointed out that a large population and gross domestic product (GDP) have contributed to medal production for the United States and other large, developed, wealthy countries. As GDP growth has shifted to other nations, all countries must raise their efficiency in sport performance. Team USA must become more efficient in global competitions as more nations are capable of winning medals.

In all twenty-two Winter Olympic Games from 1924 to 2014, the United States was second in overall medals (281) and gold medals (96) to the small country of Norway, which posted an overall medal count of 303 and a gold medal count of 107.[5] Except for the home 1932 Lake Placid Winter Olympic Games, when the United States won first place in both the gold and overall medal tally, the United States has finished second (four times) in these Games including the home Games in 2002 in Salt Lake City in terms of gold medals (however, they were first in total medals in Vancouver 2010). The Nordic (Scandinavian) and the former Eastern Bloc[6] countries disperse the medals over many more nations, and the competition for gold and overall medals is fiercer in the Winter Olympic Games.[7] Despite this, it is clear that the United States continued to dominate much of the world and Olympic sport.

It is the professional disciplines that form the main part of the market-based sports industry in the United States and provide a glimpse of why there are few

Table 3.1a USA results in the modern Olympic Games[a]

Games	Location	Gold Medals	Silver Medals	Bronze Medals	Place in terms of total medals	Place in terms of total gold medals
1896	Athens	11	7	2	2	1
1900	Paris	19	14	15	2	2
1904	St Louis	78	92	79	1	1
1908	London	23	12	12	2	2
1912	Stockholm	26	19	19	2	1
1920	Antwerp	41	27	27	1	1
1924	Paris	45	27	27	1	1
1928	Amsterdam	22	18	16	1	1
1932	Los Angeles	44	36	30	1	1
1936	Berlin	24	21	12	2	2
1948	London	38	27	19	1	1
1952	Helsinki	40	19	17	1	1
1956	Melbourne	32	25	17	2	2
1960	Rome	34	21	16	2	2
1964	Tokyo	36	26	28	2	1
1968	Mexico City	45	28	34	1	1
1972	Munich	33	31	30	2	2
1976	Montreal	34	35	25	2	2
1980	Moscow	0	0	0	DNP	na
1984	Los Angeles	83	61	30	1	1
1988	Seoul	36	31	27	3	3
1992	Barcelona	37	34	37	2	2
1996	Atlanta	44	32	25	1	1
2000	Sydney	37	24	21	1	1
2004	Athens	36	39	28	1	1
2008	Beijing	38	38	36	1	2
2012	London[b]	46	29	29	1	1

[a] databaseOlympics.com. Accessed on 8 March 2013 at http://www.databaseolympics.com/index. htm
[b] London 2012. Accessed on 8 March 2013, at http://www.london2012.com/medals/medal-count/

Table 3.1b USA results in the modern Olympic Winter Games

Games	Location	Gold Medals	Silver Medals	Bronze Medals	Place in terms of total medals	Place in terms of total gold medals
1924	Chaminox	1	2	1	3	3 (tied)
1928	St Moritz	2	2	2	2	2 (tied)
1932	Lake Placid	6	4	2	1	1
1936	Garmisch-Partenkirchen	1	0	3	6	4 (tied)
1948	St Moritz	3	4	2	4	2 (tied)
1952	Oslo	4	6	1	2	2
1956	Cortina d'Ampezzo	2	3	2	5	4 (tied)
1960	Squaw Valley	3	4	3	2	3 (tied)
1964	Innsbruck	1	2	3	8	4 (tied)
1968	Grenoble	1	5	1	8	5 (tied)
1972	Sapporo	3	2	3	6	3 (tied)
1976	Innsbruck	3	3	4	4	3 (tied)
1980	Lake Placid	6	4	2	3	3
1984	Sarajevo	4	4	0	6	3 (tied)
1988	Calgary	2	1	3	9	6 (tied)
1992	Albertville	5	4	2	6	4
1994	Lillehammer	6	5	2	6	5
1998	Nagano	6	3	4	6	4 (tied)
2002	Salt Lake City	10	13	11	2	3
2006	Torino	9	9	7	2	2 (tied)
2010	Vancouver[a]	9	15	13	1	3 (tied)
2014	Sochi[b]	9	7	12	2	4

[a] Olympic Medals: History of Olympic Medals. Accessed on 8 March 2013, at http://www.olympicsmedals.com/vancouver-olympics-medal-table-2010.php.
[b] 2014 Olympics Medal table. Accessed on 16 March 2014, at http://en.wikipedia.org/wiki/2014_Winter_Olympics_medal_table.

Table 3.2 Comparative total number of medals won by United States and selected other countries

Year	USA	Russia*	China	Germany**	UK	Australia
1952	76	71	DNP	24	11	11
1956	74	98	DNP	26	24	35
1960	71	103	DNP	42	20	22
1964	80	96	DNP	50	18	18
1968	107	91	DNP	51	13	17
1972	94	99	DNP	106	18	17
1976	94	125	DNP	129	13	5
1980	DNP	185	DNP	126	21	9
1984	174	DNP	32	59	37	24
1988	94	132	28	142	24	14
1992	108	112	54	82	20	27
1996	101	63	50	65	1	41
2000	92	88	59	56	28	58
2004	103	94	63	49	30	49
2008	110	72	100	41	47	46
2012	104	82	88	44	65	35

DNP=did not participate in these Games

* USSR from 1952–1988, Unified Team in 1992, Russian Federation from 1996.

** From 1952–1988 this is a combined total from both East and West Germanys, since then it has been a unified team

Source: databaseolympics.com, London2012

"have" and many "have not" sports in the country. A small number of profitable sports flourish, while many others struggle to develop. If we look at figures at the level of the older professional sports, especially the NFL, MLB, NBA, and NHL, we can see (Tables 3.3 and 3.4) that the revenues and operating income of these leagues dwarf many other countries' or combinations of other countries' entire sport budgets.

This results in two key facts that are unintentionally hidden. The first is that the Olympic program has more than thirty-five sports, and the majority of these sport organizations are not in a strong financial position. Revenues for the majority of sports in the United States depend on scrabbling together marketing plans and budgets to prepare athletes and teams. The second fact is that the school and higher education systems provide the structure for developing top athletes in professional and in games sport codes. That is, it is individual citizens, state-budgeted schools, colleges and universities, and municipal parks and recreation boards that are central to producing talent for the U.S. teams and their ability to remain at the top of medal tables. The professional, entertainment sports clearly enjoy a lower no-cost

Table 3.3 League revenue ($USmillions) for the four major professional sports in the United States

League	2006	2007	2008	2009	2010	2011	5 yr CAGR*
NFL	6,539	7,090	7,575	8,016	8,345	8,867	6.3%
MLB	5,111	5,489	5,819	5,898	6,137	6,464	4.8%
NBA	3,367	3,573	3,768	3,786	3,805	3,960	3.3%
NHL	2,267	2,463	2,747	2,819	2,929	3,090	6.4%

*Compound annual growth rate (over this five year period)
Source: The U.S. Professional Sports Market & Franchise Value Report 2012, p. 22

Table 3.4 Average operating income ($USmillions) for the four major professional sports in the United States

League	2006	2007	2008	2009	2010	2011	5 yr CAGR*
NFL	17.8	24.7	32.3	33.4	30.6	30.6	11.5%
MLB	16.5	16.4	16.7	17.4	16.5	16.7	0.2%
NBA	6.9	9.8	10.6	7.8	6.1	5.8	-3.3%
NHL	4.2	3.2	4.7	6.1	5.3	4.2	0.2%

*Compound annual growth rate (over this five year period)
Source: The U.S. Professional Sports Market & Franchise Value Report 2012, p. 22

development system for the athletes who compete in their leagues and events. Many of these contradictions will be discussed in the sections following.

As noted, the ongoing sections of this chapter are presented following the seven elements of the Model and indicate where the United States has borrowed ideas and programs from overseas and adapted its sport system to global challenges. *Globalization* is a new term for the essential global processes of capitalism, where labor, resources, and profits are drawn to the imperial (economic) centers; and where other sovereign nations adapt their laws, accounting, and business practices to those of the U.S. Though global ideological differences remain strong, particularly between the United States and former socialist countries such as China and Russia, the production of sport knowledge in all these nations is being improved by growing interactions in sport science, sport studies, and sport management domains. A holistic Model must attend to all of these specialized sciences for a country to lead world sport. This is especially so in the programming and funding of mass sport activities. China's sporting success is largely based on absorption of sport development methods from different parts of the world. As the following discussion shows, this is also true for the United States, but we also point to a number of international practices under-utilized in the United States, especially in the programming and funding of mass sport activities.

As a final note, the reader must be aware of the historical changes that often lead to reactive changes in the provision of mass and elite sport (e.g., draftees failing medicals, not being the top nation in the Olympics as the proxy for war). The Cold War changes were indicative of the economic and geo-political events that shape the following discussion.

Macro-level: socioeconomic, cultural, legislative, and organizational support for a national sport system by the whole of civil society and by the State

Element 1 (macro-level): balanced and integrated funding and structures of mass and elite sport

To develop any social institutional practices, a nation requires some degree of alignment between its civil society and its State. This is the base from which any society's institutional structures emanate. It is through comparing sport practices and structures of the polar cases of socialist and capitalist states that sense can be made of progress in the United States. This progress is, however, well short of that of the four major professional sports in the United States as the Model suggests. This element clearly points to how a nation provides funding for the institution of sport at both mass and high performance (HP) levels. Sport has been a central feature of United States educational institutions since the nineteenth century. This includes public, private, and military education providers. The system is very much, in the latter two contexts, inimical to the romantic notions of the muscular Christianity and athleticism of British public and Oxbridge schools and universities: and to that of Olympism.

The Victorian values attributed to sport, and used to socialize generations of young men and then women, were initially very much class-based. The current period of sport has democratized itself in the search for the best athletic talent – the key resource for a successful sport system, regardless of class, race, or nationality. Sport as an institution, both then and now, also exists to exert positive influence over young persons both in education and general societal settings; teaching discipline, leadership, and many important skills for enhanced physical and intellectual growth (Bell, 1997).

Again, these foregoing bases of sport were also strongly followed through the rational recreation movement of Britain and the rise of the YM/WCA (a Christian) movement, which started in the United States in the 1860s (Christesen, 2012, p. 253). We also see direct religious connections with sport, especially in the United States through the Catholic Youth Organization (CYO) and Jewish Community Leagues. Finally, a wide academic analysis of the connection between sport and religion exists. This literature and U.S. belief systems surround the types of relationships as seen in the mythology of Notre Dame University (see, for example, Novak, 1994; Higgs, 1995, among many others). Together these values and processes center sport as a key aspect of U.S. society. Most often religion and sport are celebrated equally (and concurrently).

The fundamental aspect of this element of the Model is not only where sport is located in society but how it is resourced. This is for both participation/mass and elite sport. Strongly liberalist, non-interventionist, and capitalist ethos and value structures resulted in a decentralized sport system in the United States, which aligns with the general U.S. ideology. The former USSR and now China, the United States's key competitors, differ greatly from the United States in terms of the State's involvement in and funding of sport. This difference can also be found in some Western nations who still maintain some welfare-state funding and structures for sport (e.g., the United Kingdom, Canada, Australia, New Zealand).

As the United States expanded across the continent, the way in which states were founded and how they operated led to high decentralization from the federal level of government, which is self-evident by the fact that the first colonies predated the War of Independence and the Constitution. Resulting from this form of federalism, the structures of governance within the U.S. sport system are organized so that they share little in common with sport in the rest of the developed world (Green et al., 2013). Sport has defaulted to state and local government levels for its organization and resourcing. It must, however, be restated the belief that individual actors operating within the free market would achieve optimal outcomes (Green et al., 2013). This meant that these lower levels of U.S. government developed and funded much of the United States's sport system.

Sport development pressures from the USSR and China

In contradistinction to the United States, in the post-revolution/WWI/Civil war (1920s), the new Soviet government established the national Physical Culture and Sport Committee that had regional and local branches across all of the republics. It was a very structured, hierarchical, and centralized department with the notion of physical culture important as a founding ideology: The development of the new Communist man/woman. This refers to the socialist ideal of Popular Culture where hygiene and discipline of the body for all citizens was established, which aligns with the IOC slogan of *"mens sana in corpore sano"* – a sound mind in a healthy body – on a national scale. As Bennett et al. (1983) noted, "the two underlying principles of the total physical culture movement in the USSR are *massovost* (mass participation) and *masterstvo* (proficiency and achievement), and the theory that *massovost* leads to *masterstvo"* (p. 117). In the case of the USSR and other Eastern bloc countries, national fitness and sport testing occurred along with sport festivals for wider citizen participation. Though such participation is very much an Eastern bloc notion, Europe and other national groups have introduced different types of "sport for all" programs. China's and Russia's current sporting successes are based on adopting the USSR principles and structures. Though embracing Western practices of commercial sport, both countries have been retaining or reviving the USSR methods of mass participation as a foundation for HP and national health. The Soviet organizational and financial structures of fostering recreation and sport are still to be fully discovered and capitalized on by the world, including the USA.

Though there are examples of fitness testing programs in many countries throughout the last century, we argue that the former USSR Sport Committee provided a holistic model of mass programs for excellence within a nation (and as the first author experienced this system first hand; all of this detail unless otherwise cited is from his direct knowledge). This committee extended the support structures for mass physical culture programs and appointed scientists and coaches to develop ways to attract all citizens to physical education, recreation, and sport.

Plans were worked out to nurture citizens to seek the highest level of physical culture they desired, including knowledge of illness prevention and physical readiness so as to be productive in the workplace and for military readiness. Sport facilities, programs, and professional instruction were made available at no or minimal costs to participants. This applied across the civil society: from kindergartens/childcare centers, schools, universities, places of work, community centers, and national networks of multi-sport societies and clubs. Emphasis was put on developing mass sport, particularly policies for guiding and rewarding lifelong progression in fitness and sport for all citizens.

Before competing in a particular sport, participants were to achieve certain results within the Ready for Labor and Defense (Gotov k Trudu i Oborone, or GTO) program. This extensive age-related program involved achieving physical outcomes in many basic skills[8] and also to demonstrate theoretical and practical knowledge of health, physical culture, sport, and national defense. GTO was first introduced in 1931. By 1985 a number of scientific evaluations and revisions were made. It comprised twenty-one gender-specific tests at six age levels for all people aged from seven to sixty. When the USSR dissolved in 1992, GTO was no longer practiced in most of the former Soviet Republics. In 2003 it was revived in Russia.

After passing the GTO tests, participants were to progress through sport-specific ranks. There were three junior and three senior mass ranks followed by four elite master ranks. Each rank required specific results against increasingly stringent criteria that were revamped in each four-year Olympic period through an immense amount of research and consultation (All-Union Sport Program GTO, 2006; Kudryashov, 1978; Kuznetsova, Kaline & Kaline, 2002; Matveev, 2008; Shkolnikova, 1978).

Russian sport scientists extended the Soviet system of ranks from 60 sports in 1980 to 143 in 2011. These long-term athlete development (LTAD) mechanisms have helped current Russia (and now China) achieve sporting success efficiently. However, the integration of LTAD with mass fitness testing emphasized by Matveev (2008) has been not fully applied by any country. U.S. athletes, coaches, and sport administrators are still to take advantage of these methods for the benefits outlined below.

The USSR government was allocating significant financial resources to the federal sport department, which reached $2.2 billion annually in the 1970s. Funding provided direct support to physical activities and was also used to attract and coordinate financial and other resources from lower levels of government, various departments and organizations, particularly within education, the military, trade unions, and youth leagues. After the breakup of the USSR, the Russian Federation continued sport and physical activity budgets. These budgets grew from $680 million in 2009 to a high of $1.8 billion in 2011 (with $1.7 and $1.6 billion budgeted in 2012 and 2013, respectively. The final installment was $1.3 billion in 2014 for final preparations for and supporting of its hosting the 2014 Winter Olympic and Paralympic Games (To, Smolianov, & Semotiuk, 2013).

This is a significant direct State input of human, infrastructural, and financial resources. Given the USA's military spending, which was about $700 billion a year in 2008–2011 according to Chantrill (2014a), Plumer (2013), and Walker (2013), similar sport and physical activity budgets would be affordable and reasonable in the U.S. It was similar to the federal government spending on health care (Chantrill, 2014b). Public polls indicated support for defense cuts, especially when participants were informed about the size of other categories in the U.S. federal budget and significantly lower military expenses of all other countries (*The Economist*, 2012a). An investment of $1 billion into a systematic sport development could be returned through reduced costs of recruiting and training of military personnel and lower public spending on health care. Besides, an objective-driven budget could hold the USOC responsible for both mass and elite sport.

Though Russia has not been able to restore the level of sport funding allocated during the time of the USSR, China now allocates considerable financial resources to sport and physical culture, originally modeled on the Soviet system. The total funding for the Chinese sport system was $2.8 billion in 2005, when the Chinese government succeeded in generating additional income from sponsorship and other commercial sources ($840,000) and lottery funding ($413 million).

By creating the National Games, similar to many Western nations, provincial and other levels of government were encouraged to invest their own sport-allocated and lottery funds into budgets for sport development, adding $1.4 billion to the total sport budget (Tan & Green, 2008). By matching the local budgets of State Games and of athlete preparation for these Games from the beginner level using world's best LTAD guidelines, U.S. federal dollars could mobilize resources of communities toward integrated mass and elite sport development.

United States sport development initiatives during the Cold War

In response to the Cold War, "military expansion and space races," and sport competition outcomes, the United States began to develop more programs in the 1950s and 1960s for excellence in both mass participation and elite sport. Platonov (2005) identified several coordinated attempts to more widely advance the U.S. sport system. He noted processes that included supporting physical education (PE) at the state level and increasing, coordinating, and applying scientific research to PE and sport. Other possibilities were expanding sports at schools, colleges, and universities, while developing a national program for preparation and participation of athletes in international competitions (particularly for the Olympic Games) and creating the U.S. Olympic Fund. Platonov (2005) also pointed to the creation of a permanent organization now called President's Council on Fitness, Sports, and Nutrition (PCFSN)[9] which has its own budget. Most of these programs align with the key ideas of this element of the Model, demonstrating significant national efforts to improve the physical performance of mass participants and elite athletes.

In parallel, the USOC adopted a program of constant training and preparation of athletes and teams in an ongoing cycle, rather than solely in the year prior to an Olympic Games or a Winter Olympic Games. Focus also shifted from individual to national team achievements, to the development of underperforming and unpopular Olympic sports, to women's sport, and to resourcing and developing a broader pool of athletes for all sports. European specialists in a number of sports were invited to prepare U.S. athletes. Training and competitions in various sports were organized abroad. There was a mass involvement of children and multi-level competitions in historically strong U.S. sports such as wrestling, swimming, and track and field. Thanks to these initiatives in the 1960s, sport and PE instructors became more respected in the U.S., reportedly almost as much as lawyers and medical doctors (Quill, 2006).

The main factory of athlete production in the U.S. has always been in its colleges and universities. From the late 1950s, however, a major change occurred in the way athletes were "compensated" for their performances. A mixed bag of scholarship-like and other compensations had regularly been used, although this was not sanctioned by governing authorities. As the Cold War escalated along with an increased sophistication and professionalization of mass and elite sport in the USSR, the NCAA in 1957 caved under pressure to subsidize athletes and voted to allow athletic scholarships, which initially covered tuition, fees, and room and board. From this point, commercialized university sports officially moved toward professionalism (Sack, 2008). However, Ivy League schools – arguably, the founders of intercollegiate athletics (the presidents of Harvard, Princeton, and Yale, among others who started the NCAA) – have never permitted athletic scholarships, maintaining the principles of amateurism and serving the mission of academic education (Crowley, 2006; Sack, 2008).

The NCAA rules first allowed scholarships to be awarded for four years regardless of performance on the field. Then scholarships took on the trappings of an employment contract. At the height of student revolts on college campuses in 1968, the association adopted rules that allowed the immediate termination of scholarship aid to athletes who challenged the authority of a coach or withdrew from sport voluntarily. Four-year scholarships were discontinued in 1973. Scholarships then became awarded on a year-to-year basis. Athletes who turn out to be recruitment mistakes could have their athletic aid terminated at the institution's discretion.

The U.S. Army advanced both mass and elite sport after WWII, when a new program of recreational athletics provided opportunities for all soldiers to engage in more than ten sports. An Inter-Service Sports Council was established in 1947 to conduct annual championships for Army, Navy, and Air Force personnel. The

U.S. Congress also approved in 1947 elite sport funding for the Army and Navy althletes, who as military personnel, meant they could receive up to $125,000 for training and participation in the 1948 London Olympic Games (U.S. Government, 1947). In 1955, Congress authorized the Armed Forces to release military personnel from service to prepare for international competitions and provided $800,000 every Olympiad (U.S. GAO, 1955). Then President Kennedy requested that the military concentrate on less-developed Olympic sports to produce more potential medal winners (Cocanour, 2007).

As a result of these many initiatives, United States athletes performed significantly better in the 1964 Tokyo Olympic Games than they had in the 1960 Rome Olympic Games. Though the USSR topped the overall medal count in 1964, the United States achieved the highest number of gold medals (thirty-six to the USSR's thirty). In the 1968 Mexico City Olympic Games, the United States finally topped the overall and gold medal tallies. This was a temporary situation that Platonov (2005) ascribed to the USSR's increasing its reliance on volunteers rather than on full-time professional coaches – a situation that was quickly rectified soon after the 1968 Games.

There were a number of attempts to enhance the U.S. sport system after 1968. Following the marred 1972 Munich Olympic Games and the partially boycotted 1976 Montreal Olympic Games, the State socialist nations, in particular the USSR and the GDR, were in ascendency. The 1976 results were a shock to the U.S. public similar to the 1956 and 1960 results. After the 1976 Games, there was energy both from the U.S. public and the government for fundamental changes. During the 1980 election campaign, President Jimmy Carter and his electoral competitor Ronald Reagan signed a joint proclamation to assist U.S. athletes morally and materially (Kolesov, 1981). In the period from 1977 to 1984 the USOC led the most significant advancements in U.S. sport to compete with Eastern European nations. In 1978, the USOC was made responsible for both Olympic preparation and mass fitness (USOC, 2011).

The USOC leaders adopted a number of practices similar to those of the USSR and Western nations with social democratic or welfare-state sport programs. These practices included establishing new sport science and medical services, along with centralized preparation of national teams (c. 1977) at a newly established U.S. Olympic training center in Squaw Valley, California. In July 1978, the USOC moved its headquarters from New York City to Colorado Springs, where a former Air Force base was made available for a nominal $1 per year rent. A national multi-sport altitude training and administrative hub was developed on this site. National governing bodies (NGBs) moved into offices that still had, ironically, maps of the Soviet Union on their walls with missile targets on them. The epicenter for the U.S. strategic response and monitoring of Cold War issues had become the center for national sport development and such historic decisions as the boycott of the 1980 Moscow Olympic Games (Badger, 2012).

In 1950 the United States Olympic Association, precursor of the USOC, managed to solicit the status of a private non-profit corporation where the donations received became tax-deductible. Then President Ford formed a commission (the President's Commission on Olympic Sports) in 1974 to study the state of the U.S. sport system. While his major goal was to help businesses operate more freely by reducing taxes and easing the controls by regulatory agencies, the Commission included a recommendation that a central sports organization should be established with authority over a vertically integrated set of sports associations (Chalip, Johnson, & Stachura, 1996). This recommendation sought to resolve disputes between the three major governing bodies overseeing amateur sports in the United States: the Amateur Athletic Union (AAU), the National Collegiate Athletic Association (NCAA), and the United States Olympic Committee (USOC). It was not until President Carter's term that the 1978 Amateur Sports Act was passed by Congress implementing many of the recommendations of the Ford Commission.

This act officially recognized the USOC as the national governing body for United States sport. The centralization of sport under the USOC helped to address the declining performance by the United States in international competition. Again, this was the limit on institutional change under the U.S.'s republicanism. Rather than a distinct government department for sport, the USOC became the key organization in matters sporting. A role we will show has expanded for the positive.

Also during Jimmy Carter's presidency the U.S. led an international (to an extent) boycott of the 1980 Moscow Olympic Games. While this saw mixed success the government agreed to contribute 50 cents for every dollar (up to a total of $20 million) the USOC raised from the public and private sectors from 1981 to 1984 in preparation for the Los Angeles Olympic Games (Bennett et al. 1983; Miller, 1984). During the bidding process and following the selection of Los Angeles as host of the 1984 Games, an intense and systematic sport development effort was made by the Reagan government and the NGBs. Any disruption was short-lived as the new USOC President, the former U.S. finance department head William Simon, reinvigorated sponsors' interest in a variety of ways and he initiated new Olympic and WOG preparation practices.

Simon called for the preparation of the strongest Olympic team ever for both versions of the 1984 Games. Each sport NGB was to include a quadrennial plan comprising: a yearly selection of prospective athletes at national sport festivals, formation of some national teams four years prior to the Games (with progress reviewed annually), and appointment of a national coach for the four-year period. Key elements of these plans were to include a wide spectrum of athlete services incorporating medicine, information technology, biomechanics, and advanced training facilities. This was to enhance centralized preparation of the athletes and teams with the latest sport, medical and scientific equipment and qualified staff. Finally, resources included a significant increase in financial support for Olympic preparation, use of praise and material rewards for athletes who achieved success, and promotional campaigns depicting winning the Games as a fait accompli.'

The USOC held its first National Sport Festival in 1978. This event was a smaller-scale version of the old European and more recent Soviet Spartakiads of mass national multi-sport competitions. All sports involved in this first National

Sport Festival were divided into three categories: prospective, developed, and underdeveloped. The prospective sports (e.g., swimming, track and field, free-style wrestling, gymnastics, volleyball, basketball, field hockey) received most organizational effort and material resources. Special attention was devoted to the preparation and participation of female athletes as the United States lagged behind the outcomes achieved by USSR and GDR sportswomen.

The U.S. system of Olympic preparation was advanced, but it was still following rather than leading the standards identified in the Model and part of many other countries practices. U.S. federal funding and support for previously hosted Olympic Games/WOGs in the United States had been provided in an *ad hoc* manner: mostly through an agency by agency or on a project by project basis, often without the benefit of an overall federal policy and systematic monitoring. As many as twenty-four federal agencies reported providing or planning to provide a combined total of almost $2 billion for Olympic-related projects and activities for the 1984 and 1996 Olympic Games and the 2002 Winter Olympic Games (U.S. GAO, 2000).

China replaces the USSR as the United States's challenger

The fall of the Berlin Wall in November 1989 was part of the demise of the socialist ideal of the Eastern or Soviet bloc nations. It was some time before reunification of East and West Germany occurred. The unification of athletes, teams, and sport systems took some time to complete. Despite this, a reunified Germany finished third in the 1992 Barcelona Olympic Games in both gold and overall medal counts and in the top ten nations overall since then. In the Winter Olympic Games since 1992, Germany placed first in total medal count four times and second twice. Many argued that the former GDR athletes benefitted from a unified Germany. Though there may be substance to this argument, both Germanys were near the top of the table for both Games for a long period.

Major change unfolded over a six-year period beginning in 1992 as the USSR ceased to exist in 1991. It disintegrated into fifteen new countries as former Soviet republics gained their independence. This led to the formation of the Unified Team that finished first in both gold and total medals at the 1992 Barcelona Olympic Games and second to the unified German team on both counts at the 1992 Albertville Winter Olympic Games. With the need to establish their economies, political structures, to deal with border issues, and fight wars, many of the former Soviet republics initially reduced their emphasis on sport. Public resources devoted to mass sport were reduced while new opportunities and priorities emerged.

In the two decades after 1990 the interaction of sport and society changed dramatically in central East Europe as the Soviet bloc dissolved. Following the 1989–1990 political and economic transition, Hungarian sport, for example, adapted to new economic and legal circumstances, particularly of how sport was financed (Gál, 2012). Bulgaria also found that the transition from a planned to a free market economy led to a withdrawal of previous subsidies and services to

Table 3.5 China's Olympic Games medals, 1952–2012

Games	Gold	Silver	Bronze	Total	Rank
1952*	0	0	0	0	NA
1984	15	8	9	32	4
1988	5	11	12	28	11
1992	16	22	16	54	4
1996	16	22	12	50	4
2000	28	16	14	58	3
2004	32	17	14	63	2
2008	51	21	28	100	1
2012	38	27	23	88	2

* only one athlete attended the Helsinki Games for the PRC
Source: databaseOlympics.com (2012). Accessed on 8 March 2013 at http://www.databaseolympics.com/index.htm

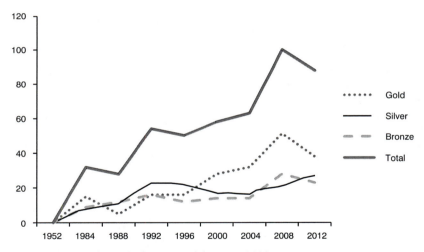

Figure 3.1 China's Olympic Games medals, 1952–2012

sport. At a time when people's real incomes were dropping, they could ill-afford to pay for sport participation. "Sport for all" changed from a way of life to a matter of choice (Girginov & Bankov, 2002). These changes had a somewhat negative effect on former socialist countries' mass participation and elite sport performance.

Though one ideologue nation, the USSR, was overcome, the rise of China has been dramatic. Since its full return to the Winter Olympic Games in 1980 and the Olympic Games in 1984, China's medal count has grown considerably and consistently (see Table 3.5 and Figure 3.1, and Table 3.6 and Figure 3.2). China's

Table 3.6 China's WOG medals, 1980–2014

Games	Gold	Silver	Bronze	Total	Rank
1980	0	0	0	0	NA
1988	0	0	0	0	NA
1988	0	0	0	0	NA
1992	0	3	0	3	15
1994	0	1	2	3	19
1998	0	6	2	8	16
2002	2	2	4	8	13
2006	2	4	5	11	14
2010	5	2	4	11	7
2014*	3	4	2	9	12

* Sochi.ru2014. Retrieved on March 8, 2014 from http://www.sochi2014.com/en/medal-standings
Source: databaseOlympics.com. Accessed on 8 March 2013 at http://www.databaseolympics.com/index.htm

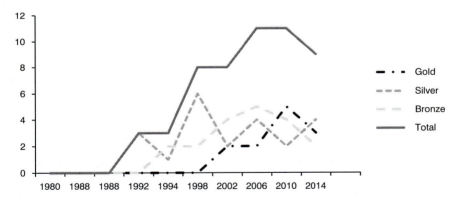

Figure 3.2 China's WOG medals, 1980–2014

success was initiated in the 1960s by borrowing the Soviet Union's concept of subsidized sport for all, among many other socialist ideas and programs. Beginning in the 1980s China also adopted some of the best of Western, particularly U.S., sports practices at all levels, from macro-organizational to micro-athlete management (Riordan, 1990; Tan & Green, 2008; Tan & Houlihan, 2006). China now integrates a mixed socialist (with five-year centralized planning) and capitalist structure for professional events and leagues, with government support of sports across all Olympic and traditional (e.g., Wushu, TaiChi, Daoyin Qigong, Sanshou) disciplines. As Chinese mass participation structures underpin its elite sport performance system, a uniform national PE curriculum focused on fitness and health promotion was established. These structures include well-educated professional coaches (from beginner level onward), affordable local training and competitions, and free outdoor fitness facilities. Programs are based on the development of an age-specific, LTAD model. All of this is supported by government programs for an integrated Olympic Strategy, a National Fitness for All Program, and a new department responsible for the development of sport (Tan & Green, 2008).

China's sport schools, colleges, and universities are subsidized from local government budgets and also by national budget input. Potential national athletes study at no cost in boarding schools similar to the expensive IMG Academies in the United States. As in the United States, less talented Chinese athletes can join specialized schools for a fee. China is further able to afford such public support thanks to lottery funding. The most important organizational structure present in China and found in all successful and progressive sport nations is a centralized, national government agency that develops sport in the same way as it supports other national policies in health and education. Federal sport agencies around the world are increasingly expected to support public health, education, and elite sport – all through mass participation.

With the election of a new leadership in 2012 change is underway in Chinese sport. The new President Xi Jinping seeks to change Chinese society around five new "pillars," that focus on the: political, economic, social, cultural, and ecological aspects of the society (personal communication, Professor Ren Hai, 22 April 2014). Rather than the strict party controlled, top-down bureaucracies dealing with issues at the local level, a broader set of NGOs, some private, but many funded through all levels of the Chinese government structure, will propose ways of delivering sport and fitness in the country. Ren also stated that new NGOs for sport would focus on the mass and elite levels, on the government departments for sport, on the use of volunteers to deliver mass and elite sport, and on ways of marketing mass and elite sport. This movement from the centralized power and control of the Communist Party is still evolving (see *The Economist*, 12 April 2014, pp. 21–24).

In terms of the "physical cultural" policy, Wang Fang (personal communication, 19–20 April 2014), stated that the central government has held meetings to move away from a Soviet-influenced, highly centralized "popular cultural" policy followed to that where NGOs develop "sport for all" and "fitness" programs. These NGOs would be funded by each level of government and by their lottery-generated funds. These NGOs would then deliver sport for all and fitness programs through local volunteers. The new policy direction in this mass area included: develop the actual NGOs and national public organziations (NPOs) and the attendant policies for their operation and governance; funding structures – government and lottery funds from each level of government; human resource development – find, train, and maintain the volunteers required to deliver programs in these areas; fitness testing – develop the standards for fitness across sex and age, deliver the testing regimes (note: some would remain along the existing GTO lines); and develop information for the new programs – advice on, knowledge of, and promotion of activities and fitness, provide advisors (PE specialists), and ideas on preventative exercise and health/lifestyle knowledge through the use of traditional and social media. Both of the above initiatives will require much change to the way Chinese civil society exists and the Communist Party operates.

The USOC changes focus and budgets

The USOC moved away from focusing on mass participation toward rewarding medal-winning performances; as have many other nations under neo-liberal conditions. This emphasis began in 1989 with the release of the Olympic Overview Report which stated that elite performance must be the USOC's primary goal (see Janofsky, 1989). Consistent with this emphasis the USOC developed a "venture capital" model in 1994 requiring member NGBs to present specific plans detailing how they intend to use financial resources from the USOC to increase their chances of winning Olympic medals (Piore, 2004). The USOC also announced it would eliminate $250,000 in guaranteed funding to each NGB beginning in 2006 (Borzilleri, 2005a). However, the USOC expanded organizational structures and financing to provide a footing for the development of a high-performance sport.

Nevertheless, some smaller NGBs receive up to 70 percent of their budget from the USOC (AP, 2000; Dittmore et al., 2008). They are concerned that the loss of guaranteed funding sent the wrong message. According to Kathy Zimmerman, former USA Badminton vice president and a retired elite player, the elimination of minimum fixed funding made the big sports stronger, while the smaller sports might drop off or disappear (Borzilleri, 2005b; Dittmore et al., 2008). According to executive directors and presidents of each of the thirty-nine NGBs governed by the USOC, financial assistance is necessary to maintain competitive success in their respective sports. Smaller NGBs preferred needs-based distribution to address an advantage that larger NGBs have in acquiring resources. Larger NGBs, with more members paying membership fees, are logically also more marketable to potential sponsors than smaller NGBs.

Non—medal winning NGBs also fear being excluded from television programming and funding in favor of NGBs with greater medal winning success. In a model that distributes resources based on actual medals won, the bigger sports will again receive the lion's share of financial resources: The "Matthew Effect" in full bloom.[10] It would also be reasonable to assume that physical fitness and participation goals will be secondary if they are considered at all. Though it is possible that the USOC is reflecting what the organization's stakeholders want (i.e., medal-winning athletes), it can be claimed that the other goals of sport are also important to a society. In response, Dittmore et al. (2008) proposed that if the goal stated in the 1978 Amateur Sports Act ("to promote and encourage physical fitness and public participation in amateur athletic activities," 36 U.S.C. § 220503) is still essential, ensuring it is adequately resourced and receiving sufficient focus and attention is also important.

Despite this notion, and soon after the 2004 Athens Olympic Games, USOC officials tried to determine which summer sports needed extra financing to win medals at the 2008 Beijing Olympic Games. Likewise, China also prepared its 119

Project in 2000. This was a focused, long-term, government-financed effort to win the most gold medals in the Beijing Olympics (Macur, 2008a). The 119 Project stood for the number of Olympic gold medals awarded in sports in which Chinese athletes have traditionally been weak; for example, track and field, swimming, and rowing (Macur, 2008a). In contrast, after 2004 Team USA focused on sports in which it had shown some success, such as fencing, triathlon, archery, and some disciplines in shooting and rowing. It also earmarked money for BMX racing, which made its Olympic debut in 2008, and for women's track cycling.

Team USA has been a strong presence at the Winter Olympics since the Salt Lake City Games in 2002, when it won thirty-four medals, second to Germany's thirty-six. At the 2006 Turin Winter Games, U.S. athletes won twenty-five medals, second to Germany's twenty-nine. In Vancouver 2010, the USA was first in overall medals (thirty-seven) but third in gold medals. Factors contributing to the USA's success included the addition of snowboarding and short-track speed skating in the WOG program. The USA is strong in these disciplines. These plans further evidence the success of the changes made in the 1980s to prepare athletes for these games.

The USOC and many of its partners are financed through donations. Though funding based on tax incentives makes the public feel good when they directly support their athletes, the accountability for these contributions is questionable because it rewards giving rather than an improved performance or increased participation. Also, donated amounts depend on economic conditions and require significant resources and special skills for soliciting funds. This leads to unstable and insufficient funding of sport, which is one of the reasons the USOC has focused less on mass participation and more on winning medals since 1994 (Janofsky, 1989).

To help rectify this shift, the USOC created the Community Olympic Development Program (CODP) in 1998. This program had initially partnered with 14 NGBs and seven Community Sports Groups. By 2011 there were 217 CODPs servicing 250,000 participants in a network of programs and facilities across the country (CODP, 2011). Sportspersons beginning to train and compete could progress through intermediate programs toward opportunities in HP and Olympic and Paralympic sports.

USOC expansion and allocations

HP and mass participation in Olympic sports is managed by the USOC and NGBs, many of which sought to increase cooperation by centralizing their operations around the USOC headquarters at the U.S. Olympic Complex in Colorado Springs. In 1998, twelve USOC member organizations located their national headquarters in this complex, while twelve other NGBs and two international sports federations located to the actual city of Colorado Springs.

The USOC's largest expense in 2010 was the $45.3 million in grants paid to 106 government and other organizations in the USA. These grants ranging from minor amounts such as $5,000 for the Casper Mountain Biathlon Club and the U.S.

Federation Handcycling, to major funding of the four NGBs which bring most of the Olympic medal tally: $2.4 million for swimming, $2.6 million for speed-skating, $3.9 million for skiing and snowboarding, and $4.4 million for track and field (Rosen, 2010). The USOC spent another $21.5 million in grants, services, and programs specifically for elite athletes (Rosen, 2010). In 2010 a combined $11.5 million of training support was allocated to the top 1,696 athletes; this included "Operation Gold" that provided $2.8 million when goals were reached, and $6.7million in health insurance and other medical benefits (Rosen, 2011). Most of these monies are devoted to athletes who achieved HP targets.

According to Mickle (2011) this approach has created uneasiness among the NGB leaders. In 2011, the USOC split NGBs into three categories, giving more money to those with higher Olympic medal potential. The USOC allocates funds across those three categories after reviewing each NGB's high-performance plan, which outlines the programs an NGB plans to run for its elite athletes and how many medals are predicted. While the USOC has been transparent about the potential cuts, it did not help Team USA compete against other nations with government support for the long-term development of NGBs. Debate will inevitably emerge about whether USOC funds should go to support elite athletes who win medals or sports that encourage participation and competition (Mickle, 2011).

Professional sports

These leagues also finance and sponsor the development of athletes through their minor and semi-professional leagues. They allow many of their contracted athletes to compete in a variety of international competitions (and for many different countries). Professional sport teams also develop athletes through multi-level development leagues and academies, which contribute to the U.S. international sporting success. The fact that the U.S. sport industry is dominated by a small number of professional sports may limit the development of other sports and create conflict in schedules. We discuss different programs and ways in which these leagues are furthering their contributions below.

Cooperation among professional sport organizations is limited as they compete for financial revenues, particularly those from television contracts. These commercial organizations also compete with the USOC. Of the USOC's 2010 revenue of $250.6 million, $105 million came from broadcast rights, $66.6 million in contributions and donations, and $71.8 million in sponsorship money (Rosen, 2011). With the absence of a central agency to coordinate and directly support sport and recreation, as proposed in the Model, U.S. sporting organizations function in a somewhat chaotic environment. Being driven by competition rather than by cooperation provides opportunities and encouragements for unique approaches but lacks communication, coordination, uniform standards, and national coherence. The need for better cooperation across sport-related organizations was stressed by the U.S. National Physical Activity Plan (NPAP, 2010), which can be facilitated by a national public agency as suggested by Bowers, Chalip, and Green (2011). A more coordinated approach to LTAD is also needed to make Team USA's performance more consistent in the increasingly competitive international sport environment (Coyle, 2007; Sparvero et al., 2008). The public makes substantial investments in sport and physical activity through the USOC, NGBs, and U.S. government initiatives, as will be discussed further in this chapter. We feel these coordinated investments would improve both the national health of U.S. citizens and the USA's international sport performance.

Nonprofit organizations

Among the thirty-four USOC-affiliated multi-sport organizations that are particularly important for mass participation at the local community level are private nonprofit entities with sport facilities and programs such as the YM/WCAs, the CYO, Boys and Girls Clubs, and Jewish Community Centers. The Y develops youths through a variety of programs, including recreational and competitive sports, and subsidizes memberships to make sport affordable for everyone. There were more than 20 million members in the Y movement; about half of them are younger than seventeen years of age, while the U.S. Ys employed 20,000 full-time staff (YMCA, 2011).

An indicative example of how this organization contributes to mass participation is the Salem Y in Massachusetts, part of a network of six YM/WCA centers on the North Shore of Boston. Collectively, they offer multiple game halls, weight rooms, swimming pools, saunas, and fitness and sport programs for all ages. The sport and other educational and cultural activities are provided through after-school programs for 200 children (North Shore Y, 2011). In 2011, the Salem Y, similar to other YM/WCAs around the country, assisted 1,000 children, adults, and families throughout their community of about 41,000 persons.[11]

The Swim Strong non-profit foundation of New York offers low-cost or free swim lessons to city residents. It does not just aim to teach children to swim but offers advanced programs with basic competition features. This approach is in line with world best practice in LTAD connecting mass and elite participation. Swim Strong is, however, administered and staffed entirely by volunteers (Foderaro, 2013). This is another good U.S. example of ways to provide mass sport at low cost to the participants.

Public organizations

Another important feature in the development of the U.S. sport system was the early formation of local and state government departments of parks and recreation. According to Walls (2009), the United States has 53 national parks and more than 6,600 state park sites, but many outdoor pursuits often begin at the playground or sports fields at nearby recreation areas. The Boston Common, designated as a public open space in 1634, is considered the nation's first city park. Bostonians enjoyed a total of sixteen parks created before 1800 (Walls, 2009). From the mid- to late 1800s, the urban park vision centered on providing quiet natural settings in an urban environment.

Beginning in the early 1900s, urban parks began to provide recreation opportunities, particularly for children, in close-to-home neighborhood parks (Walls, 2009). The recreation concept expanded to include swimming pools, ball fields, and indoor facilities in the early and middle part of the twentieth century. After World War II the interest in city parks waned as many moved to the suburbs where each house had a yard of its own. Walls (2009) concluded that close-to-home recreation opportunities are growing in importance relative to those in more distant locations. As 80 percent of the U.S. population resides in urban areas, local parks seem to be most critical for those in cities (Walls, 2009). Public departments of parks and recreation have supported mass sport participation for all ages through state-funded venues, developmental sport leagues with training programs and competitions for all age groups, and affordable children's camps during school vacations.

In terms of physical facilities, this local government and state provision is an obvious historical fact in the USA. The following are offered as examples. In Massachusetts in 2011, the Greater Boston parks maintained fifty-eight free public tennis courts, including ten with lights (Commonwealth of Massachusetts, 2012). In the same year, the City of Salem, Massachusetts, provided and coordinated leagues in fourteen sports and facilitated eighty sport programs, camps, and clinics for beginner, experienced, and world-class athletes. Though these eighty programs are not an integrated or a formal part of continuous permanent programs necessary for multi-year athlete development, they attract new participants to clubs and leagues, contributing to the process of LTAD.

Again, publicly provided sport programs are a key feature of local government. The New York City's Department of Parks and Recreation provided a variety of free aquatics programs for all ages and levels. This is a notable best mass sport practice because normally swimming lessons can cost as much as $1 a minute; so learning to swim properly can still be something of a "luxury" for most children and youth (Foderaro, 2013). Integrating mass and elite swimming, the New York City's free Swim Team program involves an ongoing competition structure for children and youths (aged from six to 18). Participants then develop competitive swimming strokes, starts and turns, and team sportsmanship concepts. Teams train most of the year and compete in the Five Borough Championship during the outdoor and the Borough Cup Championship during the indoor swim seasons (NYC Parks, 2013). This program demonstrates the important role of government-managed and financially supported (through grants) programs in providing affordable and integrated sport services.

Though being tailored to local priorities, the ability to pay, and the availability of local expertise, these programs use the infrastructure funded or supported by all levels of government across all states. Outdoor recreation-acquisition, development, and planning grants distributed $27 million in 2009, $38 million in 2010, and $47 million in 2011 for a wide range of outdoor recreation projects (Federal Grants Wire, 2011). All states are eligible for more specific grants, such as the Recreational Trails Program in which funds range from $825,000 to $4.7 million, with an average of $1.65 million for fiscal year 2009 similar to the previous five years (Federal Grants Wire, 2011). Greater efficiencies in the utilizations of park and recreation venues could be garnered and facilitated by federal, state, and local governments through better cooperation with the CODP and other long-term participation programs.

Universities

Elite sport at U.S. universities has a long history of supporting mass participation. Revenues from profitable sport teams are used to successfully subsidize unprofitable sports and programs. Since its founding in 1906, the NCAA facilitates some of the world's best conditions for 430,000 student-athletes competing in twenty-three sports at more than 1,000 colleges and universities. Most of the NCAA (2012, 2014a) revenue comes from a fourteen-year $10.8 billion agreement with Turner Broadcasting and CBS Sports for rights to the Division I Men's Basketball Championship. The NCAA revenue for 2011–2012 was $871.6 million, of which $705 million (81 percent) came from media rights payments. Most of the remaining 18 percent of revenue came from championships, mostly ticket and merchandise sales. NCAA expenses for 2010–2011 were $778 million.

A total of $480 million was distributed to Division I members, $62.6 million supported Division I championships and programs, while $31.6 million went to Division I, II, and $22 million to Division III in 2010–2011. Another $124.2 million was directed to NCAA-wide programs to fund the eighty-nine annual national championships held in twenty-three sports.

At its 1918 Convention the NCAA set out on a major mission to convince member institutions and public school systems of the need for compulsory physical education programs for their students. Significant progress was made during the 1920s and the concept is now anchored in many campuses (Crowley, 2006). In 1991 Congressman Tom McMillen (D, MD4) a former University of Maryland, U.S. Olympic team, and NBA basketball player suggested a range of initiatives to this effect. They included mandating a revenue-distribution plan favoring institutions that were working to comply with Title IX; forbidding any allocation of dollars on the basis of win/loss records; annual reporting to Congress and the Secretary of Education; establishing the NCAA board of presidents with certain control and responsibilities; and decreasing expenditures on revenue-producing sports and on athletics administration (Crowley, 2006). None of these proposals, however, traveled far in the legislative process (Crowley, 2006).

Alternative options are available; however, they are not likely to be more global with government funding under siege across the United States. This leads to an interesting anomaly in U.S. universities. As Benedict and Armen (2013, p. 185) explained:

> He's [Washington State University President] an academic to the core. His top priorities were increasing enrollment and building on WSU's reputation as a leading academic institution. He viewed football as a ticket to both. "Like it or not, football serves as the front door to institutions, with the exception of the

Ivy League," Floyd explained. "The reputation of a school is predicated on athletics. Football is first. Basketball is second. If you have a successful football program, it will support all the other revenue and non-revenue sports."

Floyd's view of college football is consistent with more and more presidents and chancellors at leading colleges and universities in America today, but the reality is that very few football programs are profitable. At that point, only 20 of the top 120 Division I football programs were in the black. The remaining programs were losing on average close to $ 10 million per year, but it is reached a point where virtually every college president has bought into the idea that in order for a university to be successful, it must have a successful football program.

The reference to the Ivy League[12] universities is instructive.

As Pennington (2011) noted the Ivy League universities do not offer the traditional U.S. athletic scholarships: for any student admitted based on grades and talents, a wide variety of aid is provided based on financial need. The Ivy League (2014) funded around 8,000 athletes competing in thirty-five sports in 2013. Harvard's Web site indicated in 2013 that the university hosts mass programs in forty-five sports and funds twenty highly competitive teams. According to Pennington (2011), in the university year of 2010–2011, the Ivy League produced 108 first-team all-Americans. He also noted that nineteen of its athletes competed at the 2010 Vancouver Winter Olympic Games, winning ten medals. This renaissance in the league can be traced to new policies that have enhanced financial aid for all admitted students. Led by endowment-rich members such as Yale, Princeton, and Harvard (which in 2012 received $30 billion in endowments; Haynie, 2013) this group of universities spent hundreds of millions of dollars in additional need-based aid.

If other U.S. colleges and universities try to utilize this "best practice" or if more approximated it, they could help their students compete through all their years of higher education. Perhaps the first step could be for the NCAA to increase athlete eligibility from four to six years, allowing athletes to represent their universities and complete their degrees (where possible). What else is feasible in terms of colleges and universities is discussed in Chapter 5.

Schools

Today public schools in the United States educate 90 percent of their children and youths. By enhancing academic learning and providing healthy lifelong habits, school PE and sport programs can contribute to the development of productive citizens (CDC, 2010). Opportunities to compete for U.S. universities and receive higher education, together with quality coaching at no cost, drives masses of high school students to compete for their schools. Coaches can create many connections between their school athletes and higher education programs.

Most U.S. high schools however develop sport as a marketing tool, similar to how universities and professional teams do, portraying glimmering teams with mascots and cheerleaders to attract students, and provide media content for the sport/media complex. High school and university sports have an exclusionary, elitist character that undermines sport participation and lifelong adherence to exercise. This is an issue with the nature and delivery of PE but also with the nature of school and university sports, in the United States and elsewhere.

To increase mass participation and integrate sport with athlete services and education, a national hierarchical public system of sport streams/classes in regular schools (as is currently occurring in Ontario, Canada) specialized sport schools/academies, and boarding schools could be created. Such a multi-level sport school system accommodated a broad spectrum of participation levels in the USSR in the second part of the twentieth century. These education/sport-linked institutions became a key factor in the global sport success of China and Cuba,[13] where their mass sport participation and international sporting success grew with their literacy rates. At the end of the twentieth century, various elements of the Soviet sport school system started to appear across Australasia and America. The NGBs, the USOC, and state and federal departments of education could utilize the experiences of the former USSR and the current Russian and Chinese sport schools and take note of how the system has been adapted in the West.

In the United Kingdom, for example, sport education is also becoming part of fostering different talents through special state schools. These schools follow the mainstream curriculum but include an emphasis on the fields of technology, music, science, language, sport, or business. The majority of secondary schools in England now have some sort of specialist status (BBC, 2004a). For example, arts and sports colleges were established in 1996. The school sport network in 2008 included 448 sports colleges, 450 school sport partnerships (groups of six schools), with 3,200 school sports coordinators and 225 competition managers (Davies, 2008). Although 38 percent of sports colleges operate an HP academy on site (Davies, 2008), they also help mass participation and tackle antisocial behavior among teenage boys and to assist in reducing obesity (BBC, 2004a). In both Australia and the United Kingdom specialized sport schools have been shown to positively influence youth in lower socioeconomic areas (BBC, 2004a, 2004b; Davies, 2008; Wynhausen, 2007).

Physical education

The U.S. government has made efforts to improve national fitness through the *Strengthening Physical Education Act 2007* aimed to get students active by making PE part of the core curriculum and requiring PE assessments throughout schooling. Forty-one states have published plans focused on physical activity and healthy nutrition aimed at reducing the prevalence of overweight and obesity: Another seventeen states have passed weight-related screening requirements for students (Merriman Curhan Ford, 2008). The National Association for Sport and Physical Education (NASPE, 2012) recommended that schools provide 150 minutes per week of instructional PE in elementary school and 225 minutes in middle and high schools. The difficulty lies in the fact that there is no uniform way to finance and implement these goals. These tasks are left to states and municipalities across the United States to deal with. Their school boards cannot afford these changes. Many school boards are now in difficult financial times, if not financially broke.

HP sport will be better supported by school PE if fitness tests and national curricula are implemented and the quantity and quality of PE are standardized. Some states already require mandatory physical education classes. According to NASPE (2012) New Jersey mandates 150 minutes of health, safety, and PE per week in all grades; New York requires 120 minutes of PE per week in the first six school years, and 90 minutes in grades seven to twelve; Illinois mandates daily PE in all grades; California requires recess and 200 minutes of PE every ten school days in grades one to six and 400 minutes in grades seven to eight and all four years of high school. While only six states require PE in every school grade and only twenty-six (51%) require some form of assessment in PE, the positive trend is that twice as many states (twenty-eight in 2012 compared with twelve in 2010) require PE grades to be included in the calculation of grade point average along with other core subjects (NASPE, 2012).

Similar requirements played an important role in the success of mass and elite sport in the former USSR as they now play in China. The school education developed in the USSR included compulsory PE with grades given as part of middle and high school diplomas. PE was based on a national uniform curriculum of forty-five-minute physical exercises twice a week and it was part of a lifelong GTO fitness program. A pass/fail PE grade was also part of any higher education graduation certificate and it was awarded after two years of preparing for and passing the GTO tests. This system of PE, multi-level fitness tests, and sport-specific ranks provided everyone with healthy paths from mass participation to HP in the USSR (Matveev, 2008; Riordan, 1980) and again was directly experienced by the first author's being a Soviet school and university student during the 1970s to 1980s.

There are a variety of schools within each U.S. neighborhood. The amount and quality of PE in public schools depends mostly on the wealth of the suburb, as property taxes pay for public schools. These schools usually have PE two times a week at best. In better charter schools and private schools, PE is scheduled every other day. In some charter and private schools, PE is scheduled every other day as recommended by the NASPE (2012). The advantage of this system lies in the fact that it allows for great variation, while the downfall is that too many children from poor families do not have the chance to receive good PE. In addition to PE, children from about age twelve can play for school teams, which typically involves practice or competition about two to three times a week during each sport season, each of a brief period of three months. The sports are broken down into fall, winter, and spring categories. Students are able to choose a different sport each season. The advantage of this system is that it is available in-house. The main downfall is that coaching is available only several months a year and, if a program is to prepare for competitions, there may be insufficient time for conditioning to avoid injuries and for recovery. Last, public school sport programs typically offer only a small number of the usual U. S. sports.

Many decision-makers have grown concerned about changing health and behavior patterns related to physical activity and nutrition. According to the Department of Health and Human Services (2008) guidelines, a healthy life implies exercising for about sixty minutes a day. In 2011 only 29 percent of high school students surveyed had participated in at least sixty minutes per day of physical activity on all seven days before the survey and only 31 percent attended PE class daily (CDC, 2012). According to the CDC (2009) children spend seven-and-a-half hours a day watching TV, resulting in or adding to one child in three being obese. About 25 percent of high school students reported that they used a computer or played computer or video games more than three hours a day, and about 33 percent of high school students reported watching television three or more hours per day on an average school day (CDC, 2009).

PE and sport can spearhead the overall improvement in U.S. school education. According to the CDC (2010) fifty studies reported a total of 251 links between physical activity and good academic performance, representing measures of academic achievement, academic behavior, and cognitive skills and attitudes. President Obama stressed in 2009 that fifteen-year-olds in the U.S. ranked seventeenth in science and twenty-fifth in math compared to their peers around the world (*USA Today*, 2010; Hechinger, 2010). The top ranked in science in 2009 was Finland (*USA Today*, 2010; Hechinger, 2010). Finland's education system is widely acknowledged as one of the best in the world where teachers have high status and where a master's degree is required to start teaching (NCEE, 2014). By 2012 the United States was twenty-first in science and twenty-sixth in math for this age group (Buchanan, 2013). The United States might consider having similar requirements for teachers (and coaches) by spending more on quality pedagogues and less on chic sport facilities and equipment, not to mention that spent on the astronomical salaries of elite athletes and coaches. In both education and sport, states might take more responsibility for re-balanced funding by moving away from the current locally funded system.

Tax and other financial incentives

States combat the lack of public and private financial support by increasing tax credits for donations to various services including public and private nonprofit schools and universities, including their sport programs. According to Hill (2012), Idaho's maximum donation tax credit increased from $100 to $200 for individuals and from $1,000 to $5,000 for corporations in 2011. The Idaho tax credit is limited to 50 percent of an individual taxpayer's state income tax liability, while the corporate credit is limited to 10 percent of the corporation's state tax (Hill, 2012). Contributions can be designated for the school district as a whole, for individual schools, or even for specific programs such as the orchestra or athletics (Hill, 2012).

The Educational Improvement Tax Credit Program in Pennsylvania allows businesses to support private and public school systems and scholarship programs in exchange for tax credits. Businesses that pledge money for one year are able to donate up to $300,000 and receive a tax break from the state for up to 75 percent of the contributed amount (Veronikis, 2012). Businesses who sign up for two years can donate up to $300,000 both years to receive a tax cut of 90 percent of the given amount (Veronikis, 2012). Significant advancements are possible in the system of tax incentives for systematic sport development across the United States.

Governments around the world economically stimulate physical activity through various personal tax incentives. The closest example for the United States is Canada. A Canadian federal government tax credit became available in 2007 that covers fees for programs that promote children's and youths' physical activity and fitness (Canada Revenue Agency, 2007). Further legislation was planned to introduce a $500 fitness tax credit for adults and doubled the existing children's fitness tax credit from $500 to $1,000 annually (Fitzpatrick, 2011). Similar incentives are being discussed in Australia and are actually being considered in the United States. Personal tax reductions would reward sport participation among the middle class. Clubs could also be given tax reductions for subsidizing participants from low-income households. NGBs under the aegis of the USOC might lobby government health departments to develop financial stimulation packages to increase sport participation for the upper-middle (e.g., through tax incentives) and lower classes (e.g., through subsidies) to reduce obesity and public medical costs.

U.S. federal government

Despite the minimal direct support for sport, the U.S. government has been attempting to encourage physical fitness as a foundation necessary for a healthy nation. Since its inception in 1956 the PCFSN has been promoting physical activity through research, education, the development of fitness tests and awards, and the encouragement of fitness, endorsed and barracked by celebrity sport figures.

The reasons for these efforts have included military readiness, elite athletic performance, the reduction of health risks, commitment to developing a higher quality of life, and motivation to live a healthier lifestyle (Franks & Safrit, 1999). However, the Council's mission of engaging, educating, and empowering all U.S. citizens across their lifespan to adopt a healthy lifestyle has not been fully supported by the necessary authority and resources. The federal government provided only about $1.2 million annually to the PCFSN within the U.S. Department of Health and Human Services (HHS, 2013). This is an insufficient amount to promote alternatives to a physically inactive lifestyle and unhealthy food. At the same time the fast food industry spent more than $5 million every day for marketing and advertising unhealthy foods to children (Kovacic, 2008) and the advertising spent on interactive video games was projected to reach $1 billion in 2014 (Chester, 2009). An egregious example was the fast food industry's aggressive lobbying of Congress that had pizza declared a vegetable to protect it from a nutritional overhaul of the school lunch program in 2012 (Wilson & Roberts, 2012).

The PCFSN, operating within the federal health department, is well positioned to promote its goals through partnerships with all possible state, profit, and nonprofit organizations toward mobilizing financial and other resources for the common goal of improving national health and fitness. In 2010, President Obama and first lady Michelle Obama intensified the activities and broadened the scope of the Council. This included the promotion of good nutrition and the launching of the "Let's Move!" campaign (see more of this progam in Element 2 below).

The Council also disseminates information on grants available in the field to a variety of organizations such as the U.S. Soccer Foundation, Bikes Belong (which pays U.S. organizations and agencies that are committed to putting more people on bicycles), and General Mills Community Action (which sponsors low socioeconomic-status schools to receive Presidential Active Lifestyle Awards). The Council also includes a sixteen-member scientific board comprising scholars who made significant contributions to the research and science of physical activity, health, sports, or nutrition (PCFSN, 2011).

The U.S. federal government estimated that the total health care costs related to being overweight and obese could reach $956.9 billion by 2030 (Merriman Curhan Ford, 2008). To reverse this problem both the public and private sectors have launched health initiatives to increase mass sport participation and hopefully develop more elite athletes. The percentage of major U.S. corporations using financial incentives to promote employer-sponsored health and wellness programs rose from 62 percent in 2007 to 71 percent in 2008 (Merriman Curhan Ford, 2008). Fifty-five percent of U.S. organizations with at least fifty employees in the public and private sectors surveyed in 2012 had a fitness program, while gym discounts and cash incentives were common ways to reward participants (Mattke, Liu, Caloyeras, Huang, Van Busum, Khodyakov, & Shier, 2013). Some employers' health insurance plans offer $150 per year for fitness club memberships, discounts for gym club memberships, and a $20 monthly gym membership credit (Harvard Pilgrim, 2014; United Healthcare, 2014). Corporations are expected to expand wellness services and incentives for participating in fitness programs (Mattke et al., 2013). Again, the debate continues in the United States over health, and within it sport, and its universality and funding. Will this ever bring fruitful results?

Government support of sport in different countries

Governments across the globe increasingly provide financial and organizational support to NGBs, clubs, educational institutions, and other organizations to develop both elite athletes and mass or recreation sport. In Russia the development of guided paths to excellence and the integration of fitness objectives into public policies started in the beginning of the twentieth century under the state departments of education, health, and defense. A highly integrated and successful system of mass and elite sport was developed by the mid – twentieth century. From this point, after realizing all the positive effects of an integrated sport system on both the holistic development of citizens and the global status of the nation, some countries followed suit. China and France borrowed many of the former USSR mass and HP structures in the 1960s, which led to successful results in the 1990s. Countries such as the United Kingdom (from the 1960s) and Australia and Canada (from the 1970s) followed both the former USSR and East German practices, which also brought success.

Governments plans, however, are often rhetoric aimed to increase a politician's popularity or win bids to host an Olympic Games. The UK government, as part of the lead-in to the 2012 London Olympic Games, announced a goal of increasing sport participation by 10 percent in the whole population: impressive but unrealistic. As noted by Girginov and Hills (2008), achieving sustainable sports participation would remain an elusive target until the rights of different communities and sport were recognized. The IOC and national governments are the key organizations that can channel collective efforts and resources effectively to create subsidized conditions for mass participation. Instead, in the United Kingdom and other countries (including the United States) the focus is still on the organization of events that benefit mostly elite athletes and corporate sponsors.

Trying to balance the development of mass and elite sport is a global issue that puzzles sport developers in the East as much as in the West. Ebishima (2012) is concerned that the result of increasing emphasis on winning medals is that top athletes are created and nurtured in the elite academies, apart from local community involvement. This phenomenon leads to the widening gap between grassroots and elite sport in some countries. Political decisions and people's recognition of how sport should exist are complex and involved. Searching for ways to understand the linkage or continuity between elite and mass sport in the United Kingdom, Ireland, and Japan, Ebishima (2012) started from the top organizational structures. In the United Kingdom, elite sport and grassroots sport are promoted by two different organizations, UK Sport and Sport England. In the Republic of Ireland, the Irish Sport Council is responsible for both categories of sport and it created a pathway from grassroots to the elite. The Japan Sport Association has two sections that promote elite sport and grassroots sport separately. In these three countries, however, sport policy appears to mirror the public value of sport (Ebishima, 2012).

In Australia and the Netherlands, sport is placed under the federal department of health, where health targets are increasingly tied to mass participation targets. In the United Kingdom there is strong local collaboration across health, education, and mass and elite sport. In Finland, there is a comprehensive integration of health and mass-oriented sport collaboration across various federal and local state agencies (Westerbeek, 2009). Finland's practices are readily borrowed by many countries because it has one of the world's fittest populations (*The Guardian*, 2005) and best school education test results (*USA Today*, 2010; Hechinger, 2010).

One of the key features identified by Houlihan and Green (2008), who analyzed elite sport development in nine successful or progressive sport nations, was the "governmentalization" of sport; particularly the attempt to balance HP with healthy mass participation policies. They noted that Japan emphasizes PE while Norway focuses on mass sport (40 to 98 percent of Norway's NGB income is devoted to mass sport) and athlete well-being (restricting, for example, competition and specialization in one sport before ten years of age). National regulations of athlete development and PE are important factors leading to international sporting success. In the absence of government leadership in the United States, sport, athlete development, and PE-mandated requirements are minimal. The U.S. government could study and implement the proven practices of countries from which the United States is facing increased competition in order to continue to succeed on the international sport stage; and to reduce obesity and medical costs, improve education, and make the nation more productive, competitive, and healthier.

Russia is now restoring the USSR-developed system of coordinated plans and actions across federal, state, and municipal levels of government. To prevent illness and improve education, these departments ensure that facilities and instruction in more than 100 sports are provided across the nation at all levels of participation. This is achieved by improving communication and coordination among organizations that nurture sport and physical activity. Better coordination in the United States would also benefit sport organizations, programs, and competitions across all elements of its sport development system.[14] Coordinating government involvement would increase opportunities for everyone to participate in a greater number of sports. This would also help to introduce a fairer balance in the U.S. media, spectator, and sponsor markets that are currently dominated by a few commercial professional sports.

Only several developed countries have halted the downward spiral toward inactive lifestyle. These include Canada and New Zealand but most notably Finland. Instead of a massive campaign telling people what not to do, Finnish officials created incentives. Local fitness competitions were organized; affordable, clean swimming pools, ball parks, and snow parks for activities such as skiing were provided; and nationwide changes in legislation encouraged healthy behavior and nutrition. The persistent renewal of existing schemes and the creation of new schemes ensured that fitness remains in the public consciousness. Hundreds of local schemes set up across Finland are either free or substantially subsidized to ensure no one was excluded. Based on a New Zealand concept, Finnish general practitioners are encouraged to prescribe physical activity to their patients along with medication. The balance between mass and elite, central and local, and public and private ensures that the Finnish central government supports a broad spectrum of unique local activities all achieving a common goal of mass sport participation.

Some countries have already adapted the Finnish strategy. In Brazil, communities have been promoting activities based around dancing (*The Guardian*, 2005; Westerbeek, 2009). Mass participation in Cuba is based on a similar concept of central support and the development of sports that are popular, affordable, and sustainable in each local community, including remote rural areas (Riordan, 1978). The PCFSN is positioned to bring together interest groups and develop a nationwide and locally focused and constantly revitalized strategy to encourage more physical activity.

The U.S. government's belief has been that the best way to engage people in physical activity is to recognize and reward it (Franks & Safrit, 1999). The President's Challenge (2005) awards are earned for participating in virtually any physical activity and self-reporting online. The rewards have included emblems, certificates, bumper stickers, magnets, T-shirts, medallions, ribbons, and pins (priced from $0.25 to $9). Similar rewards were used in the former USSR, though the Soviet approach was more direct, specific, and nurturing. This concept could be fully utilized across local communities in the United States.

The preceding discussion agrees with Kolesov, Lents and Razumovski (2003) and Platonov (2005) that the USOC, NGBs, governments, and other players within the United States sport and physical activity/education sector show significant efforts to advance the system of Olympic preparation. Despite the USOC's struggle to balance mass and elite sport investments, its Community Olympic Development Program is an important attempt to strengthen the structures connecting mass and HP sport. Different levels of government provide significant indirect support for mass and elite sport, particularly through educational systems and tax incentives. Our literature review, however, confirms that the analysis made by Sparvero et al. (2008) has substance. They concluded that the U.S. system is anything but systematic, lacking federal government involvement and the structure that this would bring; and that there is a lack of coordination among sport providers who are in competition with one another, particularly for financial resources.

We followed the recommendation of Dittmore et al. (2008) to compare the system employed in the United States with those of other countries. Both international and U.S. experiences show that a government agency, with sufficient resources, could help U.S. sport achieve vital, multiple socioeconomic goals, and most importantly improved health through better balanced and integrated mass and elite programs. The following section discusses how sporting organizations and their supporting agencies have cooperated and continue to advance their partnerships.

Element 2 (Macro-Level): Partnerships with supporting agencies

This second macro-level element shows where "sufficient resources should be obtained from, expertise exchanged, and common goals achieved" (Smolianov & Zakus, 2008, p. 7) across the sport development system. This could be achieved, as shown above, through multiple partnerships with all organizations involved in some way with sport. Partnership possibilities are numerous and include government departments (federal, state, local), all types of educational institutions, and all sport-governing organizations from local to international level.

Federal partnership initiatives

The "Let's Move!" campaign is a partnership that the PCFSN started in 2010 to mobilize public and private resources to combat the epidemic of obesity. To support "Let's Move!" and to facilitate and coordinate partnerships between states, communities, and nonprofit and for-profit private sectors, the nation's leading children's health foundations have come together to create the Partnership for a Healthier America foundation. This foundation aims to solve childhood obesity within a generation so that children born in 2010 reach adulthood at a healthy weight. Showing leadership in public-private sector cooperation, the PCFSN and the Entertainment Software Association launched the Active Play PALA+ Challenge to highlight active video games. The PCFSN could also urge coordination of the fifteen government agencies involved with food policy and the administration of the thirty food-related U.S. laws.

The PCFSN intensified its partnership efforts in 2012 in recognition that the President's Challenge Physical Activity and Fitness Awards program achieved little in encouraging a more active lifestyle. Opinions differed around the relationship between actual physical activity and fitness testing and awards. This often led to confused and fragmented programs rather than achieving consensus and a comprehensive approach for the future. Despite this, there have been many examples of cooperation through a variety of government interventions that have significantly impacted the exercise habits of the U. S. public (Franks & Safrit, 1999).

After the Surgeon General recommended in 1996 that everyone in the United States complete at least thirty minutes of exercise a day, the number of fitness club memberships increased by 8 percent between 1996 and 1997. Between 2001 and 2002, fitness club memberships increased by 7.4 percent (Merriman Curhan Ford, 2008). However, unhealthy behaviors leading to obesity have not lessened because partnerships among the health, education, and sport sectors are still lacking. One reason for this is that there are serious problems in the U.S. systems of education and health care. If President Obama succeeds in his current attempts to reform these social goods, an integrated sport development "system" might happen sooner. Improved mass fitness will give public health and education a boost when all schools provide children with a daily hour of PE and sport as recommended by the NASPE and the PCFSN. Similarly, when some form of universal health care develops in the United States, both mass and elite participants would benefit from an increase in public attention and resources relating to illness prevention through sport and recreation.

One reason for President Obama's 2010 reform of the U.S. health system was the lack of health care for all citizens (Cutler, 2009). As the U.S. federal government is assuming greater responsibility for the health care of its citizens, it might also establish a government agency for sport and physical activity (Bowers et al., 2011). Many examples exist of governments across the world mobilizing and coordinating resources from different partners for the systematic development of mass and elite sport. By coordinating numerous partners, governments of countries such as Finland and Singapore increased mass sport participation in community clubs relatively quickly (Nicholson, Hoye, & Houlihan, 2011). In the Netherlands, exemplary health, sport participation, and performance are outcomes achieved through the national government's sport funding support (Van Bottenburg, 2011).[15] The central Dutch government collects public and lottery money and then directs it to sport clubs, NGBs, and most notably to local sport projects (Van Bottenburg, 2011).

Nicholson et al. (2011) also noted the high level of sport participation rates in China. Following the former USSR model, China established a national sport department in 1954. This department had local branches that mobilized the resources of communities and places of study, work, and service for the holistic development of sport and physical activities (including the Soviet GTO tests) (Fan & Lu, 2011). Daily morning and afternoon ten-minute exercise breaks were provided and sport tournaments among workplace teams were organized (Fan & Lu, 2011). Based on this foundation, multi-level competitions in forty-three sports and sport schools with high-quality coaching were established in 1956 (Fan & Lu, 2011). In 1958 an integrated mass and elite sport plan set a target of 200 million people passing the GTO tests; 50 million to 70 million reaching competitive level; and 10 million to 15 million becoming elite athletes (Fan & Lu, 2011).

In leading sport nations from China and Russia to France, professional coaches and managers are employed through clubs by local and national governments on a permanent full-time basis. In the United States paid coaches are remunerated through indirect federal and state school and university budgets and grants. Funding for club coaches might be part of attracting funds as a charitable entity or through establishing a foundation. Many possibilities exist in the current market-based content.

At the local level, governments, schools, colleges, universities, residential communities, and businesses would provide better support and build more facilities for both mass and elite sport if partnerships were fostered though clubs and NGB branches organizing events at these facilities. The United States Tennis Association, for example, could help local governments across the United States to replicate the comprehensive support of tennis by municipalities in Florida and California. Germany provides a good example of clearly defined and agreed responsibilities in partnerships between local government and clubs for sport development, as described by Bergsgard, Houlihan, Mangset, Nodland, and Rommetvedt (2007). To maintain their relevance, NGBs need to play a more active role in local partnerships by assisting coaches and clubs across the nation to create the conditions for daily, year-round participation in a broader spectrum of sports at schools.

Clubs could better utilize school facilities, while schools could further capitalize on the resources of clubs and local communities through new sport programs and events and stronger social bonding. Highly qualified coaches and trained community leaders are needed to lead the development of partnerships between schools and the community, as exemplified by the "Mad Dog Wrestling Club" near Boston, Massachusetts, which directly helps local school wrestling programs with around-the-year training across different levels of wrestlers. Partnerships among NGBs and clubs in different sports are important in creating the conditions for everyone to participate in internationally popular sports and for gifted participants to get an opportunity to progress to HP.

Partnerships involving nonprofit, public, and private sectors in preparation for the Olympic Games provide good examples of how resources could be mobilized to develop sport and advance communities through sport. In the

2012 London Olympic Games, the government improved infrastructure and increased affordable sport offerings; Adidas and the Great Outdoor Gym Company built free fitness grounds; and wi-fi operators O2 United Kingdom, Virgin Mobile, and BT carved up public places across London, broadcasting open wireless networks in major squares, airports, and subways. The cities of Athens in 2004, Sydney in 2000, and Barcelona in 1992 all provided examples of modernizing communities through public and private resources in preparation for the Olympic Games.

The challenge for the U.S. sport system lies in adapting the best from partnership models that exist across the globe to fit local values, competitive goals, and logistics in this country. Socioeconomic development through sport could be the goal of the USOC, NGBs, and state and local governments when coordinating organizations contributing to advancement of sport. Potential partner organizations would need to be educated and kept informed about opportunities available through each sport and multi-sport programs and competitions. Better communication with organizations outside of sport is necessary for the achievement of multiple common goals and better communities – which is becoming increasingly important in North America and around the world (cf., Bloom, Grant, & Watt, 2005; Fetisov, 2005; Isaev, 2002; Vail, 2007).

The variety of geopolitical and socioeconomic conditions in which governments have been successful in coordinating sport systems suggests that concerted national efforts for healthy mass and elite sport participation do not result from a particular political agenda but rather indicate a higher level of social development. A federal sport department is probably a utopian thought for the United States today, but several agencies, the USOC, and the NGBs, could work together on one integrated plan of reducing national obesity and retaining international sport leadership.

The USOC, the NCAA, and local communities

Integrated mass and elite sport requires strong partnerships among NGBs. In 2011, the USOC and the NCAA combined forces to promote Olympic sports within NCAA organizations (Hosick, 2011). Joni Comstock, NCAA senior vice president for championships, was appointed to work with Rick Adams, a senior staff member at the USOC office in Colorado Springs. Their goal was to use the underlying structures of both organizations to provide the expertise and research needed to guide strategies for Olympic sport development. The arrangement also sought to improve the collaboration between these organizations and sport-specific NGBs to expand possible opportunities for sports to develop (Hosick, 2011).

An important connection between mass and elite sport is the growing network of the CODP mentioned in the first element of the Model. Assisted by the USOC, the CODP builds partnerships with potential supporting organizations in local communities to establish high-quality programs, particularly at the intermediate level of sport participation. The first CODP at the Georgia Amateur Athletic Foundation/Centennial Legacy Foundation was founded with proceeds from the 1996 Atlanta Olympic Games. It was then co-funded by the USOC in 1998. This program with all its assets was handed over to Atlanta's Boys and Girls Clubs in 2002. Then in 2006, the Boys and Girls Clubs of Metro Atlanta created an official contract with the USOC, giving them confirmed CODP status when they established a three-year business plan and many youth sports programs and gained further support from the community.

Recommendations from NGBs were also provided. According to the contract with the USOC, a CODP must have in place high-level educated coaches with proper credentials; structures for the delivery of grassroots sports development; events and necessary facilities; a transport plan for moving young athletes to and from the facilities; and designation by the Internal Revenue Service as a nonprofit corporation (CODP, 2014).[16]

Following the example of the University of Bath,[17] the NCAA and the USOC could help universities expand their partnerships with Team United States, professional sport teams, and mass participants from local communities.

The USOC and the armed forces

Partnerships between the USOC and the military have a strong history. Indirect government support through the military has been as important for sport performance in the United States as it has been in China, France, Germany, Italy, Russia, and many other countries across the world. The Department of Defense develops athletes for twenty-two sports as part of the Armed Forces Sports Program for personnel in the Army, Marine Corps, Navy, Air Force, and Coast Guard. More than 1.4 million U.S. military personnel are provided with opportunities to train (including free YM/WCA memberships) and compete at various levels. This includes intramural, base level, service level (All-Navy or All Air Force), the Armed Forces Championships, and through to national, international, and Olympic levels. Overall, there are eighteen Armed Forces Championships, seven national championships, and twenty international championships within the Conseil International du Sports Militaire (CISM; which encompasses 199 member nations) that are open to U.S. military personnel.

The U.S. Army World Class Athlete Program (WCAP)[18] was established in 1997 to employ more Olympic and Paralympic hopefuls and release them from service for training and competition. The U.S. Army announced its Wounded Warrior Sports Program in 2007 for its soldiers with life-altering injuries, giving them the opportunity to compete in state and national Paralympic competitions. The Army would pay for the athletes' registration fees, transportation, lodging, and athletic attire while they compete. Through such activities, the U.S. military organizations contribute significantly to mass participation and elite Olympic and Paralympic sport (Hipps, 2007). The WCAP (2005, 2011) mission changed from "provide soldiers with high national ranking or world class potential to compete for a place on the U.S. Olympic Team" in 2005 to "provide outstanding Soldier-athletes the support and training to compete and succeed in national and international competitions leading to Olympic and Paralympic Games" in 2011 to reflect this program's change.

In addition to traditional Army disciplines, the twenty-two eligible WCAP sports included diving and synchronized swimming. Between 1948 and 2012 a total of 615 Army soldiers have represented the United States at the Olympic Games as athletes (winning 142 medals) and as coaches. Since the WCAP inception in 1997, forty soldier-athletes have participated in the Olympic Games. In the 2004 Athens Games, 24 of the 538 U.S. athletes were military members.

More can be done *by* and *for* the U.S. Army military in elite sport by further emulating world best practice through these types of partnerships. A good example of these partnerships occurred in the former USSR through the spread of: centralized, rationally structured organizations; competent personnel; effective systems of training, education, and competition; and the creative application of best global practices from the army to the entire Soviet sport system (Pochinkin, 2006). In relation to the United States, thousands of athletes with the potential to represent their country could be provided with secure, flexible/part-time military jobs leading to lifelong careers within and outside of the Armed Forces. Partnerships between HP squads and military divisions, particularly those with close objectives, activity types, and geographic locations could be established. Negotiations between NGB HP managers and the top levels of central national sport, the army, and other government organizations could be fruitful (see example in footnote).[19]

As more minor sports, such as rugby, become part of the growing Olympic program, immediate opportunities can be realized with one of the most devoted USOC partners, the U.S. Army, particularly at the HP level. However, to receive greater support at mass participation level, many sports including soccer and tennis can learn from rugby to develop regular competitions within and among organizations such as the Air Force, Army, Navy, Marines, and Coast Guard. More athletes can be employed as military personnel who would further develop their sports as part of their employment duties. Competition could be expanded to the police and other law enforcement organizations and in other institutional areas.

Most successful and rapidly developing sport nations, including the United Kingdom, France, and Germany, benefit from the international performance of their military athletes. Originally, the Russian Regional Military Sport Commissions were concerned with mass fitness but since 1912 army sport teams were paid to participate in national and international competitions. This partnership and contribution to U.S. sport is growing as organizational sport structures within the U.S. Army are becoming more effective. These partnerships also have great potential for mass participation. Military athletes could contribute to the wellness of the community as leaders of programs such as Army Cadets, Civil Air Patrol, and Naval Sea Cadet Corps, which develop U.S. youths through military preparation with a strong emphasis on the physical fitness component. This partnership also veils direct government funding of sport.

U.S. police forces and communities

The various police forces across the U.S. are another important mass sport partner, as is evidenced in the Police Athletic Leagues (PAL, 2012). In the mid-twentieth century, six PAL chapters on the Eastern seaboard joined together to form an association to share ideas and resources and compete in several sports. Today there are more than 400 PAL Member Chapters servicing more than 700 cities and with 1,700 facilities throughout the USA. PAL programs also solicit funds, equipment, and volunteer help from members of the community so that the cost to taxpayers is minimized.

Although the vast majority of PAL contests are with other youths in the same city, there are regularly-scheduled national contests between teams in different parts of the country. PAL has partnered with the American Sport Education Program to provide online training and certification to PAL coaches, which is required for participation in certain NPAL tournaments.

PAL is a small-scale version of the former USSR's and now Russian Dynamo sport society (which mobilized the resources of police and security forces to provide long-term athlete development across the country in Olympic sports). The distinctive and key advantage of PALs is the close personal connection between police personnel and community members through sport participation. PAL (2012) believes that their participants are less likely to engage in crime and more likely to both praise the character of the police force and to discourage their friends from committing crimes or covering up criminal activity. Integration of PAL sporting events into school, club, and military cadet competition systems would make PAL more relevant in its contribution to both mass and elite sport.

As a membership organization, the National PAL (NPAL) provides chapters with resources and opportunities to grow their programs and enhance the quality of programming. These resources include funding opportunities through various grants, general liability protection programs, programming opportunities through affiliate organizations, and goods and services provided by corporate partners and supporting organizations.

Here again we see government funded organizations in a position to advance mass sport with hidden funding costs. The NPAL and PAL branches also exemplify the public/private nexus that is a fundamental aspect of current U.S. political and economic circumstances.

Municipal parks and nonprofit foundations

Partnerships are important to connect NGBs with public and private organizations for both mass and elite sport programs. Golf provides a good model of this. The demand for mass golf was boosted by the U.S. Golf Association, the U.S. PGA, the National Golf Foundation, and public and private course providers. As Adams and Rooney (1985, p. 438) wrote,

> once the game of the wealthy and the socially elite, golf during past three and one-half decades has undergone popularization and democratization in the United States. … In response to middle-class demands, the number of public facilities has risen so sharply that they are more widely available than private ones.

Of note was that most of the "public [golf] facilities were generally owned by entrepreneurial interests or municipalities" (Adams & Rooney, 1985, p. 427) and were courses that people could play on a fee-per-round basis. No joining or other heavy fees were demanded.

The provision of golf to the wider populations, of course, leads to a greater demand for equipment, lessons, and other consumables; and to spectatorship. A key feature in the systematic development of golf was courses built through municipal governments funded by the Works Progress Administration, an agency of the New Deal period (1935–1943) (Adams & Rooney, 1985). A result of this is that as of 1983, public courses out-numbered private ones (more than 7,000 to approximately 5,000, respectively).

Golf is now a wide-ranging industry. An SRI International Report (2011, p. 15) indicates its size and impact. In 2011 there were approximately 25.7 million participants (this includes spectators). Further, the golf industry generated $68.8 billion through goods and services economic activity. Golf also had an overall economic impact of $176.8 billion and supported 1.98 million jobs across the USA. The industry is varied and embraces real estate, capital investment, retail, tournaments, golf-related travel, endorsements, and charities. With the economic recession of 2007–2009, the golf industry has slowed down and is showing signs of shrinking.

With golf having a long history of democratic provision, one can understand current developments in the sport. The new funding model is, however, different. Fostering public programs at underutilized public parks and sport and recreation facilities has great potential for more effective and efficient use of tax and donation dollars. Pennington (2009) described practices in golf that could be used across different sports. In 2008 the New York City Parks Foundation opened its Junior Golf Center on what had been abandoned land. The center included a clubhouse with a classroom where the rudiments, rules, and etiquette of golf were taught; a twelve-stall, enclosed driving range; and a six-hole course. Use of the center and its training programs was free (and only adults accompanying their children are able to use the center) (Pennington, 2009).

The funding model for the $8-million center was through resources and sponsorships from Callaway Golf, Top-Flite, and the U.S. Golf Association. This is very much a corporate social responsibility project, although one that could reap future economic benefits with more golfers. With new Callaway junior golf clubs provided, equipment for participants' use was also free (Pennington, 2009). The foundation started a program that turned open spaces in the city parks, such as the outfield of a baseball diamond, into mini-driving ranges. About 1,500 children signed up for free training in the first year and the numbers are increasing (Pennington, 2009).

Another junior golf initiative is the First Tee program, created by the World Golf Foundation in 1997 with several corporate and golf industry partners (Pennington, 2009). It introduced the sport to 2.9 million children and teenagers nationwide, with First Tee programs being implemented in more than 2,800 elementary schools (Pennington, 2011). The First Tee of Metropolitan New York was created in 2001 as a joint venture between the Metropolitan Golf Association Foundation and the Metropolitan Section of the PGA. It provided affordable and accessible facilities to young players at several sites. Interpersonal skills, career guidance, goal setting, and learning to appreciate diversity are also taught alongside the sport of golf (Pennington, 2011). Since 1994 the Metropolitan Golf Association Foundation has also conducted a student intern program called GolfWorks. This is a program that provides more than 220 high school-age students a year with paid summer internships in the local golf clubs (Pennington, 2011)

A key feature of these programs, other than the obvious work creation for USPGA teaching members, is that these youth and children receive instruction from qualified, knowledgeable persons. This is an element of a sport delivery system we emphasized throughout this book. These programs prove that even in places where golf may not be embedded in the neighborhood culture, the game can flourish, and golfers can be nurtured (Pennington, 2009).

The above programs provide good examples of how to best connect mass and elite sport in a market-driven society. It exhibits how local (and federal) government and the private sector can blend purpose. Golf is well positioned financially and socially to expand its participant base. Most other sports need to source greater public and private subsidies for implementing such sport delivery initiatives.

Sport initiatives at places of worship

Sport programs based at places of worship have made a noticeable contribution to U.S. mass sport participation. This is historically part of the ideology of "muscular Christianity" and similar to the Rational Recreation movement in the United Kingdom (Bailey, 1978), where churches used sport as a way to develop sound morals and good behavior. The Catholic Church, through the Catholic Youth Organizations (CYO), and the Jewish faith also uses sport to proselytize and to perform a social control role by helping those in poor social and economic circumstances, or in need of sporting outlets.

White (2006) studied how the 100 largest churches in the United States attract more followers through sport. Eighty-five of the ninety-four churches responding to White's survey indicated that they offered sport as part of their overall ministry plan, using a variety of seventy-eight different sports on four days per week average. A significant amount of money and facility space was dedicated to the provision of these sports. The twelve- to eighteen-year age group were the main users of the sport ministry; however, church leaders indicated that sport can be used to reach people of all ages. The surveyed churches reported that they had averaged approximately 74 volunteers for each of their sport ministry plans (White, 2006): This does however question the quality of these programs in terms of the PE knowledge the leaders held.

Religious leaders have effectively utilized sport to grow their congregations in twenty-first-century America (McMullin, 2013; Steffan, 2013; White, 2006). Though there is evidence that some churches contribute to the delivery of recreation sport and a healthy lifestyle, it is difficult for a church to support the progression of participants to higher levels of performance. Church sport programs often lack organization and the fostering of local, regional, and national sport activities and events across congregations. This is particularly the case when programs are run by volunteers without the guidance of professional coaches and administrators. Nevertheless, sport programs at places of worship play a unique role in supporting both the physical and psychological wellness of the nation.

Philanthropy

The USA is perhaps the über-capitalist society. The concentration of capital in few persons has created severe economic inequality (this is discussed further in Chapter 5). Along with strong market fundamentalism and a republicanism that desires less government involvement in society adds to the situation where philanthropy becomes of great import. Also "underlying our charity system – and our tax code – is the premise that individuals will make better decisions regarding social investments than will our representative government" (Stern, 2013). A Web site developed to help people make donations recently claimed that:

> few people realize how large charities have become, how many vital services they provide, and how much funding flows through them each year. Without charities and non-profits, America would simply not be able to operate. Their operations are so big that during 2012, total giving was more than $316 billion (Charity Navigator, 2014).

Philanthropy, therefore, is a key characteristic of U.S. life.

The role of wealthy and powerful individuals is significant in the history and development of the sport delivery system in the United States. The influence of the wealthy benefactors began in the late nineteenth century through donations to religious and education institutions that offered some form of sport programs. These institutions were financed by donations. As individual and corporate wealth grew and became more concentrated it was tax incentives and philanthropy that led the sport development system to be more dependent on the good will of private donors.

It is often ideal when donors are not only concerned with business gains but are also passionate and knowledgeable about HP in sport. In their book on university football, Benedict and Armen (2013) classify 99 percent of "boosters" as those "representative[s] of the university's athletic interests" (p. 146): not those party to illegal or unacceptable exchanges of funds under law or NCAA guidelines. They classify this "good" portion of boosters into four categories: power brokers, jock sniffers, builders, and turbo builders. The latter category they claim has only two billionaire members, Nike Corporations Chairman Phil Knight and the oil and gas tycoon T. Boone Pickens. The following indicate their largesse (see above quote from a university president about what this philanthropy means for the viability of universities).

Former athlete, University of Oregon alumnus, and Chairman of Nike Phil Knight has been munificent. According to Benedict and Armen (2013, p. 153):

> Knight began bankrolling Oregon athletics in the 1990s. Eventually, he donated $100 million to the University of Oregon's Legacy Fund, the single largest gift in the university's history. He also contributed between $50 million and $60 million for the football stadium expansion, along with another $68 million for the construction of Oregon's new football operations facilities.

Oklahoma State graduate T. Boone Pickens is another alumnus who donated generously. Rather than leave money after his death, Pickens decided to enjoy the adulation his money could buy. It was another case of how much to donate. As Benedict and Armen (2013, p. 153) wrote:

> In 2006, Pickens, the CEO of a Dallas-based hedge fund, gave a $165-million gift to Oklahoma State athletics. It was the largest single donation for athletics to an institution of higher education in U.S. history. That was in addition to the $83 million he put into overhauling OSU's football stadium between 2003 and 2008. The combined $248 million in gifts produced a new baseball stadium; new soccer, track and tennis facilities; an equestrian center; various outdoor fields; and a multipurpose indoor practice complex. The crown jewel, however, was Boone Pickens Stadium, a sixty-thousand-seat state-of-the-art facility ringed by 101 luxury suites and 4,000 club seats that opened on September 5, 2009.

But these men are not alone. Stern (2013) noted that:

> many of the 12 other individual charitable gifts that topped $100 million in the U.S. last year were showered with similar attention: $150 million from Carl Icahn to the Mount Sinai School of Medicine, $125 million from Phil Knight to the Oregon Health & Science University, and $300 million from Paul Allen to the Allen Institute for Brain Science in Seattle, among them.

Further, if you "read the histories of grand giving by the Rockefellers, Carnegies, Stanfords, and Dukes, you would be forgiven for thinking that the story of charity in this country is a story of epic generosity on the part of the American rich" (Stern, 2013).

These excessively large donations mask two key things, aside from the nature of distribution under capitalism. First, the size of these donations indicated the wealth of the benefactors. They donated beyond what tax exemptions would absorb. A debate around how private and corporate wealth is both gained and distributed (who gets what) continues (see e.g., Nasaw, 2011).The second fact is that this is not the "normal" pattern of donating in the United States, according to Ken Stern (2013).

He wrote that it was not a story of "epic generosity" of the wealthy that fuels giving in the U.S. Rather, it is:

> one of the most surprising, and perhaps confounding, facts of charity in America is that the people who can least afford to give are the ones who donate the greatest percentage of their income. In 2011, the wealthiest Americans – those with earnings in the top 20 percent – contributed on average 1.3 percent of their income to charity. By comparison, Americans at the base of the income pyramid – those in the bottom 20 percent – donated 3.2 percent of their income.

Farther into the article, he raises the point about where the money goes. Those in the bottom 20 percent tend to donate to "religious organizations and social-service charities, while the wealthy prefer to support colleges and universities, arts organizations, and museums" (Stern, 2013): areas that reproduce their world and capital.[20]

Perhaps new philanthropic organizations and methods may contribute to the systematic support of sport; although this is unlikely. Bishop (2006) argued that billions of dollars are still being squandered by ineffective philanthropy both by the wealthy and NGOs. Hopefully, in the future, these entities will support the overall U. S. sport development system infrastructures and partnerships through philanthropic and tax-deduction-seeking capital markets and organizations (Bishop, 2006).

New philanthropists are increasingly focusing on achieving positive social results and put their money into both profit and nonprofit projects (e.g., Bill Gates). Older organizations are refocusing their philanthropic efforts; for example, the McConnell Clark Foundation in New York used to hand out grants in the traditional manner for a wide range of good causes but changed in the 1990s to achieve specific results by concentrating on youth development with a selected partner, Harlem Children's Zone (Bishop, 2006). If a "noblesse oblige" rather than pure ego identity and tax relief developed, then sport and other social goods would receive more than their current share of redistributed U.S. wealth.

Perhaps there is hope for sport. If HP managers realized this opportunity and as they learn to achieve donor objectives and better use sport to cure social, health, ecological, and other problems in our global community, the lack of government support for sport could be rectified. It will require sport managers to further focus on philanthropic foundations and organizations as part of their sponsorship and marketing plans, and universities will need to continue to look beyond alumni.

Sport betting and lotteries

Government-legislated lotteries now finance mass and elite sport across the world and they are not new in the United States. The earliest lottery held in the United States was in the eighteenth century (Lotteries of the Ancient and Medieval World, 2014). The earliest sport-related gaming on sport began in 1930 in North America. This is when The Irish Hospitals Sweepstakes ticket selling began in

Canada and the United States (Lotteries of the Ancient and Medieval World, 2014). The earliest recorded sport lottery was in 1964 when New Hampshire started a "sweepstake" around horse racing, while the first state lottery began in 1970 in New Jersey (National Gambling Impact Study Commission, 2014). As of the late 1990s, thirty-seven states and the District of Columbia had government-legislated lotteries. A key feature of lotteries, which are described as "virtual government monopoly," is that "the net proceeds [are] going to the public good" (National Gambling Impact Study Commission, 2014); that is, the largest portion of the proceeds ("a source of 'painless' revenue") of these lotteries go to social and public goods organizations; or so it is hoped.

In the United States, there are five recognized forms of gambling (with the 2007 revenues in parenthesis): card rooms ($1.18 billion); commercial casinos ($34.41 billion); charitable games and bingo ($2.22 billion); Indian casinos ($26.02 billion); legal bookmaking ($168.8 million); lotteries ($24.78 billion); and pari-mutuel wagering ($3.50 billion) (American Gaming Association, 2010). Of these forms, charitable games[21] and bingo have been mainstay of church and school fund raising, usually for sport. These types of "gambling" were widely used to fund sport and sport teams across history.

Lotteries, as was stated, are widely used for sport. In hosting the 2012 London Olympic Games, the United Kingdom, as with other Olympic host countries, took the opportunity to expand their sport system to develop competitors and to extend its TID programs and practices through a national lottery. Likewise Holland, also mentioned earlier in this chapter, directs lottery money to sport clubs, NGBs, and local sport projects. The Russian Sportloto was designed specifically to support all possible sports. We have indicated above how the Chinese lotteries aid sport development in that country. U.S. authorities could consider various international practices as possible options that could help promote fairer use of sport gambling profits in the United States and around the world.

People in the USA are able to gamble on professional and NCAA sports in Nevada, Montana, Delaware, and Oregon but not in other states. Around 1992 New Jersey turned down the opportunity to legalize sports betting when a window was open to bring sports betting to individual states. After that, a law prevented sports betting in any additional states. In 2013 New Jersey officials appealed a federal judge's decision to block legal sports betting after New Jersey legalized sports betting at the state level and began taking bets in 2012 at Atlantic City's casino and at state race tracks (Hutchins, 2013). The NCAA along with the NFL, MLB, NBA, and NHL filed a lawsuit in 2012 alleging, ironically, that legal sports betting in New Jersey would "irreparably" harm sports in the USA (Hutchins, 2013). The New Jersey officials said they were attempting to stop crime and tap into a multi-billion dollar industry. "Anyone who doesn't recognize that people are already betting on sports illegally is a fool," state Senator Raymond Lesniak (D, NJ) said "and we should make it legal here, just as it is in the state of Nevada" (Hutchins, 2013). The case indicates that gambling on sports is growing and needs better control (iGaming Business North America, 2012; Hutchins, 2013).

Some argue that legalized gambling does not regulate illegal gambling – it fuels more gambling. Others could argue that professional sport leagues have experienced huge success despite the existence of legal and illegal gambling; and, therefore, cannot claim harm if states legalize sports betting. Care needs to be taken to ensure that the incomes from gambling do actually contribute to sport development and other social improvements.

Corporations' support of sport

The lack of governmental funding makes American sport depend on corporate support. Partnerships between corporations, events, and facilities with sport organizations can be advanced into more integrated and efficient operations, as detailed below. Between 1992 and 2008. The Home Depot sponsored and employed U.S. Olympic and Paralympic athletes and potential HP athletes. More than 570 athletes were employed during the USOC's Olympic Job Opportunities Program (OJOP) (Home Depot, 2008). The Home Depot also built The Home Depot Center, a $150 million multi-sport facility for soccer, tennis, track and field, cycling, volleyball, and other sports, which opened in Carson, California in June 2003.

The Home Depot Center was the home of the 2002 MLS Cup Champion Los Angeles Galaxy and the MLS expansion team Club Deportiva Chivas United States and the 2006 expansion franchise in the Los Angeles's Major League Lacrosse 2006. This center has also become the U.S. Soccer Federation national team training headquarters, the location of the U.S. Tennis Association's HP National Training Center, and the official training site for USA Cycling and the U.S. Track and Field. The Home Depot Center represented one of the largest investments in amateur sports (Home Depot, 2008). Sponsorship of The Home Depot ranged from a $15- to $20-million-per year commitment for the 2005–2009 period (Zimmerman & Futterman, 2009).

Due to the 2007–2009 global recession, a number of USOC sponsors did not renew their contracts after the 2008 Beijing Olympic Games. This included: the Bank of America, General Motors, The Home Depot, Kellogg's, and Johnson & Johnson. These terminated sponsorships would have attracted as much as $100 million over the next Olympiad. The USOC, however, boasted nineteen new partners including Acer, Adecco, and Deloitte, with renewed contracts with Allstate, Anheuser-Busch, Hilton, Jet Set Sports, Nike, Tyson Foods, United Airlines, and 24 Hour Fitness (Gomez, 2009a, b).

Summarizing our discussion on the macro-level of the U.S. sport development, it is worth noting that U.S. people attribute great value to sport, although more to the small number of profitable spectator sports rather than to the full spectrum of Olympic and indigenous sports. A few commercial professional sports are overdeveloped whereas many other disciplines are underdeveloped. The country's sport, education, and health systems are decentralized. This results in uncoordinated effort and inefficient use of resources. Many overseas practices have been adopted in the United States, but more can be utilized, particularly with the aim of coordinating all organizations contributing to mass and elite sport as one mutually beneficial national partnership.

Meso-Level: Infrastructure, personnel, and services enabling sport programs

Element 3 (Meso-Level): Educational, scientific, medical, philosophical, and promotional support

This element plays an important role between the macro- and micro-levels in the overall Model. The macro-elements are about structural and resource matters and the interconnected aspects, relationships, and interdependencies of parts of an overall sport system. At the other end, micro-elements are about the way individuals are brought into and retained in an overall system. This intermediate element is largely about the nature of the overall sport system, as its label indicates.

Two ideas are important here. The first is that coaches in particular, but also all types of sport specialists, need to receive high-quality education and training (to expand the knowledge, skills, and abilities required for all levels of sport development). This includes attending clinics, seminars, conferences, and membership in professional and scholarly societies. Accreditation programs and ranking systems for these specialists are also required due to ethical issues that arise and for the systematic development of sport.

Second, as Smolianov and Zakus (2008) stressed, a nation's sport ideology "contributes to national values and identity and promotes excellence in and through sport" (p. 9) and serves both philosophical and educative purposes. This can be achieved by showing "leadership and global vision by striving for physical, social, emotional, mental, spiritual, and environmental wellbeing through sport" (p. 9). In the Model, we argued that all participants be educated on the values of sport (i.e., the underlying philosophy of sport). It is also important that messages are fully communicated through the media to the broader population as it acts to effectively spread ideas and support a particular political or national position. Such linking of the purpose of sport with a nation's stated constitutional purpose has placed sport in the forefront of national ideology that promotes sport widely and deeply within a country. Again, it is a linking construct in the Model between the macro and micro levels for a sport system.

Education of sport specialists

In terms of educational support, the United States has many outstanding universities researching all aspects of mass and elite sport. It was, however, a bit slow to develop national coaching programs. Though still catching up to some nations, the United States has a wide number of coaching schemes in place. These schemes, sometimes modeled after or borrowed from other nations, ensure the systematic accreditation and implementation to develop coaches who have the appropriate knowledge, skills, abilities, and ethics. Such schemes focus on the development levels of sport to ensure a flow through or "pipeline" of athletes for elite and professional competitions.

The elite coaching ranks of the United States are world leading, particularly at universities and at training centers that prepare Olympic athletes (Platonov, 2010). The USOC Coaching Education Department assists NGBs to provide educational opportunities for elite-level coaches. This includes scientific research and annual, biannual, and topical conferences to deliver applied sport sciences to Olympic-caliber athletes and coaches. The USOC also recognizes outstanding NGB coaches through its annual Coach of the Year program. However, without a centralized system of sport education, the U.S. progressive practices have been developed mostly by NGBs such as the U.S. Ski and Snowboard Association (USSA). The USSA model is very instructive as to how systematic coaching development could occur across all sports and across the nation; that is, it is an exemplar.

The USSA studied the best international practices to develop and deliver a systematic, national athlete development sport education program for all levels of coaches. Research on the USSA top athletes also provides data for this program. Tied to this, the USSA has since 2001 used its "Elite Performance Model (EPM)" to define and evaluate all aspects of its HP programs (Walshe et al., 2006). Since 2003, the EPM has informed the development of a Coaches Education Program (Walshe et al., 2006). The USSA invested heavily in cutting-edge scientific research to assist coaches and athletes at both the mass and elite levels. The EPM identifies the critical factors for elite success and then makes that information available to coaches and athletes. The creation of the USSA's multi-media educational resources and courses is the operationalization of this model.

The EPM coach certification program and its underlying continuing education goals consist of five stages (Walshe et al., 2006). Each stage includes criteria on athlete age and capability level, years of experience, and appropriate elements of sport science, medicine, management, pedagogy, and sport-specific skills and training. The USSA delivers sport-specific, advanced sport science and management courses, while general courses are offered through partner universities and the USOC. A "Physical Assessment CD" has been developed for coaches in its 320 USSA affiliated clubs. An electronic tracking system and database for all USSA athletes is part of this program. The Physical Assessment CD provides coaches with the information and tools they need to develop and implement a physical assessment program for their HP-athletes (Walshe et al., 2006).

Coaches record the results and then test their athletes again to create tailored training programs. This is completed several times a year. The areas tested are the same for the entire junior-elite development pipeline. At the elite level, the testing equipment is more expensive and sophisticated; therefore, testing is more centralized with test results and program prescriptions more detailed (Personal Interview, 2006). The success of these USSA systems is evident in USSA team members winning nine of twenty-five United States medals at the 2006 Turin

WOGs and twenty of thirty-seven medals at the 2010 Vancouver WOGs (IOC, 2011).

The following example illustrates what might be further possible in coach education at the national level (all based on the first author's direct involvement in this education). After the breakup of the Soviet Union, Russia retained its strongest centers of sport education and science. A standard coaching degree in Russia is a five-year education program similar to a combination of a coaching bachelor's degree and a sport science master's degree in the United States (though emphasis is placed on a specific sport). Also, coach education programs inherited from the former USSR require students to pass academic, referee, and fitness tests, as well as to compete in their chosen sport at a level similar to that of a top-level United States high school team. Upon graduation coaches progress through five licensing stages to progress in their careers. Each stage is awarded on the basis of competition results and athlete achievement.

The comprehensive system of coach education and support was one of the key success factors of the former Soviet sport system that continues to be so for Russia. Coaches are experts in all sport sciences but particularly in biomechanics. Compared to entrepreneurial-style U.S. system where most U.S. coaches compete with one another and have to be unique to survive, in Russia all coaches are more collaborative and compatible as they hold the same qualifications (Coyle, 2007). This is a form of quality control and standardization that is positive for the overall sport system.

Many successful sport countries, particularly those from the former Eastern Bloc, adopted Soviet-style sport education that included a government-funded network of independent universities devoted to PE and sport. In Poland, for example, the University of Physical Education in Warsaw (2014) enrolled 6,500 students and employed 400 academic staff in 2013. The Academy educates PE teachers, coaches, and specialists in physiotherapy, recreation, and tourism. It is the main center of scientific research in the field of physical culture and for sport training (The University of Physical Education in Warsaw, 2014). Similar academies exist in the Polish cities of Cracow, Gdańsk, Katowice, Poznań, and Wrocław. Sport universities are also important for successful sport systems in China, France, and Germany (Digel, 2005), but the number and variety of sport degrees in coaching science are not as available as they are in Russia.

Sport science and medicine

Some of the most fundamental sport-related scientific studies and their practical applications originated and developed in the United States. The key focus was on testing and developing advances for the military and workplaces (e.g., Taylorism; and Stakhanovism in the USSR). Over the period from 1927 to 1946, Harvard University's Fatigue Laboratory in Boston, with funding through the U.S. federal government, researched topics in the physical chemistry of blood, exercise physiology, nutritional interactions, aging, and the stresses of high altitude and climate (Harvard University, 2009). Beginning in 1941 many of the research reports dealt with the physical fitness of soldiers, the energy cost of military tasks in extreme heat and cold, and with inventing clothes and equipment for extreme conditions (Harvard University, 2009).

Similarly, the Massachusetts Institute of Technology's Institute for Soldier Nanotechnologies (ISN, 2011), founded in 2002, develops new devices and textiles for health monitoring, wound healing, and atmospheric and environmental adaptation. As the Army supports both ISN and Olympic soldier-athletes, the USOC has an opportunity to collaborate with the ISN through the U.S. Army Research Office. The USOC developed various partnership initiatives, for example, with the United States Anti-Doping Agency (USADA), MLB, and NFL for a joint $10-million anti-doping research project (Brown, 2008). The potential use of scientific findings will be realized in the United States when a permanent team, possibly under the USOC, becomes responsible for the coordination of sport research.

In the former USSR, studies of both mass and elite aspects of sport were coordinated by the Central Research Institute of Physical Culture established in 1933 in Moscow. Research was undertaken at its twenty-eight sport research institutes in all fifteen republics. This way it was able to mobilize national resources and provide local ownership in national sport policies and programs (particularly the GTO and sport-specific LTAD guidelines). Expert groups were formed in the 1970s to advise elite sport teams, bringing together coaches, sport doctors, and scientists (Polyaev, Markova & Belolipetskaya, 2005). The national USSR wrestling and boxing teams, for example, were serviced by a group of forty specialists in pedagogical science, medicine, psychology, physiology, biomechanics, biochemistry, and engineering. Four- to eight-year plans were prepared for individual athletes (Ippolitov, Mishin, Novikow, Tarasova, & Shamilov 2009).

The results of this structure and the centralized resources are evident. From the 1970s through to the early 1990s, the USSR/Unified wrestling team won more gold medals than any other country in each of the Olympic Games in which they competed. The Russian scientists of the twenty-first century applied the wrestling research results to thirteen other disciplines (Ippolitov et al., 2009). The scientific support is still centrally coordinated and financed by the Ministry for Sport, which reviews scientific programs annually to assist in prioritized sports and sport organizations.

The Russian 2012 Summer Olympic sports were supported by forty-one sport science groups, winter sports by fifteen sand Paralympic and other special needs sports by twenty-six teams of scientists. This tailored method of sport science support has been adopted by China and is being expanded given the country's increasing sport resources, scientific capabilities, and increasingly close cooperation with Russia.

According to Tan and Green (2008), the Chinese Government in 2003 required each major national training center to establish a new division of performance to coordinate coaches, scientists, and doctors for Olympic success. China has created a scientific training and monitoring structure for key national squads. The data collected from training and competition are stored to produce indicators for coaches, scientists, technicians, and doctors to develop personalized programs of training, recovery, nutrition, psychological consulting, and other services. There are six national laboratories and a team of thirty scientists to help national squads. To integrate resources the Action Project for Olympic Technology has involved institutions such as the Beijing Municipal People's Government; the Ministry of Education; the Chinese Academy of Science; and the Commission of Science, Technology, and Industry for National Defense.

These institutions invest their budgets to support scientific research and services for Olympic preparation. The direct sport science budget of the Chinese government for the 2004 Athens Olympic Games was approximately $6.14 million (Tan & Green, 2008). Of eight successful sport nations studied by Digel (2005), sport science was particularly eminent in Russia, Australia, and Germany. But he noted that special research institutes and advice centers were also established in China, France, the United Kingdom, and Italy. Sports medicine, performance diagnostics, biomechanics, physiotherapy, psychology, and organizational aspects are important research areas.

Sport research undertaken in the United States is generally completed at universities, though not at sport-specific ones. Digel (2005) pointed out that Russian sports science still plays a unique role in the world. The sport universities of St. Petersburg and Moscow and a regional network of research institutes and establishments lead the way. Language, cultural, and ideological barriers still prevent the United States from taking full advantage of the foreign sport science achievements, but benefits could still be gained from considering Australian, Canadian, and UK sport science practices. This is taking place at a micro-athlete development level, but there is also a potential of borrowing organizational practices.

If we observe a program from Canada, the point of a focused, centralized, national program to optimize outcomes is evident. The government of Canada provided funds for NGBs through Sport Canada, an organization established by an act of Parliament. Sport Canada created the Own the Podium (OTP) program to achieve greater international sport success, especially for the Vancouver Winter Olympic Games, which it hosted in 2010. In 2004 the OTP created a five-year CAN $8 million project called the "Top Secret Project." This project sought to use science and technology to optimize the Canadian winter athletes' performances.

The project combined ideas from Canada's thirteen national winter sport organizations with those of businesses and universities. Top researchers in Canada worked on fifty-five projects prioritized into four areas: competition clothing, ice sports, snow sports, and performance (Khoshnevis, 2010). The Top Secret Project looked into things such as super-low-friction bases for snowboards and whether curling brooms actually melt the ice during sweeping. Scientists used a missile guidance system to track skiers and built a giant catapult, a type of human slingshot, to hurl speed skaters into a turn to practice cornering (McGrath, 2010). Perhaps the key integration program of the country's ambitious OTP program surrounded the Canadian long-track speed skaters. These athletes raced in space-age bodysuits designed by the Japanese Descente apparel company in collaboration with the

Canadian National Research Council's Institute for Aerospace Research and the Speed Skating Canada NGB. The suits were the culmination of four years of research and testing and are more aerodynamic than human skin (Crouse, 2011).

As part of research and intelligence gathering, espionage is as important in sporting success as it is in commerce, politics, and the military. Bishop (2012) analyzed intelligence and espionage activities in different sports. In rowing, where the arrangement of a boat's rigging can affect a crew's time, everyone pays close attention to the opponents' equipment. In luge, athletes talked of how they blocked their sleds at starting lines when opposing coaches tried to sneak a peek. Someone from the U.S. BMX cycling team rode the competition course in London for the 2012 Olympic Games with a three-dimensional mapping device so the U.S. athletes could build and train on a replica of the Olympic track.[22]

The British Olympic Association claimed in late 2007 that two of its databases had been hacked into (Bishop, 2012). That same year, Chinese police officers raided weather-monitoring equipment used by the British sailing team. In Beijing, so closely guarded were the host's secrets that the 2008 Beijing Summer Games became known in some circles as the Spy Games (Bishop, 2012). In early 2008 China sequestered its top athletes at the national sports training center, a compound guarded by paramilitary and Beijing municipal police twenty-four hours a day, seven days a week (Bishop, 2012). As Olympic training became more detailed, more scientific, and more complicated, many countries formalized their sport intelligence operations.

France created an agency in its sports ministry with the nondescript name Preparation Olympique et Paralympique (POP), masking a more ambitious purpose: to boost medal counts through surveillance (Bishop, 2012). Spending upward of $121,000 for a custom-built search engine designed by a company that specializes in economic intelligence software, POP began to track news reports, government documents, Web sites, and archives in various countries (Bishop, 2012). Bishop also noted that France employed two full-time "watchers" to search for and organize the data by country and then by sport. The French agency also taught individual NGBs to perform systematic debriefings of coaches upon returning from international competitions.

It was not just happening in France. Everyone involved with Canada's Top Secret Project, engineers included, signed nondisclosure agreements lest their intelligence end up in the hands of the competition. The successful British track-cycling program, the "Secret Squirrel Club," produced a superbike made from components used in Formula One racing and the aerospace industry (Bishop, 2012). It is essential that macro-level organizational and other strategic information be gathered, analyzed, and presented, particularly in the United States.

Bowers et al. (2011) noted that there was a lack of systematic statistical and research information that would contribute to an understanding of sport in the United States. Though participation declined in most sports from 2000 to 2007, this information was not as widely available as data sponsored by commercial organizations interested in selling sporting goods. It is hard to disagree with Bowers et al. (2011) that the United States would benefit from a national sport agency. Systematic information gathering, analysis, and reporting for internal and public use is an important responsibility of many sport ministries around the world. The Web site of the Ministry for Sport, Tourism and Youth Policy of the Russian Federation (2011) published the country's current statistics on participants in 143 sports and information on results or rankings achieved by mass and elite athletes. It also provided statistics on coaches, referees, competitions, facilities, and other national data necessary for systematic sport development.

Philosophical and promotional support

The basis of a philosophy of sport was discussed in Chapter 1. It centered on the philosophical concept of "Olympism." From this, Olympic education is becoming part of school education across the world. Materials are produced in many countries to advance the goals of the Olympic movement. The first goal was to develop all individuals in physical and intellectual harmony, to make sport part of a multi-faceted education, and to help everyone achieve personal excellence. The second goal sought to spread a humanistic social philosophy that emphasizes the role of sport in world development, peaceful coexistence, international understanding, and social and moral education (Parry, 1994). The third goal was to promote peace. The fourth goal was to improve human behavior and health in collaboration with the World Health Organization, the United Nations, and other international and supranational bodies (Chatziefstathiou, 2007). And finally, from 1994, the fifth goal was the "environment" sustainability while avoiding harm to athletes and harm to the planet from hosting the Games (VanWynsberghe, 2009).

Sport ideology in many countries, including the United States, is built on nationalistic and militaristic sentiments. At the international level, sport success is a powerful tool to spread national ideology. The U.S. Department of State recognized this and uses informal sports relationships to build stronger international diplomacy. Cocanour (2007) noted three ways the U.S. international diplomacy can be further enhanced through sport. First, the increased budgets for military sports programs and global dispersion of U.S. troops allow them to participate in more international events. Military personnel are seen as solid ambassadors of U.S. ideals that the Department of State wants portrayed to the world. Likewise, there are minimal issues with conflicting schedules and absences from work.

Second, a poll of twenty-five nations showed that "one citizen in two said that the United States is playing a mainly negative role in the world" (World Public Opinion, 2007). The military provided sport clinics and training camps throughout the developing world as part of their deployment. This exposes other nations to the positive aspects of U.S. people, of U.S. foreign policy, and by improving international perceptions of the United States. And third, the U.S. military is well placed to become more involved in global anti-doping efforts and work to demonstrate to the world the U.S. commitment to fair play. Many global practices could be adopted to enhance the use of sport as a powerful ideological tool through positive sport role models and education. In many countries from

Australia and the United States to China and Russia, the ritual for celebrating Olympic champions is an important inspirational tool.

Sport has contributed to social integration and over history has acted as a type of "social glue" bonding the United States together (see Novak, 1994; Putnam, 2000). In the former USSR, sport united 100 different nationalities, each with their own language, in a peaceful effort aimed at physical, moral, and intellectual excellence. Sport is a powerful vehicle for transmitting national morals, particularly in sport-loving cultures such as Russia and the United States. Universal sport values such as justice, fair play, and teamwork are highly important in the United States.

Sport can help overcome many differences and harmonize the coexistence of various cultures within the United States. Sport can also act as an agent of sociocultural advancement through its universal appeal. The power of sport in society can be used more effectively to elevate culture. For example, the notion of competition is at the heart of both sport and U.S. culture. To make exercise a habit for everyone, the U.S. NGBs, the PCFSN, and PE curriculum developers could help people to focus on self-improvement or just having fun – rather than on simply winning.

U.S. culture and its PE curricula could be enriched by appreciating the notion of competition in ancient China, which meant a competition with oneself – not to defeat one's opponent but to perform well by overcoming one's own self-imposed limits.[23] This notion makes it easier for mass participants to maintain the self-discipline of everyday exercise and a healthy lifestyle. Similarly, the Olympic value of participating for self-development and not for winning and earning rewards could also be highlighted more by U.S. sport and national leaders to help both elite and mass participants continue competing, whether they win or lose. The strength of the Chinese sport system is that Western methods have been successfully integrated into the holistic Eastern culture.

Element 4 (Meso-Level): System of competitions and events

This element surrounds more than the hosting of major events. Smolianov and Zakus (2008) identified that sporting success first requires a balance between the objectives of commercialization and excellence and those of maximizing and coordinating domestic and international competitions for all participant ages and levels. They went on to argue that hosting international events is necessary but, even more importantly, there must be a sufficient number of international opportunities for developing athletes and "organize[d] professional well-structured high quality competitions at club, regional, national, and international levels" (p. 9). It is against these factors of this element that we see where U.S. sport varies from the Model.

Elite international competitions hosted by the United States

There have been many major international sport festivals held in the U.S. The events listed here are a mere portion of the large number of sport games and festivals that have been held in the United States. The United States has hosted the Olympic Games on four occasions. These were: St Louis (1904), Los Angeles (1932, 1984), and Atlanta (1996). Likewise, it has hosted the Olympic Winter Games on four occasions: Lake Placid (1932, 1980), Squaw Valley (1960), and Salt Lake City (2002). The USA has also hosted the Pan-American Games in Chicago (1959) and Indianapolis (1987); the Federation International de Football (FIFA) World Cup in 1994; and the world student Universiade Games (1993, Buffalo). Clearly, the United States is well placed financially, politically, and resource-wise to successfully host large multi-sport, global sport festivals. It is the other end of the participation spectrum where resources and actual competitions are lacking.

Mass participation events

Olympic-style sports festivals were a key vehicle for the integration of mass and elite sports across time. Such festivals originated in Czech and German lands in the 1860s, mainly through workers' and union movements. These types of games then spread East to Russia and later to Korea and Japan. In 1928 the former USSR advanced sport festivals through mass national Spartakiads that involved more sports than those held in the Olympic Games. By 1975 one-third of the USSR population participated in Spartakiads. Post-Soviet Russia revitalized Spartakiads in 2002 making them annual events and integrating them with school competitions. The first stage was for those in educational institutions, the second and third at municipal and regional levels, and the fourth culminating in the national finals.

The National Olympics were organized by the USOC every year from 1978 to 1995, except those years when the Summer Olympic Games took place. Bringing the best athletes from all sports to the festival and coordinating their competition schedules was initially a challenge. Some top swimmers, gymnasts, figure skaters, and basketball players failed to compete in the 1987 National Olympic festival in North Carolina. Nevertheless, it was an invaluable learning experience for U.S. sport administrators. They staged the most complex sporting event in U. S. history and were able to develop important infrastructures required.

The 1995 National Olympics held in Colorado featured 3,500 athletes competing in thirty-seven sports over a ten-day period. Lacking corporate and government support, the USOC first considered reducing the number of sports or to invite only international athletes or to hold this sport festival only once or twice in a four-year period. In the end, the USOC chose to discontinue the National Olympics (Longman, 1995; Rhoden, 1987). The National Olympics program helped to develop the U.S. Olympic team that achieved first place in both total and gold medal counts at the 1996 Atlanta Olympic Games. More importantly, the national celebration attracted people to a broad spectrum of sports.

Why did the festival come to an end? One possible reason was the end of the Cold War and the sporting arms race between the United States and USSR in 1992. The new Russia was elated at the prospect of a free market economy, prioritizing profit from sport over national fitness and international performance.

The United States could now be number one with limited effort at developing mass participation. Shifting resources from mass to elite was logical at the time for the United States and other leading sport nations, as many elite athletes and coaches from the USSR and other former Eastern Bloc countries had to search abroad for better conditions when their sport systems lost public funding. Many national teams, from Australian swimming and sailing to U.S. fencing and gymnastics, attracted former Soviet coaches, sport scientists, and athletes after 1992.

By the end of the twentieth century, China started to challenge U.S. global sport successes through a highly organized pyramidal mass-to-elite system of competitions borrowed from the USSR. To create this pyramidal system, competitions were connected so that people could participate in many local tournaments within each sport. Advanced participants could progress to regional events and then high performers could go for national and, finally, to international events. This system provides opportunities for participants to gradually progress from a number of easier events to a smaller number of increasingly difficult competitions, contributing to effective attraction, retention, and transition of sport participants (studied by Green, 2005; Sotiriadou et al., 2008).

Current state games in the USA

The State Games originated as the Empire State Games which took place at Syracuse University in New York in 1978 (Resiner, 1984). To resume the role of the national U.S. Olympics, the National Congress of State Games was established as a not-for-profit organization and a community-based USOC member. State Games were held biennially from 1999, serving as finals for state level Olympics (NCSG, 2011). More than 400,000 athletes compete annually in the State Games nationwide in various sports from the Olympic and Pan American Games programs to sports with regional popularity (NCSG, 2011). Medal winners from forty-five State Games earned the right to compete in the 2011 24-sport State Games of America in San Diego, California (NCSG, 2011).

The Empire State Games (2010) was a program of the New York State Council of Parks, Recreation, and Historic Preservation held every year for New York residents (Dowd, 2013; New York State Council of Parks, 2010). These Games consisted of summer and winter events, games for the physically challenged, and competitions for seniors. After regional trials, participants from two divisions, scholastic and open, represented six regions (New York State Council of Parks, 2010; The Empire State Games, 2010). Some 6,000 winners participated in the finals. Due to New York State's fiscal crisis, The Empire State Summer Games programs were discontinued in 2010 (Dowd, 2013; The Empire State Games, 2010).

Other states have established more stable funding for their regional Olympics and programs aimed at stimulating mass sport participation. The Massachusetts Amateur Sports Foundation (MASF, 2013) is the organizer of the Bay State Games. Established in 1982 these games attracted 7,000 participants for the Summer Games, 900 for the Winter Games, and more than 50,000 for the annual

Kids Fitness Challenge (MASF, 2013). The Bay State Games rely on private donations today more than ever. The Adopt-a-Sport program allows donations to be earmarked for use by a specified sport or team, offsetting the operational costs of the sport and helping to keep entry costs low for young athletes (MASF, 2013).

The Bay State Games stimulated participation by giving annual grants of $250, $500, or $1,000 to nine schools, the size of the grant depending on the number of participants and the school's size (MASF, 2013). The MASF also provided college and university scholarships to Bay State Games student-athletes who demonstrated outstanding achievements in academics, athletics, and community service. Through a partnership with the New Balance Athletic Shoe Corporation the MASF were able to recognize more than 200 Bay State Games participants each year. The MASF's Kids Fitness Challenge motivates children to participate in physical activity, educates them on the benefits of a healthy lifestyle, and fosters a sense of school spirit through $US4,000 in cash grants distributed to schools annually. Twice a year, four participating schools are awarded a $500 grant each to support their health and PE programs (MASF, 2013).

Variety of competitions

The State Games of America exemplified how competitions can be managed from the bottom up and that they can rely on state level initiatives and funding. These games provided communities with ownership of their sport events and freedom to develop disciplines with local popularity. However, national competition systems for gradual progression to HP are available in only a narrow spectrum of sports compared with the 50 disciplines in both the 2012 London Olympic Games and 2014 Sochi Winter Olympic Games (Sparvero et al., 2008), twenty-four sports in the national summer State Games (NCSG, 2011), and the twenty-three sports in the NCAA (2014a). As a result opportunities are limited for a broad number of mass participants and elite athletes (Sparvero et al., 2008).

National systems of developmental programs and competitions exist in professional sports (e.g., baseball, football, ice hockey, basketball, triathlon, snowboarding) and some sports supported by universities (e.g., wrestling, swimming, gymnastics) (Sparvero et al., 2008). The result of this situation, in many cases, is competition between sports to be on the menu. As a result more sports try to gain a place in the Olympics/WOGs to gain recognition and funding, while leading to the "gigantism" of these games. Competition usually leads to exclusivity rather than inclusivity. The idea is to allow as many people to participate in the disciplines they desire.

Integrated development for all levels of competition

Coleman and Ramchandani (2010) illustrated, based on evidence from the USA, UK, and Europe, the hidden financial benefits that mass participation events are capable of delivering for host cities. Their research suggested that an event does not need to be "major" in world sporting terms to become significant in economic terms. Mass participation events such as marathons can be self-financing, given that the runners are prepared to pay for taking part. In addition, such events are potentially excellent sponsorship vehicles.

Agrusa (2004) investigated the economic impact potentials of hosting marathon events. In the USA the New York City Marathon remains the biggest footrace event. In 2010, the race generated $340 million. In 2013 the New York City Marathon had more than 50,000 starters (New York Runners, 2014). The majority of marathon participants could be described as "fun runners" for whom the outcome is of little significance. These fun runners are typically happy to complete the course, beat a personal best, or simply enjoy the camaraderie while raising money for charity. Less than 0.5 percent of the 37,000 participants in the 2010 London Marathon were elite athletes, while some 20 percent were club runners (Virgin London Marathon, 2010). To meet the growing demand for distance running, there were at least twenty inaugural marathons held in the USA every year between 2002 and 2006, with the total number of races increasing from 282 to 406 (RunningUSA.com, 2011). Again, marathons show how mass and elite sport can be combined in one event.

At the elite level China provides an example of how to better integrate mass and elite competitions and to motivate local governments to support sport. China's National Games are now used as the driving force for achieving Olympic success (Tan & Green, 2008). China simulates the Olympic Games during the city, national, and most of the provincial games. From 2001 to 2004, the number of national competitions increased from 491 to 836, of which 74 percent were in Olympic sports (Tan & Green, 2008). Young, inexperienced Chinese athletes were sent to participate in the 2004 Athens Olympic Games which was regarded as preparation for success in 2008 (Tan & Green, 2008). Expansion of the U.S. State Games across all states could emulate the success of the Chinese in balancing commercialization and excellence. What is missing are affordable guided pathways from local through state and national to global competitions by age and other participant characteristics.

Element 5 (Meso-Level): training centers

Throughout the history of sport, a key element has been a place at which to play, train, and compete. A major issue in modern high-tech sport is how to rationalize and combine the construction costs and uses of mass and HP facilities, especially in multi-sport complexes. Smolianov and Zakus (2008) argued that

> sporting success depends on (a) specific high quality equipment and facilities with priority access for elite athletes; (b) regional centers of excellence; (c) a national training center; (d) accessible/distance to facilities and sport; and (e) facilities for all [sic] (p. 10). They also argued that these facilities should cater for each type of sport and for geo-climate specificities (altitude, heat/humidity), and that "centers should service all ages and levels of participation, subsidizing customers from lower socio-economic groups (p. 10).

The key points here are that the facilities are accessible to all participants and they are individualized, as best as possible, for each category of sport.

In the United States, HP is serviced by regional and national Olympic training centers, private providers such as the IMG Academy in Florida, universities, high schools, and professional league facilities. For mass participation and intermediate levels, middle schools, developmental leagues, and community facilities such as the YM/WCA provide necessary training and competition sites.

Multi-sport training hubs

The network of U.S. Olympic training centers and sites provides top-level centralized athlete preparation in different geo-climates and altitudes. U.S. Olympic Training Centers are represented by four campuses created by the USOC as training facilities for its Olympic and Paralympic athletes. The Colorado Springs Olympic Complex in Boulder, Colorado has operated since 1978. It is widely used as it provided high-altitude training for up to 557 athletes and coaches and athletes concurrently in 2012 (USOC, 2012). The Aquatics Center is used for training and testing of U.S. swimmers and water polo players and for cross-training of other athletes. An overhead catwalk and underwater cameras allow for the filming of athletes above and below the water for testing purposes (USOC, 2012). There is a flume, which is a swimming treadmill containing 50,000 gallons of water with a current that can be adjusted from zero to three meters per second, and it is built in a hyperbaric chamber and can adjust the altitude from the sea level to 8,000 feet above (USOC, 2012). Since 1993 six new gymnasiums were completed for fourteen sports, a velodrome (one of twenty-five in the United States and is rated one of the top three cycling facilities in the world), and The Olympic Shooting Center (the largest indoor shooting facility in the Western hemisphere and the third largest in the world) were added (USOC, 2012).

The Lake Placid Olympic Training Center in New York opened in 1982. It caters for training in biathlon, bobsled, figure skating, ice hockey, luge, skiing, and speed skating (USOC, 2012). In addition, athletes participating in boxing, canoe and kayak, judo, rowing, synchronized swimming, taekwondo, team handball, water polo, and wrestling can train at the site. The Sports Science division includes the departments of sport biomechanics, sport physiology, sport psychology, computer science, and engineering technology (USOC, 2012).

The third campus was established at the Northern Michigan University Olympic Training Center in 1985. This center provided the opportunity to continue education while training primarily in sports which are not very well developed at U.S. universities, such as weightlifting and boxing (USOC, 2012). According to the USOC the center also offers an Olympic Bridging Program, which assists retired athletes to transition from sport to career through education. The fourth campus was the U.S. Olympic Training Center at Chula Vista, California opened in 1995. Facilities for 4,000 athletes (and local residents) are available in archery, canoe/kayak, cycling, field hockey, rowing, soccer, softball, tennis, and athletics (track and field) (USOC, 2012).

There are also twelve Olympic training sites for specific sports (e.g., the U.S. Sailing Center in Miami), similar types of sports (e.g., the Oklahoma City Boathouse Foundation facility for U.S. Canoe/Kayak and U.S. Rowing in Oklahoma), or different sports that benefit one another (e.g., the Anschutz Southern California Sports Complex, Carson, California for cycling, soccer, and tennis) (USOC, 2012). These sites hosted Olympic or Paralympic trials and most of them have hosted World Cup or World Championship events. In 2010, these training sites were utilized by twenty NGBs, the U.S. Paralympic Association, and 473 National Team athletes (USOC, 2011).

To integrate mass participants and intermediate-level athletes for progression to HP sport, the USOC makes use of the facilities at eight CODPs representing fourteen NGBs (USOC, 2011). The CODP training centers may host one sport (Moorestown Weightlifting Club, New Jersey) or more than ten sports (e.g., World Sport Chicago in Illinois) (USOC, 2011). Facilities also differ from the franchised private non-profit Boys and Girls Clubs of Metro Atlanta, Georgia to the tax-funded Springfield Greene County Parks and Recreation, Missouri to San Antonio Sports, which develops sport and fitness programs and events on all levels in Texas (USOC, 2011). An important function of these centers is to build cooperation with multiple partners. World Sport Chicago is an independent nonprofit organization, founded as part of the Chicago 2016 Olympic and Paralympic bid, which works with eighteen organizations (USOC, 2011). The partner organizations included the Chicago Park District, Chicago Public Schools, hospitals, and nonprofits servicing various forms of recreation and sport, particularly for people with disabilities (USOC, 2011). Such partnerships pull together resources and create conditions for progression from recreational to HP level in Olympic and Paralympic sports.

Another example of the U.S. sport development system aligning with the Model is that of The Utah Athletic Foundation. This foundation incorporates an Olympic Training Center and Community Olympic Development Program in Park City. The center provided the opportunity for people of all ages and abilities to be educated and to participate and excel in winter sports (USOC, 2011). At the elite level, since 2010, this Olympic Training Center provided 2,945 training days for 149 National Team athletes and seventy-nine Development/Junior Team athletes (from the USSA, U.S. Bobsled and Skeleton Federation, US Speedskating, and USA Luge Association) and hosted twenty-nine events for 2,147 competitors including the U.S. Championships/Olympic Trials and a World Cup event in bobsled and skeleton (USOC, 2011). At the developmental youth/CODP level, the center in 2010 also serviced seventeen athletes and two coaches in bobsled/skeleton, ninety-eight athletes and sixteen coaches in Nordic skiing, thirty-five athletes and seven coaches in freestyle skiing, thirty-three athletes and nine coaches in speed skating, and forty-two athletes and sixteen coaches in figure skating (USOC, 2011). Finally, according to the USOC (2011), the Center's 2010 Outreach program involved 10,553 athletes and trained 103 coaches through ten workshops.

However, unsystematic efforts to build integrated multi-sport facilities have faltered without adequate government support for strong programming. In

Anaheim, California, for example, developers had to file for bankruptcy protection in 2002 after spending years trying to build a $150 million indoor action sports complex. This is a reality of a private provision of infrastructure.

Two sport hubs that were developed in different historical, political, and socioeconomic conditions serve as models for the integration of facilities and programs. Each occurred before the respective country hosted an Olympic Games. The first hub was built in Moscow in 1980 and the second in London in 2012. In the Izmailovo district in northeastern Moscow, a sport hub was formed around a sport-oriented university.[24] Working with multiple partners, NGBs commissioned top coaches to develop and operate the facilities as regional or national training centers and academies for all levels of participation. The second, a UK hub, is described above (see footnote 17). We refer the reader back to that sport hub model.

An important feature of both hubs was the integration of sport facilities and programs with their cities' socioeconomic infrastructures. Both hubs have been part of historical and recreational tourist destinations conveniently connected by public transport with the center of London in the United Kingdom and Moscow in Russia; thus making the hubs' facilities and events an important part of local cultural life. Both hubs attempted to attract everyone to sport by giving children the same standard of facilities and coaching used by elite athletes. Elite athletes share the facilities with recreational users, inspiring community participation while producing world records (Bath Sport, 2011; Smolianov & Zakus, 2009b).

Cities such as Melbourne, Moscow, Toronto, and Singapore placed successful bids for major events after systematic attempts to build sport hubs integrating entertainment, HP training, and mass participation utilizing public/government capabilities and resources. Many countries, from Australia, France, and Germany to Russia, China, and Cuba, contribute to equal opportunities for their citizens by publically funding the best possible training conditions at both national and regional levels. Following the practices of the former USSR, China's seven national training centers (including the Beijing Sport University and Olympic Training Center) focused on the "Three in One" principle of integrating coaching with sport science and sport medicine. One thousand athletes are serviced by twenty top Chinese sport scientists, 100 top coaches, and the best doctors and sport managers, many of whom are former athletes. In addition, the Chinese government has provided eight world-class comprehensive training centers and fifteen specialized training centers for Olympic sports, all with the best facilities, including equipment imported from the United States (Tan & Green, 2008).

Also based on the Soviet model, Cuba's sport system advanced in the 1960s with the building of regional training centers across the country and the achievement of an even higher concentration of local athlete services and facilities than did the former USSR (Pettavino [2004] and based on the first author's visit in 2008). Each of Cuba's fourteen provincial training center hubs included a university with an extensive sport department, to which athletes would go after attending two levels of sport schools: Escuela de Iniciación Deportiva Escolar (EIDE) (eight- to sixteen-year-olds) and Escuela Superior de Perfeccionamiento Atlético (ESPA) (sixteen- to twenty-year-olds) (Pettavino & Pye, 1994). These specialized centers integrated sport and academic training, with the school day adjusted to accommodate both national academic requirements and the demands of the particular sport (Pettavino, 2004). Smolianov (personal visit in 2008) noted that all services were free including room, board, and travel based on his visits and interviews with participants and coaches at these facilities. These schools are also well staffed. For example in 2008, the ESPA at Matanzas had enviable coach-athlete ratios (e.g. 100 sailors, kayakers, and canoers were trained by twenty coaches and twenty-five fencers by five coaches). As well as medical facilities with full-time personnel providing athletes with physiotherapy, manual massage, anthropometry, and performance analysis were also provided at no cost (personal visit by first author 2008).

The USOC and NGBs could raise administrative efficiencies through the creation of more sport hubs. Coaches, facility managers, school administrators and teachers, sport scientists, and medical and other sport personnel could be concentrated in these hubs. Sport and medical scientists could be invited to use sport facilities, events, and athlete data for research. Well-planned public transportation systems could connect residents with the hub's sport, educational, medical, sport science, and administrative facilities.

General provision for mass fitness

Mass fitness/sport facilities aimed more at the mass level of participation are free or affordable outdoor fitness grounds. These are often available through local, regional, or state levels of governments. Beginning an active life-style early in life is critical for a healthy nation and for flow-on effects for HP sport.

The U.S. adult playground concept was borrowed from China and parts of Europe (Hu, 2012). Outdoor fitness facilities have gained popularity in many countries including those in colder climates, such as Canada and Russia. They have been widely used in the former USSR and were part of the reason why more than a fourth of the population actively participated in sport (Smolianov & Zakus, 2008). London's outdoor fitness initiative called "AdiZones" included five outdoor gyms sponsored by Adidas and the Great Outdoor Gym Company. These outdoor fitness facilities were built to be more affordable and integrated into the community, to remove barriers to physical activity (*Horticulture Week*, 2008). In China, as part of the "Qingdao Olympic Action Plan," outdoor fitness centers were placed in public parks, squares, schoolyards, and other locations viewed as convenient for the public in an attempt to compensate for insufficient sporting facilities (Wang & Theodoraki, 2007). There are more than 50,000 outdoor fitness facilities across China located in public parks and schools, making them accessible to all adults and children in the community (Free Press Release, 2005). These facilities are considered important because they can be used by people of all fitness levels free of charge. Further, the materials they are built with are long-lasting, so that minimal maintenance is required (Free Press Release, 2005).

In the United States, some public parks, schools, colleges, and universities include purpose-built outdoor fitness facilities. The University of Arizona's outdoor fitness facility, for example, consists of ten exercise stations along a 1.6-mile loop, aiming to improve community health (Kreutz, 2007). The positive health effects of exercises are magnified when the activity takes place outdoors (Hug, Hansmann, Monn, Krutli, & Seeland, 2008).

A growing number of city and park officials, health experts, and community leaders throughout the United States are praising the health and social benefits of adult playgrounds. They say that playgrounds will succeed where treadmills have failed in combating rising rates of obesity and related illnesses (Hu, 2012). Adult playgrounds are spreading across the nation. In New York City, the $200,000, fifteen-piece Bronx playground, which opened in 2010, became so popular that the city planned to create twenty more such playgrounds in 2012–2013 (Hu, 2012). There were thirty-two playgrounds with fitness equipment in 2014 in New York City Parks (2014a).

In 2012, Miami-Dade County in Florida opened four fitness zones with advanced strength training equipment in neighborhoods with high rates of cardiovascular disease (Hu, 2012). From 2010 to 2012 San Antonio has added outdoor fitness stations to thirty parks (Hu, 2012). Los Angeles had thirty parks, with fifteen more on the way in 2012 at an average cost of $400,000 per park (Hu, 2012). New York City's adult playgrounds cost from $75,000 for the smallest ones (with five pieces of equipment) to larger ones costing over $200,000 (Hu, 2012). In contrast, children's playgrounds typically cost $500,000, with the majority running at $1 million to $2 million (Hu, 2012). Many opportunities exist to make outdoor fitness equipment more weather-durable and provide a true alternative to indoor gyms.

Municipal indoor fitness centers are valuable for health and fitness and should also be free or available at minimal cost, as they are in New York City. The city's Parks and Recreation Department maintains forty-nine recreation centers that offer indoor pools, weight rooms, basketball courts, dance and art studios, game rooms, and libraries (New York City Parks, 2014b). Annual membership is free for youth under eighteen years of age, $25 for those eighteen through twenty-four, $150 for adults twenty-five through sixty-one years old, and only $25 for seniors sixty-two and older (New York City Parks, 2014b). This is an important situation for mass fitness and health; hopefully economic conditions will not change New York's provision and other municipal governments will follow their lead.

To summarize the discussion on meso-level sport development in the United States, it is worth stressing that the involvement of governments is critical in providing affordable facilities, competitions, and other services to each type of sport participant. A more direct and centralized distribution of the U.S. tax payers' money for sport would be more transparent and efficiently allocated than through philanthropy, the current mainstay for sport. Most successful sport nations have already moved closer to the Model in balancing the central and local development of meso-level infrastructures and services. Best international practices considered in this book might appear helpful for the United States to keep up with these countries.

Micro-Level: Operations, processes, and methodologies for the development of individual participants

Element 6 (Micro-Level): Talent identification and development

A sport development system must ensure that there is a "pipeline" of new athletes. At the mass sport level this is for the full development of each individual person, the "*mens sano e coporato sano*" ideal expressed in Olympism (see Chapter 1). We want individuals to be physically active for their own health and overall development. Likewise, for the elite end of sport, the pipeline is its lifeblood ensuring continuity. For most of sport's history, talent identification and development (TID) was very much a subjective practice for most of sport history. Early "scouting" of new elite athletes was performed by retired or ex-players of a particular sport. They would go out and "beat the bushes" for new athletes. Likewise, talent development systems (i.e., LTADs) are much more rationalized and scientized: All sport sciences are now involved in the work of effective and efficient development of athletic talent (Zakus & Bird, 2002).

Career athletes go through life stages that must be considered. As most sport careers are brief, retirement and "rest-of-life" factors must be included in sport development systems to ensure that athletes have full, productive lives when they leave HP sport. Smolianov and Zakus (2008, 2009a) noted that athletic careers should be planned on a twelve- to eighteen-year basis, guiding early career development, facilitating "peaking" within the competitive phase, and developing healthy lifelong sport participation. This is based on the multi-stage methodologies recommended to coaches across most sports by such authors as Balyi (2001), Balyi and Hamilton (2010), Matveev (2008), and Platonov (2005) and by an increasing number of NGBs including USA Hockey.

U.S. TID under international influence

"Tryouts" and scouting are the main talent search processes currently in use across professional and amateur sports in the United States. Minor leagues, developmental competitions, and camps also play an important role in the selection of potential high performers. Progressive developmental programs use some elements of best international practice. School talent search was successfully used in the former USSR and later in many countries from Russia and Cuba to Canada and Australia: with some sport school initiatives beginning in the United States. In Boston, for example, recruiters for the recreational program MetroLacrosse visit schools each winter, looking for new recruits to the sport (Thomas, 2009).

Typically, though, the primary means of advancement for young athletes in the United States is competition within the following stages: child/youth athletes (recreational sports, house leagues), adolescent athletes (high school), advanced athletes (college, semi-professional), and elite athletes (national team, Olympic, professional). Those who mature and grow at a slower rate are often at a distinct disadvantage with respect to selection via competition. This is particularly so at the child/youth stage. Participants have particular needs at this age group but also form the largest pool of potential talent (Grasso, 2008). The paradox is that this age group is underserved; they are generally coached by volunteers and parents who often have little or no coaching education (Grasso, 2008). The best coaches in the United States often work exclusively with elite athletes, resulting in the lack of a development process that equally benefits and directs all youngsters (Grasso, 2008).

Health and long-term success may be compromised when more emphasis is placed on competing than on developing sport outcomes (i.e., correct technique, building endurance, flexibility, and other skills, abilities, and knowledge taught by expert coaches). Healthy age-specific recommendations similar to those developed by the Soviet medical and sport scientists and recommended by Platonov (2005; cf. Balyi, 2001; Balyi & Hamilton, 2010) are implemented to various degrees by many leading sporting nations but are rarely considered in the United States. For example, judo throws used in the United States are not allowed in Canadian competitions for six-year-olds (personal communication by the first author with Victor Sokolovski, Head Coach of Tsunami Judo Club, Ontario, Canada, June 9, 2014).

Related to the dominant role of parents and volunteers rather than professional coaches at the child/youth stage is the current trend of early child sport training. While research indicates that sport experiences at this stage of life should be unstructured and fun, there are many departures to the published growth and development knowledge. One example among thousands is the "Lil' Kickers" soccer academy, a national franchise with more than 100 locations in twenty-eight states. Here parents can enroll their children at eighteen months of age (Hyman, 2010). About 55 percent signed up in 2010 were three years or younger. Hyman also noted that there is little evidence that training in infancy accelerates overall sport ability and, in fact, there is concern about over-use injury potentials for an even younger age group.

Indicative of the free market self-managed sport system, where the potential for wealth through sports is sought, is common place. Atlas Sports Genetics offers a $149 test that aims to predict a child's natural athletic qualities (Macur, 2008b). The company is focused on testing children from infancy to about eight years of age. The test involves swabbing the inside of the child's cheek and along the gums to collect DNA and return it to a lab for the analysis of ACTN3, one gene among more than 20,000 in the human genome (Macur, 2008b). The results arrive in the form of a certificate announcing "Your Genetic Advantage," with specific human and sport indicators highlighted (Macur, 2008b). A packet of educational information suggests sports that are most appropriate and what paths to follow.

Parents might not be clear-minded about this and children are not old enough to make rational decisions (Macur, 2008b). The U.S. NGBs could also consider the current practice of Russian sport authorities who provide control over the quality of a $2,000 genetic test based on the analysis of blood and hair, accompanied by recommendations from sport scientists regarding the most suitable sport, specialization within a given sport, and optimal training and lifestyle programs (To et al., 2013). The NGBs have enough to deal with as budget troubles are extant, not to mention the potential litigation that might occur if they started dealing with genetic testing as a selection criterion.

Some U.S. NGBs are starting to establish systematic athlete and coach development models similar to those used in the USSR and Eastern Europe after World War II and adopted internationally by the end of the twentieth century (USA Hockey, 2010). USA Hockey (2010) adopted an LTAD model used by most Canadian NGBs to create the American Development Model (ADM). Launched in 2009, the ADM provides a national blueprint for optimal athlete development. It is based on long-term athlete development principles and focused on age-appropriate training (USA Hockey, 2010). USA Hockey (2010) established a team of seven regional managers in 2009–2010 to support the ADM program. The regional managers conducted hundreds of educational sessions at various locations throughout the country during the course of the 2009–2010 hockey season to help local associations implement the ADM (USA Hockey, 2010).

Printed and digital material was also produced in support of the ADM, including practice plans for age groups six years and younger (6U), eight years and younger (8U), and ten years and younger (10U) (USA Hockey, 2010). In 2009–2010 USA Hockey (2010) created a growth coordinator position for local youth hockey associations and increased new participant membership in 8U by 6 percent to 42,000 through many different initiatives. In 2009 USA Hockey (2010) started building online age-specific coaching modules and in 2010 transformed its coaching certification process in concert with the ADM to certify coaches in a five-level model. More than 700 coaching clinics were conducted for 30,000 coaches during this season (USA Hockey, 2010).

Other U.S. NGBs are also starting to develop opportunities for the gradual progression of participants. Although U.S. international successes were generated by strong mass participation numbers, all U.S. NGBs need to intensify their efforts particularly at recruitment and beginner levels of sport.

LTAD guidelines have been implemented by most Canadian NGBs and many NGBs in other English-speaking countries such as Australia, New Zealand, the United Kingdom, and South Africa and now the United States (first author's personal visits). These guidelines, authored by Balyi (2001) and Balyi and Hamilton (2010), stem from the USSR and Eastern European sport development approaches outlined by Riordan (1978, 1980) and Shneidman (1978). Theories of training (periodization) pioneered by Matveev (1964, 1977, 1983, 1991, 1997, 2001, 2008) and further developed and applied by Bompa (1983), Bompa and Harff (2009), Platonov (1988, 2005), and other sport scientists and coaches were and continue to be the basis of the physiological development of athletes. This is what we meant by the scientific rationalization of TID and LTAD.

Community Olympic Development Program

The national network of CODPs that is being built by the USOC plays a vital role in the systematic implementation of LTAD methods. From 1998–2010 CODP Community Sport Groups produced fifteen Olympians, supported the achievement of seventy National Titles, contributed 124 Senior National Team Members and seventy-six Junior National Team Members, and achieved community financial investment of $8.9 million (CODP, 2011). CODPs (2011) hosted thirty-two events and trained 440 coaches in 2010, with a community investment of $1.7 million. Integration of all levels of participant under expert coaches in partnership with local public schools occured through the CODPs. Increased investment in these programs allowed local communities to create opportunities for all talented U.S. youths to develop to their highest potential. The CODP is still very small given the size of this country as it introduced only 484,000 youths to sport in fourteen NGBs in the 2010 year (CODP, 2011).

Schools and clubs

Pools of potential HP athletes are also developed through school teams. Many middle and high schools have advanced sport programs. More than fifty university preparatory U.S. schools provide tuition at an annual cost that can exceed $30,000 (and an additional $15,000 for boarding) (IMG Academies, 2011). Funded by tuition fees, philanthropic donations, and endowments, "prep" schools invest in top-class facilities and equipment and in qualified, experienced teachers with advanced degrees. Scholarships provide for some demographic heterogeneity. Many prep schools require students to participate in one or more of the school's sport teams, and some require students to participate in a sport during all three athletic seasons. However, less than 1 percent of students enrolled in school in the United States attend such schools (Ewert, 2013).

After WWII, sport clubs across the USSR developed programs for LTAD similar to the academies and CODPs currently growing in the United States. Such multi-sport training centers have attracted some of the world's top international talents, but they are not yet developed as a regional network affordable for all gifted domestic athletes particularly when compared to China, Cuba, the United Kingdom, and other countries that adopted the USSR concept of specialized schools (CODP, 2011). Aspiring elite athletes commonly abandon regular school for home or online educational programs. More than 100 online courses were available at IMG Academies (2011) to cater for the reality that athletes travel extensively. Similarly, Laurel Springs School (2013) in Ojai, California offers private distance learning education from kindergarten through high school. Known for educating Olympic athletes and artistic performers, it has more than 300 tennis players who study at home, following an online curriculum (Laurel Springs School, 2013). Tuition at Laurel Springs School (2013) is $6,000 to $8,000 per school year. Distance learning may be good for children with self-discipline and the right parental monitoring, but other athletes need the structure of a traditional school environment. Shneidman (1978) stressed that the Soviet system of PE and sport viewed athletic and academic progress as one integrated process with the aim to enhance the overall personal, academic, and athletic development of participants. Clubs, therefore, scheduled sport practice before or after public school hours and did not allow those failing academic subjects to participate (first author's personal research, 1980). Coaches worked closely with teachers to ensure academic success and a healthy physical and nutritional lifestyle, in a way similar to the U.S. requirements for school and higher-education sport teams (first author's personal experience as participant in Moscow Spartak Swimming Club and pupil of sport class in Moscow School 431, 1980).'

Element 7 (Micro-Level): Advanced support for each participant

This final element is arguably the center of any sport development program. It has been long argued that a sport development system must be focused on the participant or athlete (i.e., the "athlete-centered" approach emphasized by Canada and Australia, among others). Programs must be priced appropriately and be age- and interest-specific. For elite athletes, a broader career, full-time involvement (professionalization) and lifestyle elements must be considered along with "injury prevention, diagnostics, and correction of [training] loads, control of adaptation, rational nutrition, pharmacology, restoration and stimulation therap[ies], and doping use prevention" when proposing a holistic system of sport development (Smolianov & Zakus, 2008, p. 11).

This level represents the bringing together of all other elements. From this, the complexity of a sport development system is evident but such a system must operate for all potential participants; regardless of circumstances (needs, age, finances, gender, ability). The effectiveness of the whole sport development system will be evident in a healthy active population with high achievements gained by its athletes.

Multidisciplinary USOC support

Reflecting the U.S. decentralized approach, the USOC does not have a ranking or carding system that rewards athletes across sports in a uniform way, contrary to the practices of countries as diverse as China and New Zealand. The USOC relies more on NGBs to decide the amount and type of support each athlete should receive from the USOC. There are also many types of grants based on need and other criteria. "Operation Gold" rewards athletes for a top-place finish in their sport's most important international competition of the year. Financial rewards range from $2,000 for eighth place to $25,000 for first place in global competitions and from $1,000 for fourth place to $2,500 for a win in Pan American events (USOC, 2011). In non-Olympic years, athletes who qualify for more than one award receive the higher award. At the Olympic Games, athletes are rewarded for multiple performances: for example, $50,000 for two gold medals (USOC, 2011).

Today, the Athlete Career Program (ACP) of the IOC consists of the USOC's career services department and Adecco human resources in the United States (Gomez, 2009c). Adecco offers athletes support to analyze career options and a personal adviser to help them strengthen resumes, develop interviewing skills, and find employers (Gomez, 2009c). Since its 2005 inception, the program has served more than 1,600 athletes. Adecco directed similar programs in forty other countries in 2009 (Gomez, 2009c). In 2012 Adecco provided services for thirty-five NOCs as part of the IOC ACP, a program led by Sergey Bubka, an ex-Soviet Olympic champion from Ukraine (Adecco, 2013).

The ACP replaced the thirty-year OJOP in the United States. The ACP has been created to better serve qualified athletes, both while they are training and competing and during their transition from sport. Athletes are provided with employment opportunities that not only are schedule-wise but have the potential for future career advancement. All ACP athletes are paid the same rate of $14/hour to prevent any job-hopping among the USOC sponsors and to create more stability for both employers and athlete-employees (USA Track & Field, 2014). A basic health benefits package is paid for by the USOC sponsor-employer and administered by Adecco, which also handles the employment administration services (USA Track & Field, 2014).

While athletes work for the USOC sponsor, they are temporary employees of Adecco so that the USOC sponsors do not have to increase their head count. To apply for an ACP position, athletes work with a personal career coach from Adecco until they are considered "job ready" for program participation. A job is not guaranteed. Athletes must go through the job interview process and be selected by the USOC sponsor, a process that forces athletes to be better prepared for job interviews and career planning both during their athletic careers and upon retirement from sport (USA Track & Field, 2014).

In 2008 the IOC renewed its commitment with Adecco USA and expanded the program to the three pillars of education, life skills, and employment (IOC, 2014). With Hilton Worldwide's extensive hotel portfolio, athletes can secure jobs without leaving their desired training destination (Adecco USA 2014). Hilton also has the ability to accommodate unusual hours. The USOC could seek similar employment opportunities with numerous other corporations across all sectors of the U.S. economy.

Ideally, athletes receive education and job-specific training utilizing their unique sport expertise and work minimal hours during their competitive career, as was done in the former USSR and is currently being attempted by the U.S. Army (WCAP, 2014). In many other leading sport nations, top Olympic athletes are free from the stress of bills and inflexible jobs (TrackTown USA, 2011a). The French practice of reserving a quota for a certain number of athletes to be employed by major organizations across the country could be emulated.

Most developed nations offer medal rewards for their athletes. This rewards many athletes who are not in a fully professionalized sport or where sponsorships are bereft. Some of this can be fairly lucrative. The national media network of Canada provided a graph that, at best, gives an indication of this "remuneration."

Based on data from international sport press and NOC sources, for gold medals in summer and winter Olympic Games across time, prizes ranged from CAN$19,716 for Australian athletes to CAN$274,664 for Kazakhstan athletes (CBC, 2014). In this same article, U.S. gold medal champions received CAN$27,450.

It is the mark of a good athlete that can turn these winnings into investments that provide lifetime earnings. As noted above with football players, it does not often happen. And then there is the government. In 2012 President Obama supported the exemption of U.S. Olympians from paying tax on their prizes and medals so that athletes could keep all of their winnings. However, the proposed exemption did not reach the President's desk and was not enacted. Athletes were still taxed on prizes and medals in 2014 (Zaldivar, 2014).[25]

The influence of professional sport

The glitter of professional sport and the wealth some athletes gain masks the reality of market-driven sport.[26] Most professional athletes in sports with players' associations (unions) receive a predetermined starting salary and are contractually bound to a particular employer for a period of time. Though some athletes do receive salaries that can or could set them up for life, there still is a lack of understanding and naiveté among them. As such it took the establishment of players' associations to regulate the sport labor market and to counterweigh for the athlete's lack of education, the need for advice, and pastoral care. The development of these associations does not, however, ensure athletes' financial and earning security over their lifetime.

Still, many athletes with big contracts or on the training teams suffer financially. Although salaries have been rising steadily during the last three decades, reports from athletes, players' associations, agents, and financial advisers indicated that by the time NFL players had been retired for two years, 78 percent of them were bankrupt or were under financial stress (Torre, 2009; Pagliarini, 2013). Discussing the above figures, Davis (2012) stressed that the NBA and NFL players go bankrupt despite making an average of $5.15 million and $1.9 million per season, respectively. Retired athletes not only suffer financial problems. In many cases substance and alcohol abuse, mental and physical health issues, and violence and suicide are prevalent (Fainaru-Wada & Fainaru, 2013). Analyses by Torre (2009) and Davis (2012) seem to agree that elite athletes would benefit from better education and assistance in managing their lives.

International influences

There are many comparisons available on the full spectrum of HP services for athletes. This advice was available in the former USSR and GDR and also in countries such as France and Cuba (Bayle, Durand, & Nikonoff, 2008; Pettavino, 2004; Platonov, 2010; Riordan, 1978; Tumanian, 2006). These might serve as useful examples for professional U.S. leagues and the USOC. Sport administrators might also consider providing the education necessary for a smooth transition to life after sport. To help maintain good health and to ensure a good life health insurance and a league demanded pension are required to keep former HP athletes financially stable in retirement; as well as ethical agents. U.S. professional leagues have created perhaps the best systems in the world for salary capping to keep teams profitable. This practice could possibly be extended to better manage salaries for the lifelong well-being of athletes.

In the Soviet/Russian system, athlete services were/are coordinated by club coaches who stay with the athletes through most of their school and college/university/army years. Teams are managed as families, with parental roles played by coaches with significant amounts of time spent together outside of training. Through partnerships with schools, colleges, and universities, coaches assist athletes with their education and career, particularly for sport-related qualifications and jobs.

Other countries offer examples. In France, the National Institute of Sports and Physical Education provides athlete services such as a range of vocational qualifications and retirement funding to assist those in transition from elite sport to life after sport (INSEP, 2014). The Australian Athlete Career and Education (ACE) program of the Australian Institute of Sport has the motto "A Balanced Approach to Sporting Excellence" (ASC, 2014). Its purpose is to help athletes combine sporting goals with education, career, and other life skills. The program was adopted by the New Zealand Academy of Sport in 2005 (NZAS, 2009). ACE advisers are trained through the Australian Institute of Sport and hold a graduate certificate in athlete career and education management when they complete the program (NZAS, 2009). The New Zealand Academy of Sport manages regional ACE coordinators and advisers who assist athletes with their sporting, career, and educational and personal commitments (NZAS, 2009). The Australian ACE program is also used in the United Kingdom (Stambulova & Ryba, 2013).

The United States could lead the world in striving for a healthier and smarter balance in the lives of its athletes. The U.S. federal tax and health care systems could be used to make support of all athletes more equal and fair across the country, so that more top athletes in a broad spectrum of sports could make as much as top doctors, lawyers, engineers, and scientists. A uniform ranking system based on best global practices from the former USSR to current China and New Zealand would be instrumental in establishing national standards for efficient compensation of participants in all sports. As a starting point, the USOC might develop a uniform ranking and rewarding system for all its Olympic and Paralympic disciplines. After their competitive career is over, all HP athletes could be supported with privileged university entry, preferential treatment in getting professional jobs, and free use of specialized medical and sporting facilities for life.

NCAA athlete services

The NCAA has increased its efforts to fight the negative perceptions of how college and university sport programs operate. The debate around paying players for their performances continues, as does the rejoinder that they receive scholarships that are worth tens of thousands of dollars: But do they receive an education? That

Table 3.7 2013 Adjusted graduation gap report: NCAA Division-1 Football

	All AGG	Black AGG	White AGG
FBS Division Mean	−18	−24	−7
FBS Division Range	−12 to −28	−16 to −34	−1 to −18
Football Championship Sub- Division (FCS) Mean	−9	−10	−6
FCS Division Range	+8 to −16	+8 to −26	+8 to −15

Source: CSRI, 2013a, pp. 6–7

aside, the debate continues on academic integrity and acceptable graduation rates. This is especially so for men's football and basketball and women's basketball athletes – the sports that generate the most revenue but also display the greatest issues. The "smoke and mirrors" behavior by many universities feeds the media frenzy.

A key difficulty of attempting to sort out this issue surrounds whose figures and press releases one believes as correct. There are figures published by the NCAA, the Department of Education, and the College Sport Research Institute (CSRI) at the University of North Carolina. The CSRI calculated and published an Adjusted Graduation Gap (AGG) report. This report shows that there is a considerable gap between the rates published by the NCAA and their own. The CSRI take many extra features (part-time students, transfer students) into their calculation that are different and more comprehensive that neither those of the NCAA (Graduation Success Rate, GSR) or the Department of Education (Federal Graduation Rate, FGR).

In their figures, the CSRI found that there are minor recent improvements in the AGG for male footballers in some conferences in 2013. In the 2013 Football Bowl Sub-Division (FBS), the AGGs are as shown in Table 3.7. If education is the benefit received for their athletic production, one would hope this is a "real" benefit. The CSRI (2013a, p. 1) claim that

> these data call into question the degree to which NCAA D-1 football players (especially those on FBS teams) have access to a meaningful education leading to a degree. This access may be compromised as a result of training and competition schedules that are akin to full-time jobs.

The situation in basketball is not really different. Again, the CSRI reports the same type of differences based on the AGG. CSRI director Dr. Richard Southall stated in an interview that "the overall gap between Division 1 men's basketball players and the general full-time male student body is once again sizable" and the gap for major conference athletes increased (Steinbach, 2011, p. 1). In women's basketball the AGG gaps are not as large but are still troubling. If there is any good news in the women's report, it is that "difference in AGGs between black and white players is not statistically significant" (CSRI, 2013b, p. 3).

Although many NCAA member institutions devote significant resources to assist athletes with their academic success this process is not without problems. While the GSR might look good according to the NCAA, there is still the need to keep the athletes eligible. The NCAA also calculates an Academic Progress Rate that "measures classroom performance and retention" (Steinbach, 2011). Both Barrett (2014) and Fainaru-Wada and Fainaru (2013) provided both the positive and negative aspects in the academic support programs for student-athletes. This system is not without scandal, as the foregoing authors make evident.

There are paper writing mills and grade changes made outside of the normal processes (Barrett, 2014). As university sport, as noted above, is big business, not all processes are efficient in producing well-rounded athletes. There are scandals involving: poor attempts to cover the facts of the recruitment processes, how acceptance standards into universities are upheld ("special admit" clauses in university admission rules, dodgy SAT scores), the standards of literacy of many student-athletes, and their ability to attend and complete assigned coursework on their own. Although the published graduation rates are higher for student-athletes than for the average student,[27] the extra tutoring they receive gives them a greater chance to graduate. Still, there are glaring differences between sports, between genders, and between races (see Table 3.7; Barrett, 2014; Fainaru-Wada & Fainaru, 2013).

Still, for football and basketball, this is the TID and LTAD system. Not all football and basketball players are academically inclined nor do many really want a university degree. They are trapped by this system. Football players can make themselves eligible for the NFL draft three years after they (or "their class") graduated from high school, basically in their sophomore or junior years in university football before their eligibility is complete (or they "graduate"). Once declaring for the NFL draft they cannot return to university football. MLB's policy – in which athletes are allowed to enter the draft either immediately after high school or three years later – could be a better model (Thomas, 2010a). The NBA requires that a player is at least nineteen years old and at least one year beyond high school before entering the league. The NBA age policy has been controversial almost since it was initiated in 2005 as part of the collective bargaining agreement between the league and the players' union. Critics have said that these policies essentially forces athletes to attend college and keep the universities in top sport talent. Many argue that this also represents a double standard because sports with a large number of black players, such as basketball, impose age restrictions while those with mostly white players, such as hockey and baseball, do not.

Another matter that links the preceding issue of student-athlete educational achievement and the next section on athlete health care was the recent approval by the National Labor Relations Board (NLRB) for the Northwestern University football team to form a union. The NRLB ruled that the football players were workers who, as they receive money (scholarships) for playing football for which they receive no university credit, they were entitled to unionize (Zirin, 2014). The players claimed "they're seeking better medical coverage, concussion testing, four-year scholarships and the possibility of being paid" and that they "want student-athletes – 99 percent of whom will never make it to the professional leagues – focused on what matters most – finding success in the classroom, on the field and in life" (Ganim, 2014).

It is hard to argue against the fact that student-athletes are mere "fodder" for the NCAA and its member universities. As the NCAA gears up for a long expensive legal battle, it raises the question of what 99 percent of football players will do with the "rest of their lives."

Athlete health care

Risk management and safety in sport are receiving a high level of priority in the United States. Sport by its very nature is risky. One can easily be injured in sport, whether it is recreational or elite (this is obvious due to the repetition of drills and fitness training required – these aspects of sport are hard on the body). How injuries are managed and how recovery is managed are keys to this section topic. As there is a huge literature on these topics, we will briefly touch on them.

Most elite sport careers are brief. Very few athletes compete for more than five years, many fewer go up to or beyond ten years; although there are exceptions to this. The post – athletic career care of sports persons is very much a personal responsibility. And it is costly, especially where universal health care (Medicare) is not available. What this implies is that the employing sport, team, club, or nation has a short-time commitment and little responsibility to care for their performers.

Currently, workplace health and safety (WHS) and risk management are reaching new heights. A debate arises here whether sport should continue for children/youths or at all. Organizations such as the NFL and NCAA have been sued multiple times for negligence regarding awareness and treatment of injured athletes or student-athletes (Vecsey, 2011). Based on the 2011 claims by college football and soccer players, the NCAA was accused of a long-established pattern of negligence and inaction with respect to concussions and concussion-related maladies sustained by its student-athletes, all while profiting immensely from those same players (Vecsey, 2011). As of 2014 a major law suit between the NFL and more than 2,000 retired players is an egregious example of this lack of responsibility toward players once they are past their "use by" date.

Many studies have linked collisions on the field to long-term cognitive problems in athletes across the collision sports (in particular). Posthumously donated brains of football and ice hockey players were found to have a newly identified brain injury, chronic traumatic encephalopathy (CTE). The NFL carried out a long cover-up and denial that concussions occur in football (Fainaru-Wada & Fainaru, 2013). It set up and funded its own concussion committee research unit and co-opted researchers who would keep this topic under their control; as big tobacco had done to cover up the fact that smoking caused serious health issues and death. (Note: if only the sport lobby was as big and well-funded as the tobacco industry's, sport would be in a better position and the nation healthier.) Finally, in 2011, a law suit was filed in Philadelphia. From this suit a class action began and eventually more than 2,000 former players were plaintiffs. Both sides hired high-priced lawyers (some from the big tobacco cases), there was a consolidation of law suits, and the NFL changed its commissioner. In 2013 both sides were ordered to mediation and soon after $765 million plus legal fees agreement evolved (NFL.com, 2013). It was however thrown out as insufficient to cover all current and future suits as the money was not enough to cover all possible players (Breslow, 2014). Currently, the NFL has a revenue stream, just from television, of approximately $26 billion to $27 billion through to 2022 (Badenhausen, 2014). Surely it can offer more.

The mantra of the new NFL Commissioner Roger Goodell included these

> new talking points: Safety is its number one priority; concussions are not confined to football; the league has made rule changes to reduce concussions and is promoting "independent and transparent [and funded] medical research"
>
> (Fainaru-Wada & Fainaru, 2013).

While there was some *mea culpa* in this, it still denies due justice to the players who are in trouble and who made football a multi-billion dollar business. Many players are destitute suffer from persistent physical and mental impairment. They need help now, not after they donate their brains to medical science.

A major result of this situation is that the Zurich Statement (McCrory, Meeuwisse, Aubry, Cantu, Dvorak, Echemendia, Engebretsen, Johnston, Kutcher, Raftery, Sills, Putukian, Turner, Schneider, & Tator, 2013) on sport concussions evolved. From this many sports have instigated more stringent rules about how to handle these injuries. For children/youths, they are to be removed from play and not allowed to return until all concussion symptoms have resolved and medical clearance is obtained. Players are not allowed to return to participation until they pass a battery of concussion tests and they receive medical clearance to return to play. They must also receive clearance from a neutral doctor (not the team's doctor as in the past, although this is not necessarily followed). Much is still to be worked out in this matter. There are still too many coaches (and parents) who risk their athletes' future health and happiness by not protecting athletes properly (O'Connor, 2012). Perhaps an increase in litigation[28] will decide how this is to operate – and to how employing organizations (universities, professional franchises) operate in the future.

It is widely debated that helmets in football, ice hockey, rugby, rugby league, soccer, or any other sport help avoid or reduce concussions. They may protect against soft tissue injuries but will not eliminate concussive and subconcussive (accumulated) injuries. For athletes of all levels, there area variety of concussion tests that can be administered prior to head injuries (baseline testing), immediately after concussion, and at a series of intervals prior to medical clearance for return to participation. Nothing can stop the brain being bashed back and forth and around inside the skull. Concussion tests and new contact rules are a start, but they will not stop these injuries. At best they can help control ways that concussions occur and are handled during training, matches, and through foul play; and that is what athletes of all age and sport deserve.

Corporate support of athletes

In addition to sponsoring athletes with cash and employing them on favorable conditions, as discussed earlier, U.S. corporations increasingly support elite athletes with in-kind services from travel and accommodation to training technology. The challenge is to cooperate in the interests of long-term mass athlete development and sustainable national success across Olympic and non-Olympic sports. It is important to grow the USOC, particularly CODP training centers, through cooperation with progressive initiatives such as the Nike Oregon Project introduced in 2001.

To address some of the key factors potentially responsible for the decline of U.S. distance runners in international competitions, Nike House was opened. It was equipped with $110,000 worth of air-thinning technology built in sea-level Portland. In the five-bedroom 3,000-square-foot bungalow, oxygen was partially removed from the air, simulating altitudes from 9,000 to 14,000 feet, which helped runners to increase their red blood cell count by 11 percent. Nike House was decommissioned in 2005, and the athletes involved with the Oregon Project found their own accommodations outfitted upon request with reduced-oxygen rooms or sleeping tents.

Then Oregon Project demonstrated an exemplary elite athlete service that should be made available to mass participants by corporations – placing emphasis on running technique, sports psychology, and healthy conditioning. Chronic injuries for vulnerable and lesser-used muscles, ligaments, and tendons are prevented through one hour of non-running daily exercises that increase strength and flexibility (TrackTown USA, 2011a).

There are interesting possibilities of ways in which corporations could support athletes beyond providing employment opportunities and outside of institutional locations (the military). Many retired athletes are providing such opportunities through the foundations they fund. Some good lateral thinking is wanted here.

Political and anti-doping athlete support

One of the challenges for the United States is to make all HP sports fully compliant with the World Anti-Doping Agency's (WADA) code and to make all sport organizations' policies consistent with international standards and regimes. The official National Anti-Doping Organization (NADO) for WADA in the United States is the US Doping Agency (USADA). USADA is a nonprofit, nongovernmental agency established in 2000 and subsequently recognized by the U.S. Congress in this role. It is responsible for "Olympic, Paralympic, Pan American and Parapan American sport" (USADA, 2014). As the WADA local branch, the USADA is responsible for upholding and delivering the three levels of anti-doping:

the World Anti-Doping Code, the International Standards, and a Model of Best Practice and Guidelines (WADA, 2014). The regime alignment of both the USA State and the USADA is part of the global initiative of the IOC to clean up sport. The USADA has had more than its share of difficulty in this.

While the IOC used moral suasion as well as institutional power to get WADA working, there were many sports initially outside of its and the IOC's purview (e.g., MLB, NHL, NFL, NBA, the AFL in Australia, IRB, ITF, a number of golf organizations, Rugby League); that is, professional sports with their own organizations and practices. It would take time and great effort to develop regime change, along with government intervention, to align these sports with global WADA practices.

In recent years, major scandals have kept the USADA busy. The first of these was with the NFL and MLB over testing and doping control. With players' agencies involved, this matter was resolved over a few years. It was baseball that proved more difficult. As documented in their book, Mark Fainaru-Wada and Lance Williams (2007) exposed the deceits and conspiracies operating in U.S. sport. Baseball fans loved the home runs and HR records being beaten, but this was drug-fueled. The BALCO laboratory was behind Barry Bonds (and Marion Jones's Olympic success). The issue blew up in the mid-2000s and took seven years to resolve. There are many disgraced athletes and several in jail. The Congressional testimony of top baseball players and other athletes caused the USADA a difficult period in the mid to late 2000s.

The other major scandal involved Lance Armstrong. As, to date, nine books have been written on the doping scandal surrounding Armstrong's bullying and deceits, only a few comments will be made here. It was Armstrong's teammate Tyler Hamilton, whose co-authored book *The secret race: Inside the hidden world of the Tour de France* (Hamilton & Coyle, 2013), that gave impetus to the downfall of Lance Armstrong. The USADA had a major role to play in this scandal by leading the sanctions against Armstrong, the reversal of his tour wins, and imposing a life ban on him from the sport (which was supported by the Triathlon NGB when Armstrong sought to compete in this sport). Slowly but successfully the USADA is gaining on athletes who choose to dope. Certainly the USADA out of intense compulsion has been a leading NADO in the world.

Virtually all sports have now signed up to WADA's goals and procedures. Some sports still require more and better doping control policies, such as the NHL. Friesen (2010) expressed alarm that there is a lack of off-season testing while during the season only one to three players per team face surprise tests. This is despite suggestions that up to 30 percent of the NHL players could be using performance-enhancing substances. Also, the NHL tests only for steroids and related substances, leaving out recreational drugs and many stimulants (Friesen, 2010).

In the NCAA, drug-testing policies vary widely. Some schools' policies barely mention performance-enhancing drugs. The NCAA, however, is increasing its efforts to prevent doping. The 2011 policy forces all Division One schools to employ one staff member who can answer questions about dietary supplements and banned drugs (Pells, 2011). These trends indicate that the United States could take a leadership role in the fight against doping. This would be beneficial for the country's international image and national health, in both physical and moral terms.

Summary

The above discussion indicates that the USOC and some NGBs are attempting to build better partnerships, access new resources, and create better conditions for the comprehensive long-term development and nurturing of all sport participants. The interdependent systems of health care, education, and sport in the United States are more private, market-driven, and less coordinated compared to other successful sport nations. Accessibility differs significantly by suburb, city, and state but good-quality service is often too expensive. However, government and corporate initiatives contributing to national fitness and sport performance are now on the rise. Reforms of the national education and health care systems are being attempted under President Obama. If the U.S. government continues to stimulate these trends and if the USOC continues to increase its efforts to bring closer cooperation among partners within and outside the sport industry a more cohesive, coherent, and efficient pyramid of athlete development will emerge. Team USA might be able to achieve the nation's ambition of being the best in the world of sport and beating the strongest opponents in the twenty-first century.

U.S. elite sport development might be stimulated by factors similar to those that fuelled the "American" Olympic glory in the past: China's growing sporting, ideological, economic, and political challenges are similar to those of the former USSR. The use of the Olympic Games to increase mass participation is also becoming more pronounced in the United States. Following the failed bids by New York and Chicago for the 2012 and 2016 Olympic Games, the USOC sent letters to the mayors of thirty-four cities in 2013 asking whether they are interested in bidding to host the 2024 Olympic Games, stressing that now, more than ever, the power of the Olympic and Paralympic Games must be used to encourage U.S. youth to be more active and engage in sport. Another promising factor is President Obama's support for hosting the Olympics, for making U.S. people fit, and for improving the national health and education systems. In 2013 President Obama presented his vision of the new U.S. role in the world. A role that avoids a muscle-bound foreign policy, dominated by the military and intelligence services, in favor of energetic diplomacy, international aid, and a calculated response to terrorism (Landler & Mazzetti, 2013).

What we observe from the material presented in this chapter is that the U.S. sport development system aligns with the Model in many places. Where it diverges, we have presented alternate possibilities to keep moving sport forward in the United States. This still does not end the discussion or the possibilities. We state here that much is good with this system but there is more that might be included. Here a "normative leap" of faith, application of knowledge, and working to break down thoughts and past practices that are unnecessarily restrictive to access to sport for all to the highest level of participation and competition in sport.

While we present how the Model can be used in a historical analytic way that is not the only way in which it can be used by present managers and academics. In the next chapter we present three empirical case studies. These case studies present the Model as a measuring stick against current sport delivery practices.

Notes

1 For ideological reasons, the IOC does not keep an outcome table. However, the media and citizens do keep track. How this is done, however, is often confusing. Is the "winner" of an Olympic or Winter Olympic Games the country with the most gold medals or with the most medals in total? We present both and leave it to the reader to determine wins and losses.

2 The "Cold War" is generally dated from 1947 to 1991 when the Soviet Union dissolved (although it started just after WWII. It was very much an ideological and economic battle over what system was better: United States-style capitalism or USSR-style socialism with communist mythology and a planned economy. There were several proxy "hot" wars during this time, but it mostly surrounded aligning other countries to one or the other side.

3 After 1952, the USSR dominated the Games except for 1964 and 1968, when the Soviet government reduced support for sport, and the support for professional coaches declined.

4 China competed in the Olympic Games as the Republic of China between 1932 and 1948. In 1952, they competed as the Peoples' Republic of China after the Chinese civil war. Due to the "two Chinas" controversy, they did not compete between 1956 and 1976. They competed again in the 1980 Lake Placid and the 1984 Los Angeles events and have done so for every Games since.

5 In the Winter Olympic Games since 1952, the USSR/Russia/Unified Team total is 123 gold and 308 overall medals, putting this amalgam of national identities in overall first place in both categories.

6 We use the term "Eastern Bloc" to refer to the former states in central and eastern Europe that were under the direct influence of the former USSR. This includes the Warsaw Pact countries of Albania, Bulgaria, Czechoslovakia, the German Democratic Republic (East Germany), Hungary, Poland, Romania, and the USSR itself. This Bloc also included the former Yugoslavia up to 1948 (which included Bosnia-Herzegovina, Croatia, Macedonia, Montenegro, Serbia, and Slovenia).

7 Mechanisms of mass participation support can be borrowed from successful sport nations with smaller populations; for example, Australia has been relatively successful in the Olympic Games summer sports (Sotiriadou, Shilbury, & Quick, 2008; Newland & Kellet, 2012) as has Norway in the Winter Olympic Games sports (Hanstad & Skille, 2010).

8 For example: running, long and high jump, pull-ups, push-ups, crawling, rope/pole/tree climbing, grenade/ball throwing, and skiing or swimming.

9 The President's Council on Fitness, Sports, and Nutrition began in June, 1956. A report of U.S. children fitness compared to European children (the Krause-Weber Report) was integral to this development. Each president since Eisenhower has appointed and fiddled with the structure and programs of this council. It is very much a promotion-based program (similar to 1970s programs in Canada [ParticipAction] and Australia ["life be in it"]). The latest legislation for this council was signed in 2010. This Congressional law states that "The Foundation is a charitable and non-profit corporation and is not an agency or establishment of the United States" and that it "may not accept any Federal funds" (National Foundation on Fitness, Sports, and Nutrition Establishment Act, 2010).

10 U.S. sociologist Robert K. Merton coined this term based on the Gospel of Matthew and how recognition in academic rewards operate. Basically, those that have shall have more, and those that have not shall give to those who have more.

11 More than $500,000 (received from 3,200 donors) was available to subsidize their memberships (North Shore Y, 2011). For example, for a two-adult family with an income of $55,000 or more, the joining fee was $99, with a monthly membership fee of $92. If household income was $25,000 or less, the joining fee was $54, with a monthly membership fee of $60. Individuals and families who were unable to afford the membership could get further financial assistance from the North Shore Y (2011).

12 The Ivy League is a group of eight elitist universities mainly in the New England states of the United States. Their long history and import in higher education in the United States is undoubted. This group consists of Brown University, Columbia University, Cornell University, Dartmouth College, Harvard University, Princeton University, the University of Pennsylvania, and Yale University.

13 For a small developing nation suffering under the current embargo, Cuba has done extremely well in the Olympic Games it has entered. After the revolution Cuba did not enter these Games until 1964 in Tokyo. At these games and the 1968 Mexico City Olympic Games, they were far down in the overall standings (30th and 31st, respectively). Since then and except for the 1984 and 1988 Games that they did not enter, they were in the top ten in five of the nine Games and in the top twenty three times in the Olympic Games they entered. Their results were poor in the 2008 Beijing Olympic Games (28th place). (All Time Olympic Games Medal Table, 2014).

14 Included here are: schools, colleges, universities, sport specific clubs, YM/WCAs, Community Olympic Development Programs, and state games and sport commissions.

15 Of the funds collected by the Dutch government 75 percent are devoted to mass sport and 25 percent to elite athletes. Local sport projects must contribute a equal 50 percent share of the project costs to be funded (Van Bottenburg, 2011).

16 The USOC's director of athlete facilities and services oversees CODPs in developing partnerships with community organizations to access additional resources, services, and facilities that positively impact athlete performance. A local CODP must assign an administrator to manage and oversee all aspects of the CODP operation and to liaise with the USOC. The USOC provides CODPs with many things. These include: operational guidelines; program review processes with oversight in collaboration with an NGB; the use of CODP trademarks; annual staff meetings for all CODP managers; access to the USOC community based multi-sport organizations (i.e., YM/WCA, Boys and Girls Clubs, Armed Forces); access to USOC resources such as International Relations, Sports Science and Coaching, Sports Medicine, Athlete Services, and Public Relations, particularly athlete services and coaching education at a discounted price; acknowledgment on the USOC Website; and invitations to the CODP Coaches Conferences (USOC, 2013; Andrasko, 2013; McConnell, 2013).

17 Exemplars such as the following case of British Pentathlon and the University of Bath (UK) help one to appreciate the value of utilizing a full spectrum of public and private partners. British Pentathlon became one of the UK's most successful sports, from having no individual Olympic medals to winning one or two medals in each of the four Games since 2000. The World Class Program (WCP) started with volunteer support from the British Pentathlon Association, which had no fulltime employees. By consolidating resources from government, higher education, and lottery organizations, an efficient structure was in place in 2005. Funds and their allocation for this sport governing body included £450,000 from the lottery for the English Institute of Sport and the University of Bath Training Center (for WCP – 11 top senior and junior performers, their three coaches, and a support team); £500,000 from the lottery to medical and coaching support through the English Institute of Sport for the Talented Athlete Program (TAP) (for thirty-three athletes fifteen to nineteen years old, their administrative manager, development coach,

and seven part-time regional coordinators); and £100,000 from the UK Sport for the management of the MPAGB, which organizes a nationwide competition of swimming and running events, that helped to identify candidates for the TAP and WCP.

Partnerships involving HPM squads, government, and higher education not only connect mass and elite sport but seem to be effective in achieving top results by elite athletes, providing them at the same time with education and career services. Through financial backing by the lottery foundation, the local council, and two NGBs, the University of Bath built a fifty-meter pool, athletics track, and indoor tennis hall. These facilities also allowed Bath to host the European Youth Olympic Days and extend the TeamBath roster. The university also built a bobsleigh push-start track with the help of the lottery and the British Olympic Association. At the same time the English Institute of Sport injected £23 million from lottery funds to extend the facilities for tennis, athletics, judo, sports science, and sport medicine. The university also attracted the nation's elite athletics, swimming, tennis, modern pentathlon, and bob-skeleton squads. NGBs for badminton, triathlon, hockey, and netball also developed programs at the university.

In terms of community outreach, anyone can become a member of TeamBath and enjoy numerous individual and community club programs. Children taking their first sporting steps can do so alongside elite "star" athletes and many talented youngsters from the region have moved into the national squad programs. Increasingly, businesses are looking to TeamBath to provide lifestyle options for their employees and help to build them into effective teams (TeamBath, 2005). TeamBath provides a model of a holistic, multi-partnered organization that bridges mass and elite sport development. It serves as a best-practice model for other countries.

18 Both U.S. Army and Air Force run a World Class Athlete Program designed to help nationally ranked athletes train toward a goal of competing in the Olympic Games. Duration and location are the two biggest differences between the services' programs. The Army allows for a training period of three years prior to the Olympic Games. Air Force athletes are limited to two years. As for location, the Army WCAP is located at Fort Carson, Colorado, near the Olympic training site, while the Air Force lets athletes train where it's best for them. The Navy and the Marine Corps' support structures for athletes are quite different from those of the Army and Air Force. Neither has a WCAP, nor do they actively recruit athletes. For the Navy, once an athlete is identified as being of Olympic caliber, he or she must request and receive a special assignment, then the program tries to relocate the athlete to a location beneficial for training purposes. Training usually begins about 18 months before the Games. If a Marine Corps athlete is invited by a sport's national governing body to participate at a training center, he or she then becomes a member of the corps' National Caliber Athlete Program. A Marine athlete is not allowed to train for more than three-and-a-half years without returning to the fleet.

19 Thomas (2008; all material below is from this reference) described a mutually beneficial partnership between the army and United States Shooting. An Army Marksmanship Unit was established in 1956 to serve as a symbol of the U.S. military prowess during the Cold War and to train and employ HP shooters. Its members won twenty-one Olympic medals. Of the twenty-two U.S. shooters who went to Beijing, six belonged to this unit. The unit's sixty-four male and four female members go through basic training, pass physical training tests, and teach marksmanship to deploying soldiers. Members of the unit compete in all three Olympic shooting disciplines: rifle, pistol, and shotgun. They typically practice about five to six hours per day, five days a week. They earn salaries based on their rank and travel to about seventy competitions each year. The unit, with an annual budget of more than $4 million, provides also has access to a licensed hypnotist and a brain wave biofeedback monitor to teach the shooters how to clear their minds.

The United States together with China and Russia lead Olympic shooting, but that was not always the case. In the 1950s, the Soviet Union seized on the poor performance of U.S. shooters as a way to demonstrate military dominance. Embarrassed by the U.S.'s weak showing and dismayed at the overall quality of marksmanship in the Army, President Eisenhower ordered the creation of the unit as a way to develop competitive shooters and to pass their skills along to other soldiers. "He wanted to beat the Russians," said Harden, who retired from the Army in 1982 and works as chief of the unit's Custom Firearms Shop. We were ordered to "build the best rifles, make the best ammunition, and get the best shooters" (Thomas, 2008). In the 1964 Toyko Olympics Games, U.S. athletes won seven shooting medals. Six of those medals, included two gold medals, went to members of the Army Marksmanship Unit.

20 Stern (2013) also noted that "of the 50 largest individual gifts to public charities in 2012, 34 went to educational institutions, the vast majority of them colleges and universities, like Harvard, Columbia, and Berkeley, that cater to the nation's and the world's elite." That the rich support that which will give them the greatest ego boost while showing their wealth, both the "Matthew Effect" and Thorstein Veblen's (1953) "conspicuous consumption" of wealth identity (e.g., buildings and other built environments with their names emblazoned on them).

21 This category is defined by the American Gaming Association (2010) as follows:" Charitable gambling is run for the benefit of non-profit organizations, although the non-profit may not necessarily be the operator of the games. Some examples of charitable gambling are PTA Monte Carlo nights and church raffles. The most popular form of charitable gambling is bingo." Another definition expands on this definition: "Charity gambling is the practice where typical gambling' games' such as bingo, roulette, lottery, slot machines, etc. are overseen by a charity or group of charities. The profits from the venture go to the charity or group of charities, rather than to a municipality or private casino. Sometimes this occurs as a 'one time event' during a casino night or such type party. In other cases, charity interests maintain ongoing gambling concerns." This last definition indicates that many casino sites can be used directly by sport organizations, much as the second author experienced in Canada.

22 As the London Games approached, the U.S. BMX team performed its reconnaissance at a test event in London – without consent of the hosts. According to national team coach James Herrera (Bishop, 2012), "we had guys on the ground, taking video, 3D, engineering-type images. So we knew how many feet it was going to be from the base of the ramp to the first obstacle, how high, how far." When Olympic officials changed the course, the U.S. team flew the same builder back to the Olympic Training Center in Chula Vista, California and altered its replica course accordingly. Officials declined to provide details but did speak to the advantages such a course provided. "Massive" is how Herrera described it, noting how the team also built a replica track for Beijing mostly from drawings; they went on win half of the six BMX medals.

23 A reminder to readers that this was known as arête in the Greek system of sport, which is the basis of Western sport (see pp.4–5 and note 7 in Chapter 1; see also MacIntyre, 1984). There are many parallel developments in Confucian China and the Aristotelian Classical Greek period (see Yu, 2007 for this development).

24 The Izmailovo sport hub is comprised of the following facilities: a twelve-pool water sports facility for swimming, diving, water polo, and synchronized swimming with two beginner "frog" pools; two twelve-meter pools for learners; four twenty-five-meter (including one outdoor) and four fifty-meter (including one outdoor) pools; a performance laboratory with equipment such as a multi-speed transparent treadmill pool; indoor and outdoor gyms/fields; saunas; medical facilities; restaurants; conference halls; offices; and a hotel. Accommodating both sport and recreational users, the facility operated from early morning to late night every day of the year with no interruptions even for the outdoor pools in severe winter conditions

25 As noted elsewhere, how much athletes in some small or non-traditional sports struggle to earn any type of financial living. It is a very small section of the elite athlete population that earn huge or even obscene amounts of money. Likewise, they do so for short time frames. Yet many see becoming a professional athlete as a life goal.

26 Top, highly marketable, highly skilled athletes have significant earning potential opportunities to earn great amounts of money, both from contracts and through sponsorships. Their career might, however, not be as easy and free. Many are dependent on and responsible to agents and sponsoring companies. Often their ability to make decisions is limited and there is a lack of knowledge and expertise on how to live on such largesse.

27 Gasgreen (2013; emphasis added) noted that, "unlike the Federal Graduation Rate, the GSR counts athletes who transfer out as graduates (it also accounts for athletes who transfer in), and *consequently shows consistently better results*. The six-year federal rate for the same cohort of athletes is 65 percent." The NCAA unremarkably argue that the trends are up. In the end it depends on whose figures and arguments one believes.

28 There are, for example, major football lawsuits involving the Riddell Helmet manufacturer after it claimed that "athletes who wore the Riddell Revolution helmet were 31 percent less likely to suffer a concussion compared to athletes who wore traditional football helmets" (Anderson, 2014). This is clearly a nonsense. Many lawsuits are against the NCAA for its long neglect of its student-athletes with concussions.

4   U.S. elite and mass tennis, rugby, and soccer

The state of the art and opportunities for development

Introduction

In the previous chapter we observed particular historical developments in U.S. sport against other sport systems and the Smolianov and Zakus Model. Comparing historical evidence against the real changes of U.S. sport filtered through that Model is one way to analyze sport and sport development. Of greater import to current practitioners is how an ideal-type model can show gaps or inconsistencies of current sport developments against "best practice" elements of a holistic model. A difficulty encountered with many practitioners is with how to use such a model. As with Allen Guttman's (1978) ideal-type model of modern sport, many people take such models as actually existing, when they are actually mental constructs. They allow one to compare what *is* with what *ought* (or rather *could* or *might*) be[1]; that is, the model is a comparative device or tool.

Both academics and, in particular, professional sport managers need such tools to improve and expand the organizations they manage. Our purpose in creating the Model was not to provide some jargon-laden academic exercise but to show how and where, through existing global examples, such improvements might ensue. The improvements depend on the ability of the sport practitioner or scientist to change the way they think (use different ideas) and how they see ways to make change. To truly display the value of this Model, we offer the following empirical studies from research completed on tennis, rugby, and soccer in the United States. We used each element of the Model to analyze the current status of the development of these sports and against advancements in other countries.

Tennis has a long and successful history in the United States. It is an individual sport and often economically exclusive; however, many individuals and organizations operate to spread opportunities for a broader range of participation. Tennis coach and instructor Nick Bollettieri founded his tennis academy in 1978 and then joined with the International Management Group (IMG) in 1987 to expand this business into other sports; this new business venture included kindergarten through to post-secondary schools. Many professional tennis players established foundations to provide either tennis (The Andy Roddick Foundation) or educational opportunities (Andre Agassi Foundation for Education) for those economically unable to play or receive a sound education. And a number of local government parks and recreation or YM/WCA initiatives expanded opportunities for all to play tennis.

Rugby is a very old code of football in the United States. As with so much other historical sport development in the nation and the world, sport originating from England provided a key source of class-based differentiation. Until the development of "American" football and the NCAA to institutionalize it, rugby (and soccer) occupied more attention. Rugby hotbeds in the northeastern states and in California, particularly at universities, continued the development of the sport.

Though rugby was once strongly associated with the upper classes, it is firmly classless today as player migration and the integration of players of non-Anglo Saxon background now dominate many national rugby teams. In terms of systems and practices, we also find that countries such as New Zealand and Australia are leading developments in this sport as opposed to China and Russia (countries that are now funding and developing rugby with ideas and personnel from elsewhere for the 2016 Rio de Janeiro Olympic Games).

Similar to rugby, soccer has a long history in the United States. In 1930 the United States was deemed to be the overall third-placed team in the first-ever FIFA World Cup hosted by Uruguay. Then, in 1994, the United States hosted the FIFA World Cup. More than 3.5 million people (an average of nearly 69,000 per match) attended the fifty-two matches held (FIFA, 2014a). Over the history of the FIFA World Cup, the U.S. men's team competed in eight tournaments: 1930, 1934, and the six held from 1990 to 2010 (as the tournament expanded first to twenty-four teams in 1982 and then to thirty-two in 1998 (FIFA, 2014b). The First Women's FIFA World Cup held in 1991 was won by the United States. Various professional leagues operated in the United States. The current Major League Soccer of nineteen teams (plus three more teams based in Canada) is the premier competition in the United States along with two other men's leagues and one women's league operating at this level. As the self-promoted "world game," soccer has a stronger foothold in the U.S. sport system than it had for many years.

This chapter presents key findings of completed empirical research on U.S. tennis, rugby, and soccer. The following sections describe the research methods before presenting the results of each sport in subsequent sections. Again, it should be reiterated that the examples given are seen as global "best practice" and not toward any national bias. We also note that our analysis is also detailed in several published articles. These include: Carney, Smolianov, and Zakus (2012); Smolianov, Gallo, and Naylor (2014); and Smolianov, Murphy, McMahon and Naylor (2014). Finally, these works exhibit the use of the Model for the analysis of a sport and a sport development system against a holistic standard.

Methods used to analyze U.S. tennis, rugby, and soccer

In the interests of achieving a more holistic analysis of the organizations and their operations in terms of the Smolianov and Zakus Model (heareafter called the "Model"), we applied both qualitative and quantitative methods in each study.

Similar previous studies employed either predominantly quantitative analysis (e.g., De Bosscher, et al., 2010), which may not capture unique or new practices, qualitative analysis (e.g., Houlihan & Green, 2008), which limits the generalizability of the findings or had no specific comparison framework (e.g., Platonov, 2010).

For each sport studied we used a quantitative survey (with space for open-ended comments), a series of semi-structured interviews with key position holders in each sport, and a content analysis of hard copy and electronic versions of organizational documents. Each element is discussed in the following sections.

Survey development

The survey used in all three studies contained fifty-four statements based on the three levels and seven elements of the Model. Validation of the first survey instrument (for rugby) involved a group of twelve international experts, including executives from the three target sport-governing bodies and academics who research and publish on high performance and sport development. Additional experts were sought to further validate the survey ahead of the tennis and soccer studies.

The experts reviewed the instrument and provided suggestions for changes to the survey. Their suggestions resulted in several items being added or removed. Other statements were clarified or adapted for the tennis and soccer versions in the final questionnaires used.

In each survey respondents were asked to indicate how often each of the desired practices occurred in their sport. Responses were put on a 5-point Likert scale, from "never" to "always." Open-ended responses were also sought in the questionnaire so that respondents could further elaborate on their sport's current practices and on whether these practices should be improved or implemented. Delivery of the questionnaire was online.

Sampling

Standard sampling techniques were used for each sport. For the tennis study the organizational directories of the National Collegiate Athletic Association (NCAA) Division I, II, and III tennis coaches and the U.S. Professional Tennis Association (USPTA) directory were used as the sampling frame. These included coaches and administrators who know the overall tennis delivery system in the United States. Though about half of the surveyed coaches worked with beginning players, the sampling frame had more high-performance coaches than in the total population of tennis coaches. This sample served the purpose of examining how high-performance staff could enhance mass participation. Seven administrators further increased the level of knowledge among the respondents and ensured the validity of this study.

The rugby sampling frame included the majority of registered USA Rugby coaches and administrators identified by e-mail addresses from various sources. These included lists from USA Rugby, colleges and universities with rugby programs, and the seven Territorial Rugby Union Web sites (which represent the regions of the USA Rugby structure). The framework provided a comprehensive sample of people with a high-level interest in rugby throughout the United States. Due to the relative infancy of rugby in the United States, there are comparatively few high performance-level staff and coaches in the country.

The sampling frame for soccer was based on e-mail addresses for the U.S. Soccer coaches and administrators from organizational directories of: USA Soccer, colleges and universities, and the four territorial regions of USA Adult Soccer Association (USASA). Having grass roots experience, most sampled coaches worked with competitive or elite players at high school and university levels. This ensured that the respondents were well informed about practices and dynamics of both mass and elite soccer systems in the U.S.

The sport-specific results tables in the following sections present the data from the online surveys. Each table displays two types of results. The first is an average of the overall 5-point Likert results for each variable (displayed in the first numeric column). The next three numeric columns summarize how respondents perceived each variable in terms of how often a practice was evident in their sport's operations or structures. In the second numeric column, we have aggregated the scores of two responses ("never" and "rarely") as both were seen as perceptions of what is "negative/lacking." The third numeric column is an aggregation of the Likert responses of "sometimes" and "do not know," which we label "neutral." It should be noted that "do not know" was a highly infrequent response. The fourth numeric column combines the responses "often" and "always," both seen as positive perceptions of what exists. This column is labeled "positive/existing." In some of the analyses we focused only on the results of the second and fourth columns.

We point out that the neutral column indicates that the sport-specific specialist respondents could not give a definitive response on their perceptions. We have included this percentage to indicate that much of each sport's community is either not aware of, or knowledgeable about, the broader aspects of their sport in the U.S. context. The neutral perception relates to lack of awareness or of confidence in what they know among those working in U.S. sport about sport structures outside their experience (Bowers et al., 2011; Green, Chalip, & Bowers, 2013). Many of the neutral responses are clarified in the written comments that are part of the analysis of each element.

Digel (2005) noted this lack of awareness as a concern not only for the U.S. sport system but for the other seven successful national sport systems he studied: Australia, China, Germany, France, Italy, Russia, and Great Britain. Even these top systems have traditionally been inward-looking and insular. Asking persons in charge of producing high-performance athletes about their knowledge concerning other nations, Digel found unfamiliarity to be the predominant feature of responses. He stressed, however, that at least part of the problem can be attributed to the complexity of sport development systems.

Semi-structured interviews

We interviewed administrators from tennis, rugby, and soccer in charge of national development, research, science, or divisional presidents representing key regions of the United States. Table 4.1 shows the breakdown of those interviewed. This was a convenience sample composed of a total of twenty sport executives from the three sports.

The feedback from U.S. rugby leaders and initial conversations with U.S. soccer and tennis administrators showed interest in the results of the coaches' surveys as this would assist in their understanding alignment with the Model (successes) and areas that needed improvement. The tennis and soccer administrators were, therefore, given results of the coaches' survey prior to obtaining their written responses. This was the only variation in the methods used.

The semi-structured interview schedule (see Appendix 1) used in this part of the research was based on the seven elements of the Model. In fact, the schedules paralleled the survey questionnaires. Their purpose was to more deeply understand what might be done in each of those elements to improve the sport in question. Also, as the interview schedule paralleled the items of the online survey, the online and telephone qualitative response data led to a straightforward analysis without a need for extensive or elaborate coding.

Seven administrators from the USTA and USPTA provided additional oral and written feedback on the state of tennis in the United States. Initial telephone conversations introduced the research and results of coaches' survey, prompting ideas on possible advancements from the administrators. Respondents were then e-mailed a document containing seven tables summarizing the results of the coaches' survey. Respondents were asked to add to the electronic document their comments and ideas for further development of their sport. They were instructed to write about specific practices that resulted in high ratings and to make suggestions on how the low ratings be improved. Follow-up calls were then made to guide respondents through the e-mailed information and ensure that the administrators understood where and how to add their comments. After the written responses were received via e-mail, additional calls were made in cases where typed comments were not clear, to confirm a respondent's point of view or details of given examples. The online responses were read and analyzed verbatim in the words that were received. This permitted a valid, accurate analysis of that data.

Table 4.1 Interview Framework for Studies on Tennis, Rugby, and Soccer

	Tennis	*Rugby*	*Soccer*
Regional heads	5	5	5
Science/research administrators	1	Nil	2
National development administrators/ CEO	1	1	Nil

Further qualitative information about rugby in the United States was obtained from five of the seven Territorial Rugby Union presidents or vice presidents and the USA Rugby CEO through semi-structured telephone interviews and e-mails. Administrators were first contacted by telephone. They were given an introduction to the research and the Model and asked their opinion about the current USA Rugby practices on the seven elements of the Model and how these practices could be advanced. These responses were recorded and then transcribed together with the more detailed written feedback, which the administrators were asked to provide.

Finally, five USA Soccer regional presidents and two research administrators provided interviews and written comments regarding problematic issues and the further advancement of U.S. soccer. The data handling was the same as for U.S. tennis described above.

Content analysis of open-responses from surveys and interviews

The analysis of the responses within the survey and data from the feedback given by top administrators was completed through a content analysis. Content analysis as used here is a way of coding or classifying different oral, written, or other observed types of communications within a conceptual framework to order the materials being observed (Babbie, 1989). The conceptual framework in this case is the Model. Further, according to Babbie, we obtained both depth (viz. validity) and specificity of understanding (viz. reliability) from the written and oral responses and from the survey replies. That is, the manifest content derived from the oral responses can be easily understood as they are part of the latent conceptual framework.

As the open responses followed the three levels and seven elements of the Model, it simplified classification of the data. This enabled us to report percentages of coaches expressing similar perceptions and to identify verbatim comments from coaches and administrators indicating commonly agreed concerns and suggestions for improvement. For example, Table 4.2 displays the common themes/descriptions from the open responses given by U.S. tennis coaches from Micro Level, Element 6 – Talent Identification and Development (Smolianov & Gallo, 2011).

These themes supported by the content analysis provide in depth information to supplement the quantitative survey data for this element (see Table 4.9). They also indicate a ranking of dimensions that have greater import and salience for improvement or use in U.S. tennis. Together the qualitative and quantitative data established a valid and reliable basis for discussion of how sport in the United States might improve its operations and structures.

Content analysis of organizational documents and Web sites

The second main area of qualitative analysis was of internal and external organizational communication processes. Unobtrusive content analysis of strategic

Table 4.2 Results from micro-level, talent identification and development responses by tennis officials (Smolianov & Gallo, 2011; relates to Table 4.9)

Theme / Description	#	%
The need of experienced coaches at the beginner level	21	22.34
It is too expensive to play tennis	20	21.28
Competition faced from other sports such as football, basketball, baseball, and soccer	13	13.83
Send out experts to look for talented tennis players	13	13.83
Improving the system of tennis in the U.S. in general	8	8.51
Poor coordination between different levels of coaching	7	7.45
Players need to be motivated and committed, and supported by their family and coaches	4	4.26
Limit scholarships given to international students and give priority to U.S. citizens	4	4.26
Coaches and players should be well paid	2	2.13
Tennis should be implemented in high schools	2	2.13
Total responses	94	100

#-number of open responses mentioning this issue
%-percent of the total open responses for this element

plans, minutes of meetings, policies, manuals, e-mail communications, and other variably available documents followed. All of these documents provided insight into an organization's culture and the unwritten values and goals that operate. Organizational Web sites have become a major tool for internal and external communications. One can easily analyze the content of an organization's Web site to gain insights into its operations and foci.

We conducted a qualitative analysis of the internal and external communication processes of each sport's national governing organizations, plus the professional bodies for tennis and soccer sites (United States Professional Tennis Association and United States Soccer Federation). The information for rugby was obtained by Mark Carney during his internship work for USA Rugby's CEO Nigel Melville at the organization's headquarters in Colorado Springs. For U.S. soccer, Peter Smolianov obtained similar information from USA Soccer through his personal contacts with USA Soccer administrators. He obtained documentation and directions to search the organization's Web site. This gave access to such materials as U.S. Soccer (2011) *Annual General Meeting Notes*, which included the full year 2012 budget of this NGB, and the *Best Practices for Coaching Soccer in the United States*, which included their *Player Development Guidelines* (U.S. Soccer, 2012). Finally, for U.S. tennis, Joe Gallo obtained organizational and member documents through his professional contacts with NCAA, USTA, and USPTA administration personnel.

The documents sought for each sport organization included annual reports, audited financial statements,[2] strategic plans, analyses and examples of best-practice plans, participation models and programs to increase participation, member journals, coaching manuals, media reports, and research reports. These documents were mainly obtained through the primary Web sites of the three organizations. Web sites of related state and regional sport governing bodies, such as Utah Tennis, Mid-Atlantic Rugby Football Union, and Nebraska State Soccer Association, were also analyzed.

The organizational documents mentioned above were searched for specific themes and then examined using conceptual and relational content analysis, as described previously for the interview and open responses. Themes used for conceptual examination included the seven elements of the Model. Relational content analysis was used to investigate how the analyzed organizations considered the seven themes/elements in regard to existing elite and mass sport development programs, policies, structures, and for potential future developments.

Each Web site was analyzed starting with the content of the "home" page. This content provides an insight into the key foci for each organization. Descriptions of the home page content could then be compared to the Model to understand where that organization aligned with or varied from the Model. There was an immediate indication of the key external relationships in this analysis and super- and subordinate organizations, from international through state/regional to local club levels. The last key element of the home page surrounds the links listed on this page. These links indicate the key areas each organization sees as important to its strategic plan, its vision and mission, its values, and program areas of import.

Analysis of each link also provided a deeper understanding of each organization's activity in terms of the integration of mass and elite sport. These links incorporated the following sport activities: organization, governance, strategic plan, finances, media, and best practices/how to coach. Table 4.3 provides the lists of links for each of the sports studied.

Though many of these links have become standardized in business-oriented sport, there are some that clearly indicate alignments with the Model.

Practices of U.S. tennis against the Model

The tennis survey was delivered online to a total sample of 398 individuals involved in USTA and other tennis bodies. A total of 107 (27 percent) valid surveys resulted. This was an acceptable response rate for online surveys. Respondents to the tennis survey proved to be diverse, both in terms of the level of players they coached and in their state of residence.

The survey participants had an average of 21.7 years of coaching experience and were coaching in fourteen of the seventeen USTA geographical sections. Forty-nine percent of respondents coached beginners, 31.7 percent coached nationally ranked players, 37.6 percent coached collegiate players, and 5 percent

Table 4.3 Key links for each of the sports studied

	Tennis	Rugby	Soccer
Home page	www.usta.com	http://usarugby.org	www.ussoccer.com
Organization and Governance	www.USta.com/About-USTA/Organization/Organization	http://usarugby.org/committees	www.ussoccer.com/about/about-home/organizational-structure/member-organizations.aspx
Strategic Plan	http://assets.USta.com/assets/1/USTA_Import/dps/USta_master/sitecore_USta/USTA/Document%20Assets/2008/07/09/USTA%20STRATEGIC%20DIRECTIONS%2010%2028%2007.pdf	http://usarugby.org/about-usarugby/strategic-plan	www.ussoccer.com/about/governance/committees.aspx
Financials	http://assets.USta.com/assets/1/15/USTA120908-Association_FINAL_SIGNED_COPY.pdf	http://usarugby.org/about-usarugby/financial-statements	www.USsoccer.com/About/Federation-Services/Resource-Center/Financial-Information.aspx
Media	www.florida.USta.com/news/?intloc=headernav	http://usarugby.org/news	www.USsoccer.com/News/News-Landing.aspx
Best Practices/ how to coach	www.USta.com/Coaches-Organizers/?intloc=headernav www.USta.com/About-USTA/Organization/Best-Practices/8365_USTA_Best_Practices/	http://usarugby.org/coaching	www.USsoccer.com/coaches/resources.aspx
Examples of sub organizations	www.newengland.USta.com www.intermountain.USta.com www.florida.USta.com	www.pacificcoastrugby.com http://rugbynortheast.org www.USarugbysouth.com	www.ntxsoccer.org www.osysa.com www.arkansassoccer.org

coached professionals. Seventy-four percent of respondents were certified by at least one governing body for tennis teaching professionals (USPTA, Professional Tennis Registry [PTR], and/or USTA).

Tennis (as does golf) has many organizational bodies governing the sport. There are the now traditional NGBs from the State and national levels through to its International Federations. Likewise, parallel bodies for professional players and coaches exist through these same levels. All of these organizations often do not clearly demarcate themselves in reality. This makes the interlocking organizational map for tennis very messy. The reader must be aware of the organization being written about in this and the sections on soccer.

Initiatives by the USTA—such as Tennis Welcome Centers, QuickStart Tennis[3] for kids ten and younger, and an infrastructure that supports development and consumer connections—are all making tennis one of the fastest growing sports in twenty-first century United States (USTA, 2010). The ever-improving quality of international competition demands, however, concerted player development efforts from the United States to remain a top tennis nation. Analysis of February 2014 Association of Tennis Profession rankings showed that among the top 50 male tennis players: 28 players were from Western Europe, 12 were from former Warsaw Pact or Yugoslavian countries,[4] nine were from other parts of the world, and only one was from the USA (ATP, 2014).'The current strength of Spain and France are evident in these rankings as they each have eight players among the top fifty (32%) and of the current United States demise in men's tennis. In the women's world rankings U.S. tennis players are much more represented in the top fifty spots. There are seven U.S. women (including the number one player), with fewer from the former "communist" countries (22) and Western European (15) than in the men's, in these rankings (plus three from China and three from other parts of the world) (WTA, 2014). The United States is not dominating at the global elite level as it had in recent years.

According to the USTA (2009), tennis participation in the United States reached 30 million players in 2008, but the Sporting Goods Manufacturers Association (2012) estimated that only about 18 million played once or more in 2008 and 2011. Demick and Haas (2011) reported that there were an estimated 14 million tennis participants in China around this time, which is a growing pool from which high-level competitive players can be drawn. The number of Russian amateur players has become similar to that of the USTA membership of 700,000 (Russian Tennis Federation, personal communication, April 3, 2013; USTA, personal communication, December 14, 2012). When tennis again became an Olympic medal sport in 1988, many countries increased investment in both mass participation and high-performance tennis, including long-standing rival Russia and new key rival China.

There are also more nations competing at the elite level, particularly after the disintegration of Central and Eastern European socialist countries into smaller independent states. For the most part, these countries retain elements of their elaborate Soviet-style sport systems where high-performance sport is integrated with mass participation. U.S. tennis is well known for its productive tennis academies and university programs. These sites are businesses that attract top international talent, that further advance the development of U.S. players with quality competition and through sharing of global practices.

We claim that the Model posits an integrated system and specific transferable international practices that would advance tennis in the United States and positively influence both international performance and public health through mass participation. To this end, we examined the current state of U.S. tennis against the Model. Below is the summary of how U.S. tennis aligns with and varies from the Model and where changes might be advisable.

Element 1: Balanced and integrated funding and structures of mass and elite sport

An analysis of organizational structures and systems of funding (see Table 4.4) contained 11 desired practices (variables) for improvement in U.S. tennis. This element was one of two in this sport that had clear and strong indications of what was lacking. There were five variables (#1, 2, 3, 5, 7) where a majority of respondents felt a gap existed. Conversely, there were only two variables (#4, 8), on which respondents (albeit slightly less than 50 percent of respondents) felt the desired practices existed in U.S. tennis to some extent.

Of the negative/lacking responses, two (#1, 3) are institutional in nature and related to the federal government. That is, these are legislative-specific matters that demand a change in the tax structure of government. Whether this is possible under current circumstances is questionable. Two other institutional variables (#2,5) surround education-related tennis opportunities. The second variable shows that more needs to be done in PE programs. This was also the case for the expansion of tennis academies.

Three variables (#7, 8, 9) exhibit near or equal responses for the negative and positive categories if one looks only at these figures. Of particular interest are the results of the seventh and eighth practices. There is a very strong bifurcation of the tennis communities around affordable programs for all and the nature of the tennis playing population. More research is required on why there is such a split in how these desired practices are viewed.

Overall and based on an $N = 107$, 43 percent responded negative/lacking, 37 percent were neutral, and 20 percent responded positive/existing in their perceptions of whether these desired practices existed.

Sixteen coaches in their open responses indicated that tennis was too expensive for mass participation and more financial support is needed. Based on the USTA Financial Statements (2010), the USTA generated $267 million in 2009, of which 90 percent (or $205 million) was generated through the U.S. Open and other elite event takings. Mass participation income such as membership fees and community tennis sponsorships amounted to more than $20 million, but this was less than 10 percent of the overall USTA revenue (USTA Financial Statements, 2010). The USTA's spending on mass tennis of almost $100 million, or about 40 percent of all income, is quite generous, especially when almost $75 million was devoted to

Table 4.4 Results of tennis survey, Level 1 – Balanced and integrated funding and structures of mass and elite sport (Smolianov, Gallo, & Naylor, 2014)

Desired Practices	Average Score	Distribution of Responses		
		Negative/ Lacking (%)	Neutral (%)	Positive/ Existing (%)
1. Corporate and philanthropic tax incentives provide sufficient support of mass and elite tennis	2.0	52	47	1
2. Participation in various sports, as a foundation for tennis development, is encouraged through physical education requirements	2.7	46	39	15
3. Sport participation, including tennis, is rewarded with reduced personal tax	1.5	69	30	1
4. Tennis programs service both recreational and high performance players	3.4	17	39	44
5. Specialized sport schools similar to the IMG Academies are available and affordable to all talented players	2.1	72	25	3
6. A multi-stage system of elite tennis player qualification is integrated with a system of fitness tests for mass participants such as the President's Challenge Awards Program	2.3	39	56	5
7. Programs affordable for all are available in various tennis clubs	2.4	51	3	46
8. Tennis participants are diverse as the general population	2.8	42	11	47
9. USTA demonstrates systematic/strategic management in developing tennis on every level	3.0	23	54	23
10. USTA is effective in fostering both mass participation and high performance in tennis	2.9	28	54	18
11. Tennis is developed in integration with Olympic and Paralympic sports to achieve sustainable competitive excellence	2.7	32	54	14
Percentage across all items in element (based on N=107 for each row)		43	37	20

community tennis (USTA Financial Statements, 2010). Additional funding from new sources could be attracted to the $15 million spent on athlete development to assist more participants to attain HP levels and to bring the portion of mass tennis expenditures closer to half of all the USTA budget for a more ideal balance for tennis development. More resources could, therefore, be devoted to systematic development and support of coaches and programs offering affordable conditions for long-term athlete progression in each community.

The key underlying sentiment of surveyed tennis coaches and administrators was that more money be devoted to the advancement of all elements of the tennis development system. The USTA appears to be in a good position to invest in these developments. In contrast with almost all other professional sports leagues and events, the U.S. Open escaped the financial wrath of the "Great Recession," generating more than $200 million a year in 2008–2010 (Weil, 2010). Event attendance in 2013 was more than 700,000 for the sixth time in its history (USTA, 2014). We also know that the median income of the spectators was $150,000, while gross sponsorship revenue rose six percent in 2010 to a record of $60 million, and corporate entertaining continued to increase with a record 157 companies purchasing hospitality packages in 2010 (Weil, 2010). As the U.S. Open retains wealthy customers and premium product sponsors, it would be wise to develop new sources of USTA funding, new partnerships, and new participant and coach support structures.

Administrator D (March 10, 2011) reflected other administrators' opinions: "I feel helping kids play tennis and making it more affordable is a major area we need to address… If you want your child to be a high level player you must spend quite a bit of money." An example of making tennis affordable has been demonstrated by the Acadia Community Tennis (ACT) in Ellsworth, ME, which is a nonprofit, tax-exempt tennis organization established to fund and foster tennis programs for children who could otherwise not afford to participate. Offering year-round programs for young people aged five to seventeen years, the ACT can charge as little as $5 for a weekly tennis lesson, depending on demonstrated financial need. This is similar to what one would pay for a swimming lesson at the YM/WCA (Fenceviewer, 2012). The challenge is to ensure quality coaching at an affordable price, which might be achieved by the USTA providing grant dollars based on best-practice community partnerships and establishing such partnerships across the nation to make tennis more accessible to all interested persons.

Another way to increase accessibility and fund tennis would be through changes to government taxation methods. This method is used by other countries to enhance access to sports that have a significant cost component. Yet, of all survey statements (see Table 4.4), the lowest rating (2.0/5) was given to the following statement: "Sport participation, including tennis, is rewarded with reduced personal tax." This indicates that overall it is not seen as a way to fund tennis in the United States. Many coaches agreed with Administrator A's[5] (February 18, 2011) statement that "it would be ideal if the government provided tax incentives for people that [sic] are developing athletes." The USTA could take the lead and promote this idea with other NGBs that are under the USOC umbrella to help government departments consider tax incentives that mimic other countries' sport development tax for both mass sport (Canada Revenue Agency, 2007; Fitzpatrick, 2011) and elite sport (Brazil's 2014 World Cup events of FIFA [2011]).

Another low-rated statement was "specialized sport schools similar to IMG Academies are available and affordable to all talented players." Seventy-two percent of coaches indicated that these situations never or rarely exist, but they noted that it was a desirable component of player development. Such progressive practices in sport schools and academies seem to be evident in Eastern Europe, China, and Cuba (Fetisov, 2005; Rhoden, 1991; Riordan, 1978, 1980; Smolianov, 2013; Smolianov & Zakus, 2008; Tan & Green, 2008). Such schools are more recent developments in Australia and the United Kingdom (BBC, 2004a, 2004b; Davies, 2008; Wynhausen, 2007) and could serve as models for the U.S. player development system, generally and specifically for tennis.

To improve organization and funding for the public sport school system in the United States, best international practices could be integrated with experiences of the IMG and other academies and "prep" schools. Top coaches from such schools as the IMG in Florida, Spartak in Moscow, and TeamBath in the United Kingdom could be employed to develop a network of sport schools in each U.S. state. The tennis school system must provide quality services, starting with coaching for every interested U.S. tennis player. As Administrator B (February 23, 2011) put it,

> the coaches who are well trained … charge significant fees for their service. There should be assistance to players that show a strong aptitude for the sport. Ten and under tennis should give greater exposure to more people at a younger age, which will give us a better opportunity to help those that show promise at 12–14 years of age.

There were thirty-six full-time tennis academies similar to the IMG Academy and about sixty different summer tennis academies for children of all ages across the United States in 2012 (mybesttennis.com, 2012). As part of a hierarchical tennis program system, special sport schools, academies, and clubs in each municipality could offer every interested person easy access to an affordable, well-educated coach. These coaches could then nurture participants from pre-school through several years of fitness and technical training into competitive tennis at school and college, on to high performance for some before gradually helping all of these participants into recreational play in their later years. Additional partnerships could provide conditions for progression as was demonstrated in many sports in the United Kingdom after lottery funding was introduced and the government increased its support to both mass and elite sport in the two decades prior to the 2012 London Olympics Games.

A well-established national network of tennis programs at public schools should improve ratings on program affordability and availability, thus making tennis participants as diverse as the general U.S. population. Greater integration with public education could also help advance tennis in underdeveloped regions and urban areas. It is important to have strong child/youth programs to develop skills for high school and tournament tennis. USTA's QuickStart program is expanding and could be brought to students of all elementary and middle schools. The consensus of our survey respondents was that lack of funds is the biggest obstacle for tennis development although the USTA makes considerable contributions in several ways. Given the country's wealth, the USTA should consider the U.S. Open income only as seed funding for maximizing both public and private funding sources, taking into account successful international experiences from countries such as Canada and China.

A low survey evaluation rating was also given to mass participation encouraged through PE. Better organized and implemented tennis programs could be brought to schools and child care centers by integrating tennis into the PE curriculum. In recognition of this, USTA developed an Internet-based *Physical Educators Guide for Teaching Tennis in Schools* (Middlestates.usta.com, 2012). USTA sport scientists could work with other sports specialists to recommend a plan for each PE class at each grade level. The USTA schools program could also introduce more comprehensive curriculum plans through synergies with other sports such as gymnastics, track and field, swimming, and some team sports.

As Administrator C (March 3, 2011) said, "We need to bring tennis to more schools. It's a sport for lifetime fitness. Tennis teaching professionals can adopt a school and help PE teachers unfamiliar with tennis. I know USTA does [sic] some of this but we could do more...." As mentioned above, the best coaches in each state could establish a network of schools with a strong tennis emphasis. Connecting top-level coaches with schools ensures that the maximum numbers of children are taught to play tennis and talent-predisposed children are nurtured to become high-performance players. Grant money could be paid to teaching professionals based on the performance results of the players whom they develop.

Together with advancing tennis in schools, it is important to develop a multi-stage system of elite tennis player qualification integrated with a system of fitness tests for all participants. A lack of such integration was reflected in the low rating of this statement. The USTA could further integrate tennis with fitness and performance testing, perhaps through further development of the President's Challenge Awards Program. Through a pyramidal system of competitions, individuals could win President's Challenge awards in general fitness, drills, and tennis. This could attract more beginners to tennis and generally make tennis players fitter.

Element 2: Partnerships with supporting agencies

Coaches' responses were highly neutral in this element (see Table 4.5). Five of the six desired practices (#2, 3, 4, 5, 6) elicited neutral responses. The only variable with a clear result was variable 1, which indicated that 60 percent of respondents felt government support for player development was inadequate (negative/lacking). Responses to variables 3 and 5 indicated that over 30 percent of respondents felt these practices were lacking. Overall, positive responses to the presence of partnerships were low, positive ratings of the second and fourth variables of around 30 percent being the only highlights.

Table 4.5 Results of tennis survey, Level 2 – Partnerships with supporting agencies (Smolianov, Gallo, & Naylor, 2014)

Desired Practices	Average Score	Distribution of Responses		
		Negative/ Lacking (%)	Neutral (%)	Positive/ Existing (%)
1. Support for tennis player development is adequate from various levels of government	2.1	60	34	6
2. Sufficient help is obtained from bodies which govern tennis and provide coach education and certification (e.g., USOC, USTA, USTPA, USPTR)	3.0	29	42	29
3. Role of clubs/community programs in tennis development is sound	2.8	37	47	16
4. Tennis is well supported by the educational sector (e.g., schools, colleges, universities)	3.1	23	46	31
5. Cooperation with agencies outside of sport industry (e.g., medical, scientific, military, philanthropic and sponsoring organizations, lotteries) is in place	2.5	40	56	4
6. USTA influences media coverage and popularity of tennis to increase support from the society	3.1	22	52	26
Percentage across all items in element (based on N=107 for each row)		35	46	19

Of particular interest, if we do not include the neutral responses, is how the tennis community replied to whether tennis NGBs and tennis coaching organizations provide sufficient help. Variable 2 shows that 29 percent see this as lacking while the same numbers see it as existing. These bodies might wish to look into this split. Also, the same situation exists for practice six on media coverage and the popularity of tennis. Why is this so?

In terms of the overall average category of response on this element, 35 percent were in the negative/lacking, 46 percent were in the neutral, and 19 percent were in the positive/existing category. Again, the neutral category appears to indicate that uncertainty surrounds whether these practices occur.

Coach 60 (January 21, 2010) indicated that "USTA is making a focused effort to reach out and work with many related agencies," Coaches 35 (February 16, 2010), 45 (February 16, 2010), 55 (January 22, 2010), 57 (January 21, 2010),

70 (January 20, 2010), and 99 (January 20, 2010) agreed that relations between USTA and supporting agencies should be improved. Coach 107 (November 19, 2009) stressed that there is "not enough cooperation and coordination between high schools, USTA, and tennis club programs," while Coaches 44 (February 16, 2010), 51 (January 24, 2010), 64 (January 20, 2010), and 70 (January 20, 2010) agreed that tennis should be better promoted through media.

The USTA has partnered with communities through its regional branches and through using the donations they receive for programs. The USTA's Adopt-A-School is a program that allows tennis advocates to donate money to help institute tennis in PE, after-school tennis programs, and no-cut school tennis teams for all levels of play. The USTA Pacific Northwest Partnership Program, for example, is an investment in communities with priorities of 10 and Under Tennis, USTA Junior Team Tennis, and other local team-based play opportunities with QuickStart Tennis in schools, clubs, sport facilities, and infrastructure development (USTA, 2012). Another example is the Mid-Atlantic Tennis and Education Foundation (MATEF), which conducted a six-week Introduction to Tennis Program for wounded war veterans and their families. MATEF also introduced a QuickStart program at a school for special needs children, providing equipment, a curriculum (thirty-five-page manual with lesson plans), and teaching aides to the school to introduce tennis in their PE program (USTA, 2012). Finally, the USTA might also extend QuickStart to pre-school programs through child care franchises and kindergartens in the vicinity of tennis clubs.

While indicating that "the corporate community does provide a great deal of financial support for mass and elite tennis," Administrator A (February 18, 2011) believed that the "USTA could do even better in fostering participation if it was willing to adopt a friendlier stance with other programs within the industry," and stressed that the U.S. government provides little to no funding for tennis player development. The USTA, colleges, parents, and coaches provide the major support. Administrator D (March 10, 2011) agreed that tennis players get virtually no help from the government and also stressed that communities really do not get involved in the development of players except in extreme cases of financial and social need. Administrator B (February 23, 2011) suggested that the main role the government can play is in the form of education funding that is earmarked for PE and the development of life skills:

> Fostering a good relationship between schools, communities, and clubs is the job of all of the governing bodies of tennis. Eliminating barriers both economically and socially will allow the sport to reach a greater population group. USTA should actively seek funding from the private sector to sponsor developing programs [sic].

At the local level, governments, schools, colleges, universities, communities, and businesses can provide better support and build more facilities if partnerships are fostered between clubs and NGBs that offer programs and organize events at these facilities. The USTA's Community Partnership Investment Grants, ranging from

$35,000 to $70,000, are awarded to organizations seeking to establish and develop community-based partnerships, to support tennis programming and equipment needs, and to match the USTA's financial investment over a three-year period (*Tennis Panorama News*, 2011). Matching funds is a great concept but, in many cases, it is not just money but the expertise and hands-on assistance to local leaders that are needed for building partnerships.

The role of clubs and community programs in tennis development can be increased. As well, assistance from organizations that govern tennis, provide coach education, certification, and manage media coverage of the game could be extended. Tennis would benefit with organizations both within their internal and external environments.

Element 3: Educational, scientific, medical, philosophical, and promotional support

Coaches indicated that the communication of sportsmanship and Olympism is the least common practice within this complex, varied element (see Table 4.6). Of the six desired practices, four were mostly identified neutral (#1, 3, 5, 6). The variable on sportsmanship and other background information (#4) was predominantly rated negative/lacking, but there also was a strong neutral response to this complex variable. Finally, the variable on USTA research (#2) was seen as positive by almost half the respondents, but neutral responses were almost equal in number.

Variable 3, if one ignores the neutral responses for the moment, shows that negative and positive responses were equal. It is interesting that those who made a clear choice of their perception felt that the communication of research results was both lacking and existing to the same degree. Likewise, variable 5 exhibits similar response rates for the way the USTA's communication adds to participants outcomes. Finally, the sixth variable shows less of a balance between the negative and positive results but does indicate an ambivalence of the tennis community about the USTA's vision and leadership. These results require more research to understand the underlying dynamic.

In terms of the overall average results by category, 47 percent indicated a neutral perception, 25 percent indicated that the desired elements were lacking, and 28 percent saw some aspects of the elements existing.

The issues that generated most open responses among both coaches and administrators related to education and research. The need for better tennis education using high-quality material was indicated by five coaches in their open responses. While one coach commented that the "USTA is very good at informing the membership" (Coach 97, January 20, 2010), four coaches suggested in their open responses that there is lack of communication, that tennis needs to be more promoted within every community, and that more coaching clinics should be implemented. The USTA, the USPTA, the United States High School Tennis Association, and other organizations offer coach certification and education; but their cooperation for a more uniform and integrated system of coach support could be improved by incorporating the useful experiences of other successful

Table 4.6 Results of tennis survey, Level 3 – Educational, scientific, medical, philosophical, and promotional support (Smolianov, Gallo, & Naylor, 2014)

Desired Practices	Average Score	Distribution of Responses		
		Negative/ Lacking (%)	Neutral (%)	Positive/ Existing (%)
1. All specialists engaged in the development of tennis players are well educated for their professional roles	3.2	16	55	29
2. USTA fosters research on all important aspects of tennis development	3.6	8	43	49
3. Research results are well communicated to coaches (e.g., by research institutes, universities, and USTA)	3.0	24	52	24
4. Principles of sportsman like conduct and Olympism and Olympic tennis history are communicated well (e.g., through mass media, school education, and through the arts as part of tennis events)	2.3	49	41	10
5. USTA's communication contributes to national values and identity by inspiring participants to strive for excellence, to show the best results and character in the world	3.0	27	48	25
6. The USTA provides vision and leadership in improving all aspects of the participants' wellbeing through tennis (e.g., physical, social, emotional, mental, spiritual, and environmental/ecological)	3.1	25	45	30
Percentage across all items in element (based on N=107 for each row)		25	47	28

tennis nations from Australia to Russia. Three coaches also commented on lack of funding in this area. Agreeing with most other respondents, Administrator D (March 10, 2011) indicated that "not all coaches are well educated in their roles and professional organizations should work with them."

Administrator A (February 18, 2011) noted that the "USTA does not fund or ask for research in tennis development. It relies on the ITF and/or TIA or other organizations...." Administrator B (February 23, 2011) agreed that little money is designated for research to enhance the sport. He also observed that "most of the breakthroughs in this area have been made by individuals outside the system" and suggested that "if more grants are available for these innovators more progress could be made." For the United States to dominate in the global tennis arena, the USTA and sport scientists from major universities that focus on tennis-specific research must collaborate. Also, to be a world leader in tennis education and science, best practices from rival progressive countries such as Australia, China, Germany, and Russia must be examined and adopted when appropriate.

One administrator believed that "the principles of conduct and tennis history are for the most part communicated to players in their schools and homes. Parents and coaches play a larger leadership role than the USTA" (Administrator A, February 18, 2011). He also suggested that "in order to improve the area of conduct, stricter rules and enforcement are necessary." The USTA together with the USOC could work with school curriculum developers to better educate all children about sportsmanship, the ethics of tennis, and the Olympic movement.

Quality and usefulness, rather than quantity, of media and educational information on tennis, need improvement. Current participants whose involvement may be particularly reinforced through the media need more details and deeper analysis of the game by expert tennis commentators. Potential participants need to be attracted, persuaded, and given advice on how to start playing tennis with limited money, time, facilities, and coaching. Presentation of new forms of competition, drills, and exercises could be taught to the public through various national media. Daily mass media fitness and wellness instructions were used decades ago in the former USSR and are now used in China to increase mass participation and improve national health. The United States has employed the mass media on a limited basis to promote mass participation. Extending the use of this method of stimulating mass participation may be worthy of further investigation. Specific approaches include broadcasting tennis fitness breaks across U.S. TV and radio channels. This could occur during the U.S. Tennis Open, in particular, using famous players to feature elements of Cardio Tennis and Slam'n'Sweat (rather than just the standard tips for playing better tennis); by showing how to warm up, cool down, and stretch; and providing information on simple recovery and illness prevention methods.

Element 4: Domestic and international competitions

In this element, along with element five, all six variables had a neutral response as the most selected response (see Table 4.7). In all but two cases more than 50 percent of coaches chose the neutral category. Interestingly, three variables (#2, 3, 4,) were also selected as evident (positive/existing) by more than 30 percent of respondents. These variables included: the structure of competitions at all levels (#2), a sufficient amount of USTA support for development events (#3), and the USTA progressive integration of amateur and professional events for all levels (#4). Just under a third of coaches felt that there were sufficient international

Table 4.7 Results of tennis survey, Level 4 – Domestic and international competitions (Smolianov, Gallo, & Naylor, 2014)

Desired Practices	Average Score	Distribution of Responses		
		Negative/ Lacking (%)	Neutral (%)	Positive/ Existing (%)
1. Hosted international events and international opportunities are sufficient for all athletes with potential to represent the country	2.9	29	53	18
2. Competitions are well structured at all levels (e.g., club/ training center, regional, and national)	3.3	16	48	36
3. USTA and its support mechanisms sufficiently assist in local and sectional developmental events (e.g., 14 and under regional)	3.2	20	45	35
4. USTA attempts to integrate professional and amateur tournaments into a progressive plan of competitions gradually preparing athletes for peak performance at "Majors", Paralympic Games, and Olympic Games	3.3	14	52	34
5. USTA tries to coordinate all domestic and international competitions for all ages and levels, between and within all possible organizations	3.3	11	61	28
6. Event sponsorship incomes are used to develop competitions for all participation levels	2.9	20	68	12
Percentage across all items in element (based on N=107 for each row)		18	55	27

opportunities and events available for all athletes (#1) and there was USTA co-ordination of domestic and international competitions for all levels and organizations (#5).

Overall, the average for this element was 55 percent neutral. Twenty-seven percent indicated that the desired practices existed to a degree and 18 percent rated the practices as lacking. These results indicate that competitions are not as problematic as the other surveyed elements.

In their open responses related to competition systems, four coaches indicated that more tournaments are needed, while eight coaches believed that it is too expensive to compete and more funds should be devoted to the development of competitions.

Together with the strong responses on this element, Administrator A (February 18, 2011) indicated that, "given the size of the USA, we need a greater number of international events and opportunities for players. This could be done by having more of the income derived from the U.S. Open used for this purpose." International events with the strongest competitors should be organized both in tennis, where U.S. Open income can be utilized, and as part of multi-sport events, where costs could be shared with other NGBs, the USOC, and hosting communities, ideally in locations where the sport is developing.

He went on to note that the USTA relies too much on volunteer help to conduct events. More resources need to be devoted to expansion, improvement, and affordability of tennis competitions staffed with paid individuals. The USTA should be developing self-sustaining events rather than just funding them from the U.S. Open budget, no matter how stable the U.S. Open income. So, what kinds of events could be developed?

Several coaches agreed in their comments that there should be more entry-level events and tournaments with prize money of $10,000 and $15,000 to allow players to fully transition into the professional ranks. This is especially so for women's tennis, where there are many $25,000, $50,000, and $75,000 tournaments, but not as many $10,000 prize entry-level events. A good comparison in this regard would be Spain, where players trying to make it to the professional level have opportunities to play a pro-entry-level tournament almost every week (Coach, 109, October 10, 2010).

In the first decade of the twenty-first century, the USTA more than doubled its number of national tournaments. The USTA and the International Tennis Federation (ITF) further professionalized the junior tournament circuit in 2004 by enacting a professional ranking system that awarded players points for advancing through rounds in tournaments. The more competitions a player enters, the greater his or her opportunity is to accrue points. Total participation has increased. The junior section competitions in the four tennis majors now use the ITF world junior rankings.

This offers junior-level players access to tournaments in the United States and 120 other countries. This gives plenty of opportunity, however, these tournaments overlap with the USTA schedule and draw players away. This "event clutter" and heavy practice schedule predisposes players to chronic physical exhaustion and injuries and illnesses associated with over-use and overtraining (Johnson, 2009). Patrick McEnroe, USTA's general manager of player development, seems to agree that it is important to improve the system but not to increase the number of youth competitions: "We have to create competition at the 8- to-12-year-old level that is inexpensive and local, with no travel. We have got to make it a game you can play while staying home and being in high school" (quoted in Alfano, 2011).

Coaches particularly commented that the USTA needs to concentrate on junior players rather than on those who are already elite. Reid, Crespo and Dimmock (2007) stressed the importance of the junior boys' circuit in the development of professional tennis players. Toward this end, amateur and professional competitions could be better integrated as Administrator B (February 23, 2011) said that elite players must currently decide if they are going to play USTA or ITF tournaments, explaining that

> you are penalized if you try to play both because they are separate ranking systems. If you can blend the two ranking systems it would provide more opportunities for international competition for U.S. players. To play just ITF tournaments without support is financially impossible for most families. Solve this issue and there will be more Americans [sic] in College Division I teams populating the top 100 pro rankings.

One coach also suggested that ITF and ATP rankings could coincide with college and university rankings (Coach 50, January 24, 2010).

Amateur, Olympic, and semi-professional event schedules must be integrated with professional tennis schedules. This will permit the development of monthly and yearly competition plans for each age group, to develop participants gradually and consistently without burning players out. The USTA, in consultation with sport scientists, could plan a calendar of competitions with progressive difficulty for each level and type of participation; for each geographic, demographic, and psychographic target market.

To integrate mass and elite sport for public health, a system of competitions for teams representing each organization and community across the country could be developed where, together with victories, each team receives points for their number of participants. Identifying that U.S. tennis might be struggling with the popularity of tournaments outside the U.S. Open, Sagatomo, Miller and Naeger (2011) suggested that the 27 million tennis participants, who could be core consumers of minor tournaments, should be given the opportunity to play on the same courts that the professionals play on: a key prerequisite for the integration of mass and elite sport development.

Element 5: Training centers and multi-facility activity hubs

A consistent problem cited in the survey was that national, regional, and local training centers are not accessible or available to athletes at affordable costs (see Table 4.8). This element, as also noted above for Element 4, had strongly neutral results. There were, however, two variables that more than 30 percent of respondents saw as being sufficiently evident. These were variables 1 and 2: access to quality equipment (#1) and facilities (#2). On the other hand, four variables (#3, 4, 6, 7) had a negative response rate of more than 30 percent. These practices related to the lack of affordable training centers at different locations, the long time needed to travel to training sites, and the lack of proximity of training sites to other sport facilities.

Again, the overall combined average for all variables in this element indicated an uncertainty about whether the desired practices exist. Fifty-six percent of

Table 4.8 Results of tennis survey, Level 5 – Training centers and multi-facility activity hubs (Smolianov, Gallo, & Naylor, 2014)

Desired Practices	Average Score	Distribution of Responses		
		Negative/ Lacking (%)	Neutral (%)	Positive/ Existing (%)
1. High performance athletes are provided with priority access to specific high quality equipment and facilities	3.4	12	49	39
2. Training centers provide specialized facilities and equipment for each age and level of participation	3.2	15	54	31
3. All national, regional, and local training centers are available to athletes at affordable costs	2.6	39	50	11
4. Travel from home to training facilities takes little time for players of all levels and types	2.5	47	49	4
5. Training facilities are close to all facilities for athlete support (e.g., school/college, medical, room & board, leisure/ entertainment)	2.9	22	64	14
6. A network of training centers is used to prepare players in different environments/socio geo-climates (e.g., high altitude/ temperature/humidity, city/ pollution, rural/resort)	2.4	39	57	4
7. Tennis training centers are located close to other sport facilities so that players participate in and learn from other sports	2.7	31	65	4
Percentage across all items in element (based on N=107 for each row)		29	56	15

coaches responded in a neutral way to the variables in this element. Fifteen percent saw some practices occurring while 29 percent saw them as lacking.

Sixteen coaches indicated in their open responses that more training centers are needed, while an additional seven said that more coaches need to be hired to work in these facilities. Eight coaches also said, as noted above, that more funds should be devoted to make tennis less expensive. It was stressed by Administrator A (February 18, 2011) that unless a player is part of a USTA national training program, he or she must pay for coaching and manage preparation for competitions without sufficient support.

In 2007 the USTA centralized its national player development program at the Evert Tennis Academy in Boca Raton, Florida. This integrated complex features twenty-three courts (fourteen lighted), dormitories, video lounge, and a staff of thirty, including a mental-conditioning coach. Tuition with room and board costs as much as $42,000 per year (Coyle, 2007). To improve affordability and attract the talented underprivileged, USTA's newly created eight regional training centers, and other tennis centers in the future, could possibly give all gifted players opportunities for development by subsidizing facility use, coaching, schooling, and room and board costs. An example of a national network of comprehensive regional training centers available for all ages and socioeconomic groups can be found in Cuba.

In the former USSR and now in Russia, the strategy has been to subsidize talented athletes, particularly from lower socioeconomic groups, from their first sport experiences, when they need direction, coaching, and financial support the most. The USTA is partnering with proven developmental programs throughout the country to provide free or subsidized high-performance training for its best junior tennis players. Regional training centers also have community outreach programs that work with local schools to establish QuickStart programming.

Significant improvement is needed with regard to transportation and the convenient location of facilities. According to Administrator D (March 10, 2011):

> Many families travel far to get the training that their children need. Not all players are provided with access to the same facilities. It depends on the part of the country. USTA has recently started regional training centers which should help give all qualified juniors better access to facilities and coaching.

The reliance on car transportation in the United States makes it difficult for most youths to travel to sport sites without the involvement of their parents. NGBs should work with transport authorities to improve access to training centers by public bus, trolleybus, tram, and subway/rail routes while encouraging new sport facilities closer to transport hubs.

The survey indicated that a network of training centers to prepare players in different environments and socio-geo-climates is also needed. Coaches suggested in their open responses that cooperation between tennis centers can be improved. The importance of utilizing Olympic Training Centers, particularly in Colorado Springs, was stressed by Administrator C (March 3, 2011). To improve and streamline cooperation between tennis centers, regular camps and competitions should be held for every age group, level of participant, and from all locations. Another possibility in this process could be an exchange program that rotates the hosting of camps and competitions at local, national, and international levels. In terms of elite players, simulations of the conditions and environment for major tennis events would provide all players representing the United States with maximal preparation.

Another area for improvement lies in the integration of training centers for tennis and other sports, as practiced at IMG Academies. It is important to share tennis facilities and athlete conditioning, sport science, and sport medical services with sport disciplines that have beneficial cross-over effects for the preparation of tennis players. Sports such as various racket sports, soccer, and baseball come to mind. The multi-sport Home Depot and Colorado Springs centers and other Olympic Training Centers, universities, colleges, and schools have great potential for such cooperation. As integration of general education with tennis is important for athlete development, one of the first considerations for tennis facility development should be the proximity of and cooperation with primary, middle, and high schools as well as colleges and universities. Administrator D (March 10, 2011) said that the regional training centers the USTA has recently started "should help give all kids equal playing ground with facilities." A variety of international practices could be used to advance the existing USTA training centers and develop new ones.

Element 6: Talent identification and development

Along with Element 2, this element had the clearest indication of which variables do and do not exist in U.S. tennis. Five of the ten variables (#1 3, 7, 8, 10) were most strongly seen as lacking and a further two (#5, 6) were also identified as lacking by more than 30 percent of coaches. As opposed to other elements, only two variables in Element 6 (#2, 6) were seen as highly neutral. Element 6 also evidenced the highest positive results. Positive perceptions related to: rewards based on age-group results/rankings, the monitoring/development of a national performance database, and offering top-ranked players full-time opportunities.

Observing the combined averages for each response category we see the most balanced results of all the tennis elements. Thirty-nine percent chose the negative/lacking category, 36 percent were neutral, and 25 percent chose the positive/existing category.

Administrator A (February 18, 2011) indicated that schools could provide a better avenue for kids to be introduced to tennis, but "schools are controlled by cities, counties, school districts, and school administrators. This makes it very difficult to coordinate and develop a national program when every area is different." The Quick Start and Under 10 (see footnote 3) are suitable programs for this level of participant and as a standardized program across the country.

In 2012 the USTA awarded more than $765,000 in Recreational Tennis Grants to twenty-two nonprofit organizations. These organizations were committed to increasing tennis participation, were well-established centers in their communities, had supported tennis programming, and were fostering diversity among their participants. Any type of nonprofit organization was encouraged to apply for these grants. Selected organizations included Community Tennis Associations, parks and recreation agencies, schools, and USTA National Junior Tennis and Learning Chapters. All funding recipients share the priority of providing: QuickStart/10 and Under Tennis programming, team tennis, and school tennis as part of PE, after-school, and summer tennis programs. Kurt Kamperman, chief executive of Community Tennis at the USTA, said that "these organizations are not only helping to grow the game using pathways such as 10 and Under Tennis and Jr. Team Tennis, they are ensuring the future growth of their communities" (*Tennis Panorama News*, 2011).

To provide the massive recreational club player market with comprehensive instructions for a gradual, healthy progression, sport scientists should be given grants to establish a ten- to twenty-year plan for player development. The plan should guide tennis coaches with age and ability level-specific recommendations for all aspects of sport performance. A distinct and important part of such plans in the former USSR and now Russia is the theoretical component that a coach must deliver, which includes broader sport history and sociology topics, together with concepts of basic fitness and training for performance. In developing such a plan, U.S. tennis scientists have a great body of knowledge to draw from, including research-based athlete development guidelines from Australia, Canada, China, France, Germany, Russia, Scandinavia, and the United Kingdom (Bergsgard et al., 2007; Canadian Sport for Life, 2011; Houlihan & Green, 2008; Platonov, 2005; Riordan, 1980; Smolianov & Zakus, 2006, 2008; Tumanian, 2006).

Athlete-ranking systems, which assist in player development, are available for full transfer or partial borrowing from around the world (e.g., the most sophisticated one was acquired by Russia and China from the former USSR). The Universal Tennis Rating System, which is currently being discussed by U.S. tennis leaders, features sixteen levels and provides tennis players worldwide a common language to determine their level of play without regard for age or gender. This system may result in the development of stronger U.S. players who are accustomed to playing at a higher competitive level. A similar system was used successfully in France. The Universal Rating system is worthy of further examination and consideration by U.S. tennis leaders.

Grants could also be focused on investment in professional preparation programs. This would help ensure that all participation levels, particularly beginners, are nurtured by well-educated, appropriately certified coaches and scouts who are better instructed on how to select tennis-predisposed children. A national talent search system could be implemented similar to the Australian practice of offering each school in the country a service of assessing and advising students on sport participation. Pre-school programs could also be part of talent search and QuickStart. Tennis could lead other sports in such initiatives under the USOC umbrella.

Despite the highly developed sport structures within the U.S. system of education, the surveyed coaches perceived the integration of tennis with school/college/university education to be problematic. Both mass participation and high-performance opportunities should be subsidized to funnel more tennis-predisposed, economically disadvantaged children into the athlete development pipeline. If more children in the United States are to receive the chance of becoming world-class, a more nurturing environment should be offered to middle school-age players of all socioeconomic classes.

This would mirror situations in other successful sport nations, at many NCAA institutions, and increasingly at high schools in the United States. National sport organizations in successful countries achieve this by cooperating with systems of public education and local governments. Ideally, all U.S. players who show promise at the age of ten to fourteen should receive free, high-quality coaching and medical, nutritional, and other athlete services integrated with their education. For this to happen, not only commercial, but public academies, similar to those in German, French, Chinese, and Russian sport schools and UK sport colleges, could be developed.

Another area for improvement based on the coaches' survey was to ensure that the development and remuneration of tennis coaches be better coordinated across all participant levels. Administrator A (February 18, 2011) suggested that "having continuing education available to part-time coaches and volunteers would increase the level of expertise." Tennis coaches are rarely paid according to multi-level certification based on coaches' education and achievements of entrusted players. Seven coaches in their open responses asked for better coordination between different levels of coaching. Administrator B (February 23, 2011) noted that tennis coaches are usually paid according to what the market will bear, but "it should be based more on certification: a one unified tennis teaching governing body in the U.S. with well-defined certifications is needed." As was noted by Administrator A (February, 18, 2010), it is difficult for the tennis-teaching professional organizations to provide more education and certification as the competitive player development market is only a fraction of the overall player market, whereas the focus for most in the tennis industry is on the recreational player, the largest market segment.

The challenge in the United States is to promote additional training and continuing education for developmental coaches who work with beginner and recreational level players. In recent years the USPTA added focus on this important initiative through their USPTA Developmental Coach Program. The USTA, USPTA, and USPTR should collaborate to share and develop strategies and methodologies to improve the education of both mass participants and elite level coaches. Ultimately, even though it would require extraordinary efforts from the foregoing NGBs, one unified tennis coach education curriculum and five-level certification could be created, as done by such successful U.S. NGBs as USSA and in a number of leading sporting nations such as Australia, Canada, China, and Russia.

Coaching requires more than having been a good tennis player. Coaches should be encouraged to get formal degrees in sport-related areas such as sport science, movement science, and tennis-specific coaching. U.S. Tennis could create a world's best system of tennis coach education that would identify those with coaching potential and support them to receive tennis-specific graduate degrees through USTA grants and scholarships. The U.S. government could develop a visa category for coaching residency programs for master coaches to teach and demonstrate best practice. Sport-specific coach education and support models are available for transfer from Chinese, Russian, and other USSR-inherited sport systems (Riordan, 1980; Smolianov, 2013; Smolianov & Zakus, 2006, 2008; Tan & Green, 2008).

The process of attracting children to the game seems to be a problematic area within U.S. tennis player development (see Table 4.9). The main barrier for youths to make their first steps in tennis was again perceived to be the high cost of this sport. Another obstruction of tennis development is competition with such sports as football, basketball, baseball, and soccer. Thirteen coaches suggested, in their open responses, that enhanced scouting programs would be the way to start identifying and attracting tennis-disposed children to the sport.

Element 7: Advanced athlete preparation and support

Again, the results indicate a high degree of uncertainty or lack of knowledge. Only one variable (#8) was clearly selected as negative, while four others (#2, 3, 4, 7) were selected by more than 30 percent of coaches as negative/lacking. Only variable 5 (that tennis players' careers are extended with proper access to medical personnel) had a positive rating of nearly 30 percent (see Table 4.10). It seems clear that the U. S. sport system does not provide sufficient support to its athletes beyond their competitive careers. Nor are there advanced processes in place that help with their life transitions.

This element again displays some interesting divisions. If we look at practice 1 we see nearly the same number of negative and positive responses on how players are ranked and rewarded. Why should the same group of tennis people see something lacking and something existing in nearly the same percentages? We could ask the same question of variable 6 and to a lesser degree of variable 5. If the people who make up the sport see these things from such different ways it makes for interesting management of them.

This is evident in the averages for all variables in this element. Taking out the neutral responses, 46 percent of remaining respondents felt that desirable practices occurred to an extent. Just more than a third felt a lack of these practices, and 14 percent felt some of these practices existed. The nexus of career development, access to medical and sport specialists, and research are not well aligned in the sport.

At an increasing number of American organizations, elite athlete employees receive conditions such as paid time off work to train and compete. This common international practice is rare in U.S. tennis, according to the surveyed coaches and administrators. In their open responses nineteen coaches indicated the need for more funds and greater athlete support, particularly with employment.

Providing all athletes with the necessary resources (money, education, work experience) is a major, global issue in sport. While a few athletes retire wealthy and manage their funds and live well, there are too many cases where this does not go well. For athletes who do not make the major professional leagues or competitions, career planning is often very limited. State NGBs in many countries initiated athlete retirement and education programs in the 1970s (or earlier for

Table 4.9 Results of tennis survey, Level 6 – Talent identification and development (Smolianov, Gallo, & Naylor, 2014)

Desired Practices	Average Score	Distribution of Responses		
		Negative / Lacking (%)	Neutral (%)	Positive / Existing (%)
1. In addition to children being introduced to tennis by themselves and parents, potential tennis players are attracted from outside the sport's participation base (e.g., by a search at schools)	2.6	47	40	13
2. Young tennis players are trained based on guidelines for multiple development stages recommended by USTA (many national governing bodies have guidelines for nurturing players from the introduction to sport through the achievement of peak performance on to retirement from sport)	2.9	27	53	20
3. Sufficient resources are available collectively from various supporting organizations for all young talented tennis players to progress through all developmental stages	2.9	57	36	7
4. A multi-stage system of player qualification based on results/rankings within age groups is used to reward player progress from beginner to top international level	3.5	39	12	49
5. Performance of tennis players in each competitive age group is monitored and developed using a national database	3.6	32	17	51
6. A high number of full-time tennis coaches are available making the athlete-coach ratio low	2.9	34	41	25
7. Tennis coach expertise is equally high across all participant ages and levels	2.4	57	36	7
8. Tennis coaches are paid according to multi-level certification based on coaches' education and achievements of entrusted players	2.5	51	37	12

continued …

Table 4.9 (continued)

Desired Practices	Average Score	Distribution of Responses		
		Negative/ Lacking (%)	Neutral (%)	Positive/ Existing (%)
9. Players with potential to represent the country (e.g. Nations top 50 players per age group) are offered the conditions to train full time with high performance standards	3.5	10	44	46
10. Tennis training is well integrated with school/college/ university education for harmonious development of athletes	2.8	39	38	23
Percentage across all items in element (based on N=107 for each row)		39	36	25

State socialist countries). Administrator A (February 18, 2011) summed this up by stating that

> only players who have achieved the highest levels are provided with a lifestyle plan and assisted with their careers outside of the sport. Members of the ATP and WTA Tours have a week long course designed for this purpose, but only players belonging to these groups are allowed to participate. The tennis schedule doesn't allow for players to work during down times or gaps in the playing schedule.

Career support of high-performance players at all stages of development is needed. The USTA could work closer with the USOC to provide athletes with employment. According to Administrator B (February 23, 2011),

> these areas are generally not addressed formally by the governing bodies of tennis in the US. Written material on players adapting to life after playing is very limited. Most teaching professionals in the United States who work with high performance players are very good at assembling a team that cares for most of the needs of the player. The Division I college opportunity gives a great number of our players the formal education and career training that they need. The only problem is that a high percentage of these opportunities go to players who have greater ITF junior exposure. This is another reason we need to support a greater number of players.

An important potential area for advancement that received a low rating was the provision of individualized lifestyle plans for athlete health at the final stages of their playing career. Sport scientists could work with health care professionals to advance this service and prolong the contribution of players to tennis. This

Table 4.10 Results of tennis survey, Level 7 – Advanced athlete preparation and support (Smolianov, Gallo, & Naylor, 2014)

Desired Practices	Average Score	Distribution of Responses		
		Negative/ Lacking (%)	Neutral (%)	Positive/ Existing (%)
1. High performance players are ranked into hierarchical levels/ pools with appropriate financial and technical support	3.1	19	59	22
2. Athletes are assisted with formal education and career outside sport	2.8	35	47	18
3. Athlete support is well shared/ balanced between coaches and advisors (e.g., coach may provide psychological, nutritional, and performance science support, while independent advisors may best assist with medicine, career, education, and personal finances)	2.8	31	52	17
4. Scientific research (e.g., biomechanics of athlete movement and psychophysiological analysis) is applied quickly and effectively to immediately benefit player performance	2.7	36	52	12
5. Player careers are prolonged by medical personnel knowledgeable in tennis (helping with such things as injury prevention, adjustment of training levels, nutrition, pharmacology, rest and stimulation therapy, doping use prevention)	3.1	22	49	29
6. Doping is controlled by the USTA based on the most recent guidelines from the World Anti-Doping Agency	3.1	14	73	13
7. Athletes leaving elite sport are provided with individualized lifestyle plans for physical and psychological health	2.1	39	59	2
8. Athletes, including tennis players, are supported at places of work and service with conditions similar to those at Home Depot and U.S. Army (paid time off given to train and compete)	2.0	58	39	3
Percentage across all items in element (based on N=107 for each row)		32	54	14

includes providing elite athletes with holistic plans for the reduction of training and competition loads toward gradual retirement from elite sport.

The survey respondents, particularly coaches, seemed to be quite open to opportunities for progressive practices, calling for greater involvement of the government in both direct support and in stimulation of sport development through tax incentives. The USTA could unite forces with the USOC and other NGBs to increase the role of government in sport development.

Tennis coach education, scientific support, and certification could be improved within current USTA resources. This could positively impact international performance in a relatively short time. To compete with Spain, France, Germany, China, and Russia, the USTA should gather world best practices and fit them together in a holistic, integrated manner. They would then have to adapt these practices for the U.S. context, thereby creating a uniquely U.S. sport development structure.

Practices of USA rugby against the Model

The questionnaire was delivered online to a total sample of 534 USA Rugby coaches and administrators. A total of 127 (24 percent) valid surveys resulted. This is an acceptable response rate for online surveys. The majority of individuals affected by policies, procedures, and decisions made by USA Rugby were in the college, high school, and youth ranks of the game. In the review of the hard data collected, 61.6 percent of respondents were located at these developmental levels of rugby, whereas 24.3 percent were associated with the elite level. The survey sample is fully geographically representative of the United States, as it was distributed to both coaches and administrators across all seven Territorial Unions (Northeast, Mid-Atlantic, South, West, Midwest, Southern California, and Pacific Coast) and the independent Unions of Alaska, Hawaii, Idaho, and Montana.

Rugby is one of the world's most popular team sports with a strong social element. This has helped rugby spread across the United States. Rugby participation in the United States has increased 350 percent since 2004. Although the number of U.S. participants reached 81,678, this is only .003 percent of the population (Chadwick, Semens, Schwarz, & Zhang, 2010). It is also interesting that 20,724, roughly a fourth of U.S. rugby participants, are female (Chadwick et al., 2010). This represents the largest number of female participants (by more than 2,500) of any rugby-playing nation.

Obviously, the level and quality of outcome in HP rugby at the international level is not similar. Where the U.S. numbers do not match is in the "Mini" or "Rookie" participation categories. The United States is reported to only have 2,216 registered members in that age group (five- through eleven-year-olds), whereas Australia has 26,664 registered members (Chadwick et al., 2010). If youth rugby participation in the United States continues to grow at the same rate as the last few years, the overall participation numbers in the United States will rival that of Japan, Argentina, and Sri Lanka. Without a clear pipeline of young players going into the youth/high school level, an introduction to rugby is perhaps already too late for many U.S. youths. There are many mainstream U.S. sports, such as American football, basketball, ice hockey, or baseball, which have the lure of more attractive professional salaries and where there are many university/ college scholarships available, to attract them (and their parents).

In terms of popularity, as reported by Miller and Washington (2012), a recent Harris Poll showed that of those U.S. sports fans surveyed, 31 percent of adults (older than age eighteen) identified the NFL as their favorite sport, MLB came in second with 17 percent, followed by college football with 12 percent (Miller & Washington, 2012). Of the other two prominent sports in the United States, the NBA received 6 percent of the vote, while the NHL received just 5 percent (Miller & Washington, 2012). It is worth noting that rugby did not register in these results. Finally, according to the National Federation of State High School Associations, there were just over 1.1 million male participants in American football in 2011–2012; compared to just over 69,000 total active rugby participants/members (all ages, all males and females) in the United States (NFHS, 2014).

Referencing global rugby practices from Tier 1 nations provided information on what USA Rugby might implement as global "best practice" to advance its HP structures, processes, programs, and organizational development (Sparvero et al., 2008). Knowledge of global practices is particularly important in light of the USOC's recent move away from grass-roots funding. This means that a decrease in mass participation will increase the challenges for USA Rugby to achieve participation numbers and realize its international aspirations (Dittmore et al., 2008).

The United States has an interesting sports landscape in that it is a nation that prides itself on its "American" sports (e.g., American football, baseball, basketball and, to a degree, even ice hockey). Even though these sports are played elsewhere, U.S. citizens idolize players and contribute to the commercial viability of these sports, making it difficult for emerging sports such as rugby to break through. Rugby in the United States competes in a cut-throat entertainment/sport industry and fights for funding and participation (e.g., see the collection of essays in Staudohar & Mangan, 1991). Best practice from these traditional U.S. sports can, however, be identified to assist rugby's growth in the U.S. market.

Currently many countries worldwide import players. This is usually not a problem for Tier 1 countries as they still develop most of their own playing compliment. Many Tier 2 countries lose players to the top tier. The same is true for Tier 2 countries importing players. Without developing a proper player development process, the long-term success of most importing nations is weakened. USA Rugby is, therefore, making a concerted effort to get away from the method of "importing" overseas and older players from other sports to focus on developing athletes from a younger age. This demands an increasing number of participants at the mass level of the sport. The implementation of Rookie Rugby has been a great success. This is an area of vital importance for USA Rugby, and where more funding is needed.

There is a lack of rugby presence in most high schools and colleges and no equivalent of the IMG tennis and soccer academies for rugby. USA Rugby has set up development camps but there are no permanent development schools across the nation. A network of training centers/schools/academies that attract mass participants and develop them into HP players would create a backbone of long-term success for USA Rugby.

As the NGB for rugby, USA Rugby has implemented a valuable set of conferences from youth development to refereeing and coaching clinics. These conferences help USA Rugby develop the support staff needed to sustain growth and research and technology services.

Element 1: Balanced and integrated funding and structures of mass and elite sport

Four desired practices (#1, 2, 3, 6) of this element displayed a strongly negative score (see Table 4.11), while variables 5, 9, 10, and 11 reflected negative responses for more than 30 percent of respondents. At least 40 percent of respondents for variables 7 and 8 indicated that desirable practices exist to an extent, although on variable 7 the positive result was matched by the number of respondents with a neutral perception. Five other variables (#4, 5, 9, 10, 11) were also neutrally perceived by about half of the respondents. It is fairly evident that many issues exist within the funding and structure of rugby in the United States.

This is also evident in terms of the overall combined average ($N = 127$) for each category in this element. Forty-seven percent saw these practices as negative/lacking in rugby, while 39 percent were neutral, and 14 percent responded positively. Clearly there are many gaps between actual practices in rugby and the desired practices recommended by the Model.

One note is required on desired practice 4. If we observe just the negative and positive responses for this variable, we see an even split in the percentage for each category. Why so many rugby community members are evenly split on whether their programs are equally serving mass and elite participants is surely odd. Rugby has to take note and sort out such an observation.

Based on USA Rugby Financial Statements (2012), the organization generated approximately $7.5 million in 2011, about half of this through mass participation sources (i.e., mostly from membership fees). Although all these funds have been reinvested into the sport, only about 30 percent of these funds were spent on all aspects of mass participation. With the growing number of televised rugby matches in the United States, funding from new sources such as sponsorships and events (only $1.7 million) could be increased and spent on the line item "game development," which received only $1.3 million in 2011. In particular, beginner and intermediate level programs could be expanded and improved to foster participation. This would increase mass rugby expenditure closer to half of all the USA Rugby budget for a more optimal balance between mass and elite player development.

Coaches' open responses and personal communication with Administrators A, B, C, D, E, and F (March 18, 19, 20, and 21, 2010) agreed that the introduction of rugby seven-a-side[6] to the Rio de Janeiro Olympic Games in 2016 is going to

Table 4.11 Results of rugby survey, Level 1 – Balanced and integrated funding and structures of mass and elite sport (Carney, Smolianov, & Zakus, 2012)

Desired Practices	Average Score	Distribution of Responses		
		Negative/ Lacking (%)	Neutral (%)	Positive/ Existing (%)
1. Corporate and philanthropic tax incentives provide sufficient support of mass and elite Rugby	1.9	71	27	2
2. Participation in various sports, as a foundation for Rugby development, is encouraged through physical education requirements	2.2	62	27	11
3. Sport participation, including Rugby, is rewarded with reduced personal tax	1.3	86	13	1
4. Rugby programs service both recreational and high performance players	3.0	26	48	26
5. Specialized sport schools similar to the IMG Academies are available and affordable to all talented players	1.7	38	60	2
6. A multi-stage system of elite Rugby player qualification is integrated with a system of fitness tests for mass participation	2.1	59	35	6
7. Dues and other "fees" affordable for all are available in various Rugby clubs	3.2	18	41	41
8. Rugby participants are as diverse as the general population	3.2	26	31	43
9. USA Rugby demonstrates systematic/strategic management in developing Rugby on every level	2.4	40	51	9
10. USA Rugby is effective in fostering both mass participation and high performance in Rugby	2.4	43	48	9
11. Rugby is developed in integration with Olympic and Paralympic sports to achieve sustainable competitive excellence	2.4	44	47	9
Percentage across all items in element (based on N=127 for each row)		47	39	14

act as a catalyst to bring rugby to public attention. Another common view was that "developing the grassroots would better facilitate HP and increase funding" (Administrator C, March 19, 2010). Existing corporate and philanthropic tax deductions have not stimulated sufficient funding for the USOC and many U.S. NGBs, such as USA Rugby. There have been relatively few donations for USA Rugby for its development. Support of rugby from federal and state governments is also lacking; and is not likely. The development of rugby through summer leagues, PE classes, after-school programs, YM/WCAs, and Boys and Girls Clubs (USA Rugby, 2012) allows some indirect public subsidization of rugby to make it affordable at the grassroots levels. USA Rugby offers materials and tools for integrating the sport into PE and to enhance training and to develop high school teams, Junior Eagle, and varsity high school programs (USA Rugby, 2012).

Element 2: Partnerships with supporting agencies

The results in this element lean strongly toward a lack of the desired practices (see Table 4.12). Five of the desired practices (#1, 3, 4, 5, 6) were clearly lacking in the sport. Only in variable 2 was the neutral score highest of all choices, but three variables (#3, 4, 5) displayed a neutral response for over 30 percent of the responses. There were no results indicating positive alignment with the Model.

If we look at the average for all variables in the element, we see how lacking the desired practices are. Fifty-eight percent chose negative/lacking responses, 32 percent were neutral in their response, and only 10 percent saw these practices as positive/existing.

USA Rugby has been actively seeking out new partners for financial support for all levels of competition. In the current economy USA Rugby has encountered some financial problems due to several sponsors going bankrupt (e.g., Setanta Sports, Canterbury USA). The U.S. market and private-sector ideology makes it very difficult to increase the support of sport from government and educational institutions.

Training academies with direct and indirect government support exist for all state/provincial teams in most Tier 1 countries. Similar support for U.S. Rugby is still to be developed. With the inclusion of rugby in the Olympic Games program, the IOC is expected to provide more support for rugby, opening opportunities for direct or indirect funding from the U.S. government. The Model assumes closer partnerships with local governments across the country to obtain more public resources for facilities and programs. Such partnerships around the world help communities deliver social inclusion and social control programs (e.g., to take youths off the streets and hopefully reduce crime at low cost to governments).

Indirect government funding is available through the educational systems. New high school and collegiate rugby teams are being created and the popularity of the game is spreading farther than the former strongholds of the East and West Coasts of the United States. The problem is that colleges do not necessarily have the resources to operate more sports or teams; this often means that no one

Table 4.12 Results of rugby survey, Level 2 – Partnerships with supporting agencies (Carney, Smolianov, & Zakus, 2012)

Desired Practices	Average Score	Distribution of Responses		
		Negative/ Lacking (%)	Neutral (%)	Positive/ Existing (%)
1. Support for Rugby player development is adequate from various levels of government	1.7	84	11	5
2. Sufficient help is obtained from USA Rugby, IRB, World Cup Sevens, and other national governing bodies such as the RFU that provide coach education and certification	2.8	32	47	21
3. Role of clubs/community programs in Rugby development is sound	2.6	49	39	12
4. Rugby is well supported by educational sector (e.g., schools, colleges, universities)	2.4	61	31	8
5. Cooperation with agencies outside of the sport industry (e.g., medical, scientific, military, philanthropic and sponsoring organizations, lotteries) is in place	2.4	57	34	9
6. USA Rugby influences media coverage and popularity of Rugby to increase support from the society	2.3	65	29	6
Percentage across all items in element (based on N=127 for each row)		58	32	10

gets the opportunity to play other than in a "club" sport that receives little to no support from the institution.

Relations with the media and corporate sponsors, which impact all other partnerships, is another important area for improvement. USA Rugby has a hard time attracting sponsors due to limited exposure to the viewing public, not being a mainstream U.S. sport, and therefore not being able to attract corporate sponsorship. Again, with rugby's recent inclusion in the Olympic Games, more rugby, especially the seven-a-side version, has aired on major channels such as NBC and ESPN. NBC Universal provided coverage of the 2011 Rugby World Cup (the major quadrennial global competition of the full form of the sport), which was an important step toward rugby's increased social presence in the United States. NBC renewed its contract to broadcast the Collegiate 7s Invitational in

June 2010 and the now annual United States leg of the IRB Sevens World Series in Las Vegas in February 2010, 2011, 2012, and 2013. With increasing exposure, rugby will gain strength within the U.S. market, and more corporate sponsors will be secured, providing the funding so much needed to develop each of the seven elements discussed.

Coaches in their open survey comments asked for a commercial message or some form of media that everyone can have access to, to improve the image of rugby in the United States, noting that we need to get away from the stereotype of "beer drinking hooligans" (Coach 16, April 13, 2010). Administrator B (March 18, 2010) stated that "when sponsorship interest arises in rugby, the rugby community needs to feel confident that USAR [sic] will not drop the ball and let precious dollars fall through the cracks of mismanagement." USA Rugby is just entering the fray in this regard. They have taken new steps forward in trying to secure some television rights and are now starting to make themselves known. In England, rugby has secured television rights with more than just one network. Specific games are played on certain channels. International games are usually covered by public television (ITV, BBC) due to anti-siphoning laws; the Aviva Premiership is usually covered by satellite/cable stations (SKY, ESPN), with the occasional game covered by the public networks. USA Rugby is trying to reach an equivalent level in the United States so that several networks pay to cover games.

The IRB has a vested interest in expanding the sport in North America. It invested earnings from past Rugby World Cups heavily in many Tier 2 countries, including those of North America. Indicative of this is the recent IRB investment of $3.12 million to establish Tier 2 competitions. This will include the United States in a schedule of regular mainstream top-tier international matches from 2012 by replacing the Churchill Cup competition, which was the mainstay North American elite rugby tournament (Rugby Canada, 2012), and is being implemented on an IRB level "Pacific Nations" competition. As noted above, full professional rugby in North America must evolve in the future. It was proposed that by 2008 cities and private investors take ownership of franchises within the United States (IRB, 2007). The competition never happened as cities/private investors did not take control of rugby franchises in the United States.

Now that rugby is part of the Olympic Games program, one of the most devoted USOC sponsors, the U.S. Army and its World Class Athlete Program (WCAP), should provide enhanced sponsorship opportunities. Rugby is already an All Army Sport, with regular competitions among Air Force, Army, Navy, and Coast Guard teams. Under the WCAP, more high-performance rugby players are expected to be employed as military personnel who would, as part of their employment duties, further develop rugby and expand competition to police and other law enforcement organizations and in other institutional areas. We have seen in recent years that the England Sevens Team has greatly benefitted from English Army athletes who play for their national team when they are not deployed.

Eric Taber, sponsorship director for USA Rugby, indicated that the U.S. Army National Guard, which was a sponsor from 2007 to 2010, has been an important partner of USA Rugby (personal communication, May 1, 2011). It particularly supported youth development by providing more than 700 high schools and colleges with jerseys, shorts, socks, and a starter kit that included balls, cones, bibs, and other training equipment (personal communication, May 1, 2011). The National Guard also supported USA Rugby's referee and coach development programs. USA Rugby still has a working relationship with the National Guard, even though the sponsorship relationship ended but would be again involved this way when and if their funding changed (personal communication, May 1, 2011).

To prevent such well-suited sponsors from leaving, USA Rugby could better understand and align with the goals of public and private organizations that can support rugby. NFL Super Bowl and Olympics organizers worked with their sponsors to develop promotional campaigns based on partner aims, through tested campaigns with sponsor's senior managers, and with targeted populations to track campaign performance (Smolianov & Shilbury, 2005). These are practices available for transfer to USA Rugby.

The Model suggests that current USA Rugby partners such as T-Mobile and Bank of America employ members and candidates of USA Rugby's national team. Australian, French, German, and U.S. companies have supported Olympic and national team hopefuls with flexible work conditions and career progression in a broad variety of jobs and locations. Opportunities are there for the USA Rugby Sevens team training in Chula Vista at the USOC center to develop a closer partnership with another current sponsor, Emirates Airline, at their Los Angeles International Airport location. According to the Model and international exemplars of deep and strong partnerships, employed players are also expected to help sponsors develop corporate rugby teams.

Various forms of lotteries and betting are critically important partners of most successful sport systems around the world but not yet in the United States. The USOC has been seeking collective effort, including USA Rugby, to help bring a sport lottery closer to reality. Lottery income is one of the most certain ways of boosting rugby development. An example of successful lottery support for sport is the implementation of this strategy by the UK Olympic teams at the beginning of the twenty-first century.

The survey showed that USA Rugby is not dealing well with its external environment and/or its stakeholders. Nearly 60 percent of respondents see a weakness here. Finally, a key issue for USA Rugby is the use of the media to popularize the sport, to get its message out, and to inform all of its members of what it is doing. The sport/media nexus is a key aspect of the success of any sport and to generate a strong revenue stream. Much more appears to be needed here.

Element 3: Educational, scientific, medical, philosophical, and promotional support

The difficult conceptual nature of this element resulted in a split in the number of variables seen as lacking or as sometimes existing (see Table 4.13). There were three variables (#2, 3, 6) indicated as not being part of the sport's delivery system and three (#1, 2, 5) where respondents felt these practices eventuated to some degree. Three neutral selections (#3, 4, 6) strongly indicated the uncertainty or knowledge of the practice, or perhaps to the actual meaning of the variable. Evidently there were many desired practices in this element that vary widely from that proposed in the Model.

Again, looking at the overall average for each result category for this element we see that the negative/lacking (39%) and neutral (43%) responses point to a lack of congruence with the Model. Only 18 percent of respondents replied that practices were positive/existing and occurred.

A consensus among the Territorial Unions (both in the survey and in personal communication with Administrators A, B, D, and E, March 18, 19, 20, and 21, 2010) was that an online USA Rugby university is needed. Further, the results indicated that national players or players in national age-grade programs must be required to take these courses to better themselves as rugby players and as individuals (similar to the practices of nations highly advanced in player and coach education, such as France and Russia). The information will also be available to all USA Rugby members (Administrators A and B, March 18, 2010). USA Rugby CEO, Nigel Melville (interview, March 18, 2010), addressed the issue further by stating that "USA Rugby is actively looking into implementing distance learning in the near future." This will improve most ratings in Element 5, particularly the communication of research results (the lowest rating of 2.3 in Table 4.13, with the highest proportion or 54 percent of respondents indicating it is never or rarely done well). Successful practices of the US Skiing and Snowboarding Association of partnering with universities and providing online education to prepare and certify coaches and other personnel are available for USA Rugby to borrow.

This element of the Model involves supporting the athlete development pipeline with experts in various fields, such as coaching and management, sporting-related sciences, and medicine (which is particularly important for rugby). There are multiple facilities in New Zealand (NZ) with doctors specializing in different types of rugby injuries, from concussion to broken bones and torn ligaments. Use of these facilities means that elite squad players return to play sooner due to decreased injury layoffs and that their comprehensive rehabilitation processes result in a decreased risk of re-injury. USA Rugby hires a full-time team doctor for all elite and age group teams, although that doctor is not necessarily a rugby specialist. Each team also has one or more physiotherapists to help players cope with the minor and recurring injuries that are common. Doctors with competitive rugby experience and education are still being developed.

To better connect rugby with medicine, USA Rugby launched the USA Rugby Medical Symposium. First held in 2009, the symposium brings medical professionals with a specific background in rugby from around the world to the United States to discuss new research in sports medicine. In 2011 the symposium was held in conjunction with the U.S. leg of the Sevens World Series in Las Vegas (Beckstrom, 2011). A more comprehensive approach is assumed in the Model and practiced around the world. In 2010 the International Rugby Board (IRB) launched their inaugural IRB Medical Conference. The conference was the

Table 4.13 Results of rugby survey, Level 3 – Educational, scientific, medical, philosophical, promotional support (Carney, Smolianov, & Zakus, 2012)

Desired Practices	Average Score	Distribution of Responses		
		Negative/ Lacking (%)	Neutral (%)	Positive/ Existing (%)
1. All specialists engaged in the development of Rugby players are well educated for their professional roles	3.0	23	55	22
2. USA Rugby fosters research on all important aspects of Rugby development	2.5	38	49	13
3. Research results are well communicated to coaches (e.g., by research institutes, universities, and USA Rugby)	2.3	54	35	11
4. Principles of sportsman like conduct and Olympism are communicated well (e.g., through mass media, school education, and through the arts as part of Rugby events)	2.7	41	37	22
5. USA Rugby's communication contributes to national values and identity by inspiring participants to strive for excellence, to show the best results and character in the world	2.7	33	45	22
6. USA Rugby provides vision and leadership in improving all aspects of the participants' well-being through Rugby (e.g., physical, social, emotional, mental, spiritual, and environmental/ecological)	2.5	45	40	15
Percentage across all items in element (based on N=127 for each row)		39	43	18

birthplace for several specialist medical groups set up to treat the major injury categories sustained while participating in the sport. The groups of medical doctors, university medical professors, and coaching and sport science specialists from various national unions and institutions focused on concussion and spinal cord injury management and on medical policies as part of overall player welfare development and management (IRB, 2010). The survey results and the Model suggest that USA Rugby be involved in coordinating scientific research on rugby across the country, similar to national sport organizations in such countries as

China and Russia, and communicate these research results to coaches through degree and certification education, seminars, and clinics.

Templates for a Geographic Union (GU) organizational structure, financial models, and bylaws were developed by a committee led by Nigel Melville, USA Rugby CEO and president of Rugby Operations. This was done after researching the highest-performing models from existing local unions and other rugby-playing nations and other NGBs. One predominant feature of the GUs that provides the central control present in many successful sport organizations is a full-time USA Rugby administrator. This administrator lives in the GU and partners with local rugby organizations to help implement USA Rugby programs (Rugby America, 2011). The 2013 National Development Summit held by USA Rugby brought best practices in rugby development to coaches, referees, and administrators around the country (USA Rugby, 2012).

New Zealand is perhaps the leader in rugby development; for example, through high-performance clinics for players and coaches led by domestic rugby experts and in the application of scientific research. New Zealanders tackled athlete burnout, a major issue in professional rugby, through Mageau and Vallerand's (2003) guidelines that promote basic needs fulfillment and help players realize a variety of positive consequences. The NZ national team, the All-Blacks, adopted these guidelines and have realized good results in recent years (Hodge, Lonsdale, & Ng, 2007).

The survey respondents, in support of the Model, seek a stronger vision, conduct, principles, ideology, and publicity for each team, event, and player. Studies found that the majority of selected rugby players in the United States honor the principles of fair play. It was noted, however, that to compete in elite rugby, more of an emphasis is placed on winning than on a fairness philosophy (Rees, 2000; Spamer, 2005).

Though nearly half of the sample was uncertain of the NGB's research on rugby-related matters, more than half did not feel these outcomes were well shared. Interestingly, results indicate that USA Rugby is providing support for participants yet could do more to communicate this to the rugby community. There appears much in this element that USA Rugby can build on to grow its systems.

Element 4: Domestic and international competitions

Results here show a pattern similar to the above element. Here the number of desired practices seen as lacking (#3, 4, 5) and those seen as neutral (#1, 2, 6) were nearly the same in number, except for the fourth variable, which was selected equally by the respondents (see Table 4.14). These two response categories also had strong preferences (more than 30 percent) on two variables each (#1, 6 negative/lacking and #3, 5 for the neutral category). There were no practices for which alignment with the Model was even a moderately strong perception.

The overall average score for each selection category supports these results. The categories negative/lacking (43%) and neutral (45%) were virtually equal. Only 12 percent of rugby people saw desirable practices as occurring to some degree.

Table 4.14 Results of rugby survey, Level 4 – Domestic and international competitions (Carney, Smolianov, & Zakus, 2012)

Desired Practices	Average Score	Distribution of Responses		
		Negative/ Lacking (%)	Neutral (%)	Positive/ Existing (%)
1. Hosted international events and international opportunities are sufficient for all athletes with potential to represent the country	2.6	40	50	10
2. Competitions are well structured at all levels (e.g., club/ training center, regional, and national)	2.8	33	46	21
3. USA Rugby and its support mechanisms sufficiently assist in local and sectional developmental events (e.g., 14 and under regional)	2.2	61	32	7
4. USA Rugby attempts to integrate professional and amateur tournaments into a progressive plan of competitions gradually preparing athletes for peak performance at "Majors" (i.e. World Cup, North American Four, World Cup Sevens, etc.), Paralympic Games, and Olympic Games.	2.5	43	43	14
5. USA Rugby tries to coordinate all domestic and international competitions for all ages and levels, between and within all possible organizations	2.6	43	41	16
6. Event sponsorship incomes are used to develop competitions for all participation levels	2.2	39	55	6
Percentage across all items in element (based on N=127 for each row)		43	45	12

Unfortunately, the premier division or Super League has been faltering for some time and is in dire need of a revamp before it fails completely. Assistance in local and sectional developmental events is an organizational issue. USA Rugby seems to be in the same trap as most NGBs over the dilemma of focusing at the top end of sport development and being bereft at the lower developmental levels. Only six percent of respondents indicated that event sponsorship incomes are always or often used to develop competitions for all participation levels.

The income from successful events is not transparently or universally shared. These are issues that affect many global sport systems. A Territorial Union President (Administrator F, March 21, 2010) suggested that USA Rugby

> go back to the model that was used in the 80's where there were four territories that played against each other multiple times a year. These territories are comprised of players from clubs within the boundaries of the respective unions, select sides if you will. Then every four years, select a U.S. Eagles team from the best players represented at the territorial level.

Nations such as England have taken the competition development to the next level with well-developed and well-executed planning. The Rugby Football Union (RFU) has created a multi-stage regional tournament for U14, U16, and U18[7] age levels sponsored by *The Daily Mail* newspaper. It is followed and publicized in the paper every week. This tournament allows the RFU to analyze each team competing for talent and it allows rugby to become a household name. Rugby is already popular in England but the publicity for this tournament has taken the sport to a new level. USA Rugby needs to find its own niche in the school competitions.

Both quantitative and qualitative results of this study indicated a lack of publicity and a lack of emphasis on developing the sport at the youth level, with clear channels for young players to continue their rugby careers in both club and college structures. To address this, and keeping in mind the preparation for the Olympic Games in 2016, USA Rugby worked on an improved club competition structure for the 2013–2014 season with the goal of creating an environment that promotes a higher level of competition for all ages and levels. The Olympic Development Program gave the start to a long-term systematic approach to rugby athlete development from 2013, including the expansion of the quality and number of seven-a-side match opportunities over the course of a year (USA Rugby, 2012). The structure of an elite domestic competition is a key factor for the national team's success (Morgan, 2002). USA Rugby will return to being among the world's best only with a constantly increasing scope and intensity of competition among its domestic teams at each level.

Element 5: Training centers and multi-facility activity hubs

It is clear from the results that the desired practices in this element are widely lacking in the US rugby system (see Table 4.15). In all but variable 1, more than 50 percent of responses indicated that the variable was lacking in rugby's development system. Responses in the neutral category exceeded 30 percent for all variables. Observing the overall averages by category, we see this skewing of the data. The scores were 60, 34, and 6 percent, respectively, for the categories negative/lacking, neutral, and positive/existing.

The inclusion of 7s rugby in the 2016 Rio de Janeiro Olympic Games will hopefully alleviate the pressure caused by lack of facilities and training hubs.

Table 4.15 Results of rugby survey, Level 5 – Training centers and multi-facility activity hubs (Carney, Smolianov, & Zakus, 2012)

Desired Practices	Average Score	Distribution of Responses		
		Negative/ Lacking (%)	Neutral (%)	Positive/ Existing (%)
1. High performance athletes are provided with priority access to specific high quality equipment and facilities	2.5	47	41	12
2. Training centers provide specialized facilities and equipment for each age and level of participation	2.2	63	31	6
3. All national, regional, and local training centers are available to athletes at affordable costs	1.9	66	32	2
4. Travel from home to training facilities takes little time for players of all levels and types	2.1	61	36	3
5. Training facilities are close to all facilities for athlete support (e.g., school/college, medical, room & board, leisure/ entertainment)	2.3	58	34	8
6. A network of training centers is used to prepare players in different environments/socio-geo-climates (e.g., high altitude/ temperature/humidity, city/ pollution, rural/resort)	1.8	66	31	3
7. Rugby training centers are located close to other sport facilities so that players participate in and learn from other sports	2.2	60	33	7
Percentage across all items in element (based on N=127 for each row)		60	34	6

Now that USA Rugby is a member of the USOC, facilities and resources are becoming available, at least for the national teams. USA Rugby now has access to the USOC Chula Vista training facilities in California, eliminating a training hub issue for USA Rugby on the West Coast of the country. The East Coast's population density, number of active USA Rugby members, and USA Rugby's documented future planning indicate the need for a hub of elite and mass rugby in one or more states including New York, Massachusetts, Pennsylvania, Maryland,

and Virginia. There is a great opportunity for integration between "rugby" as a whole, not just the seven-a-side programs, and the USOC. A well-coordinated network of training centers in different socio-geo-climates across the country is one of the most important tasks of USA Rugby development.

USA Rugby partnered with the USOC to offer twenty-three athletes (fifteen men, eight women) full-time contracts to live near and train at the USOC facility in Chula Vista (California) in 2012. Although these contracts were reserved for players specialized in the seven-a-side version of the sport, many players in this form of the game progress to compete in the full version of rugby; also, this allowed these selected athletes to prepare for the 2016 Rio de Janeiro Olympic Games. USA Rugby also created permanent high-performance development camps for women at a number of colleges throughout the United States.

USA Rugby (2012) announced the launch of the Olympic Development Program from 2013 in three phases. Phase One creates six Olympic Development Academies (ODA) in Seattle, Chicago, San Diego, Long Beach, Columbus, and Glendale (Colorado) as a pilot program to build best practice. Phase Two increases the number of centers to support the demand across the country. Phase Three establishes a National Academy facility and an expansion of the current residency program at the Olympic Training Center in Chula Vista.

Each ODA will provide a ten-month training opportunity, with two four-week recovery periods, and continuous assessment and playing opportunities throughout the year. Players attending the center will receive rugby-specific training and strength, speed, conditioning sessions, and will be put through video analysis, fitness testing, and skill development sessions. Players attending an ODA will also have bimonthly communication with USA Rugby Sevens coaching staff. Those players demonstrating the potential to play for the Eagles will be offered the opportunity to try out with the national team at Chula Vista. Such uniform local athlete development conditions across the nation provide an opportunity for the most talented players to progress to the national level. These conditions are in place for most Olympic sports in leading sporting nations. Also included in the ODAs are education and all other services necessary for nurturing young athletes for their lifelong well-being and success. The increasingly comprehensive support of training centers across the United States driven by long-term athlete development should positively influence the U.S.'s rugby development and future perceptions of rugby coaches, many of whom agreed that the NGB was not doing enough to aid the members to become better players and achieve higher levels of performance.

USA Rugby's current "home" is located in Boulder, Colorado. There is a multi-facility training center in Glendale (thirty minutes away) for elite-level players and it provides a base for various training camps and matches. Like many other governing bodies, USA Rugby also utilizes university and local city resources. For example, USA Rugby used East Stroudsburg University in Pennsylvania for a U19 team training camp. The university provides their facilities, including dorms and dining services, for a fee paid by USA Rugby. The players who attend these camps then pay a fee to USA Rugby. The Rugby Football Union uses the same types of resources for their training camp schedules as do the majority of national rugby unions, though mostly at no cost to the players.

The problem USA Rugby faces is that it is difficult to meet training facility needs equally across such a vast and decentralized country. In the former USSR, and now China, all Olympic sports received permanent federal and state support across all regions but this is not the case in the United States. Direct funding to sport provided by the U.S. government is often somewhat limited and inconsistent. The ongoing current fiscal crisis of the state and inadequate government support for sport suggest that USA Rugby should seek more favorable tax status for both itself and its participants.

Little or no training for U.S. Rugby players is available in different geo-climates. Fortunately, Boulder, Colorado happens to be just outside of Denver (labeled the "Mile High City"), so altitude training is given for the elite players based there, but there does not seem to be any emphasis put on training in other conditions prior to a competition that will be held in a specifically different environment. This is mostly due to problems with funding. It is expensive to fly an entire team and staff to a different location to train, return them to their home locations, and then bring them back to train before sending them to the competition. However, many national teams around the world, from Australia to Russia, utilize this training method even in such unprofitable sports as modern pentathlon.

Element 6: Talent identification and development

Responses indicate that more than 50 percent of coaches believe that variables 3 to 10 of the desired talent search, coaching quality, and development practices of the Model are a lacking part of the USA Rugby system (see Table 4.16). More than 40 percent of coaches also believe that variables 1 and 2 are not evident. Again, the results in the neutral category are also quite high, with responses exceeding 30 percent for variables 1, 2, 3, and 5. This is of concern as this element focuses on the mass or basic levels of the sport.

Overall averages for each category also display this trend. Sixty-eight percent of respondents selected negative/lacking, while 24 percent were neutral, and only 8 percent saw a positive/existing relationship between the practices and the Model.

These results indicate that talent pathways are underdeveloped. Other practices indicated by more than 80 percent of respondents to be negative/lacking were that there is a lack of full-time coaches, that the expertise across all age categories is poor, and that coaches are rarely paid according to their certification achievements. These are areas of focus for improvement by USA Rugby. Such results are of concern, however, as there is an insufficient number of appropriately qualified coaches available for an increasing pool of participants. From 2012 all USA Rugby coaches are required to complete a Player Protection Package that includes training in a number of critical areas of athlete safety and well-being. Perhaps the next step is to teach all coaches the LTAD guidelines followed by many English-speaking NGBs, including Rugby Canada.

Table 4.16 Results of rugby survey, Level 6 – Talent identification and development (Carney, Smolianov, & Zakus, 2012)

Desired Practices	Average Score	Distribution of Responses		
		Negative/ Lacking (%)	Neutral (%)	Positive/ Existing (%)
1. In addition to children being introduced to Rugby by themselves and parents, potential Rugby players are attracted from outside the sport's participation base (e.g., by a search at schools)	2.6	44	38	18
2. Young Rugby players are trained based on guidelines for multiple development stages recommended by USA Rugby, (many national governing bodies have guidelines for nurturing players from the introduction to sport through the achievement of peak performance on to retirement from sport)	2.6	47	35	18
3. Sufficient resources are available collectively from various supporting organizations for all young talented Rugby players to progress through all developmental stages	2.4	60	34	6
4. A multi-stage system of player qualification based on results/ ranking within age groups is used to reward player progress from beginner to top international level	2.3	59	27	14
5. Performance of Rugby players in each competitive age group is monitored and developed using a national database	2.0	59	35	6
6. A high number of full-time Rugby coaches are available making the athlete-coach ratio low	1.8	87	10	3
7. Rugby coach expertise is equally high across all participant ages and levels	2.0	81	16	3
8. Rugby coaches are paid according to multi-level certification based on coaches' education and achievements of entrusted players	1.6	88	10	2

continued …

Table 4.16 continued

Desired Practices	Average Score	Distribution of Responses		
		Negative/ Lacking (%)	Neutral (%)	Positive/ Existing (%)
9. Players with potential to represent the country (e.g. Nations top 50 players per age group) are offered the conditions to train full time with high performance standards	1.9	75	21	4
10. Rugby training is well integrated with school/college/ university education for harmonious development of athletes	2.0	75	20	5
Percentage across all items in element (based on N=127 for each row)		68	24	8

USA Rugby developed junior elite sides in the last decade, first with an U19 team, followed by the U17 and U20 teams. The national seven-a-side team is improving. Unfortunately, the Collegiate All-American team, due to funding and budget issues at USA Rugby, is struggling to compete against age-grade teams around the world. The new High-School All-American side was introduced in 2009 at both U17 and U19 age levels, which was an important step for USA Rugby to establish itself as a world-leading rugby nation. Developing the grassroots and rewarding children for excellence is how rugby programs have progressed in other successful countries. USA Rugby also took the next step of talent identification and development (TID) for the U20 age grade by having multiple camps at different locations around the country to allow more athletes to attend without undue financial hardship.

Open responses indicated that promotion and structure at the high school level of rugby have been insufficient, that many colleges do not advertise their programs to young players, and that overall USA Rugby does not focus enough on the grassroots. Territorial Union Administrator A's (March 18, 2010) suggestion was indicative of the overall survey sample: "Scrap the Eagles for the next few years and channel those resources into growing the game from the ground up, not the top down." While it is unlikely that USA Rugby would take that path of suspending the national men's team, more must be done to develop an elite national competition. Being a strongly free-enterprise market economy, there are many avenues to explore on this variable. As it stands, for far too long elite-level U.S. players have not been subsidized for their commitment to the sport and to their country. Players in certain other nations with fully professional rugby structures, such as France, England, Australia, South Africa, and NZ, are paid for their athletic services. Some U.S. players have obtained professional contracts with overseas clubs. A handful of international caliber players who prefer to play in the United States have a regular day job supplemented by small stipends to play for certain U.S. clubs (i.e., they are semi-professionals). However, the money they are paid is not enough to cover much more than travel expenses.

The literature suggests that sport leagues pursue various objectives, other than revenues, profits, and utility maximization, as they also seek financial survival, international playing success, and the maintenance of tradition (Cairns, Jennett, & Sloane, 1986). The leagues interested in maximizing revenues or profits are likely to put a much higher premium on achieving and maintaining close competition than leagues motivated primarily by utility maximization. In utility-maximizing leagues, competitive balance may take a back seat to objectives such as preserving the league status of weak but long-established teams and allowing the emergence of dominant teams that form the nucleus of successful national sides (Siebrits & Fourie, 2009). An example of this in the United States is the University of California at Berkeley. They have established one of the best rugby programs in the country by focusing resources on scouting and selectively "importing" players from overseas. Because of that, UC Berkeley has provided the national team with numerous players over the last ten years. Unfortunately, due to significant budget cuts in the athletics department at UC Berkeley and to various Title IX issues, the rugby team was downgraded to varsity club status, which puts the TID pathway to the national team in jeopardy.

Currently, there are no scouts at the elite level of USA Rugby. Instead, the elite team coaches are trained to identify prospective players at different age levels. This can be compared with NZ, which is among Tier 1 nations, where Super 16 teams employ scouts (player development specialists) throughout their elite rugby program to identify players at all age grades, leaving their coaches to focus on preparing their teams. Another method identified in the Model and available for transfer from many successful sport nations, is to train and designate the beginner-level coaches to search for talent at schools.

Countries such as England, Australia, and South Africa hone the skills of their younger rugby players far better than does USA Rugby. For example, the Australian Institute of Sport provides a national TID program that is integrated with state/regional institutes of sport. Coaches and elite players deliver sport skill and TID programs across the nation and at all levels of participation. In part, this is also due to the finances available in these countries for rugby as compared to the limited resources USA Rugby has, provides, or is able to generate. However, money is not the only factor diminishing the development of these rising prospects. It is also the huge size of the country with many regional "pockets" of highly developed rugby structures and programs. Again, Australia and South Africa are large countries and they deal with this issue through the state/provincial level rugby unions that are well connected to the school and club levels. For USA Rugby to develop talent, as is included in the Model, permanent regional centers with extant training camp facilities must be established. The Olympic Development Program launched in 2013 is designed to address this issue through the development of coordinated academies for up-and-coming players. This new talent is not yet ready for international competition but show or have the ability to play on the national team; or are players who are in the extended player pool but not part of the Eagles' residency program. They may also be domestic club-based athletes, non-collegiate age-grade athletes, or college athletes whose university programs are not delivering a high-performance rugby experience.

This program can then accommodate each age group in regional areas so players could more easily, quickly, and less expensively travel to camps. The development of regional super unions will enhance this development. USA Rugby has already started down this path with many states already establishing their own unions (e.g., Rugby Michigan). By partnering with these organizations, USA Rugby can channel resources by establishing regular coaching and refereeing clinics or by establishing a permanent presence in the states to utilize the personnel already operating at the grass-roots level of the sport. This local sport delivery will grow the game at the state level.

For player development, athletes must all be on the same program, and their progress must be recorded and stored in a database for coaches, specialist personnel, and management to review without difficulty. USA Rugby currently tracks all of its athletes in paper evaluation format that is inefficient but effective. By keeping track of athletes as they progress through the stages of development, coaches have a history of each player, their starting point, and their improvement from that point.

There are many TIDs in use currently by various rugby unions. Researchers (e.g., Vaeyens, Lenoir, Williams & Philippaerts 2008) found that those unions employing cross-sectional designs have based their work on the assumption that the important characteristics of success in adult performance can be extrapolated to identify talented youngsters. However, adolescents who possess the required characteristics will not necessarily retain these attributes through to maturation. This suggests not only that some unions have the wrong TID in effect but that scouts/coaches may not be properly trained and educated to identify talent at certain ages (Du Randt, 1993). The best international practice assumed in the Model is to discover talent at appropriate ages by constantly redefining and advancing TIDs based on most recent research and by retraining coaches to identify talent. It is also noted that with international cooperation, researchers of different countries work better together to identify the profile and characteristics of elite youth rugby players (Spamer, 2005; Spamer & Winsley, 2003).

Element 7: Advanced athlete support

As with most other elements in this sport, there is a strong response indicating that rugby does not follow the Model (see Table 4.17). For six variables (#1, 2, 3, 4, 5, 8) responses in the negative/lacking category exceeded 50 percent, with the two remaining categories (#6, 7) exceeding 30 percent. Neutral responses were the mirror image of these results, with responses around 50 percent for variables 6 and 7 and around 30 percent for all other variables. Again, the figures tell the story, with overall negative responses at 57 percent, neutral responses at 38 percent, and positive responses at 5 percent.

Table 4.17 Results of rugby survey, Level 7 – Advanced athlete support (Carney, Smolianov, & Zakus, 2012)

Desired Practices	Average Score	Distribution of Responses		
		Negative/ Lacking (%)	Neutral (%)	Positive/ Existing (%)
1. Athletes, including Rugby players, are supported at places of work and service with conditions similar to those at Home Depot and US Army (paid time off given to train and compete)	2.0	69	29	2
2. High performance players are ranked into hierarchical levels/ pools with appropriate financial and technical support	2.1	65	30	5
3. Athletes are assisted with formal education and career development outside of sport	1.9	72	26	2
4. Athlete support is well shared/ balanced between coaches and advisors (e.g., coach may provide psychological, nutritional, and performance science support, while independent advisors may best assist with medicine, career, education, and personal finances)	2.3	60	32	8
5. Scientific research (e.g., biomechanics of athlete movement and psychophysiological analysis) is applied quickly and effectively to immediately benefit player performance	2.2	62	35	3
6. Player career is prolonged by medical personnel knowledgeable in Rugby (helping with such things as injury prevention, adjustment of training levels, nutrition, pharmacology, rest and stimulation therapy, doping use prevention)	2.6	42	49	9
7. Doping is controlled by USA Rugby based on the most recent guidelines from the World Anti-Doping Agency and the IRB.	2.3	35	52	13
8. Athletes leaving elite sport are provided with individualized lifestyle plans for physical and psychological health	1.7	51	48	1
Percentage across all items in element (based on N=127 for each row)		57	38	5

Half of the survey respondents indicated that lifestyle plans are never or rarely provided to U.S. Rugby players leaving elite sport, with only 1 percent saying that it happens often or always. A study conducted by McKenna and Howard (2007) suggested that players who are forced to retire early due to increased competition demands or whose contracts were not renewed feel a sense of betrayal. Without post-career plans, these players have a hard time adjusting to life after sport. Post-career planning and programs allow current players to support the future of rugby: Many former high-profile athletes turn to managing or coaching major teams around the world after they have completed their playing career.

The RFU in England is leading the way in athlete career support. The majority of coaches and managers in the Aviva Premiership teams are former England internationals from two to ten years ago. Such career paths are still to be fully established, although there is now a path to coaching from national representation at USA Rugby. However, the quantitative and qualitative results of this study indicate that USA Rugby is still lacking the resources for the development of top-level medical doctors, sport scientists, and other specialists with rugby expertise as contained in the Model and implemented by leading rugby nations.

USA Rugby has focused in recent years on improving their coaching, medical, strength/conditioning, video analysis, and other specialist services. The desired improvements have not yet seen a significant effect in the performance of the National Teams, although performances in the Sevens World Series and Rugby World Cup for both men and women have shown that these changes have set a solid foundation from which to build successful teams.

As with many other rugby nations, USA Rugby has hired coaches with international experience to coach their national teams. However, as can be seen from the recent World Cup performance, the U.S. Eagles (Men's National 15s Team) did not raise their level of performance enough to compete with Tier 1 nations. Although the United States played well against Tier 1 nations Ireland and Italy, they still fell short and were eliminated in the pool stages of the tournament. This is yet another demonstration that even with a coach with international experience and knowledge, performance cannot be improved except with the full involvement of the national team in training. With the IRB not fully supporting Article 9 of its charter, players contracted with various professional clubs around the world are often not available for national squad training. This is a negative situation for many rugby nations but more so the Tier 2 ones such as the United States, whose top players are either inconsistently or not available for national team preparation.

Open responses confirm the quantitative results that there is not nearly enough athlete support for U.S. players and teams to compete consistently at a world-class level. The responses also suggest utilizing university sport science departments to produce research and establish agreements so students can study rugby and provide USA Rugby with valuable data. Athlete support over the years has improved dramatically, especially since rugby officially turned professional in 1995. The Super Rugby competition in the southern hemisphere consists of professional teams that pay salaries to their players and provide full, professional support systems. Many of these players also play in the Rugby Championship[8] tournament for their national teams, often with a contract supplement to reflect this selection. The training these players receive is based on the latest findings of science on elite performance, and it is synchronized with the respective countries' governing bodies (Australian Rugby Football Union, NZ Rugby Football Union, South Africa Rugby Union; combined known as SANZAR), to whom these players are also contracted, so there can be integrated athlete development at all playing levels.

Other nations with no "professional" league have a hard time competing because the onus is fully on their shoulders to keep the players at an elite standard. The U.S. has the Super League as the equivalent of the Aviva Premiership in the UK club championships. The problem is that the clubs in the Super League do not have the same level of private ownership (the so-called "sugar daddies") and sponsorship, nor does USA Rugby have the financial resources to match contracts on offer from overseas clubs. So the development of United States players is not well-balanced or even connected to the programs USA Rugby seeks to follow. The current contractual relationship between the U.S. Super League and its players is therefore lacking many important aspects of an overall athlete support system (i.e beyond suitable pay contracts).

Assistance with formal education and careers outside sport, along with individualized lifestyle plans for physical and psychological health at a later stage of a playing career, are all important improvement areas for USA Rugby. About a third of the respondents are not sure of, or do not know about, five of the eight desired supporting provisions.

In conclusion, the key areas for improvement recognized but not yet fully addressed by USA Rugby were: a lack of integration between USA Rugby and the Territorial Unions that oversee rugby in the various regions of the United States, a lack of communication between USA Rugby and its members, and a lack of development throughout the country. The focus of this development needs to be further channelled toward better coaching, academies, and facilities for youths rather than focusing more on the elite aspects of the sport, until rugby can support itself. With greater media exposure and corporate involvement in rugby, more audience creation and financial partnerships will likely evolve.

In terms of the many possibilities raised in this study and through the Model, some have begun to be addressed by USA Rugby. In 2011 after considerable problems with communication between USA Rugby and its members, USA Rugby has opened up new lines of contact. USA Rugby is now on key social media (Facebook, U-Stream, Twitter). And as noted earlier, Nigel Melville hosts a blog. Along with an increased focus on developing competition structures at the high school and college levels, USA Rugby dealt with most of the key gaps. USA Rugby also launched its inaugural USA Rugby College National Sevens Championships that served to identify and develop the national seven-a-side teams. There is much more to do.

Practices of United States soccer against the Model

The questionnaire was delivered online to a total sample of 1,000 U.S. Soccer coaches. A total of 124 (12 percent) valid surveys resulted. This was an acceptable response rate for online surveys. The soccer survey respondents represented twenty-one states of the country covering each of the four major areas in the United States Soccer governance structure: East, West, South, and Midwest. Forty-three percent of surveyed soccer coaches worked with beginner-level athletes, 60 percent coached high school athletes; 34 percent coached NCAA Division III, 17 percent NCAA Division II, and 33 percent NCAA Division I college and university players, and 23 percent coached elite-level athletes. Ninety-five percent of coaching professionals reported having a coaching certification from a national governing body of soccer such as the American Youth Soccer Organization, United States Soccer Federation (USSF), United States Soccer (U.S. Soccer), National Soccer Coaches Association of America, or the Fédération Internationale de Football Association (FIFA). Fifteen percent obtained the highest level of soccer certification, the USSF level A; 94 percent of the coaches had at least a bachelor's degree; and 55 percent had a postgraduate degree. On average, respondents were thirty-four years of age and had fifteen years of soccer coaching experience. Eighty-six percent of respondents were male and 14 percent female.

Currently, the U.S. Women's soccer team is one of the most successful national soccer teams in the world. The U.S. Women's team was ranked first in the FIFA world rankings in 2012 and won the gold medal at the London Olympic Games. The U.S. Men's team was ranked eighteenth in 2011 and did not qualify for the 2012 Olympic Games. U.S. mass soccer participation grew from 5.9 percent of the population in 2007 to 7.8 percent in 2012 (with 9,000 clubs registered in 2012) that, compared with Germany's 20 percent and 26,000 clubs with a much smaller population base, is much lower (FIFA, 2012); yet great outcomes are being achieved.

Element 1: Balanced and integrated funding and structures of mass and elite sport

Negative and neutral responses run neck and neck in this element, with variables 1, 3, 5, and 6 accorded negative responses of at least 50 percent. All other responses were neutral, to at least a 30-percent minimum level. The only variable (#4) had a positive response rate of 62 percent (see Table 4.18). It appears, therefore, that in general, these structural and funding variables of this element are not evident in the U.S. soccer system at this time.

There was one practice (#10) in which the responses, less the neutral ones, were fairly even. Negative responses were at the 32-percent level while the positive ones were at 27 percent. There is an indication here that members of the soccer community are not clear on whether U.S. Soccer and the USSF are effective in delivering programs for both mass and elite players. This situation demands further investigation.

Table 4.18 Results of soccer survey, Level 1 – Balanced and integrated funding and structures of mass and elite sport (Smolianov, Murphy, McMahon, & Naylor, 2014)

Desired Practices	Average Score	Distribution of Responses		
		Negative/ Lacking (%)	Neutral (%)	Positive/ Existing (%)
1. Corporate and philanthropic tax incentives provide sufficient support of mass and elite soccer	2.3	58	35	7
2. Participation in various sports, as a foundation for soccer development, is encouraged through physical education requirements	2.9	37	34	29
3. Sport participation, including soccer, is rewarded with reduced personal tax	1.6	84	8	8
4. Soccer programs service both recreational and high performance players	3.7	11	27	62
5. Specialized sport schools similar to the IMG Academies are available and affordable to all talented players.	2.1	80	17	3
6. A multi-stage system of elite soccer player qualification is integrated with a system of fitness tests for mass participants such as the President's Challenge Awards Program	2.3	60	34	6
7. Programs affordable for all are available in various soccer clubs	2.6	46	45	9
8. Soccer participants are as diverse as the general population	3.3	21	40	39
9. U.S.Soccer and USSF demonstrate systematic/strategic management in developing soccer on every level	2.8	33	46	21
10. U.S.Soccer and USSF are effective in fostering both mass participation and high performance in soccer	2.9	32	41	27
11. Soccer is developed in integration with Olympic and Paralympic sports to achieve sustainable competitive excellence	3.1	21	46	33
Percentage across all items in element (based on N=124 for each row)		44	34	22

Looking at the overall average response ($N = 124$) by response category, we observe that 44 percent of the surveyed coaches selected negative/lacking, while 34 percent were neutral, and 22 percent saw some alignment with aspects of the Model.

There is a lack of tax incentives for sport participation in the United States. The lowest rated statement in the survey was, "Sport participation, including soccer, is rewarded with reduced personal tax." Administrator B (April 8, 2011) from USSF commented that, "tax incentives have very little to do with our programs. In our state where education is a disaster right now, many sports programs are being removed completely. There are no tax breaks...." The United States may find the Canadian, German, Spanish, and Dutch experiences with mass participation tax incentives useful. At the elite level, tax incentives are also used to attract soccer players. After allowing nonresidents to be taxed at a flat rate of 24 percent, Spain saw an increase in the number and percentage of international players. Greece, Denmark, and Belgium have similar policies in legislation. Italy, with no such policies and a higher tax rate, witnessed a reduction in their share of foreign talent (Belsie, 2011).

According to 58 percent of surveyed coaches, corporate and philanthropic tax incentives in the United States never or rarely provide support for mass and elite soccer. The U.S. Soccer Foundation facilitates sports-based youth development programs for children in underserved, urban communities. From 1994, when it was founded, until 2012, the Foundation has provided more than $55 million to help fund programs in all fifty states. While the Foundation claimed that 80 percent of the 8,000 participants in 2011 reduced their BMI percentile and stayed out of trouble, they did not report the actual weight reductions and decreases in crime rates for the participants. No specific results in improved soccer performance were identified (The U.S. Soccer Foundation, 2012).

Respondents expressed particular dissatisfaction that soccer-specialized schools and academies are unaffordable. In the open response section of the survey, Coach 37 (March 8, 2011) made this position clear in the following comment: "We need to make the sports affordable to low income kids and to continue establishing diversity within the sport, especially in low income areas. Soccer-specific schools such as IMG and St Shattuck-St Mary's serve the ones that can pay." Administrator D (April 13, 2011) agreed with this, stating that "these places are few in number and quite expensive as well as quite exclusive for that very reason." Major concern expressed in twelve open responses was that the costs of playing soccer at most levels are too high and that many potential participants are excluded with the limited subsidization and scholarships. Coach 116 (February 9, 2011) summed this point up agreeing that "participation in soccer has increased, but support for advanced development and financial contribution has not kept pace."

Currently, the best U.S. youth players must pay anywhere between $4,000 and $8,000 a year to play in the U.S. Academy League, while Europe's top players pay nothing in their leagues. In addition, the collegiate soccer season is limited to a mere five months (Ziemer, 2011). Based on the USSF's 2012 *Annual General Meeting*

Book, the USSF generated close to $70 million in 2011, almost 90 percent through elite-level events and sponsorships (USSF AGM, 2012). Mass participation income such as member registration fees and coach and referee development programs was about 10 percent of the overall USSF revenue (USSF AGM, 2012). The USSF's spending on mass soccer does not exceed $3 million, which is only 4 percent of all expenditure (USSF AGM, 2012).

Element 2: Partnerships with supporting agencies

More than 50 percent of respondents agree on variable 2, that the governing soccer bodies in the U.S. appear to be doing a good job in providing support for the sport (see Table 4.19). Other than variable 1, where 67 percent of applicants indicate that government support for soccer is negative/lacking, the remaining variables were predominantly neutral (although both variables 5 and 6 also had negative responses in excess of 30 percent). Practice 4 outside the neutral responses was reasonably close in perception. Twenty-two percent saw support for soccer from the educational sector as insufficient (negative/lacking), while 29 percent saw it as a positive and existing. The overall average for each category reflects this result, with 43 percent of neutral responses, 35 percent of negative responses, and 22 percent of positive responses.

In their open responses, eight coaches indicated that sport participation warrants greater financial contribution, and seven coaches specifically suggested coaching education be more readily available. In addition to USSF, the organizations that govern the sport in the United States include the Major League Soccer (MLS) and the USL (United Soccer League).

The MLS is a single-entity structure where all the teams are owned by the league and revenue is shared throughout. Conversely, the USL comprises three developmental divisions to encourage participation at all levels. The U.S. Youth Soccer (USYS) is the largest youth sports organization in the United States. The second largest is the American Youth Soccer Organization. Cooperation among these national soccer organizations can be improved to provide more uniform, integrated paths for progressing participants and coaches. Soccer players in the United States are now being forced to choose between playing for their club or school teams: The USSF announced in 2012 that its eighty affiliated academies would no longer be able to participate in high school soccer. While Administrator A (April 4, 2011) stressed the need for developmental support of children's recreational soccer, Administrator B (April 8, 2011) argued that

> there is hardly anything done for players after they reach the adult level...
> except for Olympic teams or certain youth teams, there is little to no support.
> Many states have large immigrant populations for which the gifted player is
> totally overlooked. There is no support for local (upper division) teams from
> anyone. Our state would give traveling teams $US1,000 per game in which
> they had to travel, however, that would hardly pay for 18 players plus coaches
> to travel to LA from Dallas. The players had to support themselves.

Table 4.19 Results of soccer survey, Level 2 – Partnerships with supporting agencies (Smolianov, Murphy, McMahon, & Naylor, 2014)

Desired Practices	Average Score	Distribution of Responses		
		Negative/ Lacking (%)	Neutral (%)	Positive/ Existing (%)
1. Support for soccer player development is adequate from various levels of government	2.3	67	27	6
2. Sufficient help is obtained from U.S. Soccer, USSF, NSCAA, and other national governing bodies of soccer that provide coach education and certification	3.5	15	28	57
3. Role of clubs/community programs in soccer development is sound	2.9	26	58	16
4. Soccer is well supported by the educational sector (e.g., schools, colleges, universities)	3.1	22	49	29
5. Cooperation with agencies outside of the sport industry (e.g., medical, scientific, military, philanthropic and sponsoring organizations, lotteries) is in place	2.6	43	49	8
6. U.S.Soccer and USSF influence media coverage and popularity of soccer to increase support from the society	2.8	39	44	17
Percentage across all items in element (based on N=124 for each row)		35	43	22

As for other U.S. sports, soccer receives virtually no support compared to other developed sporting nations (from which U.S. NGBs and federal and state authorities could also learn to utilize soccer to improve health, enhance education, and reduce crime).

Support from partners outside the sport industry, such as medical, scientific, military, and various sponsoring organizations, can also be improved. Only 8 percent of coaches were positive that this cooperation is in place, whereas 43 percent were negative. According to Coach 8 (April 4, 2011), "the USSF could better capitalize on the popularity of the sport among young children. Too often, the lack of support of professional soccer gives too many potential partners the impression that the game is not popular." Coach 13 (March 17, 2011) also noted that "more opportunities can be utilized across the local, state, and federal governing bodies through better communication of upcoming opportunities for growth, development, and access to the sport of soccer." A similar view that internal problems result in a lack of external support was expressed by Administrator C (April 13, 2011) who stated that "adult soccer gets very little support from the various levels of soccer. We do not have the active involvement of parents to gain political support for additional fields and maintenance of facilities." Coach 6 (April 5, 2011) also saw that external support can be improved by a change of attitude within the soccer community as

> soccer people tend to be very insulated among themselves… they can develop a distorted view on how soccer is viewed by the community/media, etc. at large. Soccer people need to interact with as many other sports as possible. Fighting other sports for attention, athletes, etc. will not work in the United States. We need to understand that soccer is currently a secondary sport in the United States and probably will remain that way through our lifetimes…. Growth and changing perceptions is a very slow process. We need to embrace other sports and possibly try and work in partnership with them.

In terms of item 6, the USSF could better influence media coverage, the popularity of soccer, and increase support from society, according to coaches. In an open response Coach 31 (March 8, 2011) expressed a commonly held view by stating that

> I was not sure there is a system in place to center the attention in this area. At times, through TV, but we have lost our means of support as to what it takes for us to become a soccer nation that is supported by media, fans, and agencies in general.

Administrator B (April 4, 2011) shared that

> there is absolutely little to no media coverage for amateur or youth. One of our local TV hosts even lets it be known that he doesn't think our sport is a true sport at all. We are not even getting coverage for the Liberian project we are working on, because it is a foreign country and it is soccer.

Administrator D (April 13, 2011) responded, "I believe that this is getting better, but there isn't quite enough influence there. I think they will be able to command more influence as the National Teams gain more ground in international competitions as well as domestically."

The biggest soccer audience of 18 million viewers was attracted by a 1990 U.S. Women's World Cup match between the United States and China, so there is great potential to transfer the U.S. international success to the domestic U.S. market. In addition to ESPN coverage, NBC signed a three-year contract to televise more than forty MLS games and two U.S. Men's National Team games every year starting in 2012. The United States is catching up with nations such as Brazil, England, and Germany where soccer is regularly televised on multiple networks. The 2012 World Cup was televised live and broadcast online. The U.S. U17 World Cup was televised on ESPN television and streamed live online on ESPN3.com. Despite these new ways of promoting soccer through mass media, opportunities for the USSF to increase media exposure are still significant (e.g., streaming games live on the U.S. Soccer Facebook page).

Element 3. Educational, scientific, medical, philosophical, and promotional support

While this element in the tennis and rugby results was highly neutral, for soccer we see a different distribution of results (see Table 4.20). Perceptions of research being fostered (#3) and communication of research results (#2) were perceived by more coaches as positive/existing, the second of these by more than 50 percent. Variable 4 returned the only predominantly negative score on this element. All other results were neutral in the overall response rate.

A comparison of the non-neutral results in variables 3, 5, and 6 indicate a balance between how respondents see these variables either existing or not existing. This is an interesting result. More research into why these differences exist might provide answers to the organizational and governance structure of the sport. It seems there are two opposing views in terms of how research is fostered and how communication operates in soccer. The number of respondents who do not believe that vision and leadership exist in governing bodies is almost equal to the number who believe that they do. Perhaps this might be that there are different governing bodies for soccer. More research is demanded.

In terms of the overall averages, neutral responses were once again dominant at 40 percent, with positive responses at 33 percent and negative responses at 27 percent. This is one of the most positive averages for any element in soccer and, indeed, any of the three sports surveyed. In almost all cases, negative responses averaged across the element were higher than the positive responses.

Generally, sport-specific education and licensing of coaches is not required in the United States as is the practice in countries such as France, Russia, Spain, and the United Kingdom. However, the USSF provides education as part of their licensing, which is also not required but usually expected from U.S. coaches. Starting with youth club teams, coaches should possess a USSF "Class E" license that entails only eighteen hours of classroom instruction. Once having this license, a coach can work toward a Class D or C license that should allow for coaching youths up to the age of fourteen. Coaches at the high school and college levels need a Class B license from the USSF, which entails twenty classroom hours and forty-eight hours in field-related experience. The elite level of professional and senior developmental teams are trained by coaches who hold a Class A license (Thyberg, 2012).

A common theme across open responses was that communication must be improved, and seven coaches stressed that this should be done from the grassroots level up, which aligned with the open comments in Element 1. How the USSF provides vision and leadership in improving all aspects of the participants' well-

Table 4.20 Results of soccer survey, Level 3 – Educational, scientific, medical, philosophical, promotional support (Smolianov, Murphy, McMahon, & Naylor, 2014)

Desired Practices	Average Score	Distribution of Responses		
		Negative/ Lacking (%)	Neutral (%)	Positive/ Existing (%)
1. All specialists engaged in the development of soccer players are well educated for their professional roles	3.3	14	56	30
2. Research results are well communicated to coaches (e.g., by research institutes, universities, USSF, and U.S. Soccer)	3.4	14	34	52
3. U.S. Soccer and USSF foster research on all important aspects of soccer development	3.0	31	34	35
4. Principles of sportsman like conduct and Olympism are communicated well (e.g., through mass media, school education, and through the arts as part of soccer events)	2.7	45	36	19
5. U.S. Soccer's communication contributes to national values and identity by inspiring participants to strive for excellence, to show the best results and character in the world	3.1	27	40	33
6. U.S. Soccer and USSF provide vision and leadership in improving all aspects of the participants' well-being through soccer (e.g., physical, social, emotional, mental, spiritual, and environmental/ecological)	3.0	32	37	31
Percentage across all items in element (based on N=124 for each row)		27	40	33

being through soccer is an area for improvement, with more negative than positive responses. This relates to the respondents' comments mentioned earlier about the lack of communication and coaching education.

Coach 8 (April 4, 2011) expressed a common view: "The USSF Coaching Education Program should include more strategies and skills for communicating values that can be strengthened through soccer. There is not enough education geared toward coaching low-level athletes and teams and how to make it a positive learning experience." Coach 17 (March 15, 2011) concurred and stressed the organizational mechanisms which could make communication more effective:

> Grass root level communication needs improvement. USSF used to have a link to this through the National Staff coaches that were tasked with getting into the states and working with the educational component of each state association. Those positions are no longer involved at that level, focusing on scouting instead.

Administrators' responses were quite similar, indicating that there is lack of leadership or vision being communicated by the USSF. Or, as Administrator G (April, 28, 2011) noted, "none depending on how you see it … it is tough … the majority of support is at the elite level." This is supported by Administrator B (April 8, 2011), who wrote that

> U.S. Soccer's involvement is wonderful; however, again it is not communicated well to adult leagues at all. From my years with USL and being one of the three founders; I know most of the board, however... we have amateur teams going all the way to a semi-final with MLS teams and there was very little to no communication, coming from U.S. Soccer or, USASA. There is [sic] little to no guidelines coming from anyone for … coaches. It is their experience that guides them.

Administrator A (April 4, 2011) explained the problem with alarming pessimism:

> U.S. Soccer could not care less if U.S. Youth Soccer or any other youth organization exists or not. All they want the youth for is to pay membership fees to fund World Cup bids, worldwide travel, etc. Witness the imbalance of voting strength at the USSF AGM.

However, Coach 90 (February 17, 2011) had a constructive suggestion:

> Develop a communication system to reach out to important constituents. Then involve those constituents in creating an overall vision or create a vision that holds nearly universal acclaim in the U.S. as a quality vision. Once you have the former, you can develop a system that might actually work to advance any services.

Coach 55 (March 3, 2011) added that "USA Soccer needs to have a greater outreach through Internet, media marketing, Facebook, newsletters, Twitter, magazines, seminars"; that is, through social media that are most widely used today.

Some coaches provide individual athletes with an education that informs them about good sportsmanship, but this has a limited effect on the national scale. Principles of Olympism can be better utilized for providing vision and leadership to the U.S. soccer community through such global programs as the International Olympic Committee's Olympic Values Education Program.

Element 4: Domestic and international competitions

This element in soccer had virtually the same distribution of responses as was the case for tennis. All results for element four were predominantly neutral (see Table 4.21) with all but one exceeding 40 percent of the responses. That being said, more than 30 percent of respondents rated variables 2 to 5 positively and variables 1 and 6 negatively. All in all, and leaving aside neutral responses, perceptions of the planning and integration of professional and amateur tournaments are fairly evenly split between positive and negative.

This is reflected in the averaged overall category results, with 44 percent of responses being neutral and positive and negative responses equal at 28 percent each. This is, again, an unusual situation.

Though financial limitations hindering the development of competitions were noted by eleven coaches, Coach 37 (March 8, 2011) summed it up succinctly: "Sponsorship dollars are being included in top flight tourneys...." This was agreed to by Administrator D (April 13, 2011) stating, "my personal experience suggests that event sponsorship incomes are actually used to develop competitions for mainly the higher levels." Administrator B (April 8, 2011) explained:

> There are not enough adult events and for those that exist, there is little funding. The youth organization (USYSA) does a better job at their age levels and parents have more money than the adult players. Our state begins adult play at 18; however, many begin at 16 or less. That category is where promising players are developed for most advanced competitions.

Sponsorship money from the world's most powerful soccer competition systems, such as the English Premier League, is used to develop grass roots soccer. More needs to be done in the United States in this regard.

Another problem, according to 35 percent of surveyed coaches, is that international competition is never or rarely sufficient for all athletes with potential to represent the country. Coach 9 (April 4, 2011) suggested that

> every affiliated club teams' program should be given opportunity to send players to ODP (Olympic Development Program) and other developmental opportunities rather than invite only [sic]. Soccer is becoming extremely political.... It is not who you are but who you know in many cases.

The ODP is supposed to locate talented players who can feed U.S. Youth National Teams. It is, however, hard to integrate ODP with other soccer competitions within the U.S. decentralized sport system. For example, players can go to a two-week ODP event or trial, be deemed ineligible for the high school season, and not be able to play in any other league for two to three months while

Table 4.21 Results of soccer survey, Level 4 – Domestic and international competitions (Smolianov, Murphy, McMahon, & Naylor, 2014)

Desired Practices	Average Score	Distribution of Responses		
		Negative/ Lacking (%)	Neutral (%)	Positive/ Existing (%)
1. Hosted international events and international opportunities are sufficient for all athletes with potential to represent the country	2.8	35	46	19
2. Competitions are well structured at all levels (e.g., club/ training center, regional, and national)	3.1	23	45	32
3. U.S. Soccer, USSF, and their support mechanisms sufficiently assist in local and sectional developmental events (e.g., U.S. Youth Soccer Region I (East) Championships Lancaster, PA)	3.1	20	47	33
4. U.S. Soccer and USSF attempt to integrate professional and amateur tournaments into a progressive plan of competitions gradually preparing athletes for peak performance at "Majors" (i.e., World Cup, Superliga, North American Soccer League, FIFA Beach Soccer World Cup), Paralympic Games, and Olympic Games	3.0	27	43	30
5. U.S. Soccer and USSF try to coordinate all domestic and international competitions for all ages and levels, between and within all possible organizations	3.1	29	36	35
6. Event sponsorship incomes are used to develop competitions for all participation levels	2.8	36	44	20
Percentage across all items in element (based on N=124 for each row)		28	44	28

the high school season takes place: Or they can skip the ODP event and play for their high school. Some states allow players to be excused for ODP, but many do not.

The situation is further complicated as states play high school soccer at different times of the year. In the Southern states such as Florida and California, soccer is played mostly in the winter, generally from December to March; while the bulk of the country plays from August to November and a few states play only during spring. About twenty states complicate matters further by having either the entire state or several leagues in the state play boys' soccer in fall and girls' soccer in spring. Thus, no matter when ODP schedules an event for the players in the national pool, there will likely be a conflict with high school soccer (Kansas City United, 2011).

For amateur players (U20 and older) there are two programs. One is a state-by-state program that allows each state to select a team. Only about half the states have enough interest to field a team. These state teams compete in regional tournaments that result in the selection of regional teams, usually in late May, and the regional winners then compete for a national championship in November. The regional and national events are scouted by the national team coaches. The other is the Premier Development League, which has also been granted ODP status along with the Y League. In turn, the USYSA delegates to each of its regions, and the state associations within each region, the job of creating an ODP.

As a result, there are fifty-four separate state-run talent-scouting programs that differ in the pattern of accomplishing the objective, the process of funding the project, and the number of players participating. Larger states both in terms of population and area tend to split themselves into districts, while the largest ones add an intermediate level for the regions. In other cases a team of approximately eighteen players in each age group is chosen to compete with teams from the other districts/regions. The problem with such systems stems from the unspoken assumption that the pool of players is equal in quality and quantity in each region. This is rarely the case (United, 2011).

Coach 94 (February 17, 2011) suggested in his open response that the USSF must promote all kinds of invitational tournaments available to everyone because "there is [sic] a lot of talented players in non-affiliated leagues." U.S. Soccer attempts to integrate professional and amateur tournaments with average success according to the survey respondents, who rated this practice at 3 of 5, with 27 percent of coaches indicating that it never or rarely happens. Coach 116 (February 9, 2011) believed that youth competitions in particular should be better developed and integrated; and noted that though "there is good focus on the men's side by USSF... once the players reach 16–18 years old and beyond.... We are lacking at the youth development levels, which is why we are still far behind other nations."

Another indicative open response worthy of attention was by Coach 31 (March 8, 2011): "The problem is... more often the focus is on winning the tournament not whether... there are better players playing the game. We need to focus on games throughout the year and tone down competitive tournaments." Administrator C (April 13, 2011) noted that "the USSF is primarily involved with the National Teams and professional level. At the state level of adult soccer they receive very little support." Six coaches agreed in their open responses that competition structures could be improved when it comes to making soccer more affordable for lower-income families. Coach 10 (March 23, 2011) explained that "lots of soccer players struggle getting funds to go to these events. Kids from more affluent homes seem to get the better opportunities...."

At the level of elite (semi- and full professional) leagues, financial struggles have significantly and negatively affected elite soccer. The Women's Professional Soccer (WPS) league shut down for the 2012 season after dropping down to just five teams from eight in 2008. MLS, which charged increasing entrance fees (from $10 million in 2004 to $30 million in 2007 and proposed $100 million in 2012) for a team to join, is also facing difficulties creating new teams in the league. The premier-level tournaments will achieve long-term success when a comprehensive integrated system of youth and adult development competitions is built in the United States as it has been done in the most successful soccer nations.

Element 5: Training centers and multi-facility activity hubs

As with tennis and rugby, the results for this element are negative overall, with 5 of 7 variables (variables 3 to 7) at or above 45 percent (see Table 4.22). Only variables 1 and 2 (access and specialized facilities) show positive results greater than 30 percent. The overall average for each response category shows that negative (46 percent) and neutral (40 percent) responses dominated this element; while positive responses constituted a meagre 14 percent.

In their open responses, eighteen coaches indicated that soccer training centers are needed in new locations, while ten coaches mentioned financial limitations resulting in the lack of facilities and, therefore, problems with player development. Coach 46 (March 7, 2011) indicated that there is a need for "more soccer-specific training facilities in each state, including a number of grass and turf fields with an indoor facility." Coach 25 (March 11, 2011) offered another common opinion, suggesting that money is the issue and that it is "very expensive to accommodate the players in the entire USA."

Coach 54 (March 3, 2011) further stressed the financial challenge and raised the issue of equality: "Training centers are at a premium, especially indoor facilities used in colder climates, again feeding the discrepancy between those who can pay for soccer and who cannot. Places that have the best facilities have the most money." Administrator D (April 13, 2011) agreed with Coaches 25 and 54 on this common financial concern:

> Field time and training facilities are very expensive, especially in regions where the climate is not friendly and indoor space must be acquired. Clubs and organizations which do not have vast amounts of wealth will not have the same access to facilities, etc. that the wealthier clubs do.

The financial and social equality issues raised by many participants of this study were related to the overall attitude toward soccer player development. This was expressed by Administrator A (April 4, 2011) who believed that

> the soccer landscape today is embarrassing. The richer a family is the higher level they can afford to play at. We are not developing elite athletes to compete on a global scale! We are developing athletes that can pay for the training. And those are far from the best we can offer.

Table 4.22 Results of soccer survey, Level 5 – Training centers and multi-facility activity hubs (Smolianov, Murphy, McMahon, & Naylor, 2014)

Desired Practices	Average Score	Distribution of Responses		
		Negative/ Lacking (%)	Neutral (%)	Positive/ Existing (%)
1. High performance athletes are provided with priority access to specific high quality equipment and facilities	3.3	15	46	39
2. Training centers provide specialized facilities and equipment for each age and level of participation	3.1	25	44	31
3. All national, regional, and local training centers are available to athletes at affordable costs	2.3	63	31	6
4. Travel from home to training facilities takes little time for players of all levels and types	2.3	68	28	4
5. Training facilities are close to all facilities for athlete support (e.g., school/college, medical, room & board, leisure/ entertainment)	2.6	45	47	8
6. A network of training centers is used to prepare players in different environments/socio-geo-climates (e.g., high altitude/ temperature/humidity, city/ pollution, rural/resort)	2.4	60	38	2
7. Soccer training centers are located close to other sport facilities so that players participate in and learn from other sports	2.6	47	46	7
Percentage across all items in element (based on N=124 for each row)		46	40	14

The United Soccer Academy (2012) provides training facilities for youth players throughout New York, New Jersey, and Pennsylvania and offer camps in eight other Eastern states. A more extensive network of training centers is needed to reduce travel distances. As Coach 98 (February 15, 2011) wrote in an open response: "Those that could not afford to travel did not get to play soccer." Coach 6 (April 5, 2011) provided a reasonable suggestion in line with some best international practices: "Training centers are few and far between. Availability is by invitation only … Possibly less big extravagant Olympic training centers and more support for regional programs" are required. Yet Coach 10 (March 23, 2011) also made a valid point when stating that there is a "need [for] a center in each state … It would be nice if more sport companies would sponsor more training centers." The USSF needs to do more to provide opportunities for affordable training to all ages and skill levels. Development across regions and training centers is still uneven. The USSF could create comprehensive facilities in each state as the coaches' survey indicated that training fields are too far from sport hubs with athlete services and where players could participate in and learn from other sports.

To address the lack of and poor accessibility to comprehensive training centers, the USSF could seek partners to share facilities. This could well lead to multi-sport campuses with educational and other athlete services. To ensure equitable facility provision in each state, indoor space in the north could be subsidized. To increase the number of soccer facilities with specially trained staff as part of multi-sport hubs particularly located at or near schools, universities, and Olympic training centers, the USSF could also partner with the USASA, the USOC, and other NGBs. Professional soccer teams should be encouraged to make facilities available for all soccer players. The surveyed coaches suggested that the USSF has yet to develop soccer specific training centers in all major U.S. cities, indicating a need for more soccer-specific training facilities in each state, including a number of grass and turf fields with an indoor facility (Coach 46, March 7, 2011). Soccer facilities in the United States need to be more similar to IMG Bradenton, where players can live, train more, and still get an education. Money needs to be there so players do not have to pay to do this (Coach 22, March 13, 2011).

Element 6: Talent identification and development

One of the most significant challenges within the U.S. soccer system is related to coach competence: 80 percent of respondents indicated that the level of coach expertise was lacking equally across all participant ages and levels (see Table 4.23). Acknowledging that they receive insufficient coaching education, about half of the respondents were uncertain or not familiar with most talent identification and development practices, particularly with methods of introducing children to soccer from outside the sport's participation base and with the age-appropriate LTAD guidelines.

Seven of the ten variables (#1, 2, 3, 4, 8, 9, 10) were rated as neutral. Three (#5, 6, 7, discussed above) were rated very negatively, and six others (#1,3,4,8,9,10 – almost all of the neutral responses) had negative results of at least 30 percent. In the wash-up, 44 percent of responses for element 6 were in the negative/lacking category, 37 percent were neutral in their response, and 19 percent were positive/existing in their response.

In their open responses, eleven coaches commented on the lack of effective communication by NGBs about talent development. This is despite the fact that the highest-rated statement for Element 1 was related to the training of young soccer players based on guidelines for multiple development stages. As noted above,

Table 4.23 Results of soccer survey, Level 6 – Talent identification and development (Smolianov, Murphy, McMahon, & Naylor, 2014)

Desired Practices	Average Score	Distribution of Responses		
		Negative/ Lacking (%)	Neutral (%)	Positive/ Existing (%)
1. In addition to children being introduced to soccer by themselves and parents, potential soccer players are attracted from outside the sport's participation base (e.g., by a search at schools)	2.8	32	52	16
2. Young soccer players are trained based on guidelines for multiple development stages recommended by U.S. Soccer and USSF (many national governing bodies have guidelines for nurturing players from the introduction to sport through the achievement of peak performance on to retirement from sport)	3.1	26	46	28
3. Sufficient resources are available collectively from various supporting organizations for all young talented soccer players to progress through all developmental stages	3.0	31	43	26
4. A multi-stage system of player qualification based on results/rankings within age groups is used to reward player progress from beginner to top international level	2.9	34	41	25
5. Performance of soccer players in each competitive age group is monitored and developed using a national database	2.4	62	24	14
6. A high number of full-time soccer coaches are available making the athlete-coach ratio low	2.4	63	25	12
7. Soccer coach expertise is equally high across all participant ages and levels	2.1	80	15	5
8. Soccer coaches are paid according to multi-level certification based on coaches' education and achievements of entrusted players	2.8	35	43	22

continued …

Table 4.23 continued

Desired Practices	Average Score	Distribution of Responses		
		Negative/ Lacking (%)	Neutral (%)	Positive/ Existing (%)
9. Players with potential to represent the country (e.g. Nations top 50 players per age group) are offered the conditions to train full time with high performance standards	3.0	33	38	29
10. Soccer training is well integrated with school/college/ university education for harmonious development of athletes	2.7	39	44	17
Percentage across all items in element (based on N=124 for each row)		44	37	19

one reason behind this high rating was that in 2006, the USSF published the document *Best Practices for Coaching in the United States* (U.S. Soccer, 2012) summarizing international and domestic experiences to recommend LTAD guidelines.

The content of this document also sets broad parameters for U.S. player development; for example, it noted that while being physically strong, U.S. players should learn creativity from the Brazilians. It also contains comparisons of the level of U.S. player development to that of other countries in terms of technical and tactical skills, and physical and mental development. The United States ranked in the top three worldwide in physical and mental development, while their technical and tactical skills were ranked fifth to tenth (this was based only on testing the U.S. men's team).

Finally, within this document we also find content and some instructions on duration and type of training, competitions, travel, and rest for LTAD. Though these instructions lack a systematic scientific approach, the practical tips are quite useful, easily accessible online and are better than information available to coaches in many other U.S. sports. Together with USA Hockey, U.S. Soccer followed Canadian state-supported NGBs in educating and encouraging coaches to pursue their short-term goals from a perspective of their players' long-term needs. One national curriculum could be developed for the education of coaches. More resources from public education and professional teams could be attracted to integrate high-quality year-round coaching for all age groups with all conditions for athlete development. The most advanced multidisciplinary support is currently emerging at such expensive private centers as the IMG Academies, but they subsidize only a few top players.

In 2008 the MLS started their "Homegrown Player Initiative," a major step in creating a system more similar to those around the world, where clubs set up academies for LTAD. Prior to 2008 MLS teams were unable to sign players from their youth teams into their senior squads. Now a club may sign a player to his first professional contract without subjecting him to the MLS SuperDraft if the player has trained for at least one year in the club's youth development program and meets other league-based criteria. The USSF is also increasing its support of academies that provide systematic LTAD. Although the MLS and USSF have placed more emphasis on identifying and nurturing young talent and creating incentives for potential professionals to start their careers in the United States, more intense and concerted efforts of soccer NGBs in the United States are needed.

In terms of an LTAD, the USSF's LTAD[9] strategy is emerging, but there is still according to one coach (Nicolle Wood, personal communication, February 06, 2013),

> too much focus on winning vs. development, too many games vs. training opportunities (especially in the high schools and colleges, where players are in competition 2–3 days each week and only training 2–3 days), too many clubs that claim to be "premier" but not enough qualified coaches, adequate training facilities and events [sic]. Clubs can charge high price from parents eager to have their child on an "elite" team. Some clubs provide quality athlete development, others merely make money.

The USSF could better assist coaches to monitor and develop the performance of players in each competitive age group, which never or rarely happens according to 62 percent of coaches. One reasonable suggestion was to start from the elite by creating a national system of qualifications and standards in the United States to determine who will represent Team USA. Systems from which the United States could choose to borrow best practices include many countries from New Zealand and Scotland to China and Russia.

Organizations such as the National Collegiate Scouting Association play an important role in developing U.S. sport talent in the process of recruiting and evaluating student athletes. However, Administrator E (April 11, 2011) suggested that a specialized task force should be set up to support the needs of recruiting and training talented players:

> The real problem is that we have tried to copy the same format that we use for other sport (baseball, basketball, football) and because this is not the model other countries use for soccer in their country- we are constantly downgrading ourselves with how poorly our select teams do in international competitions. Thus we must have an inferior program and we need to put more money, time, and energy into copying the format our foreign friends use.

No improvements are going to bring long-term success without a high number of full-time coaches and low athlete-coach ratios, which is an underdeveloped area of U.S. soccer according to 63 percent of respondents.

Lack of funding to promote athlete development, indicated by seventeen coaches, was the underlying reason for most low ratings in this element. Lack of support related to the size of the country and the inability to "reach out or market to everyone at once" were also important systemic issues noted by ten coaches. Commenting on a lack of resources, of knowledgeable administrators, and of coaches, respondents pointed out that most coaches at the youth and developmental level are parents and they cannot absorb the material fast enough to effectively use the various sources of information. The respondents indicated the need for better facilitators and coaches certified by participants' age groups, particularly at the younger levels.

One coach (Coach 42, March 8, 2011) noted that there is a "lack of knowledge by some who are coaching. Too much being put on winning rather than on developing at the early stages of participation." Further, Coach 68 (March 2, 2011) indicated an important issue which exists around the world – the gap between talk and real action:

> With regards to development, age appropriate coaching is talked about and taught at coaching education courses, certifications, etc., but it's rarely practiced. The reason, I believe, is the lack of quality DOCs [directors of coaching] who are active and want to push these correct player pathways through their club on a daily basis and the lack of quality youth coaches.

Administrator B (April 8, 2011) added that:

> too many full time coaches are in those positions because of their availability and not their ability or desire. Many are paid because they want a passport renewed and true background checks are not always reviewed. Those coaches, who coach from their true desire to produce good players, usually do it for much less than they deserve. Many school coaches have never played and know very little about true coaching.

Despite having one of the most advanced sport systems at the high school, college, and university level, coaches had mixed perceptions on whether soccer training is well integrated with education for the harmonious development of athletes, rating this statement at only 2.7 of 5, with 44 percent being unaware or uncertain of this situation. Mixed responses were also given to whether players with the potential to represent the country are offered the conditions to train full-time with high-performance standards (three of five, with 38 percent unaware or not sure).

The USSF has proposed that team members of seventy-eight developmental academies should not be allowed to train and compete at their high schools, which received mixed opinions from both coaches and athletes (Borden, 2012). Better integration is needed among educational and professional soccer systems and clubs for the benefit of all player levels. Coach 23 (March 13, 2011) wrote in an open response,

I have found that high school programs don't provide those participating with any advancement opportunities. Most colleges won't even consider a player if they have not participated in a Select or Premier type youth program. This frustrates those who only have access to high school programs and are highly skilled. Also it seems there is a lot of outsourcing of players from other nations to fill spots on teams in both colleges and the MLS.

Element 7: Advanced athlete support

Doping control is a highly understood and known variable (#7) in this element, and it is the only variable predominantly scored positively (see Table 4.24). Otherwise, only two variables (#1, 8) were seen clearly as negative/lacking part of the soccer development system. Four desired practices (#2, 3, 4, 6) were viewed as predominantly neutral.

For this element, the response category averages were almost equally divided between neutral at 40 percent and negative at 39 percent. Positive responses were only 21 percent of the total number of responses. Improvement is needed to support soccer players at places of work and service with such conditions as paid time off work given to train and compete. According to 60 percent of coaches, this never or rarely occurs in the United States. In their open responses, coaches agreed that more support is necessary for drawing the best players to the sport and to higher levels of competition, noting that "many qualified individuals are hindered due to lack of monetary support from individual and corporate entities" (Coach 13, March 17, 2011). Administrator B (April 8, 2011) noted that "very few workplaces understand the sport well enough to support their young players, even with time off. Players have lost their job and some even threatened if they take time off." Effective practices of employing athletes by corporations, public organizations, and the military can be borrowed from France, Germany, and Russia. Statements three, four, and five are also rated less than three of five, reflecting the lack of advanced services available to U.S. soccer players.

Each of the seven administrators who participated in the study indicated that there is room for improvement both in education and support at workplaces such as the USASA or the athletes' own places of work. IMG Academies provide most advanced services but only for a small number of elite players. Coaches agreed that the current structures can be advanced for better support of high performance, specifying that

the focus is often on just winning not development, and since we use academies and clubs, with the best costing thousands of dollars, we lost out on potential players. The possible help is through corporate and business support or ownership similar to those in Europe (Coach 31, March 8, 2011).

Connection with the global soccer community through FIFA has been beneficial for the advancement of U.S. soccer, particularly through learning from Western European practices. This flow of intellectual capital should include Asian, Eastern

Table 4.24 Results of soccer survey, Level 7 – Advanced athlete support (Smolianov, Murphy, McMahon, & Naylor, 2014)

Desired Practices	Average Score	Distribution of Responses		
		Negative/ Lacking (%)	Neutral (%)	Positive/ Existing (%)
1. Athletes, including soccer players, are supported at places of work similar to those at Home Depot and U.S. Army (paid time given to train and compete)	2.4	60	34	6
2. High performance players are ranked into hierarchical levels/ pools with appropriate financial and technical support	2.7	38	49	13
3. Athletes are assisted with formal education and career planning outside sport	2.8	38	43	19
4. Athlete support is well shared/ balanced between coaches and advisors (e.g., coach may provide psychological, nutritional, and performance science support, while independent advisors may best assist with medicine, career, education, and personal finances)	2.7	39	47	14
5. Scientific research (e.g., biomechanics of athlete movement and psychophysiological analysis) is applied quickly and effectively to immediately benefit player performance	2.8	42	39	19
6. Player careers are prolonged by medical personnel knowledgeable in soccer (helping with such things as injury prevention, adjustment of training levels, nutrition, pharmacology, rest and stimulation therapy, doping use prevention)	3.2	17	49	34
7. Doping is controlled by the USSF and U.S. Soccer and is based on the most recent guidelines from the World Anti-Doping Agency and FIFA	3.6	15	30	55
8. Athletes leaving elite sport are provided with individualized lifestyle plans for physical and psychological health	2.3	63	31	6
Percentage across all items in element (based on N=124 for each row)		39	40	21

European, and Latin American "best practices." The USSF could also partner better with U.S. universities for advice on all aspects of soccer development.

In the end, there are many opportunities for advancement of U.S. mass and elite soccer across all key analyzed elements. New resources are required to develop athletes, coaches, and referees at all stages of participation following world best practice. If the proportion of expenditures on mass soccer were closer to half of the USSF budget, this would represent a more optimal balance between mass and elite soccer development. An increase in mass participation should provide a wider base of talent for elite level teams and lead to greater viewership and interest in elite soccer, ultimately increasing the USSF's major event and sponsorship revenues.

The surveyed coaches stressed that the U.S. soccer system should be led by one NGB with a clear direction and continuity in the development of players at all levels. The USSF could lead all other soccer NGBs, whose roles are sometimes overlapping, to build a simple and efficient organizational structure for the governance and development of soccer in this country.

An open response by Coach 118 (February 9, 2011) reflected the opinion of other surveyed coaches: "Funding is needed, there needs to be a better vision for the sport in our country and a more unified effort." Addressing this argument is fundamental for improvement not only at the micro-level of player development and support but at the meso-level of program support infrastructures and at the macro-level of organizational advancement. This comment goes beyond U.S. soccer and is relevant to the overall sport system, as evident from other chapters of the book.

Chapter summary

In terms of the quantitative data, there was a predominant trend to the neutral category. This was true for all elements and all variables in each element, while this trend provides a strong indication that elements of the ideal-type Model are not really understood, known, or exist. Perhaps this research has opened many sport specialist's minds about the complexity and elements actually operating in a sport delivery system.

Of more import for researchers and sport specialists is to look at only positive and negative responses (without the neutral ones) to gain insight into the sport system for these three sports. In some cases, there was ambiguity over whether a desired practice did or did not exist or operate. This might be an organizational issue (i.e., who runs the sport?). Or it could be geographical, age of development of the sport, or for any other number of causes.

Mass participation, elite performance, organization, and financial positions of the three analyzed sports can all be advanced. The USTA generates hundreds of millions of dollars a year but most of it through the U.S. Tennis Open – one event for a few elite athletes and an international TV audience. While attracting less than 10 percent of the U.S. population into playing the tennis (Sporting Goods Manufacturers Association, 2012), U.S. tennis is increasingly challenged by other nations to advance both mass participation and elite performance. USA Rugby generates only several million dollars as less than 1 percent of Americans play the game (Chadwick et al., 2010); and U.S. international performance in rugby needs a lot of improvement. U.S. Soccer generates tens of millions of dollars, also mostly through elite events, but also involves the participation of less than 10 percent of the country's population (FIFA, 2012).

The disparity in available resources is defined by an important similarity of the three sports: lack of government and public funding, overreliance on television, and sponsorship revenues dictated by private pocket interests, not public health concerns. These sports are also united in their opportunities to learn from other leading sporting nations on how to increase their participation bases and improve elite performance. New partners and resources are needed for the affordable healthy development of all desiring beginners into competitive lifelong players. New resources could also be used to improve and unify athlete and coach development paths. Overlapping and often conflicting organizational structures need to be harmonized, particularly in soccer and tennis.

The following chapter (Chapter 5) presents a summary of the key ideas derived from this study, along with current and potential historical changes, based on the Model.

Appendix 1: Example of survey questions (Rugby Study by Carney, Smolianov & Zakus, 2012)

Micro-Level, Desired Practice – Talent Identification and Development

1   In addition to children being introduced to rugby by themselves and parents, potential rugby players are attracted from outside the sport's participation base (e.g., by a search at schools).
2   Young rugby players are trained based on guidelines for multiple development stages recommended by USA Rugby (many national governing bodies have guidelines for nurturing players from the introduction to sport through the achievement of peak performance on to retirement from sport).
3   Sufficient resources are available collectively from various supporting organizations for all young talented rugby players to progress through all developmental stages.
4   A multi-stage system of player qualification based on results/rankings within age groups is used to reward player progress from beginner to top international level.
5   Performance of rugby players in each competitive age group is monitored and developed using a national database.
6   A high number of full-time rugby coaches are available, making the athlete-coach ratio low.
7   Rugby coach expertise is equally high across all participant ages and levels.

8   Rugby coaches are paid according to multi-level certification based on coaches' education and achievements of entrusted players.

9   Players with potential to represent the country (e.g., nations top fifty players per age group) are offered the conditions to train full time with high-performance standards.

10 Rugby training is well integrated with school/college/university education for harmonious development of athletes.

Micro-Level, Desired Practice – Advanced Athlete Preparation and Support

1   Athletes, including rugby players, are supported at places of work and service with conditions similar to those at Home Depot and U.S. Army (paid time off given to train and compete).

2   High-performance players are ranked into hierarchical levels/pools with appropriate financial and technical support.

3   Athletes are assisted with formal education and career outside sport.

4   Athlete support is well shared/balanced between coaches and advisors (e.g., coach may provide psychological, nutritional, and performance science support, while independent advisors may best assist with medicine, career, education, and personal finances).

5   Scientific research (e.g., biomechanics of athlete movement and psychophysiological analysis) is applied quickly and effectively to immediately benefit player performance.

6   Player career is prolonged by medical personnel knowledgeable in Rugby (helping with such things as injury prevention, adjustment of training levels, nutrition, pharmacology, rest and stimulation therapy, doping use prevention).

7   Doping is controlled by USA Rugby based on the most recent guidelines from the World Anti-Doping Agency and the IRB.

8   Athletes leaving elite sport are provided with individualized lifestyle plans for physical and psychological health.

Meso-Level, Desired Practice – Training centers and multi-facility activity hubs

1   High-performance athletes are provided with priority access to specific high quality equipment and facilities.

2   Training centers provide specialized facilities and equipment for each age and level of participation.

3   All national, regional, and local training centers are available to athletes at affordable costs.

4   Travel from home to training facilities takes little time for players of all levels and types.

5   Training facilities are close to all facilities for athlete support (e.g., school/college, medical, room and board, leisure/entertainment).

6   A network of training centers is used to prepare players in different environments/socio-geo-climates (e.g., high altitude/temperature/humidity, city/pollution, rural/resort).

7   Rugby training centers are located close to other sport facilities so that players participate in and learn from other sports.

Meso-level, Desired Practice – Domestic and International Competitions

1   Hosted international events and international opportunities are sufficient for all athletes with potential to represent the country.

2   Competitions are well structured at all levels (e.g., club/training center, regional, and national).

3   USA Rugby and its support mechanisms sufficiently assist in local and sectional developmental events (e.g., fourteen and under regional tournaments).

4   USA Rugby attempts to integrate professional and amateur tournaments into a progressive plan of competitions gradually preparing athletes for peak performance at "Majors" (i.e. World Cup, North American Four, World Cup Sevens, etc.), Paralympic Games, and Olympic Games.

5   USA Rugby tries to coordinate all domestic and international competitions for all ages and levels, between and within all possible organizations.

6   Event sponsorship incomes are used to develop competitions for all participation levels

Meso-Level, Desired Practice – Educational, scientific, medical, philosophical and promotional support

1   All specialists engaged in the development of rugby players are well educated for their professional roles.

2   USA Rugby fosters research on all important aspects of rugby development.

3   Research results are well communicated to coaches (e.g., by research institutes, universities, and USA Rugby).

4   Principles of sportsman-like conduct and Olympism are communicated well (e.g., through mass media, school education, and through the arts as part of rugby events).

5   USA Rugby's communication contributes to national values and identity by inspiring participants to strive for excellence, to show the best results and character in the world.

6   USA Rugby provides vision and leadership in improving all aspects of the participants' well-being through rugby (e.g., physical, social, emotional, mental, spiritual, and environmental/ecological).

Macro-Level, Desired Practice – Partnerships with Supporting Agencies

1   Support for rugby player development is adequate from various levels of government.
2   Sufficient help is obtained from USA Rugby, IRB, World Cup Sevens, and other national governing bodies such as the RFU that provide coach education and certification.
3   Role of clubs/community programs in rugby development is sound.
4   Rugby is well supported by educational sector (e.g., schools, colleges, universities).
5   Cooperation with agencies outside of sport industry (e.g., medical, scientific, military, philanthropic, and sponsoring organizations, lotteries) is in place.
6   USA Rugby influences media coverage and popularity of rugby to increase support from the society.

Macro-Level, Desired Practice – Balanced and Integrated Funding and Structures of Mass and Elite Sport

1   Corporate and philanthropic tax incentives provide sufficient support of mass and elite rugby.
2   Participation in various sports, as a foundation for rugby development, is encouraged through physical education requirements.
3   Sport participation, including rugby, is rewarded with reduced personal tax.
4   Rugby programs service both recreational and high-performance players.
5   Specialized sport schools similar to the IMG Academies are available and affordable to all talented players.
6   A multi-stage system of elite rugby player qualification is integrated with a system of fitness tests for mass participation.
7   Dues and other "fees" affordable for all are available in various rugby clubs.
8   Rugby participants are as diverse as the general population.
9   USA Rugby demonstrates systematic/strategic management in developing rugby on every level.
10 USA Rugby is effective in fostering both mass participation and high performance in rugby.
11 Rugby is developed in integration with Olympic and Paralympic sports to achieve sustainable competitive excellence.

Notes

1   This is described by Schön (1973) as the "normative leap" that is discussed more fully in Chapter 5.
2   Audited financial statements, for example, included: an independent auditors' report statements of financial position, activities, and cash flows of the United States of America Rugby Football Union, Ltd. and its subsidiaries for the 2009 and 2010 years (by Johnson Kightlinger & Company) and publically disclosed tax statements

(e.g., Form 990, Return of Organization Exempt From Income Tax Under section 501(c) of the Internal Revenue Code, Department of the Treasury, Internal Revenue Service).

3 QuickStart is a tennis development program for kids under ten. It is played on a shorter court with smaller rackets and softer low-compression balls. Ten and Under Tennis follows the same logic as other youth sports such as baseball or soccer, which use child-sized fields and child-sized equipment. Children learn to play baseball by first playing T-ball; they use shorter, lighter bats and larger, softer balls. Children learning basketball shoot baskets with child-sized balls on lowered backboards, and they play soccer on smaller fields with smaller goals. Now with 10 and Under Tennis, balls bounce lower, do not move as fast through the air, and are easier to hit. Children's tennis racquets are sized for small hands and courts are smaller. By using this format, within a short time children are rallying, playing real tennis, and having more fun, which contributes to player retention.

4 These are male and female players from the Czech Republic, Serbia, Croatia, Poland, Russia, Latvia, Bulgaria, Ukraine, Belarus, Romania, Slovakia, and Estonia.

5 Of all of the tennis respondents, this individual provided substantial, and we feel well thought through written comments. We use his responses widely in this chapter as he states clearly what is needed to align more to the Model but also to what is likely to be best for tennis in the U.S. in the future.

6 The sport of rugby union is normally a competition between two teams of fifteen players per team. The game is played for eighty minutes and recovery from matches is long. A derivative version with seven players per team playing a fifteen-minute match gained import resulting in the IRB sanctioning a now popular professional circus of teams playing around the world for both men and women. The IRB long lobbied the IOC to include rugby in the Olympic Games and, with the advent of a women's global competition and more countries playing this version of the sport, rugby union will be part of the 2016 Rio de Janeiro Olympic Games.

7 This usage implies an age-specific team. For example, U14 is a team of players younger than fourteen years of age by a specific date. Other age categories (U16, U18, U19, U20) are used in rugby for local, national, and international competitions.

8 This was the Tri-Nations tournament until 2012, when the Argentine national team, the Pumas, became part of the now named Rugby Championship competition. It is still very much a South Africa, New Zealand, and Australian Rugby Union operation.

9 This document is available on the following Web site: http://www.ussoccer.com/Teams/Development-Academy/Academy-Overview.aspx.

5 Reality and possible advancements for U.S. sport

Improving health and performance

The United States has been effective in its sport achievements and outcomes. It is always at or near the top of Olympic Games and WOG results tables or in other major global sport contests. While effectiveness is apparent, the efficiency of the U.S. sport development system is questionable. With increasing competition for success across sports and major competitions, the United States, we argue, might do better with its resources and its sport development system than it currently does.

Academics studying sport often neglect the wider, or macro-level as we call it, view of sport within the broader society. Sport does not exist outside of society. It is a part of the social and cultural bases of a country and, in the U.S. case, of its professional and many NCAA sports, and the capitalist economy. We discuss this wider context to summarize the situation in the United States and to show where advances were made and where future possibilities exist.

In terms of health the picture is not so rosy. Like many nations, the United States is struggling with developing strategies to combat the rising health care costs and at the same time provide cutting-edge health care that the nation is known for. In the absence of universal health care and the presence of strong medical, pharmaceutical, and insurance lobby groups, the health needs of U.S. citizens are not always efficiently met. Lifestyle choices around diet and exercise do not portend well for the country.

The PCFSN is working on these issues through policies of moral suasion. When, however, the fast food industry lobbied Congress to recognize pizza as a vegetable so it would remain part of the school lunch program (thereby maintaining its rent seeking), it made a mockery of Congressional decision making. This Council (PCFSN) is not only struggling against the advertising and lobbying industries but also the inherent political and economic institutions and practices (e.g., the lobbying industry, the U.S. and global plutocracies, and wealthy members of Congress) of the United States. The U.S. health care system is being reformed toward universal coverage, even if it has not done that well under Obama. The current health care changes create better conditions for systematic sport development, giving health care to all, and increasing the role of preventative measures including sport. Therefore, we can now be more optimistic about the future of U.S. sport and health.

Sport is an integral part of the U.S. culture. Comparatively speaking, this is no different from many, if not most, nations of the world (but it is not a panacea as many try to make it). Where there is difference is how the various sport organizations interlock with their external environments. In many ways, there is a public (government) linkage through the schools, colleges, and universities and local parks and recreation bodies funded in this manner. The United States, however, is strongly public/private or private in the way both participant and elite sport are funded. One needs to look no further than the revenues of the major professional sport leagues and that of major NCAA competitions but, as will be discussed below, there is little "trickle-down" or "rising tide" effect to the developmental levels of the U.S. sport system.

This final chapter will take a somewhat different profile as is common in most books. Before we can begin to suggest what might be done to enhance the U.S. sport system, we will discuss certain realities of the context. Some of these realities were introduced in Chapter 1 and have been discussed in Chapters 3 and 4 but they will be expanded upon here. It is within this context that sport operates and this cannot be disavowed. The following three sections will discuss the ideological, economic, and political aspects of the United States that constrain how the sport system could actually exist against the Model's elements. Once this "ground clearing" is completed, we will go through the seven elements of the Model against the historical and empirical evidence provided in the third and fourth chapters.

Ideological constraints

Many ideologies are circulating at any time and place in a country. That is, the system of ideas that govern thought and action in the United States has been long held and is different in many ways from the ideas used in other nations. This difference is the basis of the claim of "American exceptionalism," a claim made by many different nations and civilizations throughout human history. There is no singular or correct definition of what is meant by the ideology of exceptionalism (Caeser, 2012); in fact, there is a major academic publishing industry around this concept. This latter point is mainly due to its appropriation by politicians over time but more so in recent times (e.g., Obama and Romney in the 2012 election). As this book is focused on sport, we will mention this ideology only briefly, as it impacts and limits future choices for the sport system.

The following are basic ideas that make up this ideology. Most generally, Walt (2011) noted that "most statements of 'American exceptionalism' presume that America's values, political system, and history are unique and worthy of universal admiration. They also imply that the United States is both destined and entitled to play a distinct and positive role on the world stage" and that the "United States is a uniquely virtuous nation, one that loves peace, nurtures liberty, respects human rights, and embraces the rule of law" (Lipset, 1996).

According to U.S. sociologist Seymour Lipset (1996) this uniqueness was:

born out of revolution; the United States is a country organized around an ideology that includes a set of dogmas about the nature of a good society ... the nation's ideology can be described in five words: liberty, egalitarianism, individualism, populism, and laissez-faire. The revolutionary ideology that became the American Creed is liberalism ... [but] what Europeans have called "liberalism," Americans refer to as "conservatism": a deeply anti-statist doctrine emphasizing the virtues of laissez-faire ... [that] focuses on the rights of individuals and ignores communal rights and obligations.

This ideology began with the foundation of the United States and is expressed in its Constitution.

The historical thread was analyzed by Caesar as it evolved in many different ideological forms and that it is based on and has a "theological source – namely, the belief that God provides a warrant for America's mission – many identify it as having a naturally self-righteous dogmatic form" (p. 3). As noted above, this ideology has a long history in the United States as a "line runs from seventeenth-century Puritan thought, to the Revolution, to the mid-nineteenth-century doctrine of manifest destiny, to late nineteenth-century American imperialism, to Wilsonian idealism, to cold war anticommunism, and finally to George W. Bush's unilateralism" (Caeser, 2012, p. 3). Caeser (2012, p. 4) wrote that "exceptionalism packs different ideas under the same label. Sometimes it refers to matters of domestic affairs, at other times to matters of foreign affairs." Or with George W. Bush's stand that if other peoples and countries are not with the United States and their foreign affairs and purposes, they are against the United States and will be treated as needed by the United States. (Thankfully, global sport has a moderating effect on this position, however limited it might be.) Lipset (1996) earlier stated a parallel condition for those born in the USA when he stated that "being an American, however, is an ideological commitment. It is not a matter of birth. Those who reject American values are un-American.".

The key points to take from this for the purpose of sport are that the United States seeks a "more limited government, which they consider to be the cornerstone of liberty; they favor an economy in which incomes reflect market forces, not government decisions" (Caeser, 2013, p. 3). This results in a fairly strong, clear, and present block to many of the comparisons, especially those emanating from former "communist/socialist" countries' sport systems, specifically in terms of government intervention and funding of sport. While ideologies provide gestalts for citizens, they also lead to difficulties. Noam Chomsky (2013) argued that, as German-U.S. political scientist Hans Morgenthau understood, "America is unique among all powers past and present in that it has a 'transcendent purpose' that it 'must defend and promote' throughout the world: 'the establishment of equality in freedom.'" It is however "the transcendent purpose of America that is 'reality'; the actual historical record is merely 'the abuse of reality.'" If U.S. sport specialists see ideas and alternatives we present from the Model as less because they do not emanate from the United States, this could be a problem. While it is not our purpose here to critique U.S. internal and external affairs, we urge readers, as Migranyan (2013) cautioned, that "it is perilous for politicians and society to fail to notice the moment in which the gap between ideology and reality becomes an abyss."

There are many slogans used in the United States that point to this exceptionalism. Populist notions that "the cream rises to the top" or that individuals can achieve great things if they have the "right stuff" pervade. This liberal notion that every citizen has the ability to rise to the top of U.S. society is a key element of the "American dream." Actually, the degree of social mobility in the United States has declined (Migranyan, 2013; Walt, 2011). This, along with a declining middle class, foreshadows more concerns for the U.S. sport system. We will use these ideas in concluding discussions of the elements of the Model.

Economic constraints

Likewise, the ideology of capitalism is supreme. As an economic system, capitalism has shown its strength over history; but it also has many shortcomings. The track of neo-liberalism and its attendant process of financial globalization have, since the 1970s, led to greater class differences and to greater difficulty for the government to operate (Panitch & Gindin, 2013).

That ones' individual character will allow each person in the United States to rise as high as they are capable of, misses the point that there is an extant and highly unequal class system. Recent public protests (the "Occupy" movement, e.g., Occupy Wall Street) indicate that the "99 percent" are unhappy about this inequality and the "hollowing out" of the middle classes. One must emphasize that it was a large, vigorous middle class that provided human resources and was the driving force behind the sport system. When one observes the difference between income and wealth of the "1 percent" versus the "99 percent," it is widening and dismaying.

In a 2010 report economist Edward Wolff wrote that

> between 1983 and 2007, the top 1 percent received 35 percent of the total growth in net worth, 43 percent of the total growth in non-home wealth, and 44 percent of the total increase in income. The figures for the top 20 percent are 89 percent, 94 percent, and 87 percent, respectively.

In a recent article, U.S. Nobel Prize winning economist Joseph Stiglitz (2011) updated these figures:

> The upper 1 percent of Americans are now taking in nearly a quarter of the nation's income every year. In terms of wealth rather than income, the top 1 percent control 40 percent. Their lot in life has improved considerably. Twenty-five years ago, the corresponding figures were 12 percent and 33 percent.

From 1997 to 2005, the top 1 percent's annual income has grown by over $673 billion, almost equal to the total income losses ($743 billion) of the bottom four quintiles (Hacker & Pierson, 2010, p. 157). And the wealthy weathered the "Great Recession" much better than other quintiles (Stiglitz, 2012). Wolff (2010, p. 37) disclosed that the Gini coefficient[1] for wealth distribution in the United States swelled from 0.834 in mid-2007 to 0.865 by June, 2009, and is likely higher now.

Why is this situation so? While many in the United States are aware of this extreme inequality, Norton and Ariely (2011, p. 12) wrote that

> Americans appear to drastically underestimate the current level of wealth inequality, suggesting they may simply be unaware of the gap. . . . .they may also hold overly optimistic beliefs about opportunities for social mobility in the United States. . . . beliefs which in turn may drive support for unequal distributions of wealth.

Most citizens of the United States are not the only naïve population in this regard in the world. Yet, on a sad note, "Americans may remain unlikely to advocate for policies that would narrow this gap" (Norton & Ariely, 2011, p. 12) or that "those in the 99 percent could come to realize that they have been duped by the 1 percent: that what is in the interest of the 1 percent is not in their interests" (Stiglitz, 2012, p. 287). So reigns ideological constraint in the USA.

The key factor for growth and success of the U. S. sport development system was that it had a robust middle class. As noted above, there has been a "hollowing-out" of the U.S. middle class this century.[2] Wolff (2010) provided evidence that "the years 2001 to 2004 witnessed an explosion of household debt and gave evidence of the middle-class squeeze" (p. 34). Living on credit compounds this issue of where the money will come from to take part in sport. The 2007–2009 "Great Recession" only made matters worse. Stiglitz (2011) put this into perspective stating that "growing inequality is the flip side of something else: shrinking opportunity. Whenever we diminish equality of opportunity, it means that we are not using some of our most valuable assets – our people – in the most productive way possible." And sport is about people – participants and athletes.

Where the United States is deficient in its sport delivery system is in fully understanding that not all children have an equal opportunity to access sport. Sport, along with education and health, has to be re-visioned as a socially necessary public good that all citizens must enjoy: They are not market goods that only parts of civil society can access (leaving aside spectatorship of sport events). If issues of obesity, diabetes, and heart disease are to be properly addressed, this situation must move beyond markets and beyond the lobbying strength of corporations.

How might this change? Again, Stiglitz (2012, p. 267) argued that "a more efficient economy and fairer society will also come from making markets work like markets – more competitive, less exploitive – and tempering their excesses." In terms of helping the bottom four quintiles of the population, he emphasized the need for improved access to education, helping to establish savings, "health care for all," and the "strengthening of other social protection programs" (p.275-277). Ultimately Stiglitz (2011) argues that "we can achieve a society more in accord with our fundamental values, with more opportunity, a higher total national income, a stronger democracy, and higher living standards of most individuals."

We have spent much time on discussing the economic challenges and changes required for the future success of mass and elite sport in the United States. Panitch and Gindin (2013, p. 340) argued that the "secular struggle between classes is ultimately resolved at the political – not at the economic or cultural – level of society." It is now to this level we turn.

Political constraints

The political situation in the United States leads some U. S. academics to criticize that elections and political party platforms that have as their "real aim to ensure continuity, to keep intact the institutions and arrangements" that actually "serves to underwrite the status quo" (Bacevich, 2009, p. 171). Many academics write of the plutocracy that operates in Washington, DC (Bacevich, 2009; Harvey, 2014 are two such examples). The need to "renew institutions" requires both internal and external policy change: And perhaps a fundamental change in the Constitution, the way the electoral process operates, and the manner in which the system of checks and balances functions in the government of the United States. Popular activism exists and politicians respond to populism for re-election purposes. As a form of the fundamental change required in the United States and most of the world, it is not sufficient (Harvey, 2014). Harvey argued that a fundamental change to global capitalism is vital for real change to occur. Liberal politicians are often derided and marginalized in U.S. politics, but a return to U.S. constitutional values and away from myths of "American exceptionalism" (see Walt, 2011 for a discussion and refutation of these myths).

Stiglitz (2012) also argued for political reform as currently the 1 percent and interest groups (lobbyists) control what happens in government. This would require the reduction of rent seeking and a change in "the rules of the game that are tilted to advantage those at the top" (pp. 268–269). Many academics decry, as noted elsewhere, that a plutocracy runs the United States. The "smooth functioning of our democracy [is] perhaps, the most important public good of all" (p. 285). The U.S. government is "too gridlocked to re-distribute, too divided to do anything but lower taxes" (Stiglitz, 2011). The mainly supply-side policies, ironically, will affect the plutocracy in negative ways. If demand-driven policies are not implemented (i.e., through stimulus funding – that could happen by consistently reducing military spending), then there will be a crisis of overproduction and ultimately a lack of realization of profits (Krugman, 2009; Harvey, 2014).

The United States developed, often concomitantly, many similar processes and programs as identified in the Model and implemented in State socialist societies. In terms of the latter comparison, it is not to imply that past and present State socialist governments (USSR, China, Eastern Bloc, Cuba, etc.) are or were better or preferred. It was that these societies attempted to make the necessities of life available to all citizens; including fitness and sport. Likewise, and until the neo-liberal versus social democratic (Keynesian) economic war, many Western societies have done a better job of (initially) publicly providing sport social goods to their populations. Yet, many of these nations are now pulling back under austerity budgeting demanded by structural adjustment directives, uni- or multi-lateral free trade agreements, and/or their own supply-side economic ideology and policies.

According to previous comparative studies that mostly focused on macro- and meso-levels of sport development, most nations have converged with global trends in elite and mass sport, irrespective of their ideological, economic, and political characteristics. The historical examples provided in Chapter 3 and suggestions in the above section on ideology demand that history be understood and lessons from it be applied to current circumstances in a sound way.

Most current written U.S. history is conservative and narrow as it

> only tells a small part of the story. It may convince those who don't probe too deeply [but] historical understanding defines people's very sense of what is thinkable and achievable. . . . as a result, many have lost the ability to imagine a world that is substantially different from and better than what exists today (Stone & Kuznick, 2012).[3]

These U.S. authors go on to state that "Americans believe they are unbound by history. . . . historian Christopher Lasch saw as a reflection of their 'narcissism'" (see the above ideological section). Understanding through a critical reading of history will help progress the U.S. sport development system by those who can make the normative leap and see beyond what *is* to what *ought* to be.[4]

As evidenced in Chapter 4, the Model provides an alternative way to understand particular sports in the United States. It also adds historical understanding of sport evolution in the United States and that alternate national sport histories were widely successful. What is demanded in the future analysis of sports in the U.S. is to refine the Model and to look at points where meaningful change can occur. There is no perfect, better, or ideal sport delivery system. As we noted above, the best one can do is approximate and emulate as many of the elements of the Model as possible. As change is constant, there will be many opportunities to improve the institutions, structures, policies, and practices in the future.

In the next section, we offer some suggestions about what *is* and what *might be* done to alter the U.S. sport development system. Only sport practitioners can decide what might be introduced to the system. The next section follows the elements of the Model.

Element 1 (Macro-Level): Balanced and integrated funding and structures of mass and elite sport

Key to this is an integrated sport body to develop and monitor a coherent strategy for better international sport performance *and* domestic mass participation. This would also abet developments in health and education. It demands "perhaps most important . . . 'collective action' – it needs government to invest in infrastructure, education, and technology" (Stiglitz, 2011). Above all, this element focuses on

Table 5.1 Average score for all Element 1 variables by sport

	Negative %	Neutral %	Positive %
Tennis	43	37	20
Rugby	47	39	14
Soccer	44	34	22

what institutional and organizational changes can be made to structure and fund sport more efficiently.

The empirical study showed that there is a clear funding issue (variable one) across all three sports, although less so for tennis. From this, we suggest that corporate and philanthropic contributions are not enough despite the tax incentives offered. The third variable (reduced personal tax for participants) also showed this situation in the United States as expected and strongly so. The last variable of mention in this element concerns the lack of availability of specialized sport schools, although rugby respondents were neutral on this as perhaps it was not seen as conceivable. As shown in Table 5.1, there were few overall positive responses while the neutral and negative categories were more balanced. Readers should also see variable one of Element 2 for the very strong critique of funding in the sports studied in this project.

We discuss particulars of the historical impacts identified in Chapter 3 below. What will be seen is that the United States has been active in the process of change within the possibilities of its ideological, economic, political, and cultural milieux: and that there are strong possibilities for the expansion of its sport system.

Institutional and organizational changes

Calls for institutional change in the United States are acknowledged as not being a likely or viable option at least in the short term. There are many demands for a change to the way the U.S. government predominantly favors a small fraction of the population. As noted above, the lobbyists and the wealth already in Congress are not working for "we the people." Changes to the political and legislative processes, again, will take some time to occur, but change is required and widely called for in U.S. academic literature (Bacevich, 2009; Hacker & Pierson, 2010; Harvey, 2014; Krugman, 1999, 2008; Stiglitz, 2010, 2011; Wolf, 2007).

The current untenable economic state of the United States will take time to resolve. It is unlikely legislation in key sport areas will soon happen. With a reduced role for government as a founding ideology and a neo-liberalist privatization push, it would be hard to hope for a centralized, funded department of sport. As noted in Chapter 3, the USOC acts as the central organizing (institutional) body for sport in the United States. The establishment of CODPs to conduct mass and development-level sport activities, and the holding of more inclusive sport festivals, might be a way to obtain more direct government involvement in sport without these activities being seen as "socialist". Certainly their focus on outcomes is within the current economic ideology and accountability, but hopefully this can be overcome over time.

The USOC at least provides a centralized agency for sport. This situation, for the moment, will alleviate many of the structural issues in the United States. In many countries, especially smaller and certain "developing" nations (e.g., Norway, the Pacific islands of Tonga, Fiji, Manu Samoa), their NOCs play a similar omnibus role. So the USOC's role in this regard is not new or unusual.

And a private NGO may well have more latitude to operate and fund itself. Since its inception, the USOC has expanded its roles, functions, and operations. All of this portends positively for the future. As with other organizations in the United States, it will have to operate as a business and seek revenues from the market while also seeking tax-deductible donations and other types of grants. This is what more and more sport government departments and clubs have had to do for the last three decades under austerity budgeting (e.g., Sport Canada in the 1980s, Australian Sport Commission more recently). This expansion would eventually locate the United States closer to the Model in terms of this key institutional idea.

The other institutional area with more possibilities for change is physical education (PE). While there is an intriguing privatization of education under neo-liberalism, it is a fraught process. Within this movement, PE is an area seen as expensive and highly risky in its undertaking. If schooling retains a public function as a public good, then a key aspiration for PE must involve a paradigm shift. Shifts that are seen as possible include: those surrounding the existing role of PE within schools (mandatory or elective), in the purpose and nature of the PE curricula (lifelong fitness and health versus sport-based), and in how PE is delivered at all levels of schooling (quantity and quality of that delivery). This paradigm shift would be significant, as much of PE is about sport, and the "regular" non-athlete student is often underserved and often alienated. And there is too much focus on talented athletes and on school teams.

The surveyed tennis, soccer, and rugby coaches were dissatisfied with a lack of structure in the form of a system of affordable schools where sports are taught all year round. Training and competition seasons in many U.S. school sports last two or three months a year, which is useful for trying different sports. However, practising year-round would be more effective in reducing obesity, getting students into a habit of constant exercising, and assisting participants in a gradual, uninterrupted progression to higher levels in a chosen sport.

The possibility of extending the school year is currently being discussed. PE and school sports could be extended into the summer months to provide the option of participating in government-funded or partially subsidized programs to improve students' health and fitness levels. There are opportunities for both private sector and government agencies to cooperate and expand summer camp programs. Grants, tax relief, partial subsidies, and other incentives could help improve both mass health and international performance through qualified coaches advancing participants' fitness and sport performance in year-round programs.

Sport academies have become a major business enterprise. In the U.S. many sport, educational, and business organizations have established academies to extend their business operations. In many ways, they are an extension of summer camp enterprises for children and youth. As such, sport academies of all stripes would be a logical way to identify and capture talented youth as well as to extend business investments. While the USSA has entered this market, more sports could seek out public/private funding to establish academies. It must be noted, however, that this still does not solve the mass sport and wider opportunities for all young people in the United States. Unless a young athlete is talented enough to receive a scholarship to an academy, many academy programs are costly and thus prohibitive for many. Academies, clubs, and NGBs could create investment funds that they manage for the long-term development of each sport and subsidization of talented children from low income families.

Finally, the NCAA monopoly has to be re-envisioned along the lines of the Ivy League universities. We realize that education institutions are suffering under austerity budgeting. The use of football and basketball to ameliorate budget demands is antithetical to the purpose of colleges and universities. Their first purpose is to educate and prepare young people for careers. From the data provided in Chapter 3, it is dubious that this occurs or occurred often enough. The Northwestern University (Evanston, IL) situation clearly pointed out that football athletes are employees. If 99 percent of players do not make it to the NFL, then what will their educational backgrounds permit them to do for the rest of their lives? The NCAA seems to be operating like a corporation. Using the direct producers of football, the players as underpaid employees is a cynical consumption of these young peoples' lives for the billions of dollars gained by universities. We suggest the NCAA and virtually all universities regain their purpose and ensure a proper and useful education for student-athletes.

Funding

The neo-liberalism currently behind many economies and its concomitant agenda of austerity budgeting permeates most of the financially "globalized" world. Several myths surround this economic/political philosophy that have serious negative repercussions for sport. Myths like "a rising tide lifts all boats" or "trickle-down" economics and that austerity budgeting is necessary to control inflation (cf. Blyth, 2013) were shown to be false (Stiglitz, 2012). None of these economic policies is viable or necessary, except for ensuring the wealthy become obscenely wealthier (Harvey, 2014). The money is clearly not flowing down to the grassroots level of sport development. Nor are wages keeping up with either inflation or productivity, and fewer people are now working. And stimulus funding has declined severely under austerity so that state and federal governments are spending less on public support programs, education, health, and sport. It has become much harder for families to spend on sport opportunities. As with many social provisions in the United States, sport is currently regressing at this key level of sport development.

In 2011 Stiglitz claimed that the "more divided a society becomes in terms of wealth, the more reluctant the wealthy become to spend money on common needs," which was evident in our discussion of philanthropy in Chapter 3. Although donations are a more important part of culture and economy in the

United States than in most countries in the world, the surveyed tennis, rugby, and soccer coaches indicated that corporate and philanthropic tax incentives rarely provide sufficient support for mass and elite sport. Philanthropy is not the answer for funding sport. It is a palliative measure at best but far from enough to rectify this situation.

The consensus of the tennis, rugby, and soccer studies' respondents is that lack of funds is the biggest obstacle for sport development. This is despite the extreme wealth in the United States and even more so in the case of upmarket sports such as tennis. Revenue sharing is a form of cooperation that worked well for commercial leagues (e.g., the NFL) and for nonprofit organizations like the NCAA and the USOC; or even small, cross-funded community programs such as Sail Salem in Massachusetts. Better revenue sharing and reinvestment into development are important tasks of each U.S. sport-related organization. Teams, certain sports, mass participants, and coaches struggling for funds all need to be better supported for long-term success by revenue-generating teams (which might be foreign to neo-liberal thinking, but this is a good compromise for the broader functioning of sport).

As with the organizational structure of U.S. sport, the financing of sport is also disorderly and could be more efficient. The coordination and integration of organizational structures and activities to develop both mass and elite sport as one system would be a good starting point if the USOC can rationally expand. Allocation of all moneys to sport, including continuous public and private support, grants, and tax deductions, need to be transparent and accountable. Most of all, they must be enhancing the sport system.

Led by international governing bodies and developmental, humanitarian, and philanthropic agencies (e.g., IOC, FIFA, UN, UNESCO, Council of Europe, USAID, Right To Play) and progressive national governments and NGBs, the role of sport around the world will further deepen and broaden across the wide spectrum of functions. Sport development will be measured by yearly growth or decline of multiple socioeconomic indicators, particularly health and education ones (Fetisov, 2005; Isaev, 2002; Keller, Lamprocht, & Stamm, 1998; Smolianov & Zakus, 2008; Svoboda, 2005; Wankel & Sefton, 1994).

As noted, perhaps *ad nauseum* above, the 1 percent control governments' ability to change the tax structure that would allow more demand-driven funding across the United States. The calls are just as great for the ending of rent seeking. An obvious example of this practice is for huge sport facilities that are only normally usable by professional sport teams, while the public have to find grant or sponsorship money to build local sport facilities for the wider use. In New York, the construction of the new \$1.3 billion Yankee Stadium was publicly subsidized in the form of tax exempt bonds. The city also issued bonds on behalf of other new stadiums, allowing the teams, which are responsible for making the annual payments on the bonds, to save millions of dollars a year in financing costs. This is again a form of corporate welfare through subsidized rent seeking, which is more and more a tradition of professional sport franchises and their owners.

While these suggestions overlap with Element 5, we feel they are a way in which the public financing of private capital can assist mass sport and fitness. If these monuments to sport are to be publicly financed, then they must include facilities for public use. They do not need to access the playing surfaces, but there could be gymnasia, fitness rooms, and a variety of other facilities (pools, indoor running tracks, etc.) for community use. It is not difficult to conceptualize such adaptations. It is only a matter of including these things in contractual wording (and massaging the egos of franchise owners, civic leaders, and other capitalists) to ensure such adaptations occur.

This is part of a trend that turns state and local governments into investment bankers for rich commercial teams (rent seekers) and gives these private sport corporations access to tax exemption status prohibited by the 1986 Tax Reform Act (Humphreys & Matheson, 2008). Taxpayers also subsidize some professional sports leagues; for example, the NFL, because they operate as nonprofit entities. Not much has changed since Shneidman (1978) suggested taxing U.S. professional sports and diverting the money to amateur participation. He believed that professional sport organizations and professional athletes make unreasonable incomes and should give more back to mass participant activities and sport. As with U.S. philanthropy generally, this proposal will not alleviate issues for children/ youth and mass sport. The questions of who would decide the focus of these funds and how would they be distributed arise. This is a similar matter with corporate social responsibility (CSR). We would point out that CSR creates a tax break and will likely be distributed to groups or organizations that will provide maximum attention or tax relief to the donor rather than being equitably distributed or effectively applied to deal with the social inequities and wider social issues that ensue from the current capitalist operation of U.S. society. While such practices are welcome, they are necessary but not sufficient.

On a final note, as we stated in Chapter 3, "the U.S. sport system is anything but systematic." This is not a difficult situation to resolve for the better. Certainly the knowledge of organizational structure and operations is widely available in the United States. Someone needs to stand back, look at the big picture, and then sort it. A formidable task, but one we feel will make better use of all sport resources.

Element 2 (Macro-Level): Partnerships with supporting agencies

The long-term nurturing of sport and recreation participants is achieved through partnerships across the systems of health care, education, and sports; which in the United States are more private, market-driven, expensive, and less coordinated than in other successful sport nations. Concomitant with the above element's focus on funding, responses to Variable 1 in this element also showed a major lack of funding from government. We feel any further comment is unnecessary.

Of the other variables, there are some of note, although most were predominantly neutral. Tennis seems to be well served by the school system (Variable 4). As tennis is a lifelong sport, this is a doubly good state of affairs. Coaching certification

Table 5.2 Average score for all Element 2 variables by sport

	Negative %	Neutral %	Positive %
Tennis	35	46	19
Rugby	58	32	10
Soccer	35	43	22

in tennis seems to be operating to a good level although the responses were ambivalent (Variable 2). Rugby has many structural and organizational issues to deal with. Only Variable 2 – support from IRB affiliated bodies – was scored well (21%). Of the three sports, soccer showed the highest level of agreement on six variables. This was especially so for soccer NGBs helping with education and certification of coaches (Variable 2). Overall, as Table 5.2 exhibits, rugby has the lowest alignment with the Model, while soccer shows a stronger alignment and tennis is much the same as on other elements.

There are many good examples of these relationships. Articles by Susan Vail (2007) and Hal A. Lawson (2005), among other sport development researchers, indicated what is possible. Vail (2007) suggested a possible process of tailored partnership building. Tennis Canada and eighteen communities across Canada agreed to participate in a study on tennis development.[5] A three-year grant totalling $280,000 from Sport Canada (a federal government agency) was matched by Tennis Canada. During the 2000–2007 period, the program helped Tennis Canada and its provincial associations introduce 71,920 new participants to tennis across fifty-three communities (Vail, 2007). U.S. Hockey has done this, and the USOC could easily lead NGBs to be more hands-on by sharing these examples of best practice. It does not take much funding to really grow a participant base.

Lawson (2005) provided a solid argument for the role sport and education physical educators (SEPE) could play in community sport development. He stated that "SEPE professionals, policies, programs, and practices facilitate both empowerment and community development. In turn, empowerment and community development–oriented SEPE professionals and their operations contribute to sustainable development" (p. 4). He proposed that SEPE professionals must work collaboratively with other professionals and with community groups. But more importantly, these SEPE specialists must receive the education and training to do this type of development work.

As a development specialist in sport, Lawson points out the promise of non-"Prolympic" sport. He extrapolates the wish that many have for sport:

> The essence of SEPE work lies in liberating and empowering people, enabling them to eliminate terror, find joy, maximize their freedom, and improve their health and well-being. If you want SEPE professionals and their programs and practices to empower people and contribute to community development, you'll have to design them accordingly. (p. 26)

Lawson points to another aspect of grassroots or community sport development that must be addressed. He provided a list of seventeen points that mirror those Vail later outlined but more fully. He also has much more to say about the production of SEPE professionals than can be outlined here. We recommend both of these articles toward sound sport development structures and practices. Both of these authors provide important ways to expand mass sport.

We have noted above the importance of the CODP, USOC, and NGB partnerships. These are key developments. If they could be expanded to include USOC and professional sport facilities, another major deficit could be reduced. The models provided at the University of Bath (UK) and at the Izmailovo sport hub (Russia) exemplify the types of partnerships at the facility and program levels. U.S. universities are extremely well placed to expand this provision beyond what they currently do.

Many sports in the United States are providing rationally planned coaching certification programs (e.g., US Hockey, USSA). This will expand naturally and for the benefit of the whole sport system. Providing paid educated coaches for all of children's and youth sport is something that will have to be worked out at the economic and ideological level within the country. Certainly the raw human resources exist in the United States. More of this topic is discussed in the next element.

There are strong existing partnerships that could be expanded in the United States. These are NGBs that need to adopt a more strategic approach to sponsor partnerships. This is particularly the case for developing sports such as rugby and soccer. Though the ideology of state intervention in U.S. society implies minimal government involvement and assistance, there are many strong indirect mechanisms for government support of sport. The key instrument is allocating public tax revenues to schools, colleges, universities, the military, police, and park and recreation departments. This allocation of funds would stimulate demand and help directly and indirectly to promote economic growth and improved funding for sport.

How economies, societies, and sports develop around the world will be influenced less by the United States and more by Asian approaches, including the philosophy of holistic fitness and prevention of illnesses. Although China has not solved many of its problems related to health, particularly industrial pollution, the Chinese advancement of mass fitness and elite sport is something to be learned by the world. Also, China's seeking new mass and elite sport policy goals with NGOs delivering what they see as necessary social public goods will provide future ways that the United States can enhance its sport system. Both are following market principles in this adventure.

In the current globalized world, the level of sport development is less defined by a particular economic or political system and more driven by both societies' devotion to fitness and sport and the government's ability to adopt practices that make other countries successful. The United States has been applying some European practices without investing in the development of comprehensive approaches suitable for U.S. conditions and culture: while China has been aggressively adopting best European and U.S. practices. In recent talks with the second author and Chinese colleagues at the Beijing Sport University, China's recently appointed government leadership want "reform." There are ideas here for the United States that align with those described and argued by Vail (2007) and Lawson (2005).

Finally, the public/private ventures for golf discussed in Chapter 3 are sound ways for mass, lifelong sport provision. While it is truly centered in the expansion of capital, that is to be expected in the United States. As Harvey (2014) would argue, the unused public space can be revived for the broader young population. Although we sound anti-capitalist in our critique here, such partnerships are of benefit for all constituencies concerned.

Element 3 (Meso-Level): Educational, scientific, medical, philosophical, and promotional support

As this element is very complex, the perceptional results from the surveys (Chapter 4) provided a complicated picture on how the analysed sports varied from the Model. This element perhaps needs refinement in the way the variables are phrased. The tennis and soccer results indicated that specific research is reaching its membership. This was not the case for rugby, but this is likely due to little research being completed on this sport in the United States. Countries where rugby is a mainstream sport publish research that USA Rugby shares through the conferences it organizes. The U.S. university system is world leading in many sport research fields. It appears that this information is not adequately reaching practitioners.

As would be expected, rugby again displayed divergence from the Model in virtually all variables. Interestingly, tennis did not show many positive alignments to the Model. Responses by soccer informants indicated that 30 percent felt that four variables were positively occurring. Again, as Table 5.3 displays, the overall averages for each sport pointed to the somewhat positive situation in soccer, less so for tennis, but not so for rugby. These aspects are discussed below along with suggestions for the future.

Here again, we observe coaching education as central to an effective and efficient sport system. The NGBs will have to establish a more advanced system of coach education, as noted above. The constant upgrading of coaching certification occurs and is a positive way to educate as well as recognize and reward volunteer coaches. Along with those in other Western nations, U.S. volunteer coaches must be nurtured wisely. For paid coaches, continuing education is necessary. Canada's

Table 5.3 Average score for all Element 3 variables by sport

	Negative %	Neutral %	Positive %
Tennis	25	47	28
Rugby	39	43	18
Soccer	27	40	33

National Coaching Certification Program has many ways (both "carrots and sticks") to ensure that both volunteer and paid coaches upgrade their knowledge. NGBs could also assist in organizing coaching clinics, seminars, conferences, colloquiums, and round-table discussions held in a central location (in all regions of the county), with invited international experts. Also, additional local sessions could be held at regional training and educational centers.

As many high schools and colleges with athletic programs have struggled to afford a sufficient number of coaches, some academic programs have reduced coaching education considering it to not be a promising occupation. According to the U.S. Bureau of Labor Statistics (2012a), there were only 243,900 coaches and scouts for over 200 million Americans who might wish sport instruction. Coaches' median pay in 2012 was only $28,360 per year compared to the median annual wage for all workers of $34,750. However, employment of coaches and scouts was projected to grow from 243,900 in 2012 by 15 percent or 36,200 in 2022, faster than the 11 percent average for all occupations (U.S. Bureau of Labor Statistics, 2012a). There would have to be a paradigm shift in order to increase the number of good coaching jobs in the U.S. and to boost the reputation of the coaching profession. For all but the elite level coaching pay is quite poor. It is not a viable career for many in the U.S. unless they have an additional role as a teacher or administrator. To stimulate the projected growth of coaching jobs is a relatively easy correction of the sport system.

An interesting aspect of the U.S. university system is that it does not have a dedicated sport university (or universities). Current examples are the German Sport University in Cologne; St. Petersburg and Moscow Sport universities in Russia; and the Beijing and Shanghai Sport universities (and fourteen others) in China. These institutions are unique in that they focus on all aspects of sport, from educating PE teachers and coaches through high-level specific research for elite athletes. Such research occurs in the United States and it is world class. Perhaps one or more dedicated sport universities would advance the overall sport system with the necessary human resources and new knowledge. The United States Sports Academy in Daphne, Alabama has emerged as an institution dedicated to sport studies, but it offers coaching courses in only twelve sports compared to fifty-five at Moscow Sport University. Further growth of such universities could be better supported through partnerships with NGBs and various levels of government, as is well done at the University of Bath in the United Kingdom.

A more efficient national coordination of world-class sport science and education would be beneficial for all NGBs. The USOC is well positioned to achieve it for all Olympic sports through its partnership with the NCAA and certain sponsoring corporations. This could be a unique solution to problems arising from the underutilization of science and educational resources as was the case for rugby. When universities, corporations, and sporting organizations develop this initiative, governments may also provide better state support once economic conditions permit, reflecting the bottom-up management of United States sport.

For Team USA to dominate the global sporting arena, U.S. NGBs need to become world leaders in educating sport-specific coaches, physicians, and scientists. Global competition demands that U.S. NGBs create some sort of sport specific "brain centers" or specialist tennis, rugby, or soccer universities and science centers. These organizations could then coordinate research for the needs of mass and elite sport and publish findings in journals that would deliver medical and scientific support to coaches and athletes in all sports.

Element 4 (Meso-Level): System of competitions and events

The United States has generally been successful in hosting major sport events. According to the tennis and soccer respondents, there is much alignment with the Model in terms of the structure of competitions at all levels; the support is there for developmental events and for the integration of progressive events, although both of these sports would like expanded hosting of international events and opportunities for their athletes. These sports need to simply advance what they are already providing. Rugby, on the other hand, varied widely from the Model across all elements. There is much to be done with developing all types of rugby competitions. Certainly hosting the Las Vegas World 7s leg is important. It appears that rugby needs a rationalized structure of internal national competitions as was mentioned in Chapter 4.

Of all of the elements, this one seems to have the overall greatest alignment with the Model when observing the total average for all variables in each sport (see Table 5.4). In both the tennis and soccer totals, there are many more positive than negative results displaying this alignment.

There are good examples of how U.S. sport can become more effective in this element. The National Olympics is one. The U.S. National Congress of State Games is a good model of development games and could be expanded to all summer and winter Olympic sports at state and national levels. As with other factors in the U.S. sport system, funding is an issue. With governments and nonprofit organizations at the state level struggling to support their State Games, there is a question of continuity. Without serious national media coverage and expanded funding, they are unlikely to continue. Perhaps to advance the State Games, teams representing public and private organizations could be added to the current competitions.

Sponsorship revenue from commercial professional and mega events must be used for the systematic development of lower-level amateur and grass roots

Table 5.4 Average score for all Element 4 variables by sport

	Negative %	*Neutral %*	*Positive %*
Tennis	18	55	27
Rugby	43	45	12
Soccer	28	44	28

tournaments. All major events and leagues need to attract and nurture their athletes through several lower stages of competition. The prerequisite for systematic elite player development is an optimal number and regularity of events (Crespo, Reid, Miley & Atienza, 2003). Most U.S. NGBs suffer from focusing on the top level of sport development and lacking systematic development at the youth level.

Another factor complicating effective and efficient sport development is the content of state and national games. Compared with the thirty-five disciplines competed in at the 2012 London Olympics, there are only thirteen sports with significant professional opportunities (Sparvero et al., 2008) and twenty-three NCAA sports that are widely competed in the United States. This too suggests that the United States could decline in its Olympic standing if more sports are not developed through a regular, structured series of competitions.

Element 5 (Meso-Level): Training centers

In this element we again see that tennis and soccer are better developed and more in alignment with the Model in two key areas. The first of these is priority access for high-performance (HP) athletes to high-quality equipment and facilities. The second is provision of specialized facilities and equipment of all age level of athletes.

All sport respondents were emphatic that the variables were at variance with the Model. This was especially so in soccer and rugby in terms of access, affordability, proximity (to homes and to other training facilities and services) of training centers, and centers that prepare athletes for competition in different environments (Variables 3–7). In terms of the overall average for each sport across all variables of this element, it is much the same outcome except for rugby, which had fewer neutral scores but a greater number of negative scores, indicating that rugby has a major problem in terms of training centers (see Table 5.5). Training centers are being developed for rugby, as seen in Chapter 4; however, the tyranny of distance operates strongly in this sport.

We have provided examples of successful experiences from across the world in both Chapters 3 and 4. These examples included the current municipal tennis developments in Florida and California, Germany's policies for concerted efforts of local governments and sport clubs (Bergsgard et al., 2007), and Bath (UK) and Izmailovo (Russia) sport hubs that were discussed previously in the book. The USOC is developing and centralizing training facilities in several locations, as are CODP programs. There are local and regional groups doing likewise and

Table 5.5 Average score for all Element 5 variables by sport

	Negative %	*Neutral %*	*Positive %*
Tennis	29	56	15
Rugby	60	34	6
Soccer	46	40	14

attempts at private sport hubs exist. Overall, it perhaps is the disjointedness of this provision that creates the most difficulty in developing training center hubs.

Academies such as those connected with the MSL clubs, IMG, NCAA, and USOC are another positive development in facilities provision. There might also be opportunity to use these facilities for mass participation and public health. Through its current support of parks, the federal government provides significant resources to local recreation departments for the construction of facilities. This could perhaps be expanded to programs and activities as well.

Current research suggests that there is a strong need for more local training centers providing facilities, coaching, sport science services, and competition for juniors without participants having to travel long distances. U.S. NGBs could coordinate the development of commercial and public academies by partnering with the USOC's CODPs, YM/WCAs, Boys and Girls clubs, and departments of education and local governments in each state.

Under current conditions of environmental degradation, better public transportation is strongly recommended to be incorporated into the planning of facilities. Can we end the idea of "mum's taxi" being a key element in sport development? New facilities will ideally be built to guarantee even coverage in each state. Funding of training centers should depend on their success in achieving both mass fitness and HP results. All Olympic facilities, particularly for expensive sports such as sailing, equestrian, and modern pentathlon, could be subsidized for affordability by both elite and mass participants.

What Gilbert (1980) noted about North American facilities is still true in the twenty-first century: There is a focus on appearance rather than on affordability and performance. Gilbert described a swimming pool in the former GDR's Berlin that was heated by thermal effluents from a nearby factory and had a roof on wheels allowing the pool to be open to the weather in summer and closed in winter. Such low-cost sport facility solutions could be interesting to consider, as too many outdoor pools in America operate for only several months a year. Facilities are sometimes not built because only expensive extravagant options are considered.

Finally, U.S. public parks should consider providing outdoor exercise equipment and programs. Departments of recreation can ensure that the most important apparatuses are provided (through assistance from HP coaches and sport scientists) and are supported by instructional programs for mass fitness. Outdoor elements could be integrated into conventional buildings, allowing fresh air exercise indoors in sheds, under awnings, on verandas, and on outdoor fields or using removable roofs, walls, and windows. The Muscle Beach weight training facility in Santa Monica, California is a good example of a removable roof. Much of this type of design is beginning to occur in strongly sunny or cold climates. This would be a good trend to continue.

Element 6 (Micro-Level): Talent identification and development

At the micro-level we encounter the key element for any sport development system, the participant-athletes, and HP athletes. Much is made of democracy and of "athlete-centered" sport development systems. Again, rhetoric supplants reality.

The quantitative data resulted in many interesting variances from the Model. For tennis, there were only two variables with very negative results reflecting lack of athlete development resources and coach expertise (Variables 3 and 7). IIt appears that tennis players are well monitored (Variable 5) and those with the potential are able to train full-time at HP standards (Variable 9). Of note, the age group results/rankings system showed both a strong negative and positive alignment with the Model. The various tennis bodies and its NGB must delve further into that anomaly. Seven of 10 variables showed more negative than positive scores, indicating that most of the current tennis structure and operation varies from the Model. Ability, availability, and pay for coaches were far from alignment with the desired practices of the Model

The results from the rugby community again indicate that this sport is underdeveloped and some distance from the variables in this element – and strongly so. Only three variables had double-digit positive responses and these were low. Rugby is very far away from the Model's suggested elements in matters related to coaching (educated/certified coaches for all players, coach/athlete ratios, and pay for coaches). These three variables were negatively rated in the 80-percent levels. The availability of specialized focus on talented athletes is also far from the Model's recommendations (those for Variables 3, 4, 9, and 10). The first two variables on youth development were nearly at the 50-percent level of negative response. Clearly, the early stages of introducing rugby to children and youth are lacking.

Soccer presented some interesting anomalies. Four variables were rated closely positively and negatively. The variables on LTAD, resource availability, player multi-stage rankings, and the potential to represent the United States displayed percentages that were between 2 and 9 percent different. Otherwise, most felt that soccer is not approximating the Model. Coaching expertise and availability and athlete-coach ratios in rugby and soccer were particularly viewed as far from ideal.

All sports respondents felt their sports were far from the notion of a national database being employed to track their respective athletes. This situation is also evident in many other countries' sports systems. If an advanced database exists at all in the United States, it is for the major professional sports and in the upper stages of TID for Olympic athletes. In terms of the overall average percentages for each sport (Table 5.6), the relative balance between positive and negative responses in tennis (with few neutral scores) was notable.

The above results show an uneven development of TID practices. This along with a lack of LTAD processes is not ideal. U.S. Hockey developed its ADM (see Chapter 3) system that is sound and will carry the sport forward. With age

Table 5.6 Average score for all Element 6 variables by sport

	Negative %	Neutral %	Positive %
Tennis	39	36	25
Rugby	68	24	8
Soccer	44	37	19

groupings standard in rugby, it will likely rationally develop playing talent in the future. LTAD programs take time to develop and then to implement.

According to Johnson, Wojnar, Price, Foley, Moon, Esposito, and Cromartie (2011), most countries use an athlete development system that focuses on performance outcomes. This involves getting as many young athletes as possible into training programs and then focusing on the elite performers. The authors stress that the problem with this method is that NGBs rely on early maturing youngsters: those who are simply bigger and stronger than their peers and therefore almost inevitably perform better in sport. However, only an estimated 25 percent of youngsters identified as potential "elite athletes" at an early age were ranked the same way at a later date.

In fact, people who develop later in life can become elite athletes given enough time. Johnson et al. (2011) suggest making a conscious effort to keep all athletes involved through stage-appropriate modifications in training and competition. Those NGBs that provide a better sport experience for everyone increase the likelihood of developing elite athletes who would otherwise have dropped out of sport. Not only does this enlarge the pool of talent but it increases the likelihood that athletes will continue to be physically active throughout life. As youths progress into adulthood, they acquire the skills and knowledge from organized sports to remain healthy and physically fit (Johnson et al., 2011).

Inner-city programs have great potential for discovering talented young athletes. The future development of these participants depends largely on being subsidized by the family or, in rare instances, by owners of private academies that see enough potential to invest in the athlete. The age at which sport talent and specialization are identified and supported by academies and emerging sport investment funds will continue to become younger (Downie, 2008; Smith & Westerbeek, 2004). The result could likely lead to over-commercialization of talent development, concentration of resources only on a gifted few, further domination of elite over mass sport, and the unrealized potential of sport in advancing life in society.

The interconnected advancement of macro-, meso-, and micro-conditions, particularly in education and health care practices, could make sport TID more socially accepted, particularly when used as part of the development of all talents and interests. The following actions could be considered as part of an integrated TID and LTAD strategy. Research findings from sport scientists on best global practices on multi-year human development stages (i.e., those identifying the age at which certain sport-related activities begin; for example, starting weightlifting before thirteen years of age and after reaching certain body parameters) must be followed. Other factors strongly age-related and in need of communication surround: the maximum hours and types of training and competitions for different age levels; the ranking of athletes according to achieved results other than winning; valid research findings on how to eat, drink, rest, and recover from vigorous training or competition; place a stronger emphasis on sport ethics; and avoid early specialization of athlete development. Finally, two aspects that will sound very repetitive are required. First, look for ways to pay coaches according to their knowledge and success in long-term healthy development of participants as part of uniform national coaching education and certification. Second, look for ways to subsidize, in a balanced way, and spread resources among all children and youth so they may fully realize their sport potentials.

Element 7 (Micro-Level): Advanced support for each participant

Much of the above research identifies what attracts and keeps children and youth in sport. If a sport system is to fully identify, attract, and support athletic talent, it must do so in ways that maximize the potential both of those who might become Olympians or professional stars and those who are lifelong participants. Many countries and their national sport systems fail to do this because their approach to sport is mainly exclusionary. Though science is improving the way in which sporting talent is identified, there is still much to be done.

The variables in this element are perhaps too socialist to consider, although they exist in capitalist societies and in recently professionalized sports such as rugby. The neutral percentages in tennis exhibit this and its long development as a professional sport. It is scary to think of the lack of knowledge around doping issues (Variable 6) in the sport. Again we see a split decision on ways to prolong tennis playing careers (Variable 5), even though nearly 50 percent responded neutrally. Overall, the responses from tennis experts indicate that this sport varies from the Model.

Rugby respondents again supported the claim that this sport is in its early stages of development in the United States. There was only one double-digit positive percentage in the sport. Between the neutral and strongly negative percentages, it is not difficult to state that rugby varies widely from the Model's premises.

Finally, the resulting percentages from soccer respondents showed less understanding of the variables of this element, as shown by the neutral responses. Soccer aligned more with the Model in terms of anti-doping control and to a lesser degree in the extension of careers through adequate medical knowledge by soccer personnel. Clearly, soccer does not provide career advice and opportunities. U.S. soccer shows variance against most of the variables in this element of the Model.

The overall averages for all variables in this element for each sport (Table 5.7) again show rugby less developed than that of the other two sports. The average for tennis indicates a lack of knowledge or understanding of the element's variables or simply that tennis is a professional sport whether at the college and university level or at the elite level. This result indicates that tennis players should win enough

Table 5.7 Average score for all Element 7 variables by sport

	Negative %	Neutral %	Positive %
Tennis	32	54	14
Rugby	57	38	5
Soccer	39	40	21

money or go to coaching. The right-hand column clearly displays the variance from the Model.

Multidisciplinary support

The strong individualistic liberal ideology implies that people in the United States should be responsible for their lives and their ability to support themselves. If one is not in a fully professionalized sport, then one must ensure to obtain a wage or salary that permits a full life. If one is a professional athlete, then one should save to support oneself throughout life (after sport). The Republican Right decries a "nanny" state, so many of the aspects of this element depend on individual responsibility.

This situation would be alleviated if college and university athletes all received a full, meaningful education that abetted employability. If sound middle-class occupations are found, then health contingencies and retirement planning can be fully met. Once again, personal economic matters are the responsibility of the individual. Career planning as provided through the partnership between the USOC and Adecco is important for all athletes in the United States, not just for athletes outside of the four major professional sports. The NCAA should also lift its game in this regard. Likewise, such opportunities exist with military and CODP programs. Plans are also required and necessary to gradually reduce the impact of competitive activities on the health and lives of elite athletes; this is an important health issue as athletes need to be de-trained in a programmed way. Counseling is also required to dissolve the social context of elite sport; to reduce the tribal nature of sport teams and, to a degree, the "celebrity" lifestyle, in order to reenter "normal" society.

A final comment on the recent issue of the concussion-related – as one of many other physically debilitating – injuries in HP sport is necessary. In the United States and in other countries, medical and psychological care is required for retiring and retired athletes. HP sport puts unreasonable stress on the human body. Yes, this is accepted as part of competing in sport. Despite this complicity, athletes might be provided with full medical insurance and support in their post-career lives. Surely a small percentage from each sport team and NGB is not outside of the realm of possibilities to make such coverage possible. And this would be within the market principles that guide life in the United States.

Chapter Summary

For U.S. sport to continue to positively, successfully, and efficiently advance, there are larger societal factors that need to be considered and hopefully transformed. We have mentioned these as the reality of the context of the United States allows one to see future possibilities for U.S. sport. Being a market-based, liberalist-capitalist republic, the United States does not provide equality of opportunity for many U.S. children and youth. The decline in the size of the middle-class and austerity budgeting, in particular, are limiting the number of athletes from which the United States can draw on for international sport competitions. Fortunately, some adaptations and subsidized support exist, which helps increase the flow of talented athletes and more healthy citizens.

The question is how can conditions be improved for all of sport in the United States? It will demand an overhaul of both the economic and political institutions of the society: "Of all the costs imposed on our society by the top 1 percent, perhaps the greatest is this: the erosion of our sense of identity, in which fair play, equality of opportunity, and a sense of community are so important" (Stiglitz, 2011). These are the global and historic values attributed to sport and through which sport delivers a better life through friendly competition for those involved. Sadly, this feature of current community life disproves this myth except for a few cases.

Much of what we observe in the U.S. sport system still depends on market principles and capitalist individualism. As U.S. republicanism demands there is less government support for and oversight of sport in the U.S. sport system, a more private sector approach shapes the way that sport is delivered and structured. This leads to economic and ideological domination by a small number of revenue-generating sports such as baseball, football, basketball, and hockey that are sold as entertainment by elite teams. Rather than being active participants, many U.S. citizens choose to be supporters of these popular sports in the form of paid spectators, purchasing the products and services of corporate sponsors, and subsidizing the rent-seeking construction of stadiums through tax dollars.

Elite sport also receives indirect public support (hidden externalities) through park and recreation departments, schools, colleges, and universities where talented children from all social classes receive opportunities to become elite athletes. Tax-reduction incentives for donors also would help subsidize participation among the poor through nonprofit organizations such as YM/WCA and Boys and Girls Clubs. However, some of the best potential athletes are not identified and developed because the system allocates most funding to elite programs, especially in the more expensive sports. Elite teams receive significant public support, but they profit only a small group of individuals rather than increasing mass participation within their communities.

To achieve consistent global success and improve national health, resources in the U.S. sport system need to concentrate on the development of participants and instructors at beginner, intermediate, and pre-HP levels rather than paying astronomical salaries to a few top players and coaches. The larger number of professional players and coaches in each sport, particularly developing sports such as rugby and soccer, must be supported with full-time pay and advanced services in each state. This large wealthy capitalist country has given rise to a fluid, entrepreneurial system that is both praised as the athletes' greatest advantage and blamed for their shortcomings (Thomas, 2010b). The U.S. sport system is influenced by the tradition of paying professional athletes their market price rather than providing them with comprehensive education and health care. In schools, colleges, and universities this could be addressed by allowing coaches whose athletes are successful academically to spend more time with athletes in the off-season while barring teams from playing in the postseason for poor academic progress (Thomas, 2010a).

The U.S. sport delivery system, overall, will also likely need to re-envision how it is to operate. While sport is not a true public good, it might require federal government stimulus funding if opportunities are to exist for all in the United States. Stimulus funding will result in more resources for the development of participants and instructors at beginner, intermediate, and pre-HP mass levels and advanced services in unprofitable mass participation sports (particularly through USOC/private sponsorship agreements). Nonetheless, as Berman (2006a) cautions, the sort of change demanded to redirect the United States politically will not happen in the short term and is likely to require a cycle of forty to fifty years to occur. Can the U.S. citizens see beyond dominant national ideologies and more fully embrace global sport practices? There are signs that this is happening; therefore, optimism exits.

This funding will also support the commissioning of sport scientists to develop and reinforce the comprehensive pedagogical components of training so that coaches deliver specific knowledge about healthy training and lifestyle (as well as sport history, organization, and ethics of sport). University researchers can be better utilized by forming multidisciplinary scientific groups to work together with university and pro-team coaches and sport service specialists to provide competitors with individualized healthy lifestyle plans. We also promote the idea that sport managers, coaches, participants, and all school students and their parents understand fundamental concepts related to exercise (e.g., short-term and long-term effects of training, periodization, as well as healthy restoration and illness prevention). U.S. individualism is key here: It is up to each participant to know more of what is involved in producing sport performances, whatever the level of involvement.

Finally, the participant/athlete must be protected and encouraged. The sport system should provide athletes with education outside of the playing field to enable their smooth career progression on a variety of sport-related fields from coaching and management to journalism, medicine, and various sport sciences. University researchers can be better utilized to this end.

As highlighted throughout this book, American athletes have benefited from many progressive foreign methods, particularly at the micro- and meso-levels. There is no reason to fear integrating the successful macro-level sport approaches utilized by other nations as they are not based on capitalism or U.S. republicanism. Opportunities for the further advancement of U.S. sport using the practices of other leading sport nations were evident across all key analyzed elements. Many successful international practices have already been adopted in the United States, particularly to develop elite athletes in a small number of commercial professional competitions: at high schools, universities, elite training centers, academies, and in the military (especially the Army). The USOC is taking a greater, central role in organizing sport in the United States. Many local, regional, and state populist organized groups are successfully providing sport for development and for recreationists. However, some mass participation practices remain to be implemented. As noted throughout the book, the unity of mass and elite sport forms the backbone of a truly well-functioning system.

Likewise, with a capacity for critically reflecting and learning, the sport practitioner can operate in complex, fast-changing situations and make the "normative leap from data to recommendations, from fact to values, from 'is' to 'ought'" (Schön & Rein, 1994, p. 31). The Model is a device that hopefully will stimulate further critical reflection on the current U.S. sport system. We see it as being a device that will aid problem setting, allowing sport practitioners to name and frame the changes required to better the U. S. sport development system. And toward learning organizations that will be more effective.

The knowledge and policies exist to achieve the goals of effective and efficient sporting outcomes. It is up to those working as sport specialists in this system to identify, implement, and manage those outcomes in the most beneficial way. We hope that this book provides a framework for a constructive national debate, particularly by sport-related societies and associations, on how the United States could lead the world in systematic and efficient sport development.

Notes

1   The Gini coefficient or Gini ratio is a summary statistic that measures relative (not absolute) inequality of income or wealth in a population. It ranges from 0 (perfect equality of income or wealth) to 1(total inequality of income or wealth).

2   The following is further evidence of the dire position of the U.S. middle class and their ability to access participatory and sport opportunities, especially for their children and youth. If liberal individualism demands that everyone pay their way, then the affordability issue is greater. The extensive and regularly updated report by Edward Wolff (2010, p. 34) provides other key evidence for this decline. He wrote that "households with zero or negative non-home wealth rose substantially, by 2.5 percentage points, from 2001 to 2004. Median income also fell by 1.6 percent from 2001 to 2004".

> Of further evidence of the middle-class squeeze is that for the middle three wealth quintiles there was a huge increase in the debt-income ratio from 100 to 157 percent from 2001 to 2007 and an almost doubling of the debt-equity ratio from 31.7 to 61.1 percent. Moreover, total stocks as a share of total assets fell off from 12.6 to 7 percent for the middle class. The debt-equity ratio in 2007 was also much higher among the middle 60 percent of households (at 0.61) than among the top 1 percent (0.028) or the next 19 percent (0.121). Moreover, the evidence suggests that middle-class households, experiencing stagnating incomes, expanded their debt almost exclusively in order to finance normal consumption expenditures (p. 36).

> Stiglitz (2012) criticized what the middle class have done as "people outside the top 1 percent increasingly live beyond their means. Trickle-down economics may be a chimera, but trickle-down behaviorism is very real;" advertising and soap-operas have a serious effect on peoples' minds and purchasing. Panitch and Gandin (2012, p. 337) added that "so much consumption was dependent on credit" leading to the unsustainability of middle class lifestyles. How this will affect sport development in the U. S. is still to be seen. From our examples in Chapter 3, there are more charities and foundations involved today.

3 Bacevich (2009, p. 7) states this more directly. He quotes Reinhold Niebuhr in that "our [U.S.] dreams of managing history" is "born of a particular combination of arrogance and narcissism". Bacevich sees a potential mortal threat to the country as Neibuhr's type of realism "implies an obligation to see the world as it actually is, not as we might like it to be" and warns not to "remake the world in what we imagine to be America's image" (p. 7). Berman (2006b) advanced this idea, noting that "Cicero wrote that 'Not to know what happened before one was born is always to be a child.' Most Americans don't seem to know what's happened during their own lifetime" (p. 295). But those in the United States, again, are not alone in this ahistorical position.

4 The normative leap necessitates a bit of explanation. First, all sport practitioners have some form of "frame" (sets of perceptions and ideas) with which to observe and act in the world. This frame results from one's background (history), education, and ability to break down (critique) other frames that exist. A frame helps us construct a particular social reality, such as a way of understanding sport and how it operates in society. But it is important that we do not just take basic, existing observations or interpretations as being adequate. Acting in this way leads to problem solving and hampers real change. It avoids what Argyris and Schön (1974) identify as organizational learning. Errors and mistakes are part of learning and life. How we detect and correct them demands a starting point beyond the use of existing strategies, policies, and practices used in sport. Employing old frames limits possibilities of new ideas, strategies, policies, and actions. They defined this as "single-loop learning." Here the feedback loop returns to identifying errors or problems within current thinking, rules, and concepts rather than questioning those currently operationalized organizational actions: And as Schön and Rein (1994, p. 38) further note: "Frame reflection is a crucial step in the reframing that helps resolve conflicts and controversies practitioners meet in practice."

They propose problem setting, or the naming and framing of the situation, to go beyond the current narrow and often ideologically-bounded ones that limit possibilities. They suggested "double-loop learning" where "governance" elements (the goals, values, plans of strategic planning and operational rules) are questioned. This is often difficult due to power (especially political power) exercising itself in negative and disastrous ways, but this also leads to ineffective and inefficient policies, practices, and ways of thinking and, therefore, does not lead to progress.

5 While we do not have the space here to elaborate on this study, we encourage readers to source this work and take note of its simplicity and its focus on community sport development. The purpose of the research was to develop community capacity to ensure the continuity of these programs.

Bibliography

24 Hour Fitness. (2011). Retrieved August 11, 2011, from http://www.24hourfitness.com/company/press_room/press_releases/20080501.html.

Adams, R. L. & Rooney Jr., J. F. (1985). Evolution of American golf facilities. *Geographical Review*, 75(4), 419–438.

Adecco. (2013). IOC Athlete Career Programme. Bringing elite athletes together with great companies. Retrieved July 20, 2013 from http://athlete.adecco.com/en-US/Documents/index.html#what.

Adecco USA. (2014). Hilton Worldwide and Adecco partnership. Retrieved March 22, 2014 from http://www.adeccousa.com/articles/Hilton-Worldwide-and-Adecco-partnership.html?id=142&url=/pressroom/pressreleases/Archives/Forms/AllItems.aspx&templateurl=/AboutUs/pressroom/Pages/Press-release.aspx.

Agrusa, J. (2004). Marathon economic impact could rise. *Pacific Business News*. Retrieved December 13, 2004, from www.bizjournals.com/pacific/stories/2004/12/13/daily55.html.

Agus, D. (2011). *The End of Illness*. New York, NY: Free Press.

Alfano, P. (2011). ESPN. Wimbledon. American tennis in a nosedive. Retrieved June 20, 2011, from http://espn.go.com/espnw/news-opinion/6670519/wimbledon-american-tennis-nosedive.

All-time Olympic Games medal table. (2014). Retrieved March 11, 2014 from http://en.wikipedia.org/wiki/All-time_Olympic_Games_medal_table.

All-Union Sport Program GTO. (2006). *RIA Novosti*. Retrieved August 4, 2010, from http://www.rian.ru/spravka/20060812/52549966.html.

American Gaming Association. (2010). Types of gambling. Retrieved March 16, 2014 from http://www.americangaming.org/sites/default/files/uploads/docs/facts_at_your_fingertips_12022010.pdf.

American Sports Data Inc. (2007). The superstudy of sports participation. Cortland Manor, NY: ASDI.

Anderson, P. D. (2014, February 28). NFL concussion litigation: Eliminating false marketing campaigns. Retrieved March 17, 2014, from http://nflconcussionlitigation.com

Andersen, S. S., & Ronglanb, L. T. (2012, April-July). Same ambitions–different tracks: A comparative perspective on Nordic elite sport, *Managing Leisure*, 17, 155–169.

Andrasko, A. (2013). USOC Coordinator, Community Outreach. Interviewed by Brooke Pinkham on March 22, 2013.

AP (Associated Press). (2000). USOC soothes fears over sports shakeup. Retrieved April 16, 2000, from http://www.deseretnews.com/article/755332/USOC-soothes-fears-over-sports-shakeup.html?pg=all.

Argyris, C.& Schön, D. A. (1974). *Theory in practice: Increasing professional effectiveness*. San Francisco: Jossey-Bass.

ASC (Australian Sport Commission). (2014). The Australian Sports Commission: The Athlete Career and Education (ACE) program. Retrieved March 21, 2014, from http://www.ausport.gov.au/ais/athlete_career_and_education/about/background.

Askdefine (2013). Dictionary definition. Heuristic. Retrieved January 10, 2004, from http://heuristic.askdefine.com/.

ATP (Association of Tennis Professionals). (2014). Web site of the ATP World Tour. Retrieved March 2, 2014, from http://www.atpworldtour.com/Rankings/Singles.aspx.

Babbie, E. (1989). *The Practice of Social Research* (5th ed.). Belmont, CA: Wadsworth.

Bacevich, A. J. (2009). *The limits of power: The end of American exceptionalism*. New York: Metropolitan Books.

Badenhausen, K. (2014). The NFL Signs TV deals worth $27 billion. Retrieved March 24, 2014, from http://www.forbes.com/sites/kurtbadenhausen/2011/12/14/the-nfl-signs-tv-deals-worth-26-billion/

Badger, E. (2012). How Colorado Springs became the heart of the US Olympic Movement. Retrieved June 21, 2012, from http://www.fastcompany.com/1840907/how-colorado-springs-became-heart-us-olympic-movement.

Bailey, P. (1978). *Leisure and Class in Victorian England: Rational Recreation and the Contest for Control, 1830–1885*. London: Routledge & K. Paul.

Baker, A. (2012). Despite obesity concerns, gym classes are cut. *The New York Times*. Retrieved from http://www.nytimes.com/2012/07/11/education/even-as-schools-battle-obesity-physical-education-is-sidelined.html?_r=0&adxnnl=1&pagewanted=all&adxnnlx=1367953337-Hz//MZ/MOLcgryul7tHN8Q

Balyi, I. (2001) Sport System Building and Long-term Athlete Development in British Columbia. Canada: SportsMed BC. Retrieved from http://iceskatingresources.org/SportsSystemDevelopment.pdf.

Balyi, I., & Hamilton, A. (2010). Long-term athlete development: trainability in childhood and adolescence. *American Swimming*, 2, 14–23.

Barrett, P. (2014, February 27). Fake Classes Scandal, UNC Fails Its Athletes–and Whistle-Blower. *Business Week*. Retrieved March 15, 2014, from www.businessweek.com/articles/2014-02-27/in-fake-classes-scandal-unc-fails-its-athletes-whistle-blower.

Barrow, H. M., & Brown, J. P. 1988. *Man and Movement: Principles of Physical Education* (4th ed.). Philadelphia, PA: Lea & Febiger.

Bath Sport (2011). Retrieved June 3, 2011, from http://www.bathsport.org/aboutbathsport.shtml.

Baumann, A. (2002). Developing sustained high performance services and systems that have quality outcomes. *12th Commonwealth International Sport Conference Abstract Book*, 62–71.

Bayle, E., Durand, C., & Nikonoff, C. (2008). France. In B. Houlihan, & M. Green, (Eds.). *Comparative elite sport development: Systems, structures and public policy* (pp.147–165). Butterworth-Heinemann, Burlington, MA.

BBC. (2004a). Sport 'improves boys' behaviour. Retrieved June 14, 2004, from http://news.bbc.co.uk/2/hi/uk_news/education/3804793.stm.

BBC. (2004b). Specialist schools now a majority. Retrieved January 29, 2004, from http://news.bbc.co.uk/2/hi/uk_news/education/3438825.stm.

BBC. (2011). America's child death shame. Retrieved October 17, 2011, from http://www.bbc.co.uk/news/world-us-canada-15288865.

Beckstrom, J. (2011). Medical Symposium. USA Rugby. Retrieved December 29, 2011 from http://www.USARugby.org/newsarchive.

Bell, C. C. (1997). Promotion of mental health through coaching competitive sports. *Journal of the National Medical Association, 89*(8), 517–520.

Belsie, L. (2011). Incentives matter: Soccer player file. Retrieved March 28, 2011 from http://antidismal.blogspot.com/2011/03/incentives-matter-soccer-player-file.html.

Benedict, J. & Armen, K. (2013-09-17). *The system: the glory and scandal of big-time college football.* Knopf Doubleday Publishing Group. Kindle Edition.

Bennett, B., Howell, M., & Simri, U. (1975, 1983). *Comparative Physical Education and Sport.* Philadelphia, PA: Lea & Febiger.

Benson, D. (2007, October 8). Taking a hit: While women's programs flourished under Title IX, men's athletics suffered. *Fort Wayne News Sentinel.* Retrieved October 8, 2007, from http://fwnextwebl.fortwayne.com/ns/projects/titleC/titleQlO.php.

Bergsgard., N. A., Houlihan, B., Mangset, P., Nodland, S. A., & Rommetvedt, H. (2007). *Sport policy: A comparative analysis of stability and change,* Oxford, UK: Butterworth-Heinemann.

Berman, M. (2006a). *The twilight of American culture.* New York: W. W. Norton.

Berman, M. (2006b). *Dark ages American: The final collapse of empire.* New York: W. W. Norton.

Bishop, G. (2012). Long before London Games, James Bond tactics. *The New York Times.* Retrieved July 22, 2012, from http://www.nytimes.com/2012/07/23/sports/olympics/countries-try-anything-for-olympic-edge-including-spying.html?nl=todaysheadlines&emc=edit_th_20120723.

Bishop, M. (2006, February 26). A survey of wealth and philanthropy. *The Economist, 378*(8466), 3–16.

Bloom, M., Grant, M., & Watt, D. (2005). Strengthening Canada: The socio-economic benefits of sport participation in Canada. Ottawa: The Conference Board of Canada.

Blyth, M. (2013). *The myth of austerity: The history of a dangerous idea.* New York: Oxford University Press.

Bompa, T. O. (1983). *Theory and Methodology of Training: The key to Athletic Performance.* Dubuque, IA: Kendall/Hunt.

Bompa, T. O., & Haff, G. G. (2009). *Periodization: Theory and Methodology of Training.* Champaign, IL: Human Kinetics.

Borden, S. (2012, March 3). High school players forced to choose in soccer's new way. *The New York Times.* Retrieved March 4, 2012 from http://www.nytimes.com/2012/03/04/sports/soccer/soccers-all-year-model-forces-high-school-players-to-choose.html?_r=1&nl=todaysheadlines&emc=tha27.

Borzilleri, M.-J. (2005a). USOC says NGBs must show cause to get cash. *Colorado Springs Gazette.* Retrieved September 12, 2005, from http://usoc.gazette.com/fullstory.php?id=4291.

Borzilleri, M.-J. (2005b). Federations worried by funding plan from USOC. *Colorado Springs Gazette.* Retrieved September 12, 2005, from http://usoc.gazette.com/fullstory.php?id=4923.

Bowers, M. T., Chalip, L., & Green, B. C. (2011). Sport participation under laissez-faire policy: The case of the United States. In M. Nicholson, R. Hoye, & B. Houlihan (Eds.). *Participation in sport: International policy prospectives* (pp. 254–267). London and New York: Routledge.

Bravo, G., Orejan, J., Vélez, L., & López de D'Amico, R. (2012). 'Sport in Latin America'. In M. Li, E. Macintosh, & G. Bravo (Eds.). *International sport management* (pp. 99–133), Champaign, IL: Human Kinetics.

Breslow, J. M. (2014, January 14). Judge rejects $765 million NFL concussion settlement. Retrieved March 17, 2014, from http://www.pbs.org/wgbh/pages/frontline/sports/league-of-denial/judge-rejects-765-million-nfl-concussion-settlement/.

Broad, W. J. (2012). How yoga can wreck your body. *The New York Times*. Retrieved January 5, 2012, from http://www.nytimes.com/2012/01/08/magazine/how-yoga-can-wreck-your-body.html?pagewanted=1&_r=1.

Brooks, K. (2005). Re-interpreting social capital–a political hijack or useful structural concept in community regeneration. Retrieved November 17, 2012 from http://www.engagingcommunities2005.org/ab-theme-6.html.

Broom, E. F. (1986). Funding the development of the Olympic athletes: A comparison of programs in selected Western and socialist countries. *Proceedings of the 3rd International Seminar on Comparative Physical Education and Sport*, 21–24. Champaign, IL: Human Kinetics.

Brown, M. (2008). MLB Partners with NFL, USOC, USADA on PED Research. *The Biz of Baseball*. Retrieved August 13, 2011, from http://www.bizofbaseball.com/index.php?option=com_content&task=view&id=1827&Itemid=42.

Buchanan, P. (2013). Is the sun rising in the East? *Townhall Magazine*. Retrieved December 6, 2013, from http://townhall.com/columnists/patbuchanan/2013/12/06/is-the-sun-rising-in-the-east-n1758363/page/full.

Budberg, A. (2005). Breakfast with a champion. *Moskovskii Komsomolets*. Retrieved October 28, 2005, from http://www.mk.ru/.

Busbee, J. (2014). Russia gives all its gold medalists $120,000, a new Mercedes. Yahoo Sports. Retrieved March 21, 2010, from http://sports.yahoo.com/blogs/olympics-fourth-place-medal/russia-gives-all-its-gold-medalists--120-000--a-new-mercedes-174223357.html.

Caeser, J. W. (2012). The origins and character of american exceptionalism, *American Political Thought: A Journal of Ideas, Institutions, and Culture*, 1, 1-26.

Cairns, J., Jennett, N., & Sloane, P. J. (1986). The economics of professional team sports: A survey of theory and evidence, *Journal of Economic Studies*, *13*(1), 3–80.

Canada Revenue Agency. (2007). Children's fitness tax credit. Retrieved July 10, 2008, from http://www.cra-arc.gc.ca/fitness/.

Canadian Sport for Life. (2011). LTAD stages: A clear path to better sport, greater health, and higher achievement. Retrieved June 3, 2011, from http://www.canadiansportforlife.ca/coaches/ltad-stages.

Carney, M., Smolianov, P. & Zakus, D. H. (2012). Comparing the practices of USA Rugby against a global model for integrated development of mass and high performance sport. *Managing Leisure: An International Journal. Special issue: The Management of Excellence in Sport*, *17*, 181–205.

Carlton, E. (2000, September 22). Degrees of success. *Times Higher Education Supplement*, *1454*, 8.

CBC (Canadian Broadcast Corporation). (2014). Sochi 2014: Cash for gold. Retrieved March 23, 2014, from www.cbc.ca/sochi2014/features/.

CDC. (2008–2013). The Centers for Disease Control and Prevention. Retrieved from: http://www.cdc.go

Chadwick, S., Semens, A., Schwarz, E., & Zhang, D., (2010). Economic impact report on global rugby: part III. *Strategic and Emerging Markets*. Retrieved January 2, 2012 from http://www.irb.com/mm/Document/NewsMedia/MediaZone/02/04/22/88/2042288_PDF.pdf.

Chalip, L. (1995). Policy analysis in sport management. *Journal of Sport Management*, *9*(1), 1–13.

Chalip, L., Johnson, A., & Stachura, L. (1996). National sports policies. In *National sport policies: An international handbook*. London-Westport, CT: Greenwood Press.

Chantrill, C. (2014a). Defence: US FY 2004-2019. Retrieved March 30, 2014, from www. usgovernmentspending.com/spending_chart_2004_2019USb_30t.

Chantrill, C. (2014b). Health: US FY 2004-2019. Retrieved March 30, 2014, from www. usgovernmentspending.com/spending_chart_2004_2019USb_15s2li111mcn_30t_Health.

Charity Navigator. (2014). Giving statistics. Retrieved March 15, 2014, from www. charitynavigator.org/index.cfm?bay=content.view&cpid=42.

Chatziefstathiou, D. (2007). The history of marketing an idea: The example of Baron Pierre de Coubertin as a social marketer. *European Sport Management Quarterly*, *7*(1), 55–80.

Chester, J. M. K. (2009). *Digital Marketing: Opportunities for Addressing Interactive Food and Beverage Marketing to Youth*. Berkeley, CA: Berkeley Media Studies Group.

Chomsky, N. (2013). Noam Chomsky: The Obama doctrine. *Truthout*. Retrieved on April 15, 2014 form http://truth-out.org/opinion/item/19251-the-obama-doctrine.'

Christesen, P. (2012). *Sport and Democracy in the Ancient and Modern Worlds*. New York, NY: Cambridge University Press.

Coalter, F. (2007a). Sports clubs, social capital and social regeneration: Ill Defined Interventions with Hard to Follow Outcomes. *Sport in Society*, 10, 537–559.

Coalter, F. (2007b). *A wider social role for sport: Who's keeping score?* London and New York: Routledge.

Cocanour, S. C. M. (2007). Sports: A tool for international relations. A research report submitted to the in partial fulfillment of the graduation requirements, Air Command and Staff College, Air University, USAF, Maxwell Air Force Base, Alabama.

CODP. (2011). Community Olympic Development Program 2011 Fact Sheet. Retrieved August 2, 2011, from http://s3.assets.usoc.org/assets/documents/attached_file/filename/41103/2011_CODP_Fact_Sheet.pdf?1302640380%20.

CODP. (2014). CODP Designation Plan 2013-1014. Downloaded March 11, 2014, from http://www.teamusa.org/codp.

Coleman, R., & Ramchandani, G. (2010). The hidden benefits of non-elite mass participation sports events: An economic perspective. *International Journal of Sports Marketing and Sponsorship*, *12*(1), 24–36.

Collins, B. (2005). Marathon training: The ultimate achievement. *Sun Wellness*. Retrieved from http://www.sunwellness.com/articles/051feat4.html.

Coloradofusion. (2012). Colorado Rapids Adidas alliance. Retrieved March 22, 2012 from http://www.coloradofusion.org/aboutus/rapidsadidasalliance/index_E.html

Commonwealth of Massachusetts. (2012). Tennis Courts. Boston Region. Retrieved July 2012, from http://www.mass.gov/eea/agencies/dcr/massparks/recreational-activities/tennis-courts.html.

Conzelmann, A., & Nagel, S. (2003). Professional careers of the German Olympic athletes. *International Review for the Sociology of Sport*, *38*, 259–280.

Coyle, D. (2007). How to grow a super-athlete. *New York Times Play Magazine*. Retrieved March 4, 2007, from http://www.nytimes.com/2007/03/04/sports/playmagazine/04play-talent.html?emc=eta1.

Crespo, M., Reid, M., Miley, D., & Atienza, F. (2003). The relationship between professional tournament structure on the national level and success in men's professional tennis. *Journal of Science and Medicine in Sport*, *6*, 3–13.

Crouse, K. (2011). Boys swimming on girls teams find success, then draw jeers. *The New York Times*. Retrieved March November 18, 2011, from http://www.nytimes.

com/2011/11/19/sports/boys-swimming-on-girls-teams-find-success-then-draw-ire. html?nl=todaysheadlines&emc=tha27.

Crowley, J. N. (2006). The NCAA's first century in the arena. Digital edition. Retrieved from http://www.ncaapublications.com/p-4039-in-the-arena-the-ncaas-first-century. aspx.

CSRI (College Sport Research Institute). (2013a). 2013 Adjusted graduation gap report: NCAA Division-1 Football. Retrieved March 16, 2014, from http://csri-sc.org/wp-content/uploads/2013/09/CSRI_2013_AGG_NCAA_D-I_FB.pdf.

CSRI (College Sport Research Institute). (2013b). 2013 Adjusted graduation gap report: NCAA Division-I Men's and Women's Basketball. Retrieved March 16, 2014, from http://csri-sc.org/wp-content/uploads/2013/09/CSRI_2011_AGG_NCAA_D-I_MBB-WBB.pdf.

Cutler, D. (2009). David Cutler, former health advisor to President Obama speaking on *Hardtalk* program, BBC World News, TV broadcast 11.30 pm EST, July 30, 2009.

Dalleck, L. C., & Kravitz, L. (2012). The history of fitness. Retrieved August 1, 2012, from http://www.unm.edu/~lkravitz/Article%20folder/history.html).

Davies, G. (2008). Specialist sports colleges make the grade. *Telegraph.* Retrieved February 1, 2008, from http://www.telegraph.co.uk/sport/2290634/Specialist-Sports-Colleges-make-the-grade.html.

Davis, N. (2012). An athlete and his money are soon to part. Retrieved April 2, 2012, from http://www.gq.com/sports/guides/201204/athletes-millionaires-bankrupt-spending#ixzz1quK2cmFh

De Bosscher, V., Bingham, J., Shibli, S., Van Bottenburg, M., & De Knop, P. (2008). *The global sporting arms race.* Oxford: Meyer & Meyer Sport.

De Bosscher, V., & De Knop, P. (2004). De prestatiebepalende factoren van topsport volgens atleten, coaches en topsportcoördinatoren. [Sports policy factors leading to international sporting success: The opinion of athletes, coaches and performance directors in Flanders.] Internal Report for the Flemish Ministry of Sport. Belgium: Vrije Universiteit Brussel.

De Bosscher, V., De Knop, P., & Heyndels, B. (2003). Comparing tennis success among countries. *International Sports Studies, 25,* 49–68.

De Bosscher, V., De Knop, P., Van Bottenburg, M., & Leblicq, S. (2004). Why the Netherlands are successful and Belgium is not? A comparison of the elite sports climate and policies. *Proceedings of the 12th Congress of the European Association for Sport Management,* 239–241. Ghent, Belgium.

De Bosscher, V., De Knop, P., Van Bottenburg, M., & Shibli, S. (2006). A conceptual framework for analyzing sports policy factors leading to international sporting success, *European Sport Management Quarterly, 6*(2), 185–215.

De Bosscher, V., Shibli, S., Van Bottenburg, M., De Knop, P., & Truyens, J. (2010). Developing a method for comparing the elite sport systems and policies of nations: A mixed research methods approach. *Journal of Sport Management, 24,* 567–600.

De Knop, P. (1992, July). New trends in sport tourism. Paper presented at the Olympic Scientific Congress, Malaga, Spain.

De Knop, P., De Bosscher, V., & Leblicq, S. (2004). Topsportklimaat in Vlaanderen [elite sports climate in Flanders]. Brussels: Vrije Universiteit Brussel.

Demick, B., & Haas, B. (2011). China cheers Li Na, an unlikely tennis champ. *Los Angeles Times.* Retrieved from http://articles.latimes.com/2011/jun/05/world/la-fg-china-tennis-li-20110605.

Department of Health and Human Services. (2008). 2008 Physical Activity. Guidelines for Americans. Retrieved December 23, 2008, from http://www.health.gov/paguidelines/pdf/paguide.pdf.

Digel, H. (2002). Resources for world class performances in sport: A comparison of different systems of top level sport policy. Institut National du Sport Expertise in Elite Sport 2nd International Days of Sport Sciences, 46–49.

Digel, H. (2005). Comparison of successful sport systems. *New Studies in Athletics, 20*(2), 7–18.

Dittmore, S. W., Mahony, D. F., & Andrew, D. P. S. (2008, May). Financial resource allocation in U.S. Olympic sport: National governing body administrators' fairness perceptions. 23rd Annual Conference of North American Society for Sport Management, Toronto, Canada.

Donnelly, P. (2012). Turning Canada's Olympic success into increased participation in sports. *Toronto Star*. Retrieved July 23, 2012, from http://www.thestar.com/opinion/editorialopinion/article/1230769--turning-canada-s-olympic-success-into-increased-participation-in-sports.

Dowd, T. (2013). Postponed again, Empire State Games hope for 2014 rebirth. Retrieved March 20, 2014, from http://blog.silive.com/hssportsextra/2013/04/esg_postponed.html

Downie, A. (2008). Trading in soccer talent. *The New York Times*. Retrieved July 19, 2008, from http://www.nytimes.com/2008/07/19/business/19soccer.html?th&emc=th.

Drugfree.org. (2012). The partnership at Drugfree.org. Retiring Olympic athletes may be at risk of substance abuse, studies suggest. Retrieved March 20, 2014, from www.drugfree.org/join-together/addiction/retiring-olympic-athletes-may-be-at-risk-of-substance-abuse-studies-suggest.

Dubrovski, A. I. (1991). *Reabilitatsiya v Sporte* (Rehabilitation in Sport). Moscow: Physical Culture and Sport.

Duffy, P., Lyons, D., Moran, A., Warrington, G., & Macmanus, C. (2001). Factors promoting and inhibiting the success of high performance players and athletes in Ireland. Retrieved January 20, 2002, from http://www.nctc.ul.ie/press/pubs/Success%20Factors%20STUDY.doc.

Du Randt, R. (1993). Sport talent identification and development and related issues in selected countries. An updated contract research report conducted on behalf of the Federation for Movement and Leisure Sciences for the Department of National Education. Port Elizabeth: University of Port Elizabeth.

Ebishima, H. (2012, July). Linkage between elite sport and grassroots sport: Who decides which is which? Glasgow Caledonian University: World Congress of Sociology of Sport.

Eisenberg, M. E., Wall, M., & Neumark-Sztainer, D. (2012). Muscle-enhancing behaviors among adolescent girls and boys. *Pediatrics*. DOI: 10.1542/peds.2012-0095. Retrieved November 20, 2012, from http://pediatrics.aappublications.org/content/early/2012/11/14/peds.2012-0095.full.pdf+html.

Engle, E. (2013). Honolulu Marathon generated $132.8M in spending. *Star Advertiser*. Retrieved March 20, 2014, from www.staradvertiser.com/news/breaking/20130129_Honolulu_Marathon_generated_1328M_in_spending.html.

ESPN.com News Services. (2002) Flames and flickers: Hey, we can get this at home. Retrieved February 12, 2002, from: http://sports.espn.go.com/oly/winter02/gen/story?id=1330653.

Evans-Wents, W. T. (1967). *Tibetan Yoga and secret doctrines*. New York: Oxford University Press.

Ewert, S. (2013). The decline in private school enrollment. U.S. Census Bureau. Social, Economic, and Housing Statistics Division. Retrieved March 23, 2014, from www.census.gov/hhes/school/files/ewert_private_school_enrollment.pdf.

Fainaru-Wada, M. & Fainaru, S. (2013). *League of denial: The NFL, concussions, and the battle for truth.* New York: Crown Archetype.

Fainaru-Wada, M. & Williams, L. (2007). *Game of shadows: Barry Bonds, BALCO, and the steroids scandal that rocked professsional sports.* New York: Gotham Books.

Fan, H., & Lu, Z. (2011). China. In M. Nicholson, R. Hoye, & B. Houlihan (Eds.). *Participation in sport: International policy prospectives.* London and New York: Routledge.

Federal Grants Wire (2011). Federal grants, government grants and loans. Retrieved August 10, 2011, from: http://www.federalgrantswire.com/.

Federation International De Football Association. (2007, May 30, 31). Fifa financial report 2006. Retrieved November 23, 2010, from http://www.fifa.com/mm/document/affederation/administration/51/52/65/2006_fifa_ar_en_1766.pd.f

Fenceviewer. (2012). Subsidized tennis for children offered at ETC. Retrieved January 27, 2012, from http://fenceviewer.com/site/index.php?option=com_k2&view=item&id=71735:subsidized-tennis-for-children-offered-at-etc&Itemid=1505

Fetisov, V. A. (2005). *O Kriteriyah i Pokazatelyah Razvitiya Fizicheskoj Kul'tury i Sporta v Zarubezhnyh Stranah* (On Criteria and Indicators of Development of Physical Culture and Sport Internationally). Moscow: Soviet Sport.

FIFA (Fédération Internationale de Football Association) (2011). FIFA awarded tax-free in Brazil to organize 2014 World Cup. Retrieved June 20, 2011, from http://fifa.zimaa.com/2010/12/fifa-awarded-tax-free-in-brazil-to.html.

FIFA (Fédération Internationale de Football Association) (2012). Federation International De Football Association. Retrieved September 23, 2012, from http://www.fifa.com/worldranking/rankingtable/; http://www.fifa.com/worldfootball/bigcount/allplayers.html.

Fish, D., Gallo, J., & Smolianov, P. (2011, December). Bringing 'Moneyball' thinking to American player development: Building an evidence-based approach. Intercollegiate Tennis Association Coaches Convention, Naples, Florida.

Fitzpatrick, M. (2011). A fitness tax credit with a catch or two, no pun intended. *CBC News.* Retrieved April 4, 2011, from http://www.cbc.ca/news/politics/canadavotes2011/realitycheck/2011/04/a-fitness-tax-credit-with-a-catch-or-two-no-pun-intended.html.

Foderaro, L. W. (2013). Hurricane Sandy crept up on a boy who couldn't swim. Guess what he did. *The New York Times.* Retrieved August 11, 2013, from http://www.nytimes.com/2013/08/12/nyregion/surrounded-by-beaches-and-finally-learning-to-swim.html?nl=todaysheadlines&emc=edit_th_20130812.

Footballacademy. (2012). Projects. Retrieved March 22, 2012, from http://www.footballacademy.ru/eng/projects.

Foster, C. (2000). Guidelines for health-enhancing physical activity promotion programs. Written for the British Heart Foundation Health Promotion Research Group. Oxford, UK: University of Oxford.

Franks, B. D. & Safrit, M. J. (1999, May). The president's challenge in the new millennium. *Quest (Human Kinetics), 51*(2), 184-191.

Free Press Release. (2005). Outdoor fitness combats national health and fitness crisis. Retrieved October 22, 2008, from http://www.free-press-release.com/news/200510/1130729365.html.

Friesen, P. (2010). NHL needs to step up drug testing: WADA. *Toronto Sun*. Retrieved February 11, 2010, from http://www.torontosun.com/sports/hockey/2010/02/11/12844511-qmi.html

Gál, A. (2012, July). Society and sport in Central Europe, particularly in Hungary. Glasgow: World Congress of Sociology of Sport, Glasgow Caledonian University.

Ganim, S. (2014, March 27). Labor board: Northwestern University football players can unionize. Retrieved March 27, 2014, from http://edition.cnn.com/2014/03/26/us/northwestern-football-union/

Gardner, A. (2010). 30% of overweight Americans think they're in normal range, HealthDay USA Today. Retrieved December 28, 2010, from http://www.usatoday.com/yourlife/fitness/2010-09-09-fat-perception_N.htm.

Gasgreen, A. (2013, October 25). Athlete grad rates back up. Inside Higher Education. Retrieved March 17, 2014, from www.insidehighered.com/news/2013/10/25/after-slight-dip-athletes-graduation-rates-back.

Gearin, M. (1999). Help a mate–Raiders style. *Sport for Life*, *6*, 16–17.

Gilbert, D. (1980). *The miracle machine*. New York: Coward, McCann & Geoghegan Inc.

Girginov, V., & Bankov, P. (2002). Bulgaria: Sport for all from a way of life to a matter of choice. In L.P. DaCosta, & A. Miragaya, (Eds.). *World experiences and trends of sport for all*. Oxford: Meyer & Meyer Sport.

Girginov, V., & Hills, L. (2008). A sustainable sports legacy: Creating a link between the London Olympics and sports participation. *The International Journal of the History of Sport*, *25*(14), 2091–2116.

Golubitsky, S. (2004). *Fencing is My Life*. Staten Island, NY: SKA SwordPlay Books.

Gomez, B. (2009a). Major economic cuts implemented by USOC nationwide. *The Gazette*. (Colorado Springs, CO). Retrieved March 20, 2009, from http://education.tmcnet.com/news/2009/03/20/4072700.htm

Gomez, B. (2009b). USOC loses another high-profile sponsor. *Gazette, The* (Colorado Springs, CO). Retrieved June 3, 2009, from http://gazette.com/usoc-loses-another-high-profile-sponsor/article/55654.

Gomez, B. (2009c). USOC program helps athletes prepare for the future. *Gazette, The* (Colorado Springs, CO). Retrieved August 19, 2009, from http://gazette.com/usoc-program-helps-athletes-prepare-for-the-future/article/60438.

Grasso, B. (2008). Talent identification & development on an international basis, athletes' acceleration. Retrieved July 1, 2008, from http://www.athletesacceleration.com/youthtalentidentification.html.

Green, C. (2005). Building sport programs to optimize athlete recruitment, retention, and transition: Toward a normative theory of sport development. *Journal of Sport Management*, *19*, 233–253.

Green, C., Chalip, L., & Bowers, M. T. (2013). United States. In I. O'Boyle, & T. Bradbury, (Eds.). *Sport governance: An international case study perspective* (pp. 20–36). London and New York: Routledge.

Green, M., & Houlihan, B. (2005). *Elite sport development. policy learning and political priorities*. London and New York: Routledge.

Green, M., & Oakley, B. (2001). Elite sport development systems and playing to win: Uniformity and diversity in international approaches. *Leisure Studies*, *20*, 247–267.

Greenleaf, C., Gould, D., & Diefen, K. (2001). Factors influencing Olympic performance with Atlanta and Nagano US Olympians. *Journal of Applied Sport Psychology*, *13*, 154–184.

Grosch, J. W., Alterman, T., Petersen, M. R., & Murphy, L. R. (1998). Worksite health promotion programs in the U.S.: Factors associated with availability and participation. *American Journal of Health Promotion, 13,* 36–45.

Guba, V. P. (2008). *Teoriya and Praktika Otbora i Rannej Orientatsii v Sporte* (Theory and Practice of Sport Selection and Early Orientation within Sports). Moscow: Soviet Sport.

Guttmann, A. (1978). *From ritual to record: The nature of modern sports.* New York: Columbia University Press.

Guttmann, A. (1984). *The games must go on: Avery Brundage and the Olympic movement.* New York: Columbia University Press.

Hacker, J. S., & Pierson, P. (2010). Winner-Take-All Politics: Public Policy, Political Organization, and the Precipitous Rise of Top Incomes in the United States. *Politics & Society, 38*(2), 152–204.

Hale, J. (1994). *The civilization of Europe in the Renaissance.* New York: Maxwell Macmillan International.

Hamilton, T., & Coyle, D. (2013). *The secret race: Inside the hidden world of the Tour de France.* New York: Bantam Books.

Hannan, D. (2013, November 19). 150 years ago today, Abraham Lincoln praised 'government of the people, by the people, for the people' – but the words were not his. *The Telegraph.* Retrieved March 30, 2014, from http://blogs.telegraph.co.uk/news/danielhannan/100246622/150-years-ago-today-abraham-lincoln-praised-government-of-the-people-by-the-people-for-the-people-but-the-words-were-not-his/.

Hanstad, D. V., & Skille, E. Å. (2010). Does elite sport develop mass sport? A Norwegian case study, *Scandinavian Sport Studies Forum Proceedings, 1,* 51–68.

Harder, P. (2004). Developing world championship ice hockey in the USSR: The inside story, 1946–1972. (Unpublished master's thesis) Carleton University, Canada, MAI.

Hartocollis, A. (2013). New York City ties doctors' income to quality of care. *The New York Times.* Retrieved January 11, 2013, from http://www.nytimes.com/2013/01/12/nyregion/new-york-city-hospitals-to-tie-doctors-performance-pay-to-quality-measures.html?nl=todaysheadlines&emc=edit_th_20130112&_r=0.

Harvard Pilgrim (2014). Fitness pays! Retrieved March 6, 2014, from www.harvardpilgrim.org/pls/portal/docs/PAGE/EMPLOYER/MARKETING/CC2762_FITNESS_REIMB_FLYER.PDF.

Harvard University. (2009). Harvard Fatigue Laboratory. Retrieved March 15, 2014, from http://oasis.lib.harvard.edu/oasis/deliver/~med00120

Harvey, D. (2014). *Seventeen contradictions and the end of capitalism.* New York: Oxford University Press.'

Hay, D. (1986). *The age of the Renaissance.* London: Thames and Hudson.

Haynie, D. (2013). Universities with the largest financial endowments. U.S. News & World Report. Retrieved October 1, 2013, from www.usnews.com/education/best-colleges/the-short-list-college/articles/2013/10/01/universities-with-the-largest-financial-endowments-colleges-with-the-largest-financial-endowments.

Hechinger, J. (2010). U.S. teens lag as China soars on international test. Bloomberg News. Retrieved Dec 7, 2010, from www.bloomberg.com/news/2010-12-07/teens-in-u-s-rank-25th-on-math-test-trail-in-science-reading.html.

Herrmann, L. (2011). In latest cycling doping scandal, Hamilton gives up gold. *Digital Journal.* Retrieved August 30, 2011, from http://digitaljournal.com/article/307004.

HHS (2013). Department of Health and Human Services. Fiscal Year 2013. Retrieved March 6, 2014, from www.hhs.gov/budget/fy2013/hhs-general-budget-justification-fy2013.pdf

Higgs, R. J. (1995). *God in the stadium: Sports and religion in America.* Lexington, KY: University Press of Kentucky.

Hill, B. (2012). Madison high school boys soccer. Retrieved from http://www.bobcatsoccer.org/donations-and-tax-credit-savings.html

Hipps, T. (2004). Military bolsters Team USA for Athens Games. Retrieved December 29, 2004, from http://www.army.mil/article/6588/

Hipps, T. (2007). Army to launch Wounded Warrior Sports program. Retrieved August 14, 2011, from http://www.army.mil/article/6588

Hodge, K., Lonsdale, C., & Ng, J. (2007). Burnout in elite rugby: Relationships with basic psychological needs fulfillment. *Journal of Sports Sciences, 26*(8), 835–844.

Hognestad, H. K. (2012, July). Mutuality or patronage? A critical view of sport and development projects. Glasgow: World Congress of Sociology of Sport, Caledonian University.

Home Depot (2008). Olympics. Retrieved July 21, 2008, from: http://corporate.homedepot.com/wps/portal/Olympics.

Horticulture Week. Editorial. (2008, September 18). AdiZones bring fitness equipment into London communities. *Horticulture Week, 8.*

Hosick, M. B. (2011). A meeting of the missions. NCAA and USOC combine forces on a 'win–win' endeavor. NCAA.org. Retrieved Aug 2, 2011, from: http://fs.ncaa.org/Docs/NCAANewsArchive/2011/august/a%2Bmeeting%2Bof%2Bthe%2Bmissionsdf30.html.

Houlihan, B., & Green, M. (2008). *Comparative elite sport development: Systems, structures and public policy.* Oxford, UK: Butterworth-Heinemann.

Hu, W. (2012). Mom, dad, this playground's for you. New York City installed an adult playground at Macombs Dam Park in the Bronx. *The New York Times.* Retrieved June 29, 2012, from http://www.nytimes.com/2012/07/01/nyregion/new-york-introduces-its-first-adult-playground.html?nl=todaysheadlines&emc=edit_th_20120701.

Hug, S., Hansmann, R., Monn, C., Krütli, P., & Seeland, K. (2008). Restorative effects of physical activity in forests and indoor settings. *International Journal of Fitness, 4*(2), 25–37.

Humphreys, B. R., & Matheson, V. A. (2008, December). PILOTs and public policy: Steering through the economic ramifications. College of the Holy Cross Department of Economics Working Paper Series. Paper No. 08-17. Retrieved June 16, 2011, from http://academics.holycross.edu/files/econ_accounting/Matheson-Humphreys_PILOTS.pdf.

Hutchins, R. (2013). N.J. appeals decision in federal sports betting case. Retrieved March 14, 2013, from http://www.nj.com/politics/index.ssf/2013/03/nj_appeals_decision_in_federal.html.

Hyman, M. (2010). Sports training has begun for babies and toddlers. *The New York Times.* Retrieved November 30, 2010, from http://www.nytimes.com/2010/12/01/sports/01babies.html?nl=todaysheadlines&emc=a27.

Ibbitson, J. (2012, September 24). What the rise of Asia means for Canadians. *The Globe and Mail,* A4.

iGaming Business North America. (2012). Retrieved August 11, 2011, from http://www.igamingbusinessnorthamerica.com/webinars/usa-new-jersey-legalized-sports-betting

Illion, T. (1991). *In Tibet.* Stelle, IL: Adventures Unlimited Press.

IMG Academies. (2011). Retrieved September 10, 2011, from http://www.imgacademies.com

Ingham, A. G. (1978). American sport in transition: The maturation of industrial capitalism and its impact on sport. (Unpublished doctoral dissertation), University of Massachusetts.

International Health, Racquet & Sportsclub Association (2011). About the Industry. Retrieved December 29, 2011, from http://www.ihrsa.org/about-the-industry/.

International Sports Programming Initiative. (2011). International Sports Programming Initiative (ISPI) Washington, DC: US Department of State. Retrieved June 10, 2013, from http://www.grants.gov/search/search.do?mode=VIEW&oppId=134573.

IOC (2008). The International Olympic Committee. Historical Archives. Retrieved July 15, 2008, from http://www.olympic.org/historical-archives.

IOC (2011). The International Olympic Committee: Event results. Retrieved July 20, 2011, from www.olympic.org/.

IOC (2014). Athletes. IOC Athlete Career Programme. Retrieved March 21, 2014, from www.olympic.org/ioc-athlete-career-programme.

INSEP. (2014). Institut National du Sport et de l'Education Physique en France. Retrieved March 16, 2014, from www.insep.fr.

Ippolitov, J. A., Mishin, A. A., Novikov, A A., Tarasova, L. V., & Shamilov, G. S. (2009). Innovative technologies of athletic preparation. *Sports Science Bulletin, 5*, 3–5.

IRB. (2007). International Rugby Board. Retrieved December 3, 2009, from http:/ /www.irb.com.

IRB. (2010). IRB Groups tackle key player welfare issues. International Rugby Board. Retrieved August 22, 2011, from http://www.irb.com/newsmedia/mediazone.

Isaev, A. A. (2002). *Sportivnaya Politika Rossii* (Sports Policy of Russia). Moscow: Soviet Sport.

ISN. (2011). Institute for soldier nanotechnologies. Retrieved August 10, 2011, from http://web.mit.edu/isn/index.html

Iskanderov, S. (2006, September 19). Eternal skating rink. *West-East, 38*(317), 12.

Ivy League (2014). 0. Retrieved December 1, 2013, from www.ivyleaguesports.com/history/overview

Janofsky, M. (1989, February 20). Steinbrenner report faults U.S. progress. *New York Times*, C1.

Jeffries, S. C. (1984). An analysis of the organizational structure of the Soviet youth sports system. Olympic Scientific Congress, Eugene, OR. In *Sport and politics* (pp. 51–57). Champaign, IL: Human Kinetics Publishers.

Johnson, D. V. (2009). The career path to pro tennis often passes high school. *The New York Times*. Retrieved August 30, 2009, from http://www.nytimes.com/2009/08/31/sports/tennis/31school.html?pagewanted=all&module=Search&mabReward=relbias%3Aw&_r=0

Johnson, K. N., & Ali, A. (2002). A tale of two seasons: Participation and medal counts at the summer and winter Olympic Games. Retrieved February 15, 2003, from http://www.wellesley.edu/economics/wkpapers/wellwp_0010.pdf. Wellesley, MA: Wellesley College.

Johnson, S. R., Wojnar, P. J., Price, W. J., Foley, T. J., Moon, J. R., Esposito, E. N., & Cromartie, F. J. (2011). A coach's responsibility: Learning how to prepare athletes for peak performance. *The Sport Journal, 14*. Retrieved from http://thesportjournal.org/article/coachs-responsibility-learning-how-prepare-athletes-peak-performance.

Kansas City United. (2011). Kansas City united about ODP. Retrieved December 25, 2012, from http://www.kansascityunited.net/about/parents/odp.html.

Katzmarysk, P., Gledhill, N., & Shephard, R. (2000). The economic burden of physical inactivity in Canada. *Canadian Medical Association Journal, 163*, 1435–1440.

Kaup, D. (2011, June 3). Providence Medical Center partners with Sporting Kansas City. *Kansas City Business Journal*. Retrieved March 17, 2012, from http://www.bizjournals.com/kansascity/news/2011/06/03/providence-medical-sporting-kansascity.html.

Keller, H., Lamprocht, M., & Stamm, H. (1998). *Social Cohesion through Sport.* Strasbourg: Council of Europe, Committee for the Development of Sport (CDDS).

Kennedy, P. (1988). *Rise and fall of great powers.* New York: Random House.

Khoshnevis, K. (2010). Top secret contributions. Retrieved March 23, 2010 from www.capitalnews.ca/index.php/ news/top-secret-contributions.

Kimmelman, M. (2010, August 25). How power has transformed women's tennis. *The New York Times.* Retrieved August 25, 2010, from http://www.nytimes.com/2010/08/29/magazine/29Tennis-t.html?pagewanted=all.

Kirk, P., & Shutte, A. M. (2004). Community leadership development. *Community Development Journal, 39,* 234–251.

Knox, R. (2013). US ranks below 16 other rich countries in health report. NPR. Retrieved January 9, 2013, from http://www.npr.org/blogs/health/2013/01/09/168976602/u-s-ranks-below-16-other-rich-countries-in-health-report.

Kolesov, A.I. (1981). Osnovnie puti povishenija effektivnosti raboti sportivnih organizatsij v razvitii visshego sportivnogo masterstva (Key ways to increase efficiency of sport organizations in high performance sport development). *Sport Science Bulletin,* 4, 3.

Kolesov, A. I., & Ponomarev, N. I. (1979). Fizicheskaya kul'tura i sport (Physical culture and sports). *The Great Soviet Encyclopedia* (3rd ed. 1970–1979). New York and London: Macmillan.

Kolesov, A. I., Lents, N. A., & Razumovski, E. A. (2003). *Problemy Podgotovki Sportsmenov Vysshej Kvalifikatsii v Vidah Sporta s Tsiklicheskoj Strukturoj Dvizhenij* (Process of Preparation of High Performance Athletes in Sports with Cyclic Structure of Movement). Moscow: Physical Culture and Sport.

Kotler, P., Haider, D. H., & Rein, I. (1993). *Marketing places: Attracting investment, industry, and tourism to cities, states, and nations.* New York: Free Press.

Kovacic, W. (2008). Marketing food to children and adolescents: A review of industry's activities, expenditures and self-regulations. A Federal Trade Commission Report to Congress. Federal Trade Commission.

Kovacs, M. S., Ellenbecker, T. S., & Kibler, W. B. (2010). Tennis recovery: A comprehensive review of the research. United States Tennis Association. Retrieved December 21 2012, from http://assets.usta.com/assets/1/dps/usta_master/sitecore_usta/RECOVERY%20PROJECT%20FINAL.pdf.

Krause, M. D. (2012). History of US army soldier physical fitness. Retrieved December 4, 2012, from http://www.ihpra.org/col_krause.htm.

Kreutz, D. (2007, September). UA exercise trail is fit to be tried: Outdoor stations are free and open to the general public. *Arizona Daily Star.* Retrieved October 17, 2008, from http://corvette.salemstate.edu:2048/login?url=http://search.ebscohost.com/login.aspx?direct=true&AuthType=cookie,ip,cpid&custid=ssc&db=nfh&AN=2W62W63526341553&site=ehost-live&scope=site.

Krüger, A. (1984). To Moscow and back: International status of comparative research in regard to physical activity outside of schools. *Proceedings of the 4th International Seminar on Comparative Physical Education and Sport,* 213–227. West Germany: Malente-Kiel.

Krugman, P. (1999). *The accidental theorist and other dispatches from the dismal science.* London: Penguin.

Krugman, P. (2008). *The return of depression economics and the crisis of 2008.* New York: W. W. Norton.

Kudryashov, V. (1978). *Sportivnaya Atributika* (Sport Attributes) (2nd ed.). Moscow: Physical Culture and Sport.

Kuper, G. H., & Sterken, E. (2003). Olympic participation and performance since 1896. Research Report, No. 03C19. University of Groningen, Netherlands: Graduate School/

Research Institute Systems, Organizations and Management. Retrieved September 15, 2003, from http://som.eldoc.ub.rug.nl/reports/themeC/2003/03C19.

Kuznetsova, Z., Kaline, I., & Kaline, G. (2002). Russia: Traditions, political interventions and the educational system as foundations of sport for all. In L. P. DaCosta & A. Miragaya (Eds.). *World experiences and trends of sport for all.* Oxford: Meyer & Meyer Sport.

La Crosse, Y (2013). Financial assistance. Retrieved on January 4, 2013, from http://www.laxymca.org/index.php?option=com_content&view=article&id=235&Itemid=293.

Landler, M., and Mazzetti, M. (2013). For Obama's global vision, daunting problems. *The New York Times.* Retrieved May 24, 2013, from http://www.nytimes.com/2013/05/25/us/politics/for-obamas-global-vision-daunting-problems.html?nl=todaysheadlines&emc=edit_th_20130525.

Larose, K., & Haggerty, T. R. (1996). Factors associated with national Olympic success: An exploratory study. (Unpublished master's thesis), University of New Brunswick, Canada.

Laurel Springs School. (2013). Accredited online private school. Retrieved July 20, 2013, from http://laurelsprings.com/.

Lavallee, D. (2005). The effect of a life development intervention on sports career transition adjustment. *The Sport Psychologist, 19*(2), 193–202.

Lawrence, S. J. (2011). Om in the army: The US military gets yoga. *Guardian.,* Retrieved August 31, 2011, from http://www.guardian.co.uk/commentisfree/cifamerica/2011/aug/31/yoga-army-us-military.

Lawson, H. A. (2005). Empowering people, facilitating community development, and contributing to sustainable development: The social work of sport, exercise, and physical education programs. *Sport, Education and Society, 10,* 135–160.

Lee, R. (2008). Keeping track of technology. Retrieved September 18, 2008, from http://www.eis2win.co.uk/pages/news_keepingtrackoftechnology.aspx.

Lee, R. (2009). EIS sport sciences develop with skill acquisition. English Institute of Sport. Retrieved April 29, 2009, from http://www.eis2win.co.uk/pages/news_eissportsciencesdevelopwithskillacquisition.aspx.

Lelore, E. (2012, July). New forms of governance of the sporting elite: Between deterritorialization and systemic integration. Glasgow: World Congress of Sociology of Sport, Glasgow Caledonian University.

Lipset, S. M. (1996). American exceptionalism: A double edged sword. *Washington Post.* Retrieved on April 20, 2014 from http://www.washingtonpost.com/wp-srv/style/longterm/books/chap1/americanexceptionalism.htm#TOP.

London2012. (2012). Medal count. Accessed on March 8, 2013, at http://www.london2012.com/medals/medal-count/.

Longman, J. (1995). Olympics; future is cloudy for U.S. festival. *The New York Times.* Retrieved July 20, 2009, from: http://www.nytimes.com/1995/07/21/sports/olympics-future-is-cloudy-for-us-festival.html.

Lotteries of the Ancient and Medieval World. (2014). History of lotteries. Retrieved March 15, 2014, from www.lotteries-of-the-world.com/HistoryofLotteries/historyofthelottery.html%20March%2015.

Luzi, L. (2012). What's new with physical exercise in 2012? *Sport Science for Health, 7,* 1–3.

MacAloon, J. J. (2008). *This great symbol: Pierre de Coubertin and the origins of the modern Olympic games.* London and New York: Routledge.

MacIntyre, A. (1984). *After virtue: A study of moral theory.* Notre Dame, IN: University of Notre Dame Press.

Mackay, D. (2011, January 18). Putin backs Russian athletes preparations for Sochi 2014 with massive cash injection. Inside the Games. Retrieved January 18, 2011, from http://www.insidethegames.biz/olympics/winter-olympics/2014/11683-putin-backs-russian-athletes-preparations-for-sochi-2014-with-massive-cash-injection.

Macur, J. (2008a). USOC looking to diversify medal count. *The New York Times*. Retrieved June 1, 2008, from www.nytimes.com/2008/06/01/sports/olympics/01usoc.html?_r=0.

Macur, J. (2008b). Born to Run? Little ones get test for sports gene. *The New York Times*. Retrieved November 29, 2008, from www.nytimes.com/2008/11/30/sports/30genetics.html?pagewanted=all&_r=0.

Macur, J. (2012). Details of doping scheme paint Armstrong as leader. *The New York Times*. Retrieved on October 10, 2012, from http://www.nytimes.com/2012/10/11/sports/cycling/agency-details-doping-case-against-lance-armstrong.html?pagewanted=1&nl=todaysheadlines&emc=edit_th_20121011&_r=0.

Mageau, G. A., & Vallerand, R. J. (2003). The coach–athlete relationship: A motivational model. *Journal of Sport Sciences*, *21*(11), 883–904.

Markel, U. (1995). The German government and politics of sport and leisure in the 1990s: An interim report. In S. Fleming, M. Talbot, & A. Tomlinson, (Eds.). *Policy and politics in sport, physical education and leisure* (pp. 95–108). Eastbourne, UK: Leisure Studies Association.

MASF. (2013). The Massachusetts Amateur Sports Foundation: Bay State Games. Retrieved July 2013, from www.baystategames.org/index.cfm?fuseaction=home.main.

Mason, B. (2008). Doping scandal taints famed bike race, PBS. Retrieved July 4, 2008, from http://www.pbs.org/newshour/extra/features/july-dec07/cycling_8-01.html.

Mattke, S., Liu, H., Caloyeras, J. P., Huang, C. Y., Van Busum, K. R., Khodyakov, D., & Shier, V. (2013). Workplace wellness programs study. RAND Health sponsored by the U.S. Department of Labor and the U.S. Department of Health and Human Services. Retrieved on October 26, 2013, from http://www.dol.gov/ebsa/pdf/workplacewellnessstudyfinal.pdf.

Matveev, L. P. (1964). *Problema Periodizatsii Sportivnoj Trenirovki* (Periodization of Sport Training). Moscow: Physical Culture and Sport.

Matveev, L. P. (1977). *Osnovy Sportivnoj Trenirovki* (Foundations of Sport Training). Moscow: Physical Culture and Sport.

Matveev, L. P. (1983). *Aspects fondamentaux de l'entrainement*. Paris: Vigot.

Matveev, L. P. (1991). K teorii postroeniya sportivnoj trenirovki (On the theory of construction of sport training). *Theory and Practice of Physical Culture*, 12, 11–20.

Matveev, L. P. (1997). *Obshchaya Teoriya Sporta* (General Theory of Sport). Moscow: Voenizdat.

Matveev, L. P. (2001). *Obshchaya Teoriya Sporta i ee Prikladnye Aspekty* (The General Theory of Sport and its Applications). Moscow: Izvestia.

Matveev, L. P. (2008). *Teoriya i Metodika Fizicheskoj Kul'tury* (Theory and Methodology of Physical Culture). Moscow: Physical Culture and Sport-SportAcademPress.

McCarthy, M. (2011, June 7). NBC wins U.S. TV rights to four Olympic Games through 2020, *USA Today*. Retrieved from http://content.usatoday.com/communities/gameon/post/2011/06/olympic-tv-decision-between-nbc-espn-and-fox-could-come-down-today/1. 17 November 2012.

McConnell, A. (2013, March 24). USOC director, Athlete Services and Programs. Interviewed by Brooke Pinkham on March 24, 2013.

McCrory, P., Meeuwisse, W., Aubry, M., Cantu, B., Dvorak, J., Echemendia, R. J., Engebretsen, L., Johnston, K., Kutcher, J. S., Raftery, M., Sills, A., Putukian, M., Turner, M., Schneider, K., & Tator, C.H. (2013). Consensus Statement on Concussion in Sport–the 4th International Conference on Concussion in Sport Held in Zurich, November 2012. *Clinical Journal of Sport Medicine, 23*, 89–117.

McGrath, C. (2010). Canada's medal quest: Gold, and lots of it. *The New York Times.* Retrieved February 9, 2010, from: http://www.nytimes.com/2010/02/10/sports/olympics/10podium.html?th&emc=th.

McKenna, J., & Howard, T. (2007). Enduring injustice: A case study of retirement from professional rugby union. *Sport, Education & Society, 12*(1), 19–136.

McMullin, S. (2013). The secularization of Sunday: Real or perceived competition for churches. *Review of Religious Research, 55*(1), 43–59.

Mellalieu, S., Trewartha, G., & Stokes, K. (2008). Science and rugby union. *Journal of Sports Sciences, 26*(8), 791–794.

Merriman Curhan Ford. (2008). Fitness and wellness. Consumer/Internet/Media Equity Research Report. Retrieved August 13, 2011, from http://www.physicventures.com/files/news/pdf/Fitness%20and%20Wellness%20Industry%20Rpt.pdr.pdf.

Michaelis, V. (2009). U.S. Olympic athletes help pitch fundraising campaign. *USA Today.* Retrieved June 3, 2009, from http://www.usatoday.com/sports/olympics/2009-06-02-usolympiccampaign_N.htm.

Mickle, T. (2011). USOC funding strategy worries small NGBs. *Street and Smith's Sports Business Journal.* Retrieved October 3, 2011, from http://m.sportsbusinessdaily.com/Journal/Issues/2011/10/03/Olympics/NGB-funding.aspx.

Migranyan, A. (2013). The myth of American exceptionalism. *National Interest.* Retrieved on April 16, 2014 from http://nationalinterest.org/commentary/the-myth-american-exceptionalism-9223?page=1.

Miller, F. D. (1984, February). The blueprint for success in 1984. *The Olympic, 7*, 5.

Miller, R. K., & Washington, K. (2012). *Sports marketing.* Loganville, GA: Richard K Miller & Associates.

Ministry for Sport, Tourism and Youth Policy of the Russian Federation. (2011). Retrieved July 25, 2011, from http://sport.minstm.gov.ru/.

Mission: Readiness. (2010). Too fat to fight. A report by Mission: Readiness. Military Leaders for Kids. Retrieved 2010 from http://cdn.missionreadiness.org/MR_Too_Fat_to_Fight-1.pdf

MLB. (2011). Minor League Baseball. Retrieved September 5, 2011, from http://web.minorleaguebaseball.com/index.jsp.

Morgan, M. (2002). Optimizing the structure of elite competitions in professional sport–Lessons from rugby union. *Managing Leisure, 7*(1), 41–60.

Muir, H. (2005). Sporting drive sees drop in crime for Olympic borough: Bid money helps lure kids into clubs and off the streets. *The Guardian.* Retrieved August 8, 2005, from http://www.guardian.co.uk/uk/2005/aug/08/olympics2012.ukcrime.

Müller, B., Georgi, K., Schnabel, A., & Schneider, B. (2009). Does sport have a protective effect against suicide? *Epidemiology and Psychiatric Sciences, 18*(4), 331-335.

Murray, M., & Pizzorno, J. (2012). *Encyclopedia of natural medicine* (3rd ed.). Rocklin, CA: Prima Publishing.

mybesttennis.com (2012). Tennis Academy Directory. Retrieved December 29, 2012, from http://www.mybesttennis.com/tennis-academy-directory/

Nasaw, D. (2011). Looking the Carnegie gift horse in the mouth: The 19th-century critique of big philanthropy. Retrieved March 15, 2014, from www.slate.com/articles/

news_and_politics/history_lesson/2006/11/looking_the_carnegie_gift_horse_in_the_
mouth.html.

NASPE (National Association of Sport and Physical Education) (2012). National Association
for Sport and Physical Education. Retrieved November 27, 2012, from http://www.
aahperd.org/naspe/.

National Foundation on Fitness, Sports, and Nutrition Establishment Act. (2010).
U.S. Congress Public Law No: 111-332, 111th Congress, 124 Stat.3576. Retrieved
March 24, 2014, from www.gpo.gov/fdsys/pkg/PLAW-111publ332/pdf/PLAW-
111publ332.pdf.

National Gambling Impact Study Commission. (2014). Lotteries. Retrieved March 16,
2014, from http://govinfo.library.unt.edu/ngisc/research/lotteries.html.

Nature. (2008). A level playing field? Editorial. *Nature, 454*, 667. Retrieved on August 7,
2008, from http://www.nature.com/nature/journal/v454/n7205/full/454667a.html.

NCAA (2012). The National Collegiate Athletic Association. Revenue. Retrieved December
10, 2012, from: http://www.ncaa.org/about/resources/finances/revenue.

NCAA (National Collegiate Athletic Association). (2014a). The National Collegiate
Athletic Association. Revenue. Retrieved March 5, 2014, from: www.ncaa.org/about/
resources/finances/revenue.

NCAA (National Collegiate Athletic Association). (2014b). The National Collegiate Athletic
Association: Sports. Retrieved March 20, 2014, from www.ncaa.com/.

NCEE (National Center on Education and the Economy). (2014). Best performing nations.
Finland. Retrieved March 6, 2014, from www.ncee.org/programs-affiliates/center-on-
international-education-benchmarking/top-performing-countries/finland-overview/
finland-teacher-and-principal-quality/.

NCSG. (2011). National Congress of State Games. Who we are. Retrieved August 7, 2011,
from http://www.stategames.org/about.

Newland, B., & Kellet, P. (2012, April-July). Exploring new models of elite sport delivery:
The case of triathlon in the USA and Australia. *Managing Leisure, 17*, 155–169.

New York City Parks. (2014a). City of New York Parks and Recreation. Recreation Center
Membership. Retrieved March 20, 2014, from www.nycgovparks.org/programs/
recreation-centers/membership.

New York City Parks (2014b). Fitness Equipment. Retrieved May 20, 2014, from http://
www.nycgovparks.org/facilities/fitnessequipment.

New York Runners. (2014). New York City Marathon. Retrieved March 20, 2014, from
www.nyrr.org/.

New York State Council of Parks, Recreation and Historic Preservation. (2010). New York
State Council of Parks, Recreation and Historic Preservation. 2009 Annual Report.
Retrieved March 20, 2014, from http://nysparks.com/state-council/documents/2010
StateCouncilAnnualReport.pdf.

NFHS (National Federation of State High School Associations) (2011). About NFSHA.
Retrieved August 12, 2011, from: http://www.nfhs.org/Activity3.aspx?id=3260.

NFHS (2014). *National Federation of State High School Associations Handbook*. Retrieved March
7, 2014, from http://www.nfhs.org/2013-14%20NFHS%20Handbook_pgs52-70.pdf.

NFL.com. (2013). Static: NFL, retired players resolve concussion litigation; court appointed
mediator hails "historic" agreement. Retrieved March 13, 2014, from http://static.nfl.
com/static/content/public/photo/2013/08/29/0ap2000000235504.pdf.

NFL. (2010). NFL Play 60: The NFL movement for an active generation. Retrieved August
13, 2011, from http://www.nfl.com/news/story?id=09000d5d80b4a489&template=w
ith-video&confirm=true.

Nicholson, M., Hoye, R., & Houlihan, B. (2011). *Participation in sport: International policy prospectives*. London and New York: Routledge.

North Shore Y. (2011). About the YMCA of the North Shore. Retrieved August 29, 2011, from: http://www.northshoreymca.org/about/.

Norton, M. I., & Ariely, D. (2011). Building a Better America–One Wealth Quintile at a Time. *Perspectives on Psychological Science*, *6*, 1, 9–12.

Novak, M. (1994). *The joy of sports: End zones, bases, baskets, balls and the consecration of the American spirit*. Lanham, NY: Rowan & Littlefield.

Novikov, A. A., & Ippolitov, J. A. (2008). Development of scientific basis for sports in VNIIFK. *Sports Science Bulletin*, *4*, 32–35.

NPAP. (2010). US National Physical Activity Plan. Retrieved on December 29, 2010, from http://www.physicalactivityplan.org/.

NYC Parks. (2013). City of New York Parks and Recreation. Swim Programs. Retrieved August 12, 2012, from http://www.nycgovparks.org/programs/aquatics.

Nys, K., De Knop, P., & De Bosscher, V. (2002). Prestatiebepalende factoren in topsport [Factors determining international success in elite sports]. (Unpublished master's thesis), Vrije Universiteit Brussel, Belgium.

NZAS. (2009). New Zealand Academy of Sport. Retrieved July 15, 2009, from nzas.org. nz/

O'Connor, A. (2012). Trying to reduce head injuries, youth football limits practices. *The New York Times*. Retrieved June 14, 2012, from http://www.nytimes.com/2012/06/14/sports/pop-warner-football-limits-contact-in-practices.html?nl=todaysheadlines&emc=edit_th_20120614.

Oakley, B., & Green, M. (2001). The production of Olympic champions: International perspectives on elite sport development system. *European Journal for Sport Management*, *8*, 83–105.

Olsen, L. (1983). Frontispiece. *Arête: Journal of Sport Literature*, *1*(1): i

Olympic Medals: History of Olympic Medals. (2012). Retrieved March 8, 2013, from http://www.olympicsmedals.com/vancouver-olympics-medal-table-2010.php

Osborne, T. (2008). Behind the Olympics. *American Fitness*, *26*(4), 48–50.

Pagliarini, R. (2013). Why athletes go broke: The myth of the dumb jock. *CBS News*. Retrieved March 20, 2014, from www.cbsnews.com/news/why-athletes-go-broke-the-myth-of-the-dumb-jock/

PAL. (2012). The National Police Athletics/Activities Leagues, Inc. Retrieved September 10, 2012, from http://www.nationalpal.org/

Palaelogos, K. (1976). *The Preparation of Athletes. The Olympic Games in Ancient Greece*. Athens: Ekdotike Athenon S.A.

Panitch, L., & Gindin, S. (2012). *The making of global capitalism: The political economy of American empire*. London and New York: Verso.

Parker-Pope, T. (2010). As girls become women, sports pay dividends. *The New York Times*. Retrieved February 15, 2010, from http://www.nytimes.com/2010/02/16/health/16well.html.

Parker-Pope, T. (2013). Suicide rates rise sharply in U.S. *The New York Times*. Retrieved May 2, 2013, from http://www.nytimes.com/2013/05/03/health/suicide-rate-rises-sharply-in-us.html?nl=todaysheadlines&emc=edit_th_20130503&_r=0.

Parry, J. (1994). Olympism at the beginning and end of the twentieth century-immutable values and principles and outdated factors. International Olympic Academy: 28th Young Participant Session. International Olympic Academy, 81–94.

Pate, R., Pratt, M., Blair, S., Hakwkk, W., Macera, C., Bouchard, C., et al. (1995). Physical activity and public health: A recommendation from the Centers for Disease Control and Prevention and the American College of Sports Medicine. *Journal of the American Medical Association, 273*, 402–407.

Pavlov, S. P. (1975). Perspektivy razvitiya sovetskoj sportivnoj nauki (Development perspectives of Soviet sport science). *Theory and Practice of Physical Culture*, 11, 2, 137–157.

Payne, N., Jones, F., & Harris, P. (2002). The impact of working life on health behavior: The effect of job strain on the cognitive predictors of exercise. *Journal of Occupational Health Psychology, 7*, 342–353.

PCFSN. (2011). President's Council on Fitness, Sports and Nutrition. About PCFSN. Retrieved August 11, 2011, from http://www.fitness.gov/about-pcfsn.

Pells, E. (2011, March 30). NCAA College Drug-Testing all over the map. *The Huffington Post.* Retrieved November 24, 2011, from http://www.huffingtonpost.com/2011/03/30/ncaa-college-drugtesting-_n_842524.html.

Pennington, B. (2009). Open spaces for kids, with tees and greens. *The New York Times.* Retrieved August 9, 2009, from www.nytimes.com/2009/08/10/sports/golf/10pennington.html

Pennington, B. (2011). Financial aid changes game as Ivy sports teams flourish. *The New York Times.* Retrieved December 22, 2011, from http://www.nytimes.com/2011/12/23/sports/financial-aid-changes-game-as-sports-teams-in-ivies-rise.html?pagewanted=1&_r=1&nl=todaysheadlines&emc=tha27.

Peterson, K. (2009). College athletes stuck with the bill after injuries. *The New York Times.* Retrieved July 15, 2009, from http://www.nytimes.com/2009/07/16/sports/16athletes.html?th&emc=th.

Pettavino, P. J. (2004). Cuban sports saved by capitalism? *NACLA Report on the Americas*, Mar/Apr, *37*(5): 27–43.

Pettavino, P. J., & Pye, G. (1994). *Sport in Cuba: The diamond in the rough.* Pittsburgh: University of Pittsburgh Press.

Pettavino, P. J., & Pye, G. (2014). Sport in Cuba: Diamond in the rough. Retrieved April 5, 2014 from www.pbs.org/stealinghome/sport/diamond.html.

Pfutzner, A., Reib, M., Rost, K., & Tunnermann, H. (2001). Internationale und nationale Entwicklungstendenzen auf der Grundiage der Ergebnisse der Olympischen Sommerspiele in Sydney mit Folgerungen fur den Olympiazyklus 2004. *Leistungssport, 1*, 20–36.

Piore, A. (2004, August 16). Sink or swim. *Newsweek.* Retrieved February 21, 2006, from http://www.msnbc.msn.com/id/5636114/site/newsweek.

Platonov, V. N. (1988). *L'entrainement sportif: Theorie et methode.* [Sport training: Theory and method.] Paris: Ed. EPS.

Platonov, V. N. (2001). Perspektivy sovershenstvovaniya sistemy olimpijskoj podgotovki v svete urokov igr XXVII Olimpiady (Prospects of advancing the system of Olympic preparation as learned from the 27th Games). *Science in Olympic Sport, 2*, 5–17.

Platonov, V. N. (2005). *Sistema Podgotovki Sportsmenov v Olimpijskom Sporte* (System of Preparation of Athletes in Olympic Sport). Moscow: Soviet Sport.

Platonov, V. N. (2010). *Sport Vysshikh Dostizhenij i Podgotovka Natsional'nykh Komand k Olimpijskim Igram* (High Performance Sport and Preparation of National Teams for Olympic Games). Moscow: Soviet Sport.

Platonov, V. N. & Guskov, S. I. (1994). *Olimpijskij Sport.* (Olympic Sport). Kiev: Olympic Literature.

Plumer, B. (2013). America's staggering defense budget, in charts. Retrieved January 7, 2013, from www.washingtonpost.com/blogs/wonkblog/wp/2013/01/07/everything-chuck-hagel-needs-to-know-about-the-defense-budget-in-charts/.

Pochinkin, A. V. (2006). *Stanovlenie i Razvitie Professional'nogo Kommercheskogo Sporta v Rossii* (Formation and Development of Professional Commercial Sport in Russia). Moscow: Soviet Sport.

Polyaev, B. A., Makarova, G. A., & Belolipetskaya, I. A. (2005). *Zarubezhnyj i Otechestvennyj Opyt Organizatsii Sluzhby Sportivnoj Meditsiny i Podgotovki Sportivnyh Vrachej* (International and National Experience of Organizing Sports Medicine Service and Preparing Sports Physicians). Moscow: Soviet Sport.

Poole, L. (1965) *History of Ancient Olympic Games*. London: Vision Press.

Portugalov, S. N., Ozolin, E. S., & Shustin, B. N. (2010, May). *Innovatsionnye tehnologii v podgotovke sportsmenov-olimpijtsev* (Innovative technologies in preparation of Olympic athletes). Conference on Problems in Sport and Physical Culture, Minsk, Belorus.

Putnam, R. D. (2000). *Bowling alone: The collapse and revival of American community*. New York: Simon & Schuster.

Quenqua, D. (2012). Muscular body image lures boys into gym, and obsession. *The New York Times*. Retrieved on December 29, 2012, from http://www.nytimes.com/2012/11/19/health/teenage-boys-worried-about-body-image-take-risks.html?nl=todaysheadlines&emc=edit_th_20121119&_r=0#h.

Quill, S. (2006, October). Saving generaiton XXL. Seven ways to reform America's physical education and transform kids from fat to fit. *Men's Health*, 148–154.

Rees, C. R. (2000). School sport in America: the production of 'winners' and 'losers.' In S. Bailey (Ed.). *Perspectives: The interdisciplinary series of physical education and sports science, volume 1: School sport and competition* (pp. 31–39). Oxford: Meyer & Meyer Sport.

Reid, M., Crespo, M. A. F., & Dimmock, J. (2007). Tournament structure and nations' success in women's professional tennis. *Journal of Sports Sciences*, *25*(11), 1221–1228.

Reid, M., Crespo, M., Santilli, L., Miley, D., & Dimmock, J. (2007). The importance of the International Tennis Federation's junior boys' circuit in the development of professional tennis players. *Journal of Sports Sciences*, *25*(6), 667–672.

Resiner, M. (1984, August 11). Empire State Games set to open Wednesday. The Evening News. Associated Press. p. 1B. Retrieved March 20, 2014, from http://news.google.com/newspapers?nid=1982&dat=19840811&id=R15GAAAAIBAJ&sjid=yzENAAAAIBAJ&pg=5737,1054116.

Rhoden, W. C. (1987). Olympic Festival: Attendance marks bring satisfaction. *The New York Times*. Retrieved July 27, 1987, from: http://www.nytimes.com/1987/07/27/sports/olympic-festival-attendance-marks-bring-satisfaction.html.

Rhoden, W. C. (1991). Pan American Games; The secret of Cuba's sports success? Spot the children who are athletes, *The New York Times*. Retrieved July 27, 2010, from http://query.nytimes.com/gst/fullpage.html?res=9D0CEFD9133FF93AA2575BC0A967958260&sec=&spon=&pagewanted=all.

Rice, E. A., Hutchinson, J. L., & Lee, M. (1958). *A brief history of physical education*. New York: The Ronald Press Co.

Ridpath, B. D., Yiamouyiannis, A., & Lawrence, H. (2009). Changing sides: The failure of the wrestling community's challenges to Title IX and new strategies for saving NCAA sport teams. *Journal of Intercollegiate Sports*, *1*, 255–283.

Riordan, J. (1978). *Sport under communism: The USSR, Czechoslovakia, the GDR, China, Cuba*. London: C. Hurst.

Riordan, J. (1980). *Sport in Soviet Society: Development of sport and physical Education in Russia and the USSR.* Cambridge: Cambridge University Press.

Riordan, J. (1982a). Sport and the Soviet state: Response to Morton and Cantelon. In H. Cantelon, & R. Gruneau (Eds.). *Sport, culture and the modern state* (pp. 265–280). Toronto: University of Toronto Press.

Riordan, J. (1982b). Sport and communism-on the example of the USSR. In J. Hargreaves, (Ed.). *Sport, culture and ideology* (pp. 213–231). London: Routledge & Kegan Paul.

Riordan, J. (1988). Sport made to measure: The formal organization of sport in the Soviet Union. *Arena Review, 12*(2), 105–115.

Riordan, J. (1989). Soviet sport and perestroika. *Journal of Comparative Physical Education and Sport, 6*(2), 7–18.

Riordan, J. (1990). Playing to new rules: Soviet sport and perestroika. *Soviet Studies, 42*(1), 133–146.

Riordan, J. (1991). *Sport, politics and communism.* Manchester: Manchester University Press.

Rohlin, S. M., Corbin, L. & Rafferty, N. (2013) The 2013 Half Moon Bay International Marathon: An Economic Impact Analysis. Department of Economics. Kent State University. Retrieved March 20, 2014, from http://halfmoonbayim.org/files/6413/8732/1187/Economic_Impact_for_the_2013_HMBIM.pdf.

Rosen, K. (2011). USOC tax return reveals decline in executive pay, compensation. *The Sport Digest.* Retrieved May 25, 2011, from http://thesportdigest.com/2011/05/usoc-tax-return-reveals-decline-in-executive-pay-compensation/.

RT. (2012). Bones and confidence grow with Soviet orthopedic technique. Retrieved July 8, 2011, from http://rt.com/news/features/ilizarov-surgery-still-center.

Rugby America. (2011). GU's here to confuse things even further? Retrieved on August 18, 2011, from http://rugbyamerica.net/2011/08/18/gus-here-to-confuse-things-even-further.

Rugby Canada. (2012). Final bow for Churchill Cup. Retrieved on January 2, 2012, from http://www.churchillcuprugby.net/leagues/newsletter.cfm?leagueID=10901&clientID=3731&stype=1&page=53572&newsFrom=01%2F08%2F2012&newsTo=01%2F22%2F2012#.TxzZEv-IBmU.gmail.

RunningUSA.com. (2011). Statistics. Retrieved July 2011, from www.runningusa.org/

Russian Express. (2011, May 27). Canadiana. Unhealthy lifestyle, *694*, 7.

Sack, A. (2008). Should college athletes be paid? *The Christian Science Monitor.* Retrieved December 1, 2012, from www.csmonitor.com/Commentary/Opinion/2008/0307/p09s01-coop.html.

Safai, P. (2009, May). A healthy anniversary? Exploring narratives of health in the 1968 and 2008 Olympic Games. Olympic Reform: A Ten-Year Review Conference, Toronto, Canada.

Sagatomo, T. S., Miller, J., & Naeger, D. (2011). They play but do they watch? An examination of tennis consumers. 26th Annual Conference of North American Society for Sport Management, London, Canada.

Sayers, M. (2003). Running mechanics of elite rugby players. In *Proceedings of the International Conference on the Science and Practice of Rugby*, Brisbane, QLD, 44.

Schmidt, M. (2011, November 22). Baseball strides forth on H.G.H., but carefully. *The New York Times.* Retrieved November 22, 2011, from http://www.nytimes.com/2011/11/23/sports/baseball/baseball-strides-forth-on-hgh-but-carefully.html?nl=todaysheadlines&emc=tha27.

Schön, D. A. (1973). *Beyond the Stable State.* Harmondsworth: Penguin.

Schön, D. A., & Rein, M. (1994). *Frame Reflection: Toward the Resolution of Intractable Policy Controversies*. New York: Basic Books.

Schwetschenau, H. M., O'Brien, W. H., Cunningham, C. J. L., & Jex, S. M. (2008). Barriers to physical activity in an on-site corporate fitness center. *Journal of Occupational Health Psychology, 13*(4), 371–380.

Schwirtz, M. (2008, August 2). Russia will address doping bans after the Games. *The New York Times.* Retrieved August 28, 2011, from http://www.nytimes.com/2008/08/02/sports/olympics/02doping.html.

Sedlacek, J., Matousek, R., Holcek, R., & Moravec, R. (1994). The influence of the political changes on the high performance sport organization in Czechoslovakia. In Wilcox, R. (Ed.). *Sport in the global village* (pp. 341–347). Morgantown, WV: Fitness Information Technology Inc.

Semotiuk, D. (1975). The sport system of the Union of Soviet Socialist Republics: An illustrated analysis. *Proceedings and Newsletter,* (pp. 50–51) Lemont, PA: North American Society for Sport History.

Semotiuk, D. (1990). East bloc athletics in the glasnost era. *Journal of Comparative Physical Education and Sport, 9*(1), 26–29.

SGMA. (2012). SGMA says the Olympics do impact sports participation. Retrieved March 12, 2012, from http://www.sgma.com/press/431_SGMA-Says-The-Olympics-Do-Impact-Sports-Participation.

Shephard, R. J. (1996). Worksite fitness and exercise programs: A review of methodology and ealth impact. *American Journal of Health Promotion, 10*, 436–452.

Sheppard, J. M., & Young, W. B. (2006). Agility literature review: Classifications, training and testing. *Journal of Sports Sciences, 24*, 919–932.

Shkolnikova, N. (1978). The rungs of prowess: An introduction to the Unified Sports Classification System of the USSR, *Olympic Panorama, 7*. Retrieved May 20, 2010, from http://www.gymn-forum.net/Miscellaneous/Soviet_Sport_Rankings.html.

Shneidman, N. N. (1978). *The Soviet road to Olympus: Theory and practice of Soviet physical culture and sport.* Toronto, Canada: The Ontario Institute for Studies in Education.

Siebrits, K., & Fourie, J. (2009). An application of attractiveness measures to evaluate the structure of the Currie Cup. *South African Journal for Research in Sport, Physical Education & Recreation, 31*(1), 95–113.

Slaughter, M. (1998). *Out on the Edge: a Wake-up Call for Church Leaders on the Edge of the Media Reformation.* Nashville, TN: Abingdon Press.

Sleight, S. (1989). *Sponsorship: What It is and How to Use It.* London: McGraw-Hill.

Smith, A. & Westerbeek, H. (2004). *The Sport Business Future.* NY, NY: Palgrave Macmillan.

Smolianov, P. (2005). Systemy obespecheniya sporta vysshih dostizhenij. Analiz mezhdunarodnogo opyta v organizatsii Olimpijskoj podgotovki (Systems for provision of high sport performance. Analysis of international experience in organizing Olympic preparations. *Sports Science Bulletin, 3*(8), 49–52.

Smolianov, P. (2013). Russia. In O'Boyle, I. & Bradbury, T. (Editors). *Sport governance: An international case study perspective* (pp.74-89). London and New York: Routledge.

Smolianov, P., & Gallo, J. A. (2011, June). Comparing practices of USA Tennis against a global model for integrated development of mass and high performance sport, 26th Annual Conference of North American Society for Sport Management, London, Canada.

Smolianov, P., & Shilbury, D. (2005). Examining integrated advertising and sponsorship in corporate marketing through televised sport. *Sport Marketing Quarterly, 14*(4), 239-250.

Smolianov, P., & Zakus, D. H. (2006, September). Developing a global model of high performance management in Olympic sports. Paper presented at 14th Congress of the European Association for Sport Management, Nicosia, Cyprus.

Smolianov, P., & Zakus, D. H. (2008). Exploring high performance management in Olympic sport with reference to practices in the former USSR and Russia. *The International Journal of Sport Management, 9*(2), 206-232.

Smolianov, P., & Zakus, D. H. (2009a, May). Integrated development of mass and high performance sport: A global model. Olympic reform: A ten-year review conference, Toronto, Canada.

Smolianov, P., & Zakus, D. H. (2009b, September). Olympic training centers as part of sport development and mass participation–a case of Moscow, USSR. 17th Conference of the European Association for Sport Management, Amsterdam, Netherlands.

Smolianov, P., Gallo, J., & Naylor, A. (2014). Comparing the practices of USA Tennis against a global model for integrated development of mass and high performance sport. *Managing Leisure: An International Journal.* DOI:10.1080/13606719.2014.929402.

Smolianov, P., Murphy, J., McMahon, S. and Naylor, A. (2014, in press). Comparing practices of USA Soccer against a global model for integrated development of mass and high performance. *Managing Leisure: An International Journal.*

Smolianov, P., Murphy, J., McMahon, S., & Naylor, A. (2014). Comparing practices of USA soccer against a global model for integrated development of mass and high performance sport. Presented at 27th Annual Conference of North American Society for Sport Management, Seattle, Washington.

Snyder, K. (2011). Soccer academy for sale, again. *The Morning Soccer Journal.* Wednesday October 12, 2011. Retrieved March 17, 2012 from http://www.morningjournal.com/articles/2011/10/12/news/mj5132902.txt.

Sochi. (2010). Department of International Affairs and Protocol, Sochi City Administration. Retrieved June 15, 2010, from http://www.sochi-international.ru/.

Sochi.ru2014. (2014). Official web site of the 2014 Sochi Olympic Winter Games. Retrieved March 8, 2014, from www.sochi2014.com/en/medals.

Sotiriadou, K., Shilbury, D., & Quick, S. (2008). The attraction, retention/transition, and nurturing process of sport development: Some Australian evidence. *Journal of Sport Management, 22* (3), 247–272.

Spalding, B. T. (1924). *The Life and Teaching of the Masters of the East, Vol.1.* Merina del Ray, CA: Devorss & Co.

Spamer, E. J. (1999). Talent identification in sport: a present-day perspective with reference to South Africa. *African Journal of Physical Education, Health, Recreation and Dance, 5*(2), 69-95.

Spamer, E. J. (2005). Ethical behaviour in sport: Fair play versus winning among elite rugby players. *Journal of Human Movement Studies, 48, 125-132.*

Spamer, E. J., & Winsley, R. (2003). Comparative characteristics of elite English and South African 18-year-old rugby players with reference to game-specific skills, physical abilities and anthropometric data. *Journal of Human Movement Studies, 43*, 187-196.

Sparvero, E., Chalip, L., & Green, B. C. (2008). United States. In B. Houlihan, & M. Green, (Eds.). *Comparative elite sport development: Systems, structures and public policy.* Butterworth-Heinemann, Burlington, MA.

Sporting Goods Manufacturers Association (2012). 2012 Sports, fitness and leisure activities topline participation report. Retrieved from http://assets.usta.com/assets/1/15/SGMA_Research_2012_Participation_Topline_Report.pdf.

SRI International Report. (2011). Golf 20/20: The 2011 golf economy report. Retrieved March 15, 2014, from www.golf2020.com/media/31624/2011_golf_econ_exec_sum_sri_final_12_17_12.pdf.

Stambulova, N. B., & Ryba, T. V. (2013). *Athletes' Careers Across Cultures*. London and New York: Routledge.

Starodubtseva, E. S., & Gordon, S. M. (2004). Parametricheskaya trenirovka plovtsov v godichnom makrotsikle (Parametric training of swimmers in a yearly macrocycle). *Physical Culture: Pedagogy, Education, Training, 4*, 28–29.

Staudohar, P.D., & Mangan, J.A. (1991). *The Business of Professional Sport*. Urbana and Chicago: University of Illinois Press.

Steffan, M. (2013). The main reason for declining church attendance: children's sports? *Christianity Today*. Retrieved April 8, 2013 from http://www.christianitytoday.com/. gleanings/2013/april/main-reason-for-declining-church-attendance-childrens.html

Steinbach, P. (2011, December). Record NCAA graduation rates don't tell the whole story. *Athletic Business*. Retrieved March 17, 2014, from www.athleticbusiness.com/Governing-Bodies/record-ncaa-graduation-rates-don-t-tell-the-whole-story.html.

Stern, K. (2013, March 20). Why the Rich Don't Give to Charity: The wealthiest Americans donate 1.3 percent of their income; the poorest, 3.2 percent. What's up with that? *The Money Report*. Retrieved March 15, 2014, from www.theatlantic.com/magazine/archive/2013/04/why-the-rich-dont-give/309254/.

Stiglitz, J. E. (2010). *Freefall: Free markets and the sinking of the global economy*. London: Allen Lane.

Stiglitz, J. E. (2011, May). Of the 1%, by the 1%, for the 1%. *Vanity Fair*. Retrieved March 25, 2014, from www.vanityfair.com/society/features/2011/05/top-one-percent-201105.

Stiglitz, J. E. (2012). *The price of inequality*. London: Allen Lane.

Stone, O., & Kuznick, P. (2012). *The Untold History of the United States*. Gallery Books. Kindle Edition.

Stuckler, D. & Basu, S. (2013). *The Body Economic: Why Austerity Kills*. New York: Basic Books.

Sturkenboom, M., & Vervoorn, C. (1998). Diagram of the multidisciplinary support staff in top sports. Paper presented at NOC*NSF Symposium, Ahrnem, the Netherlands.

Svoboda, B. (2005). *Sport and Physical Activity as a Socialization Environment, Scientific Review Part 1*. Strasbourg: Council of Europe, Committee for the Development of Sport (CDDS).

Taliaferro, L.A., Rienzo, B.A., Miller, M.D., Pigg, R.M., & Dodd, V.J. (2008). High school youth and suicide risk: exploring protection afforded through physical activity and sport participation. *Journal of School Health, 78*, 545–553.

Tan, T., & Green, M. (2008). Analysing China's drive for Olympic success in 2008, *International Journal of the History of Sport, 25*(3), 314–338.

Tan, T., & Houlihan, B. (2006, September). Chinese sports policy & globalisation: The case of the Olympic movement. Paper presented at 14th Congress of the European Association for Sport Management, Nicosia, Cyprus.

Tatz, C. (1995). *Obstacle Race*. University of New South Wales Press, Sydney, Australia.

Tavernise, B. (2012). Life expectancy rises around the world, study finds. *The New York Times*. Retrieved December 13, 2012 from http://www.nytimes.com/2012/12/14/. health/worlds-population-living-longer-new-report-suggests.html?nl=todaysheadlines&emc=edit_th_20121214

Taylor, B., & Ogilvie, B. C. (1994). A conceptual model of adaptation to retirement among athletes. *Journal of Applied Sport Psychology, 6*, 1–20.

TeamBath (2005). Sport. Retrieved June 21, 2005, from http://www.teambath.com/sport/3_3_9.cfm.

Tennis Panorama News. (2011). USTA awards $450,000 in recreational tennis grants. Retrieved on January 11, 2011, from http://www.tennispanorama.com/archives/2137.

The 2011 International Sports Programming Initiative. (2010). Department of State. Retrieved from http://www.grants.gov/search/search.do?mode=VIEW&oppId=59017.

The Economist. (2012a, May 15). Defence spending cuts. The informed majority. Retrieved May 15, 2012, from http://www.economist.com/blogs/democracyinamerica/2012/05/defence-spending-cuts.

The Economist. (2012b, September 8-14). Asian welfare states, 23–26.

The Economist(2014, 12 April). Chinese civil society: Behind the glacier. 21–24.

The Empire State Games. (2010). About the Empire State Games. Retrieved July 20, 2009, from www.empirestategames.org/.

The Empire State Games. (2011). Retrieved August 2, 2011, from http://www.empirestategames.org/.

The Guardian. (2005). Fat to fit: how Finland did it. Retrieved June 22, 2012, from http://www.guardian.co.uk/befit/story/0,15652,1385645,00.html.

The University of Physical Education in Warsaw. (2014). Study in Warsaw. The Józef Piłsudski University of Physical Education in Warsaw. Retrieved March 15, 2014, from www.studyinwarsaw.pl/index.php?option=com_content&task=view&id=1&Itemid=12&uczelnia_id=9.

The U.S. Professional Sports Market & Franchise Value Report 2012. (2012). WR Hambrecht, San Francisco, CA. Retrieved from www.wrhambrecht.com/pdf/SportsMarketReport_2012.pdf.

The US Soccer Foundation. (2012). The US Soccer Foundation Grants. Retrieved from http://www.ussoccerfoundation.org/our-grants/past-grant-recipients.

Thoma, J. E., & Chalip, L. H. (1996). *Sport Governance in the Global Community*. Morgantown, WV: Fitness Information Technology.

Thomas, K. (2008). Army sharpshooters have Olympic medals in their sights, *The New York Times*. Retrieved July 10, 2008, from http://www.nytimes.com/2008/07/10/sports/olympics/10marksmen.html?pagewanted=1&_r=1&th&emc.

Thomas, K. (2009). Using teamwork to bring girls into the game, *The New York Times*. Retrieved June 14, 2009, from http://www.nytimes.com/2009/06/15/sports/15girls.html?th&emc=th.

Thomas, K. (2010a). Education chief criticizes N.B.A. and the N.C.A.A., *The New York Times*. Retrieved: January 14, 2010, from http://www.nytimes.com/2010/01/15/sports/15ncaa.html?th&emc=th

Thomas, K. (2010b). Olympic glory, led by stars hardly on the team. *The New York Times*. Retrieved February 27, 2010, from http://www.nytimes.com/2010/02/28/sports/olympics/28olympics.html?th&emc=th.

Thomas, K. (2012). Drug shortages persist in U.S., harming care. *The New York Times*. Retrieved on November 16, 2012, from http://www.nytimes.com/2012/11/17/business/drug-shortages-are-becoming-persistent-in-us.html?pagewanted=2&nl=todaysheadlines&emc=edit_th_20121117.

Thyberg, D. (2012). What education do you need to become a soccer coach. Retrieved on December 20, 2012, from http://www.ehow.com/info_7743802_education-do-need-soccer-coach.html.

Tierney, J. (2008). Let the games be doped. *The New York Times*. Retrieved on August 11, 2008, from http://www.nytimes.com/2008/08/12/science/12tier.html.

Tierney, M. (2013, April 13). At a college, dropping sports in favor of fitness. *The New York Times.* Retrieved on April 13, 2013, from http://www.nytimes.com/2013/04/14/sports/at-spelman-dropping-sports-in-favor-of-fitness.html?pagewanted=1&_r=0&nl=todaysheadlines&emc=edit_th_20130414.

To, W. W. H., Smolianov, P., & Semotiuk, D. M. (2013). Comparative high performance sport models. In P. Sotiriadou, & V. De Bosscher (Editors). *Managing high performance sport.* London and New York: Routledge.

Topdrawersoccer. (2012, January 11). How is USSF identifying and developing the best. Retrieved on December 24, 2012 from http://www.topdrawersoccer.com/article/?categoryId=26&articleId=23641&articleTitle=how-is-ussf-identifying-developing-the-best.

Toronto Star. (2005, June 21) Editorial. New report says millionaire's club growing worldwide, A22.

Torre, P. S. (2009). How (and why) athletes go broke. *Sports Illustrated.* Retrieved March 23, 2009 from http://vault.sportsillustrated.cnn.com/vault/article/magazine/MAG1153364/1/index.htm.

TrackTown USA (2011a). Nike Oregon Project: Salazar applies the latest technology to distance training. Retrieved Aug 25, 2011 from http://www.tracktownusa.com/track.item.5/the-oregon-project.html.

TrackTown USA (2011b). Phil Knight-University of Oregon Booster Extraordinaire. Retrieved September 11, 2011 from http://www.tracktownusa.com/track.item.39/Phil-Knight-University-of-Oregon-Booster-Extraordinaire.html.

Tumanian, G.S. (2006). *Strategija Podgotovki Chempionov* (Strategy of Preparing Champions). Moscow: Soviet Sport.

UN International Year of Sport and Physical Education (2005). Retrieved from http://www.un.org/sport2005/.

United Healthcare (2014). Fitness Reimbursement Program. Retrieved March 6, 2014, from www.uhctogether.com/uhcwellness/16181.html.

United Soccer Academy. (2012). Recreation soccer training. Retrieved December 5, 2012, from http://unitedsocceracademy.com/club-soccer-services/recreation-soccer-training.html.

UPI. (2012). Hidden costs of U.S. prisons in billions. Retrieved on June 10, 2012, from http://www.upi.com/Top_News/US/2012/01/30/Hidden-costs-of-US-prisons-in-billions/UPI-84191327900935/.

U. S. Bureau of Labor Statistics. (2012a). American time use survey 2011 results. Retrieved August 1, 2012, from http://www.bls.gov/news.release/atus.htm.

U. S. Bureau of Labor Statistics (2012b). Occupational Outlook Handbook. Entertainment and Sports. Coaches and Scouts. Retrieved April 25, 2014 from: http://www.bls.gov/ooh/entertainment-and-sports/coaches-and-scouts.htm.

U. S. Department of Defence (2004). 2004 Summer Olympics. Retrieved December 29, 2004, from http://www.defense.gov/specials/2004Olympics/.

U. S. GAO. (1955). United States General Accounting Office. 84th Congress, Public Law 11 (Washington, DC: Government Printing Office, 1955) sect. 3.). Retrieved from http://www.gpo.gov/fdsys/pkg/STATUTE-69/pdf/STATUTE-69-Pg11-2.pdf.

U. S. GAO. (2000). United States General Accounting Office. Olympic Games: Federal Government Provides Significant Funding and Support. Retrieved from http://www.gpo.gov/fdsys/pkg/GAOREPORTS-GGD-00-183/pdf/GAOREPORTS-GGD-00-183.pdf.

U. S. Government (1947). Public Law 159, ed. 80th US Congress.

U. S. Soccer. (2011). U.S. Soccer Federation 2011 Annual General Meeting Notes. FY'12 Budget Executive Summary. Pp. 68-95. Retrieved from http://resources.ussoccer.com/n7v8b8j3/cds/downloads/2011AGMBook.pdf.

U. S. Soccer. (2012). Best practices for coaching soccer in the United States: Player development guidelines. Retrieved January 29, 2012 from http://www.ussoccer.com/Coaches/Resources.aspx.

USA Hockey. (2010). 2009–2010 annual report. Retrieved August 5, 2011 from http://www.usahockey.com/uploadedFiles/USAHockey/Menu_About_USA_Hockey/2010%20USAH%20Annual%20Report_FINAL2.pdf.

USA Rugby. (2012). USA Rugby News. Retrieved December 25, 2012 from http://www.usarugby.org/news.

USA Rugby Financial Statements (2012). Audited Finanical Statements from USA Rugby. Retrieved December 15, 2012 from http://usarugby.org/.
about-usarugby/financial-statements

USA Today. (2010). In ranking U.S. students trail global leaders. Retrieved July 12, 2010, from http://usatoday30.usatoday.com/news/education/2010-12-07-us-students-international-ranking_N.htm.

USA Track & Field. (2014). Team USA Career Program. Retrieved March 21, 2014, from www.usatf.org/groups/HighPerformance/AthleteSupport/TeamUSACareer.asp.

USADA. (2014). USADA: the United States Anti-Doping Agency: About USADA. Retrieved March 24, 2014, from http://www.usada.org/about.

USOC. (2011). About the USOC. Retrieved August 5, 2011 from http://www.teamusa.org/About-the-USOC.

USOC. (2012). Training Centers & Sites. Retrieved December 20, 2012, from www.teamusa.org/About-the-USOC.

USOC. (2013). CODP. Retrieved May 10, 2013 from http://www.teamusa.org/About-the-USOC/In-the-Community/Partner-Programs/CODP.

USSF AGM. (2012). United States Soccer Federation 2012 Annual General Meeting Book. Retrieved December 5, 2012, from http://www.ussoccer.com/about/governance/2012-annual-general-meeting/agm.aspx.

USTA. (2009). U.S. tennis participation tops 30 million people for first time in more than 25 years. Retrieved on June 20, 2011, from http://www.itatennis.com/AboutITA/News/U_S__Tennis_Participation_Tops_30_Million_People_for_First_Time_in_More_than_25_Years.htm.

USTA Financial Statements (2010). Retrieved 10 December 2012 from http://assets.usta.com/assets/1/15/USTA120908-Association_FINAL_SIGNED_COPY.pdf.

USTA (2012). About USTA. Retrieved 10 December, 2012, from http://www.usta.com/About-USTA/?intloc=headernav.

USTA. (2014). Web site of the U. S. Tennis Association. Retrieved March 2, 2014, from http://2013.usopen.org/en_US/about/history/years.html.

Vaeyens, R., Lenoir, M., Williams, A.M., & Philippaerts, R.M. (2008). Talent identification and development programmes in sport: Current models and future directions, *Sports Medicine, 38*(9), 703.

Vail, S. E. (2007). Community development and sport participation. *Journal of Sport Management*, 21(4), 571–596.

Van Bottenburg, M. (2000). *Het topsportklimaat in Nederland* [The elite sports climate in the Netherlands]. 's Hertogenbosch: Diopter-Janssens en van Bottenburg bv.

Van Bottenburg, M. (2002, October). Sport for all and elite sport: do they benefit one another? Paper for the IX World Sport for All Congress, Papendal, The Netherlands.

Van Bottenburg, M. (2011). The Netherlands. In, M. Nicholson, R. Hoye, & B. Houlihan, (Eds.). *Participation in sport: International policy prospectives.* London and New York: Routledge.

Van den Berg, M. (2001). The support structure for top sports: Perspectives from national team sport coaches. Unpublished thesis for the European University Diploma of Sport Management. Utrecht, the Netherlands.

VanWynsberghe, R. (2009, May). The Olympic Games impact study and the 2010 Winter Olympic Games: A study in monitoring the Games' sustainability. Olympic Reform: A Ten-Year Review Conference, Toronto, Canada.

Veblen, T. (1953). *The Theory of the Leisure Class.* New York: New American Library.

Vecsey, G. (2011). College athletes move concussions into the courtroom. *The New York Times.* Retrieved November 29, 2011 from http://www.nytimes.com/2011/11/30/sports/ncaafootball/college-players-move-concussions-issue-into-the-courtroom.html?pagewanted=1&_r=1&nl=todaysheadlines&emc=tha27.

Veronikis, E. (2012, August 11). School districts turn to nonprofit foundations for help. Retrieved December 10, 2012 from http://www.pennlive.com/midstate/index.ssf/2012/08/education_foundations_schools.html.

Virgin London Marathon. (2010). Media guide. London Marathon Limited.

WADA. (2014). World Anti-Doping Agency: Play True: Retrieved March 24, 2014, from www.wada-ama.org/en/World-Anti-Doping-Program.

Walls, M. (2009). Parks and Recreation in the United States. Local Park Systems. Retrieved March 29, 2010, from www.rff.org/rff/documents/RFF-BCK-ORRG_Local%20Parks.pdf.

Walker, D. (2013). Trends in U.S. Military Spending. Council on Foreign Relations. Retrieved July 30, 2013, from www.cfr.org/defense-budget/trends-us-military-spending/p28855.

Walshe, A., McCann, D., Lundstrum, P., Weatherford, Z., Parker-Simmons, S., Keller, L., & Gundersen, F. (2006, April). The "Elite Performance Model™" approach to the development and implementation of a comprehensive, nation-wide sport education program. National Convention of the American Alliance for Health, Physical Education, Recreation and Dance, Salt Lake City, USA.

Walt, S. M. (2011, October 11). The myth of American exceptionalism. *Foreign Policy.* Retrieved on April 10, 2014 from http://www.foreignpolicy.com/articles/2011/10/11/the_myth_of_american_exceptionalism.

Wang, W. & Theodoraki, E. (2007). Mass sport policy development in the Olympic City: The case of Qingdao–host to the 2008 sailing regatta. *The Journal of the Royal Society for the Promotion of Health, 127,* 125–132.

Wankel, L. M. & Sefton, J. M. (1994). *Physical Activity, Fitness and Health.* Champaign, IL: Human Kinetics.

WCAP (World Class Athlete Program). (2005–2014). U.S. Army World Class Athlete Program. About us. Retrieved March 21, 2010, from www.thearmywcap.com/about.

Weber, M. (1949). *The Methodology of the Social Sciences.* New York: The Free Press.

Weber, M. (1978). *Economy and Society.* Berkeley, CA: University of California Press.

Weil, D. (2010). U.S. Open tennis beats the recession, thanks to the rich. Retrieved September 9, 2010, from http://www.bnet.com/blog/business-news/us-open-tennis-beats-the-recession-thanks-to-the-rich/3753.

Wells, H. J. C. (1991). Developing sporting excellence in Hong Kong. *Journal of Comparative Physical Education and Sport, 1,* 28–34.

Westerbeek, H. M. (2009). *Using Sport to Advance Community Health: An International Perspective.* Nieuwegein, the Netherlands: ARKO Sports Media.

White, M. B. (2006). Sports Ministry in America's one hundred largest churches. Doctoral Dissertation, Asbury Theological Seminary. Retrieved May 1, 2013 from http://place. asburyseminary.edu/cgi/viewcontent.cgi?article=1276&context=ecommonsatsdisserta tions.

Wilson, D. & Roberts, J. (2012). Special report: How Washington went soft on childhood obesity. Reuters. Retrieved Apr 27, 2012 from http://www.reuters.com/ article/2012/04/27/us-usa-foodlobby-idUSBRE83Q0ED20120427.

Winniczuk, L. (1983). *Ludzie, Zwyczaje, Obyczaje Starozytnej Grecji I Rzymu.* (People, Traditions and Customs of Ancient Greece and Rome). Warszawa: Panstwowe Wydawnictwo Naukove.

Wolf, N. (2007). *The end of America: Letter of warning to a young patriot.* White River Junction, VT: Chelsea Green.

Wolfe, P. (2012). Olympians win with Hilton jobs. *Lodging Hospitality.* Retrieved Jul 17, 2012, from http://lhonline.com/news/olympians_hilton_jobs_0717/.

Wolff, E. N. (2010). Recent trends in household wealth in the United States: Rising debt and the middle-class squeeze–an update to 2007. Working Paper No. 589 Levy Institute of Bard College. Annandale-on-Hudson,NY: Levy Economics Institute.

Wong, N. C. (2008). Selling the nonski slopes. *The Boston Globe.* Retrieved January 31, 2008 from http://www.boston.com/travel/explorene/specials/ski/articles/2008/01/31/ selling_the_nonski_slopes/?page=full.

World Health Organization. (2011). Promoting sport and enhancing health in European Union countries:A policy content analysis to support action. Retrieved August 1, 2012, from http://www.euro.who.int/__data/assets/pdf_file/0006/147237/e95168.pdf.

World Public Opinion (2007). World View of the US Role Goes from Bad to Worse. Retrieved July 29, 2010, from http://www.worldpublicopinion.org/pipa/articles/ international_security_bt/306.php?nid=&id=&pnt=306.

World Sport for All Congress. (2002). Declaration. 9th World Sport for All Congress. Sport for all and elite sport: rivals or partners? Retrieved from: http://www.olympic. org/Documents/Olympism_in_action/Sport%20for%20all/9th-World-Sport-for-All-Congress---Declaration.pdf.

WTA. (2014). Web site of the Women's Tennis Association. Retrieved March 2, 2014, from www.wtatennis.com/singles-rankings.

Wuest, D. A., & Bucher, C. A. (1995). *Foundations of Physical Education and Sport.* St. Louis, MO: Mosby.

Wynhausen, E. (2007). Crossing the greatest of divides, *The Australian.* Retrieved December 1, 2007, from http://www.theaustralian.news.com.au/story/0,25197,22850153-2722,00. html.

YMCA. (2011). The YMCA organizational profile. Retrieved August 2, 2011, from: http:// www.ymca.net/organizational-profile.

Young, D. C. (1984). *Olympic Myth of Greek Amateur Athletics.* Golden, CO: Ares.

Young, E. (2010). FC gold pride we hardly knew you. Retrieved December 10, 2010 from http://www.bizjournals.com/sanfrancisco/blog/2010/12/fc-gold-pride-we-hardly-knew-you.html.

Yu, J. (2007). *The Ethics of Confucius and Aristotle: Mirrors of Virtue.* New York and London: Routledge.

Zakaria, F. (2011). *The Post-American World.* New York, NY: W.W. Norton & Company Inc.

Zakus, D. H. (2005, July). The Philosophy of Olympism. Keynote speech at the Singapore Olympic Academy, Singapore.

Zakus, D. H., & Bird, M. (2002, November). Integrating Sport Science Specialists Structures and Systems into Sport Organisations: The Exemplar of the Brisbane Lions. Paper presented at the 2002 Sport Management Association of Australia and New Zealand Conference, Rockhampton, Australia.

Zaldivar, G. (2014). In Russia, earning an Olympic medal at Sochi Means a Mercedes and pile of cash. Bleacher Report. Retrieved March 21, 2010, from http://bleacherreport.com/articles/1977004-in-russia-earning-an-olympic-medal-at-sochi-means-a-mercedes-and-pile-of-cash.

Ziemer, B. (2011). Comparing the US soccer environment to the world's soccer environment. Retrieved December 12, 2012 from http://www.oregonyouthsoccer.org/assets/coaches/Comparing_the_US_Soccer_Environment_to_the_World.pdf.

Zigmund, E. (2010, July 16). Radical freedom. *Gezeta Plus, 448*, 22–24.

Zimmerman, A. & Futterman, M. (2009). Home Depot ends program for Olympics. *Wall Street Journal, 253*(6), B2.

Zirin, D. (2014, March 26). The Northwestern University football union and the NCAA's death spiral. *The Nation.* Retrieved March 28, 2014, from www.thenation.com/blog/179042/northwestern-university-football-union-and-ncaas-death-spiral.

Zuosheng, H., & Yonghe, Z. (1990). Reform steps for Russian sports in recent several years and their reminders to us. *Chinese Sports Science and Technology, 2*, 25–29.

Index